JUSTICE LEAGUE™

THEIR GREATEST TRIUMPHS

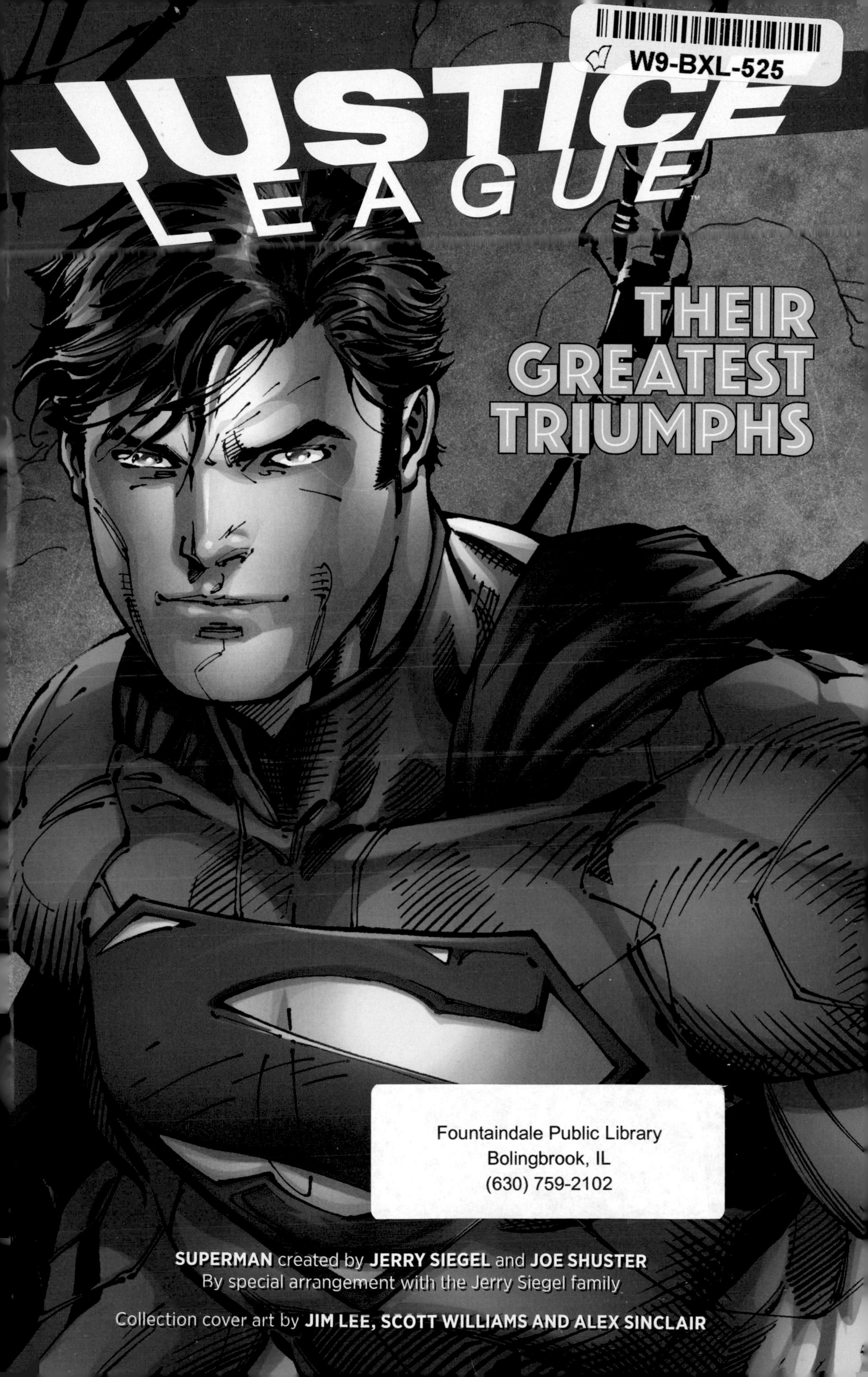

SUPERMAN created by **JERRY SIEGEL** and **JOE SHUSTER**
By special arrangement with the Jerry Siegel family

Collection cover art by **JIM LEE, SCOTT WILLIAMS AND ALEX SINCLAIR**

EDDIE BERGANZA
DAN RASPLER
BRIAN CUNNINGHAM
MIKE CARLIN
Editors – Original Series
TONY BEDARD
REX OGLE
Associate Editors – Original Series
KATE DURRÉ
KATIE KUBERT
JEANINE SCHAEFER
MICHAEL SIGLAIN
AMEDEO TURTURRO
Assistant Editors – Original Series
JEB WOODARD
Group Editor – Collected Editions
ROBIN WILDMAN
Editor – Collected Edition
STEVE COOK
Design Director – Books
SHANNON STEWART
Publication Design

BOB HARRAS
Senior VP – Editor-in-Chief, DC Comics
PAT McCALLUM
Executive Editor, DC Comics

DIANE NELSON
President
DAN DiDIO
Publisher
JIM LEE
Publisher
GEOFF JOHNS
President & Chief Creative Officer
AMIT DESAI
Executive VP – Business & Marketing Strategy, Direct to Consumer & Global Franchise Management
SAM ADES
Senior VP & General Manager, Digital Services
BOBBIE CHASE
VP & Executive Editor, Young Reader & Talent Development
MARK CHIARELLO
Senior VP – Art, Design & Collected Editions
JOHN CUNNINGHAM
Senior VP – Sales & Trade Marketing
ANNE DePIES
Senior VP – Business Strategy, Finance & Administration
DON FALLETTI
VP – Manufacturing Operations
LAWRENCE GANEM
VP – Editorial Administration & Talent Relations
ALISON GILL
Senior VP – Manufacturing & Operations
HANK KANALZ
Senior VP – Editorial Strategy & Administration
JAY KOGAN
VP – Legal Affairs
JACK MAHAN
VP – Business Affairs
NICK J. NAPOLITANO
VP – Manufacturing Administration
EDDIE SCANNELL
VP – Consumer Marketing
COURTNEY SIMMONS
Senior VP – Publicity & Communications
JIM (SKI) SOKOLOWSKI
VP – Comic Book Specialty Sales & Trade Marketing
NANCY SPEARS
VP – Mass, Book, Digital Sales & Trade Marketing
MICHELE R. WELLS
VP – Content Strategy

JUSTICE LEAGUE: THEIR GREATEST TRIUMPHS

DC Comics, 2900 West Alameda Ave, Burbank, CA 91505
Printed by LSC Communications, Kendallville, IN, USA. 9/1/17. First Printing.
ISBN: 978-1-4012-7351-4

Library of Congress Cataloging-in-Publication Data is available.

PEFC Certified
Printed on paper from sustainably managed forests, controlled sources
PEFC
PEFC/29-31-337
www.pefc.org

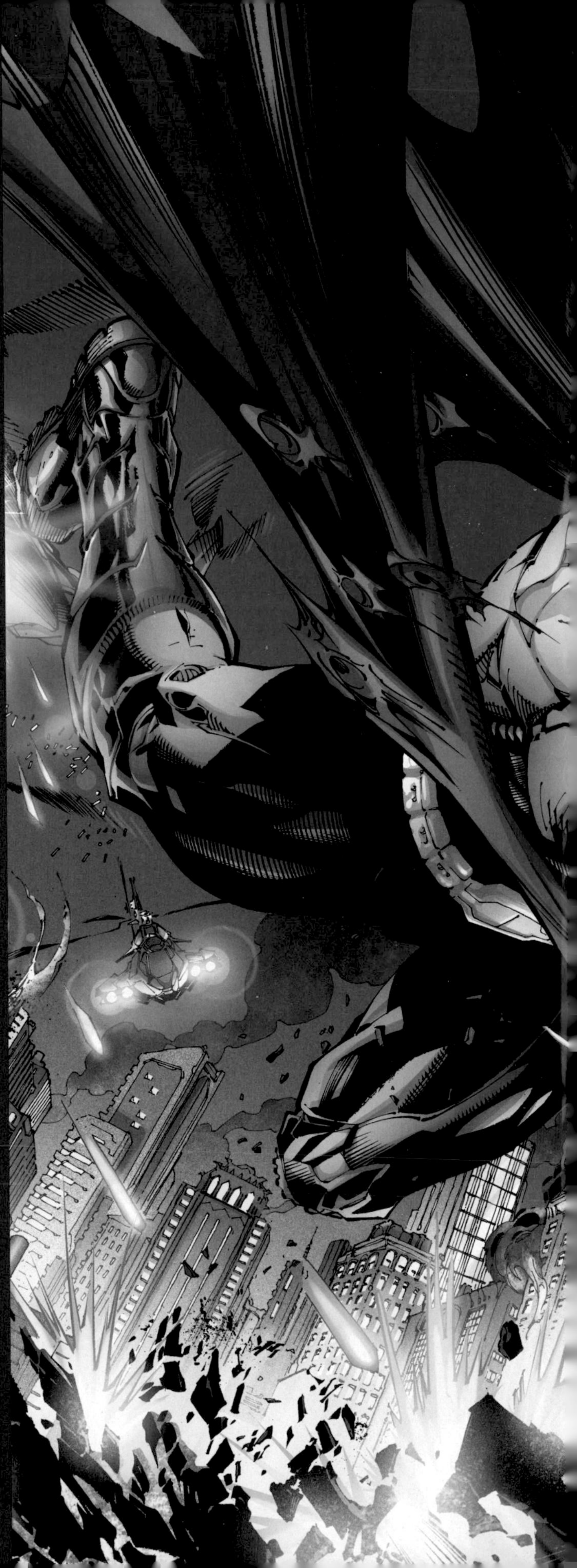

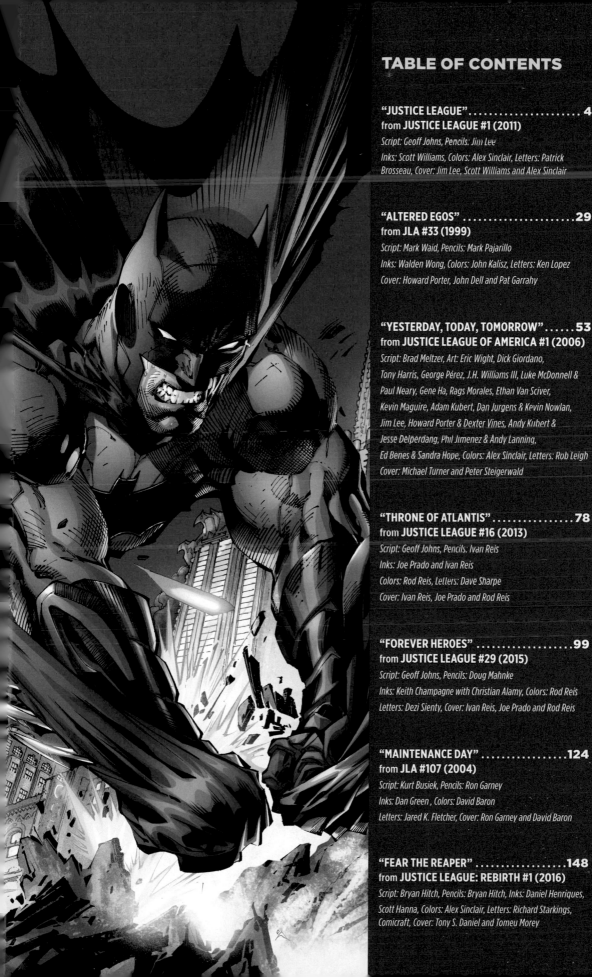

TABLE OF CONTENTS

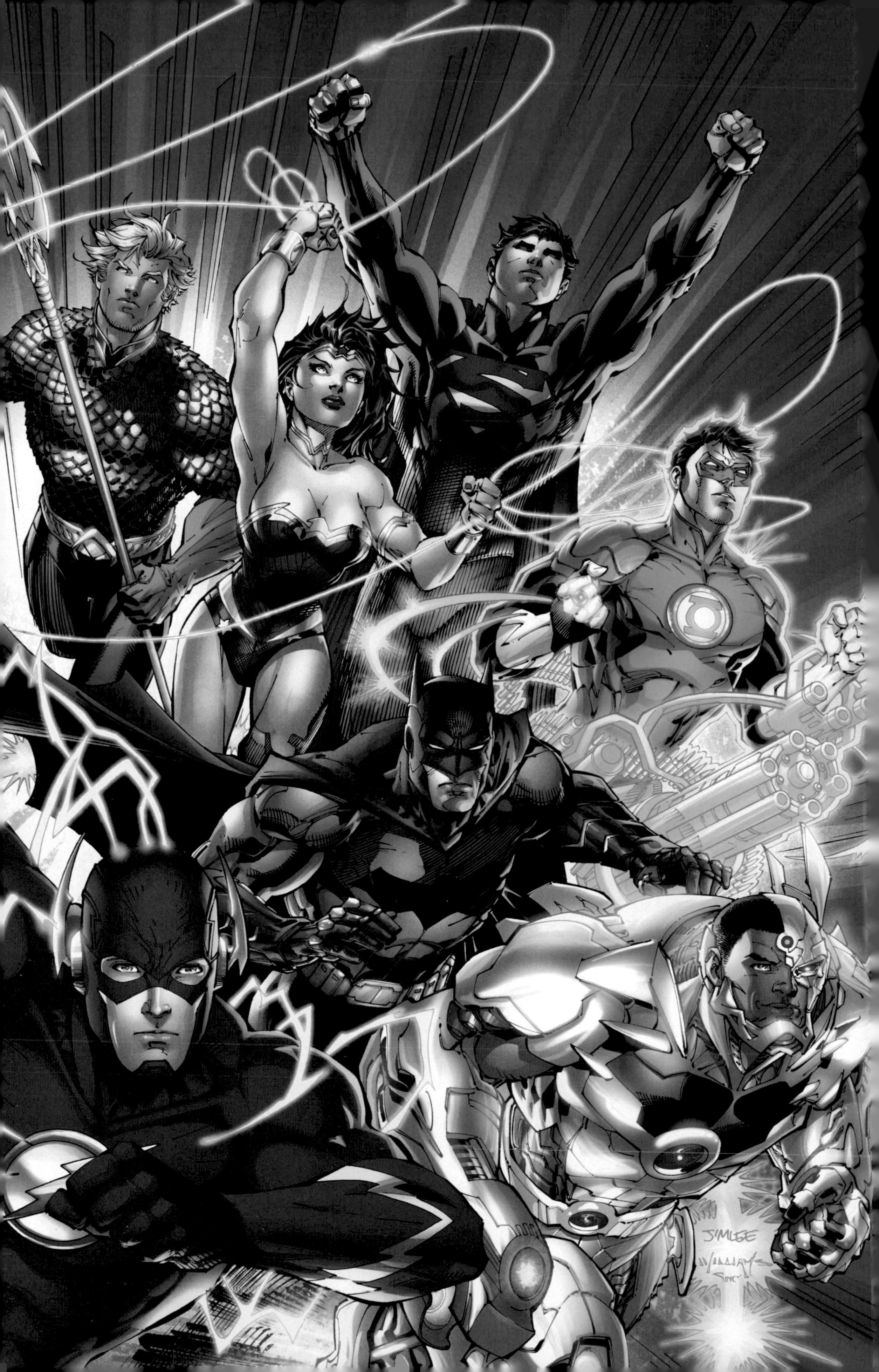

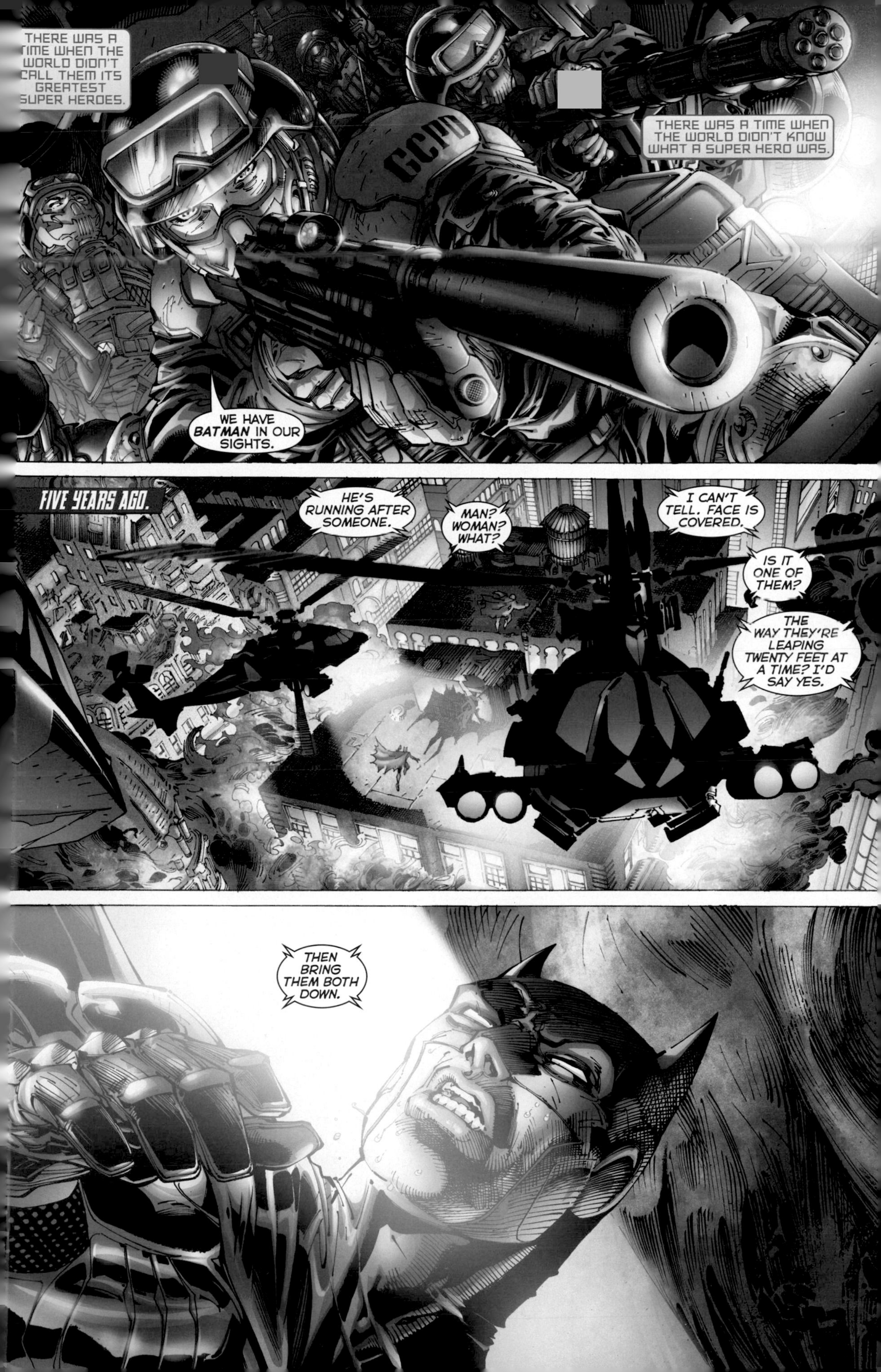
THERE WAS A TIME WHEN THE WORLD DIDN'T CALL THEM ITS GREATEST SUPER HEROES.
THERE WAS A TIME WHEN THE WORLD DIDN'T KNOW WHAT A SUPER HERO WAS.
GCPD
WE HAVE BATMAN IN OUR SIGHTS.
FIVE YEARS AGO.
HE'S RUNNING AFTER SOMEONE.
MAN? WOMAN? WHAT?
I CAN'T TELL. FACE IS COVERED.
IS IT ONE OF THEM?
THE WAY THEY'RE LEAPING TWENTY FEET AT A TIME? I'D SAY YES.
THEN BRING THEM BOTH DOWN.

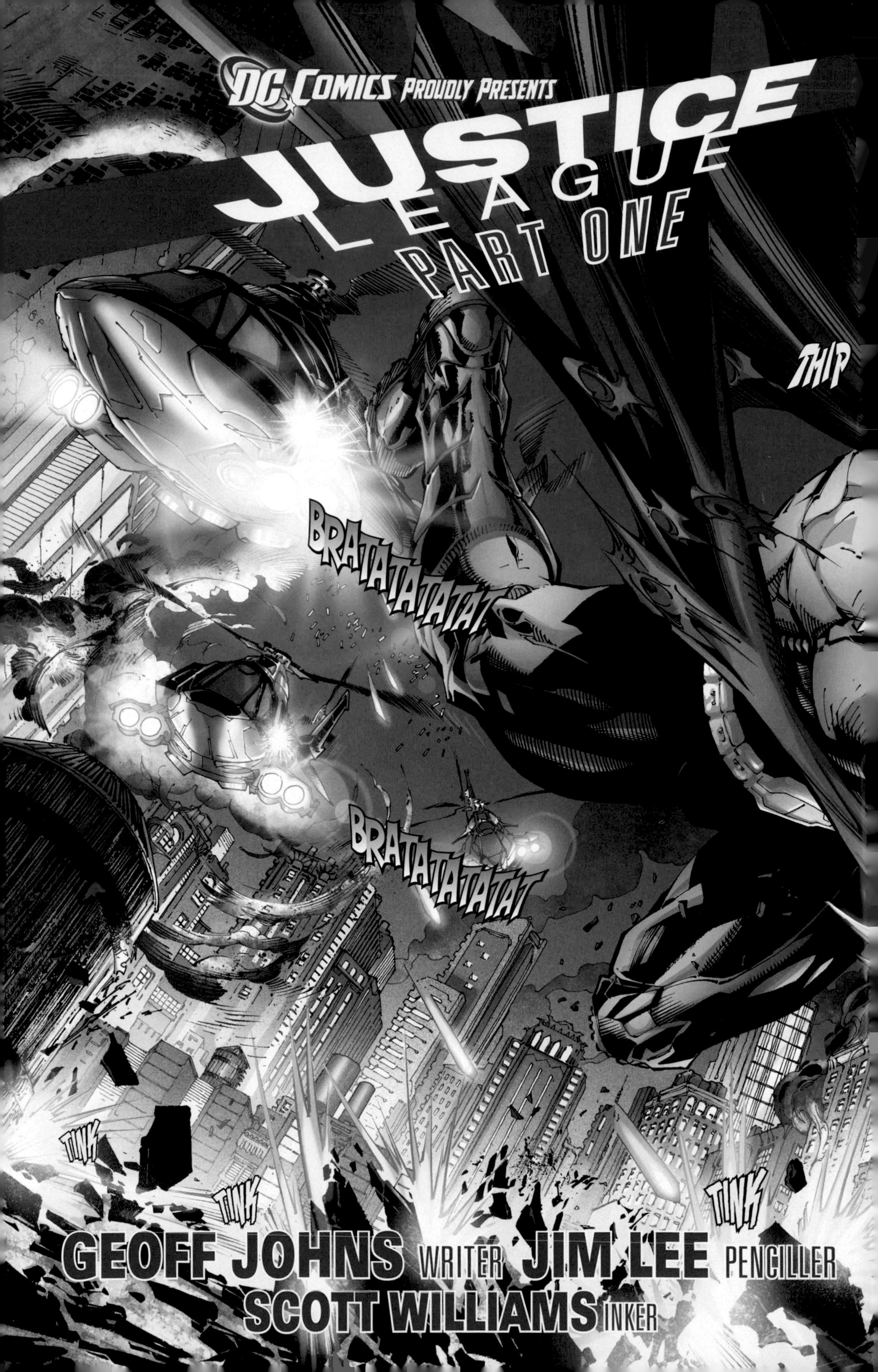
DC COMICS PROUDLY PRESENTS
JUSTICE LEAGUE
PART ONE
THIP
BRATATATATAT
BRATATATATAT
TINK
TINK
TINK
GEOFF JOHNS WRITER JIM LEE PENCILLER
SCOTT WILLIAMS INKER

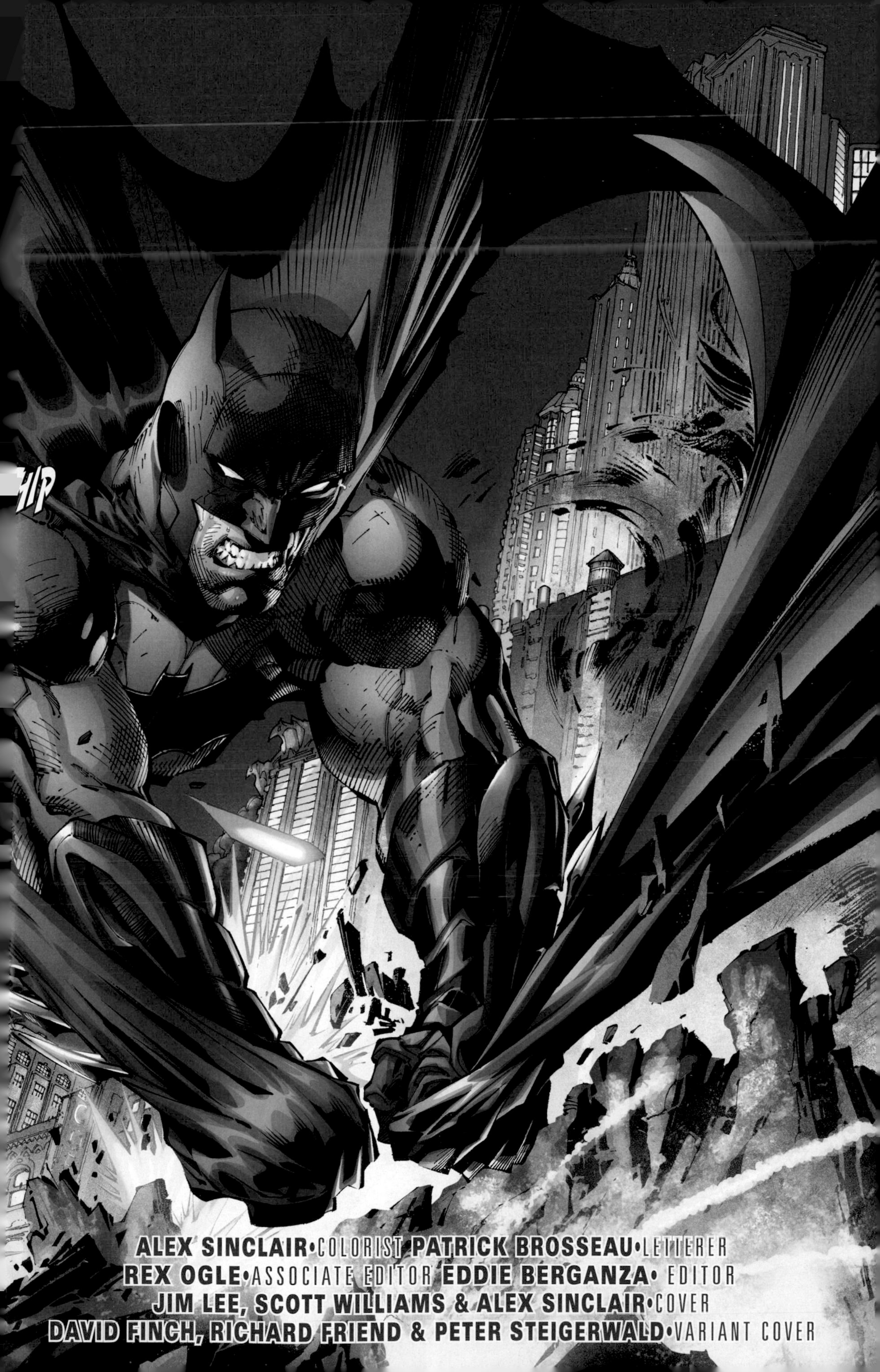

ALEX SINCLAIR•COLORIST PATRICK BROSSEAU•LETTERER
REX OGLE•ASSOCIATE EDITOR EDDIE BERGANZA• EDITOR
JIM LEE, SCOTT WILLIAMS & ALEX SINCLAIR•COVER
DAVID FINCH, RICHARD FRIEND & PETER STEIGERWALD•VARIANT COVER

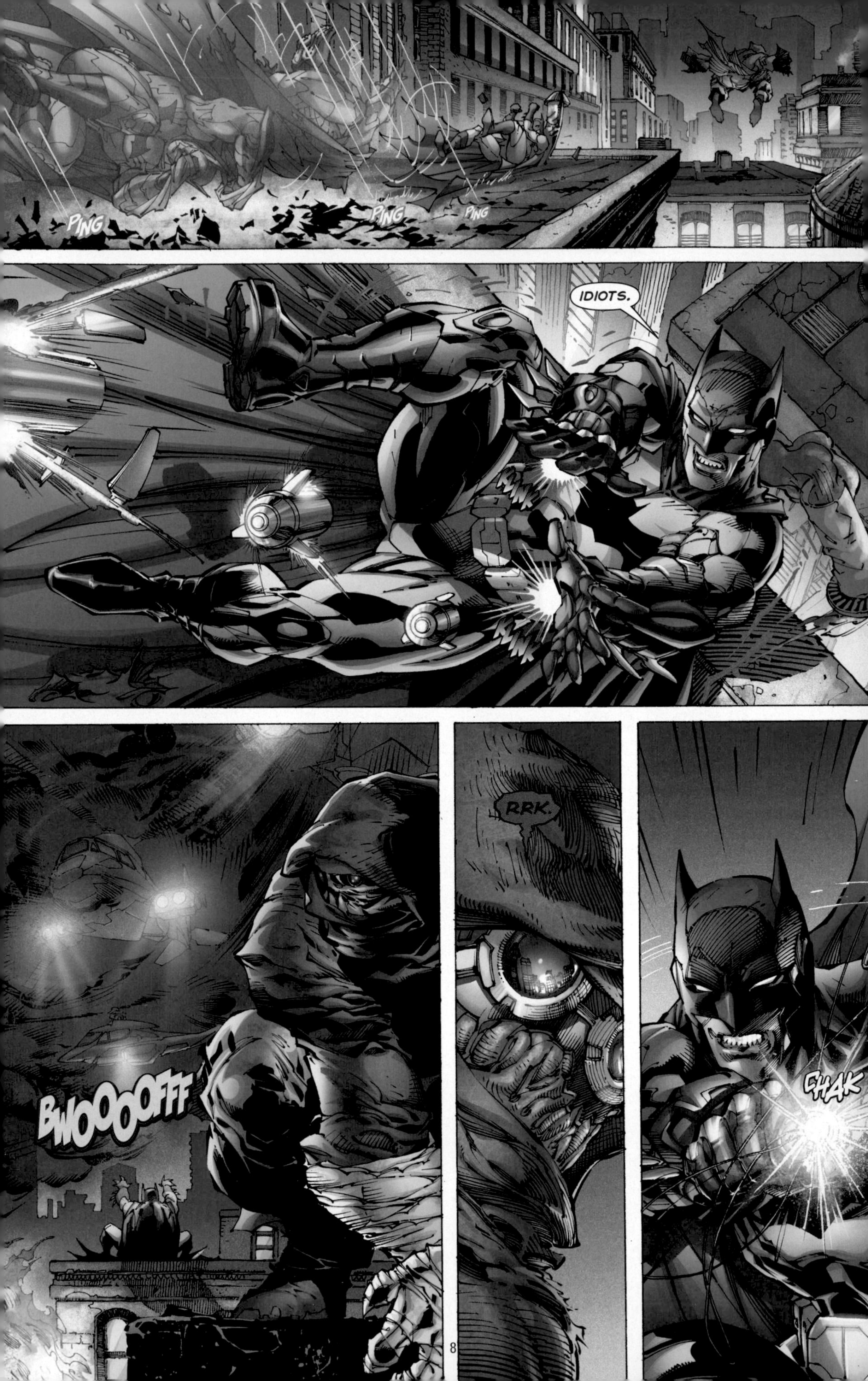
PING
PING
PING
IDIOTS.
KLINK
KLINK
BWOOOOFFF
RRK.
CHAK

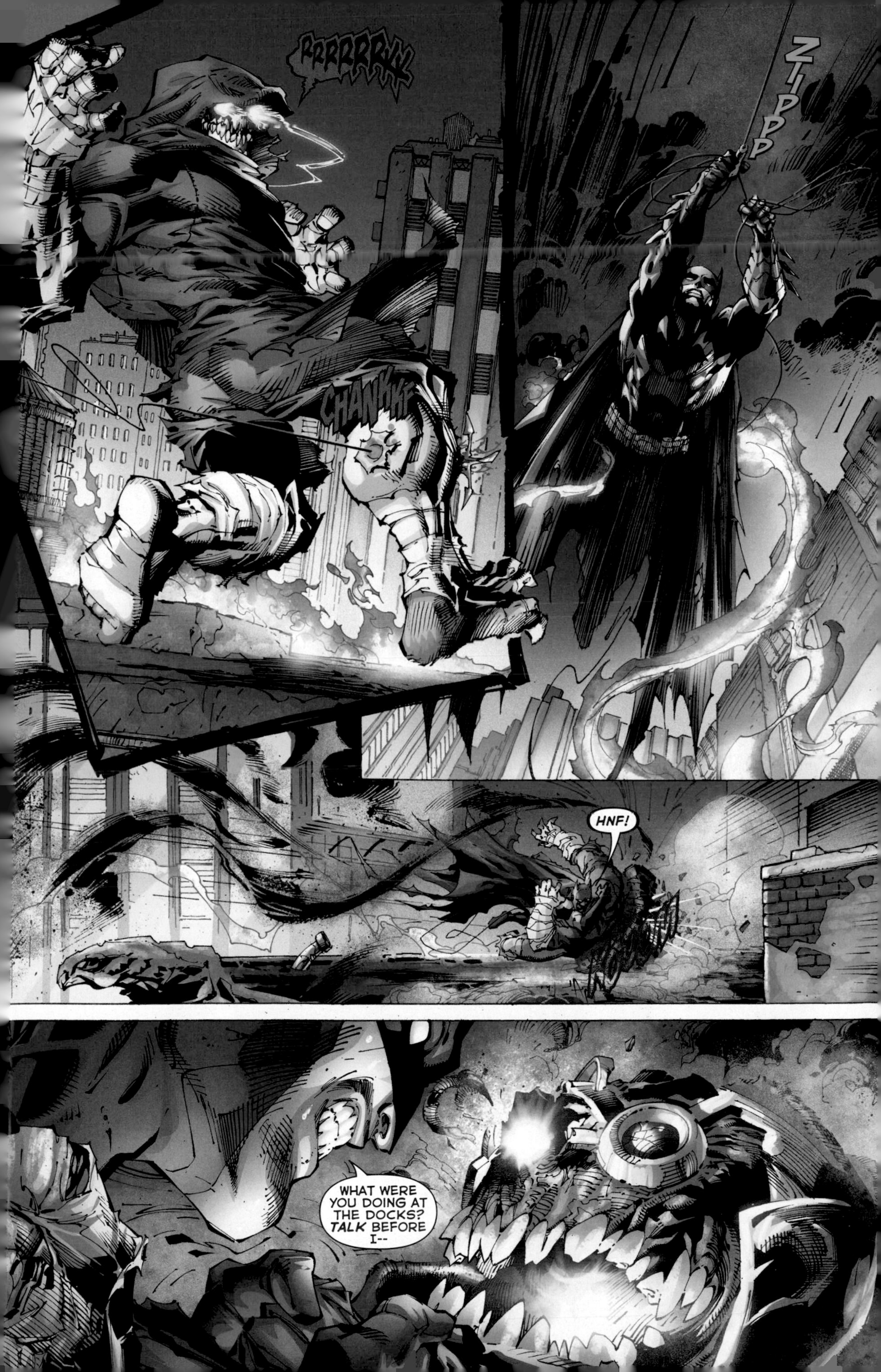
RRRRRKK
ZIPPP
CHANKK
HNF!
WHAT WERE YOU DOING AT THE DOCKS? *TALK* BEFORE I--

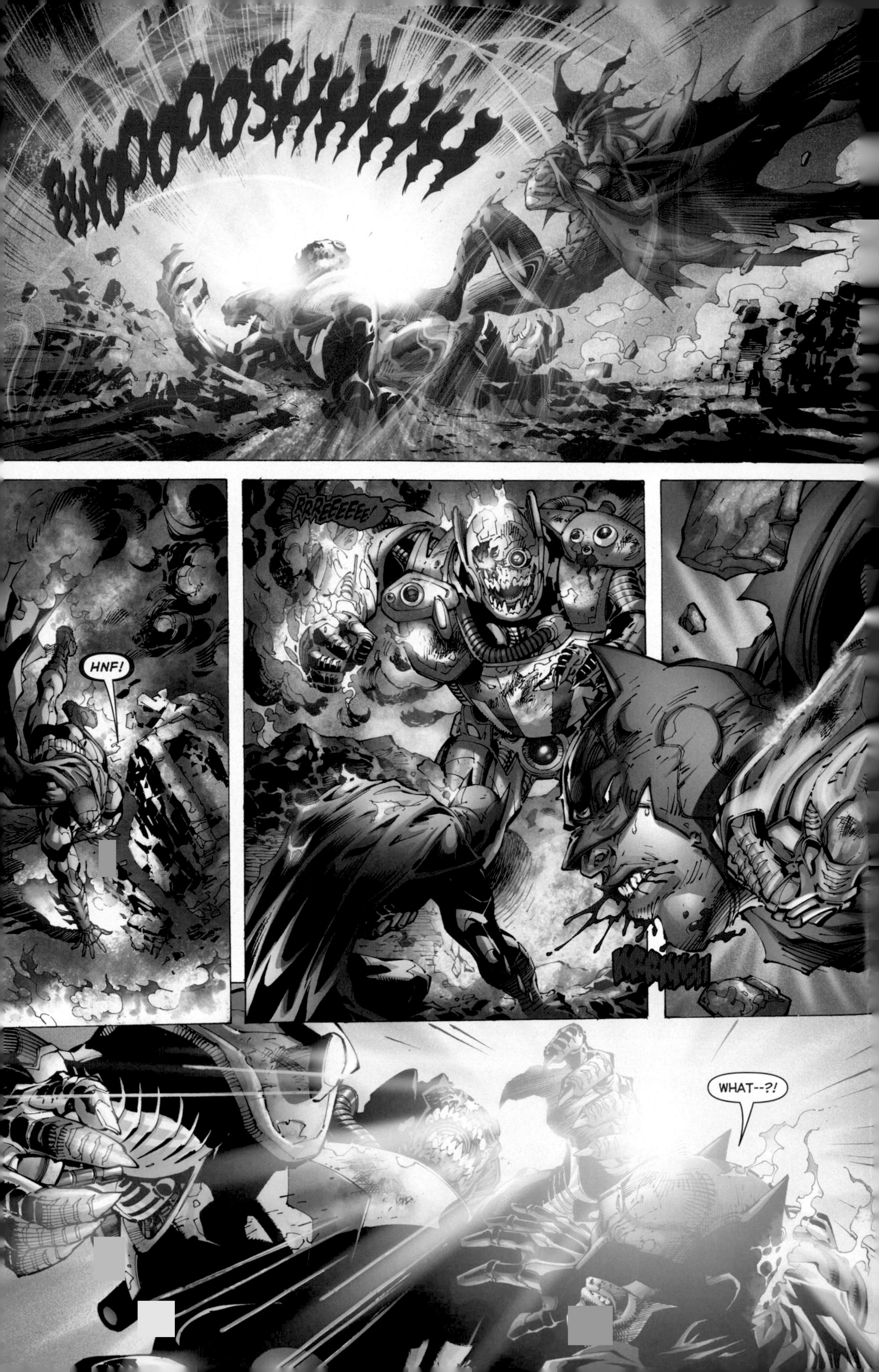
BWOOOOSHHHHH
HNF!
RRREEEEEEE!
WHAT--?!

BAMMM

KRRRKKK

BATMAN?

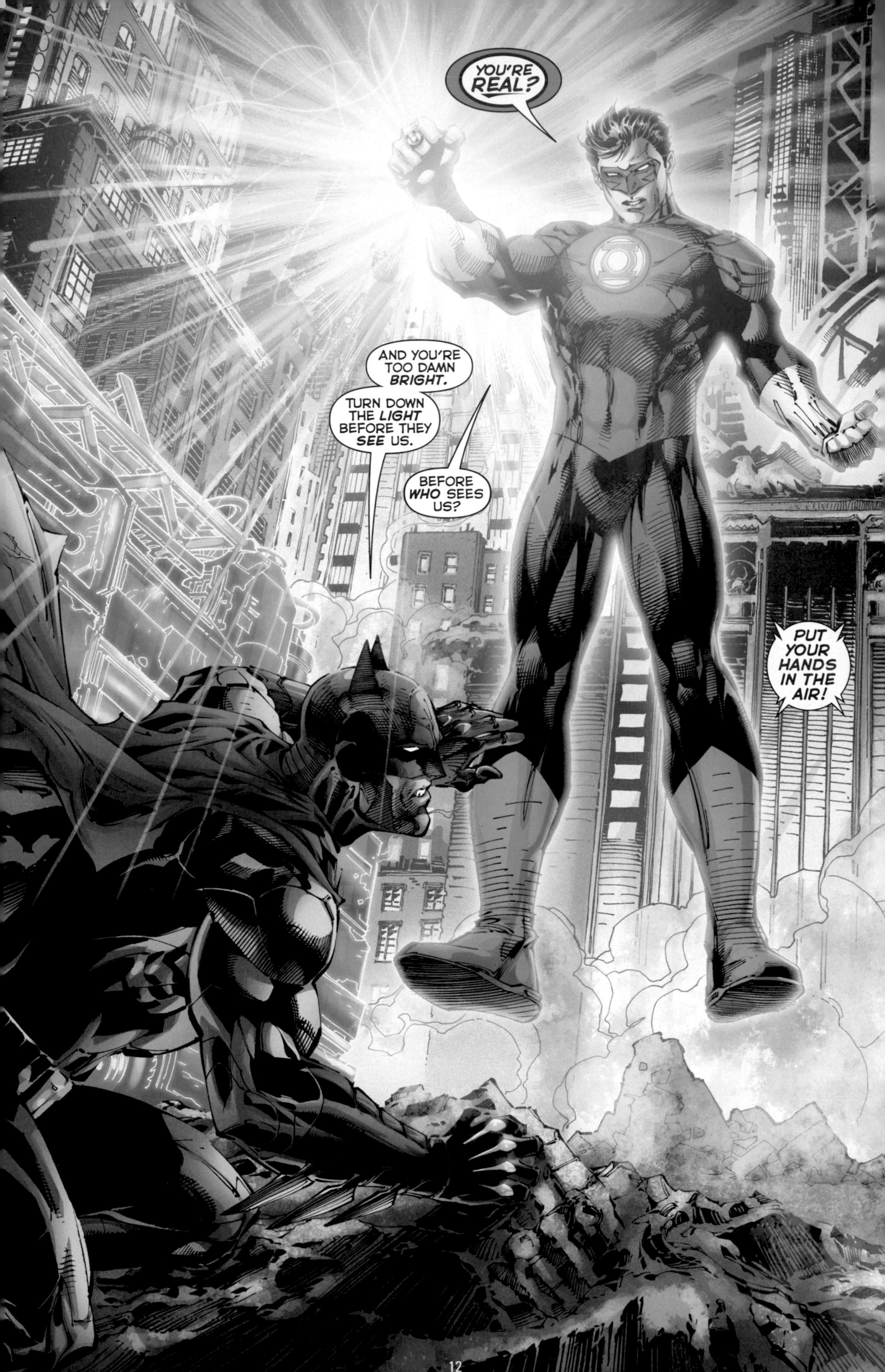
YOU'RE REAL?
AND YOU'RE TOO DAMN BRIGHT.
TURN DOWN THE LIGHT BEFORE THEY SEE US.
BEFORE WHO SEES US?
PUT YOUR HANDS IN THE AIR!

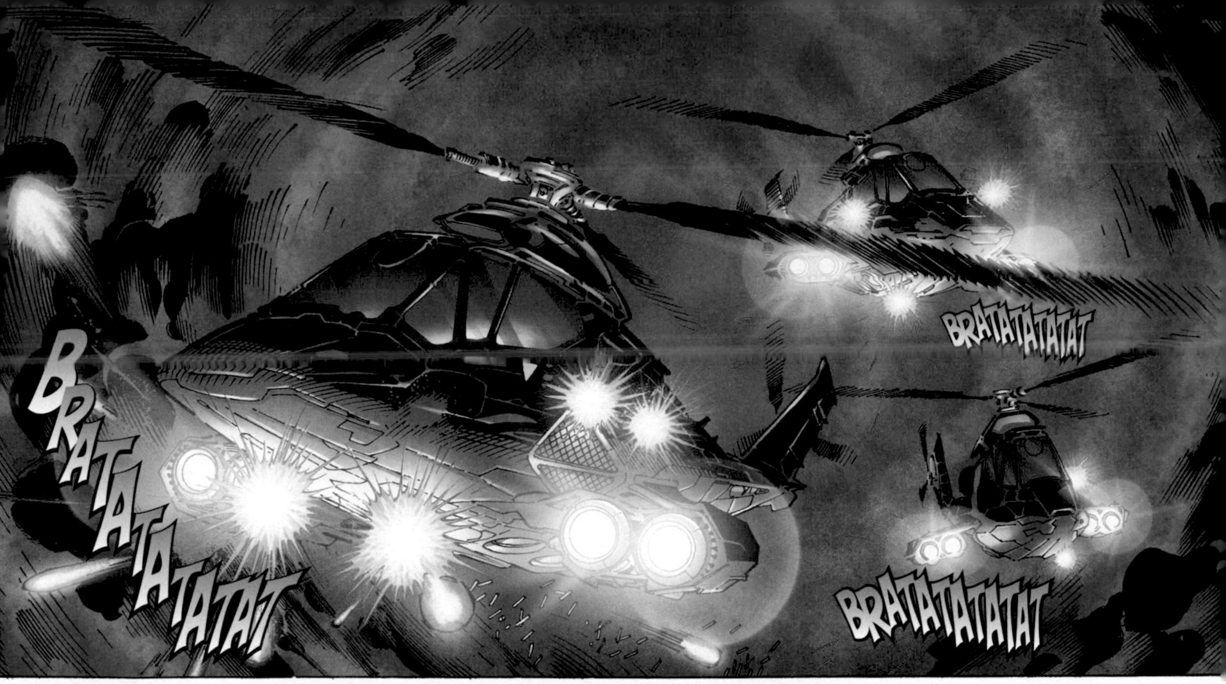
BRATATATATAT
BRATATATATAT
BRATATATATAT

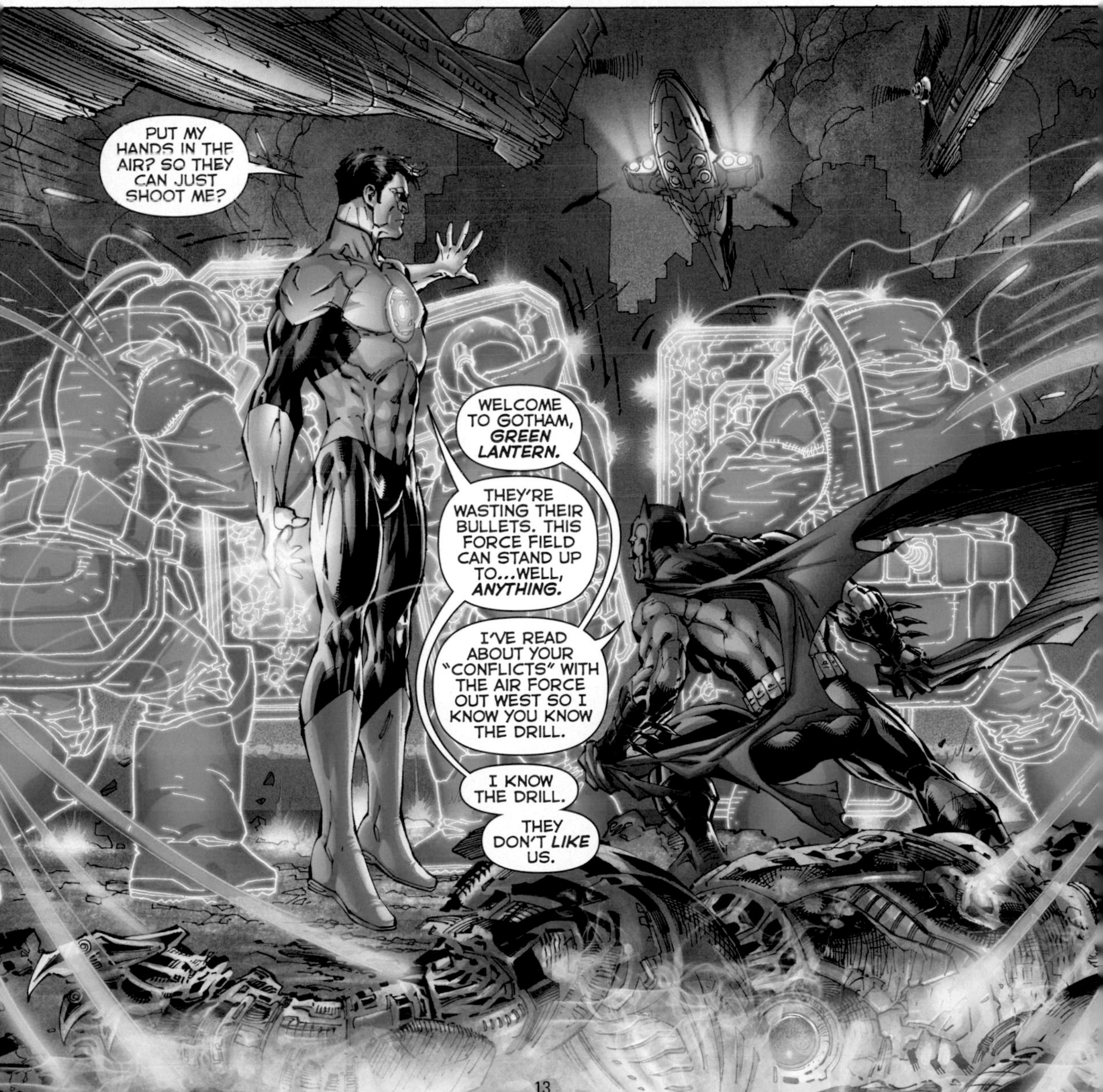
PUT MY HANDS IN THE AIR? SO THEY CAN JUST SHOOT ME?
WELCOME TO GOTHAM, *GREEN LANTERN.*
THEY'RE WASTING THEIR BULLETS. THIS FORCE FIELD CAN STAND UP TO...WELL, *ANYTHING.*
I'VE READ ABOUT YOUR "CONFLICTS" WITH THE AIR FORCE OUT WEST SO I KNOW YOU KNOW THE DRILL.
I KNOW THE DRILL.
THEY DON'T *LIKE* US.

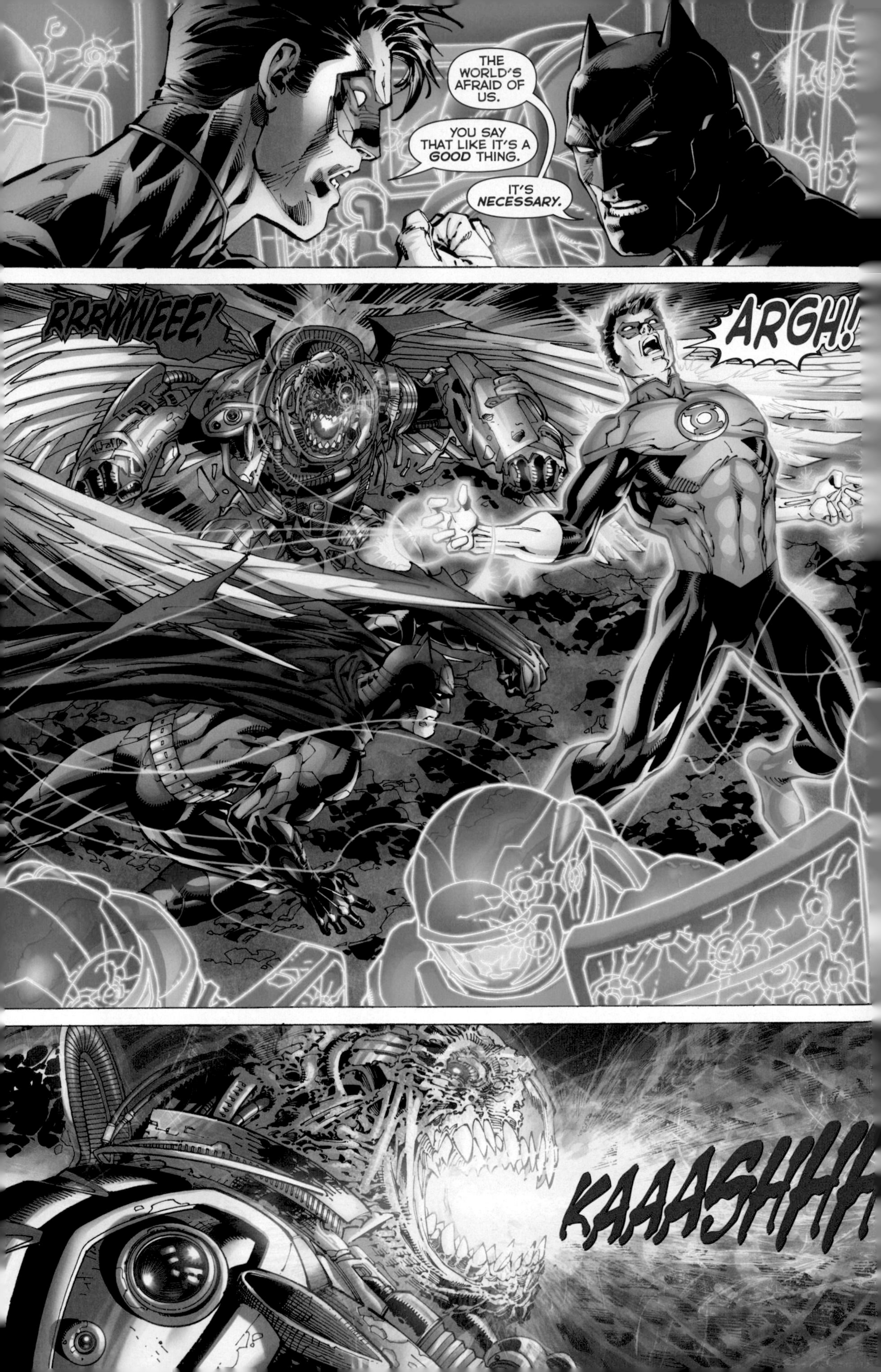

THE WORLD'S AFRAID OF US.
YOU SAY THAT LIKE IT'S A GOOD THING.
IT'S NECESSARY.
RRRWWEEE!
ARGH!
KAAASHHH

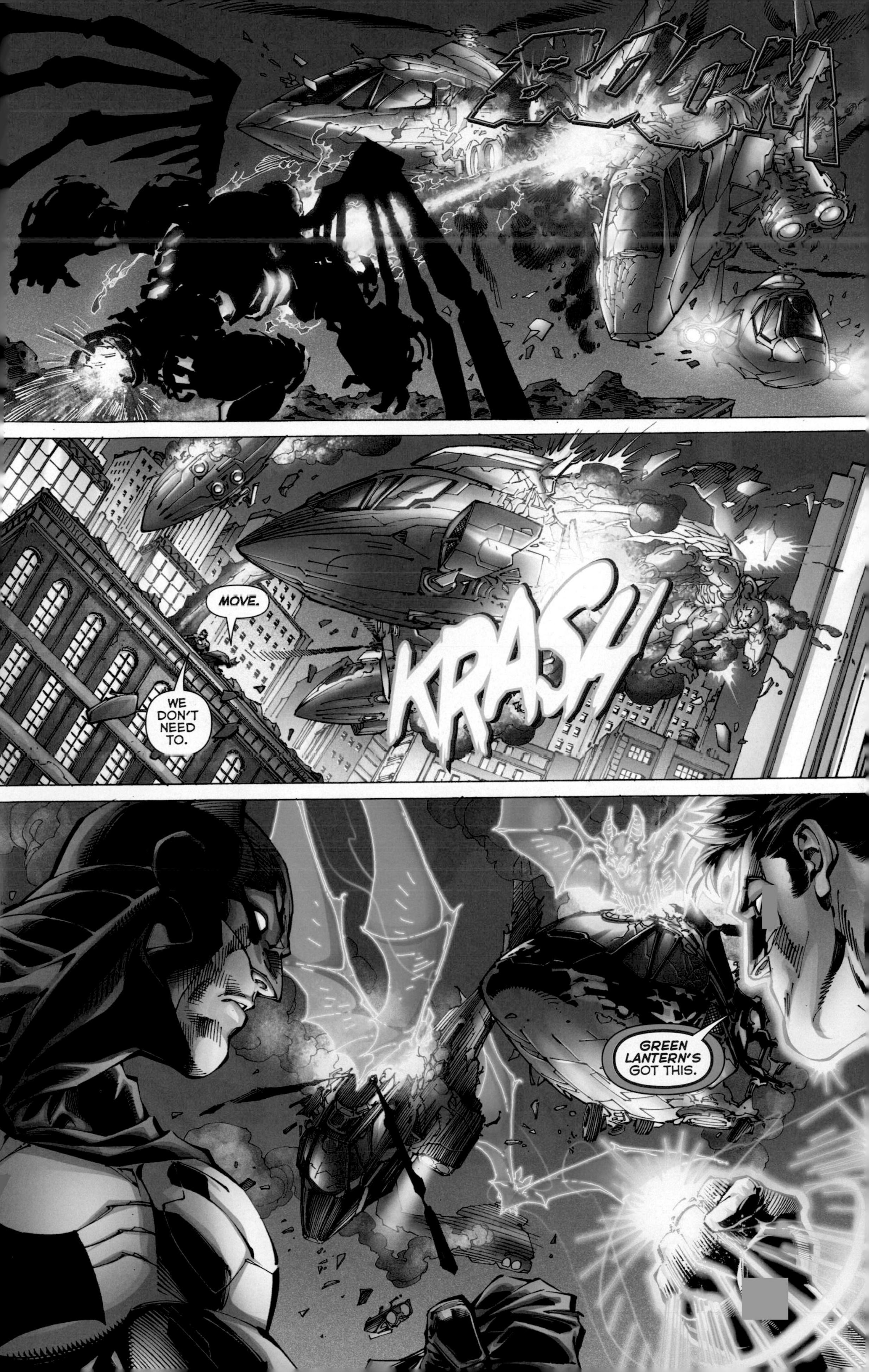
KRASH
MOVE.
WE DON'T NEED TO.
GREEN LANTERN'S GOT THIS.

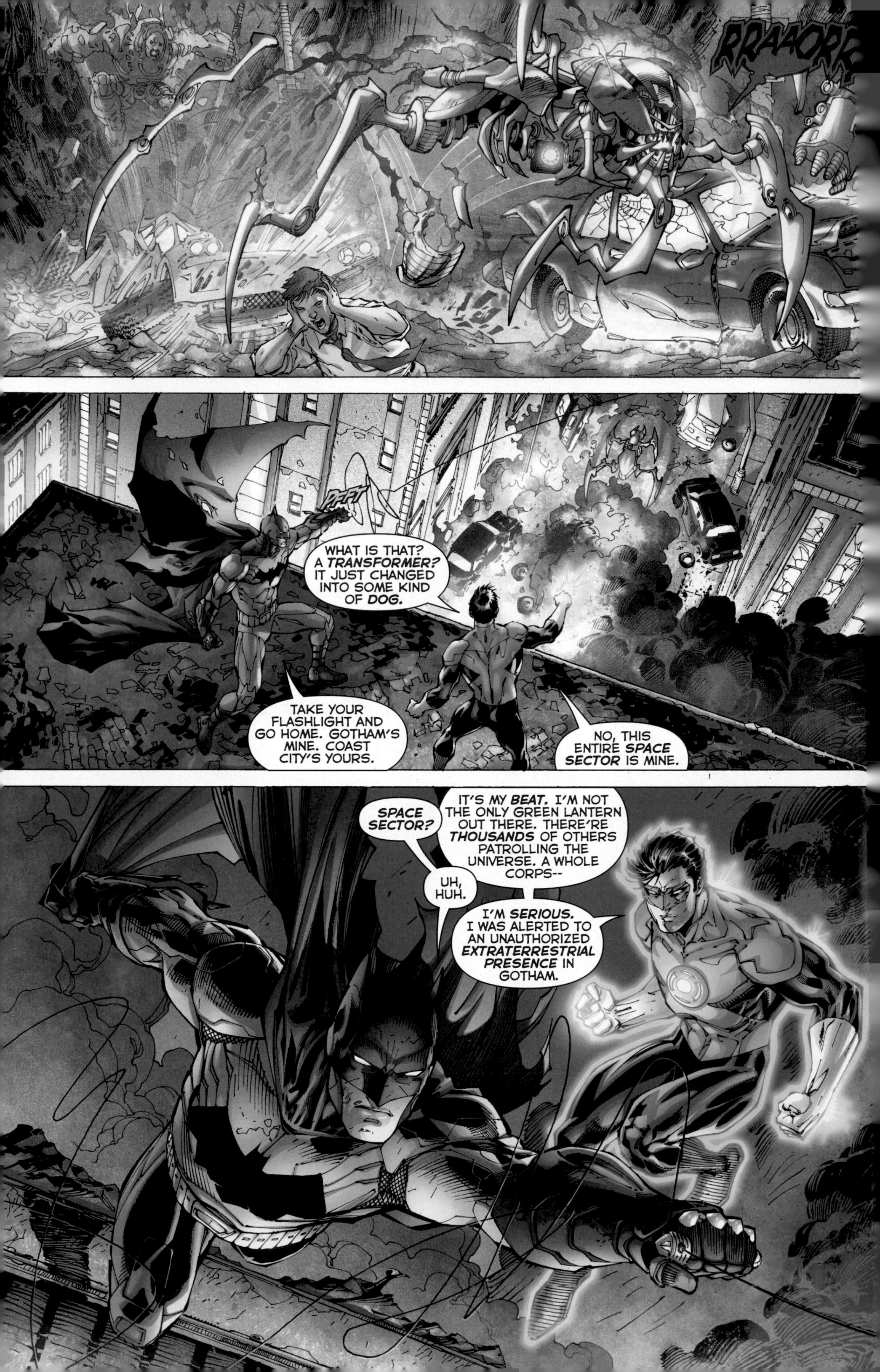
RRAAORR
PAFT
WHAT IS THAT? A TRANSFORMER? IT JUST CHANGED INTO SOME KIND OF DOG.
TAKE YOUR FLASHLIGHT AND GO HOME. GOTHAM'S MINE. COAST CITY'S YOURS.
NO, THIS ENTIRE SPACE SECTOR IS MINE.
SPACE SECTOR?
IT'S MY BEAT. I'M NOT THE ONLY GREEN LANTERN OUT THERE. THERE'RE THOUSANDS OF OTHERS PATROLLING THE UNIVERSE. A WHOLE CORPS--
UH, HUH.
I'M SERIOUS. I WAS ALERTED TO AN UNAUTHORIZED EXTRATERRESTRIAL PRESENCE IN GOTHAM.

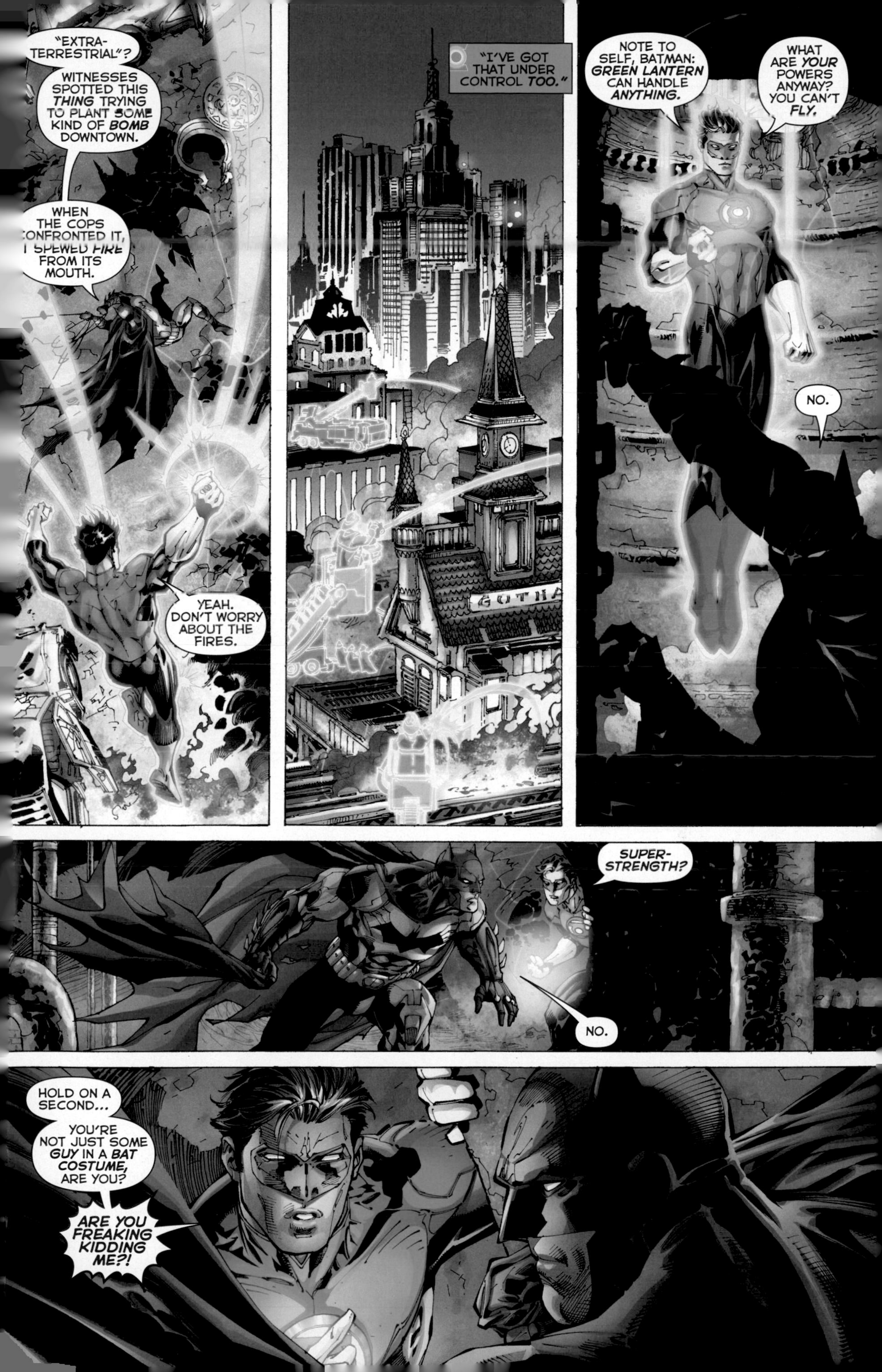
"EXTRA-TERRESTRIAL"?
WITNESSES SPOTTED THIS *THING* TRYING TO PLANT SOME KIND OF *BOMB* DOWNTOWN.
WHEN THE COPS CONFRONTED IT, IT SPEWED *FIRE* FROM ITS MOUTH.
YEAH. DON'T WORRY ABOUT THE FIRES.
"I'VE GOT THAT UNDER CONTROL *TOO.*"
GOTHA
NOTE TO SELF, BATMAN: *GREEN LANTERN* CAN HANDLE *ANYTHING.*
WHAT ARE *YOUR* POWERS ANYWAY? YOU CAN'T *FLY.*
NO.
SUPER-STRENGTH?
NO.
HOLD ON A SECOND...
YOU'RE NOT JUST SOME *GUY* IN A *BAT COSTUME,* ARE YOU?
ARE YOU FREAKING KIDDING ME?!

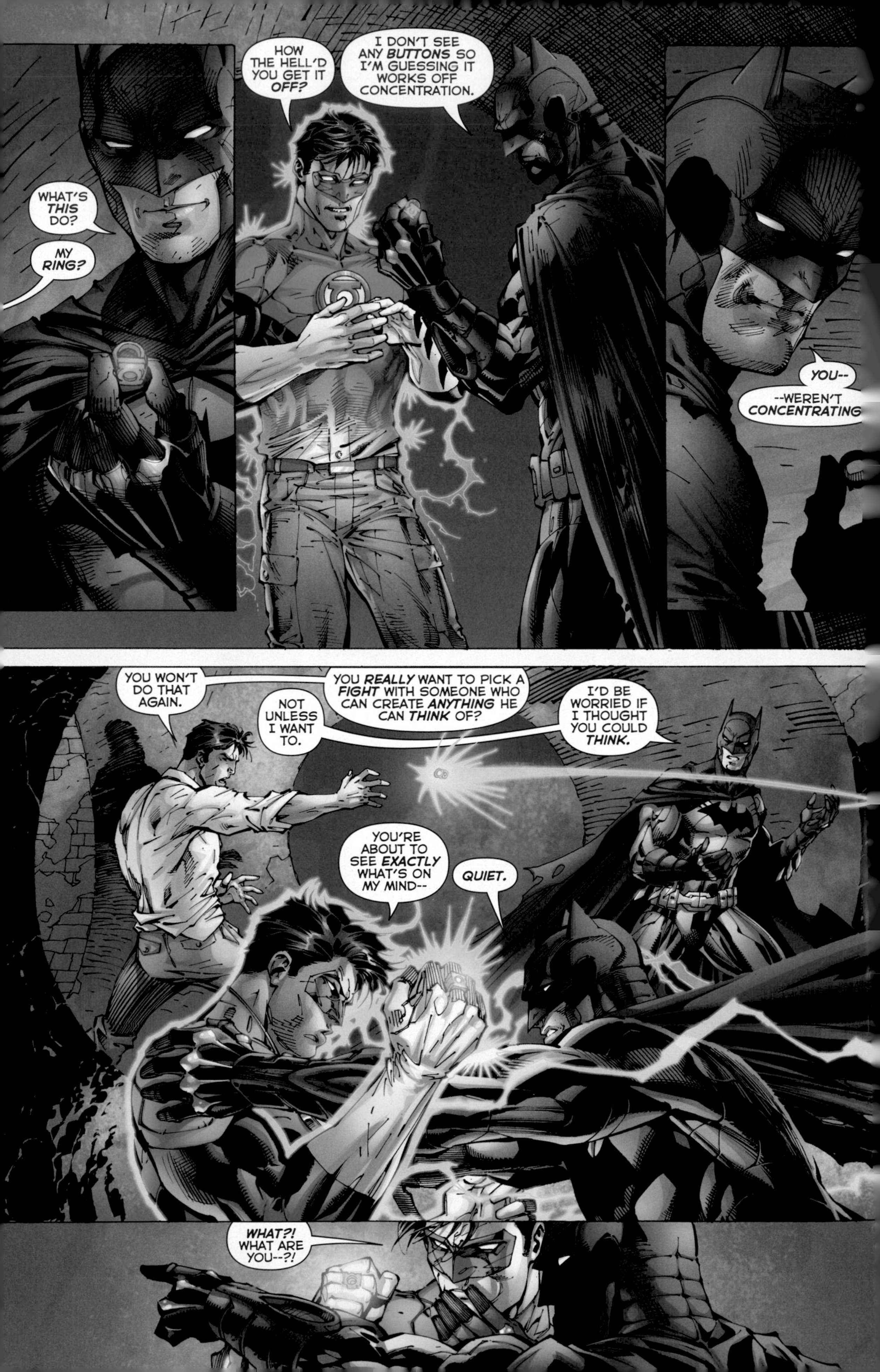

WHAT'S THIS DO?
MY RING?
HOW THE HELL'D YOU GET IT OFF?
I DON'T SEE ANY BUTTONS SO I'M GUESSING IT WORKS OFF CONCENTRATION.
YOU--
--WEREN'T CONCENTRATING
YOU WON'T DO THAT AGAIN.
NOT UNLESS I WANT TO.
YOU REALLY WANT TO PICK A FIGHT WITH SOMEONE WHO CAN CREATE ANYTHING HE CAN THINK OF?
I'D BE WORRIED IF I THOUGHT YOU COULD THINK.
YOU'RE ABOUT TO SEE EXACTLY WHAT'S ON MY MIND--
QUIET.
WHAT?! WHAT ARE YOU--?!

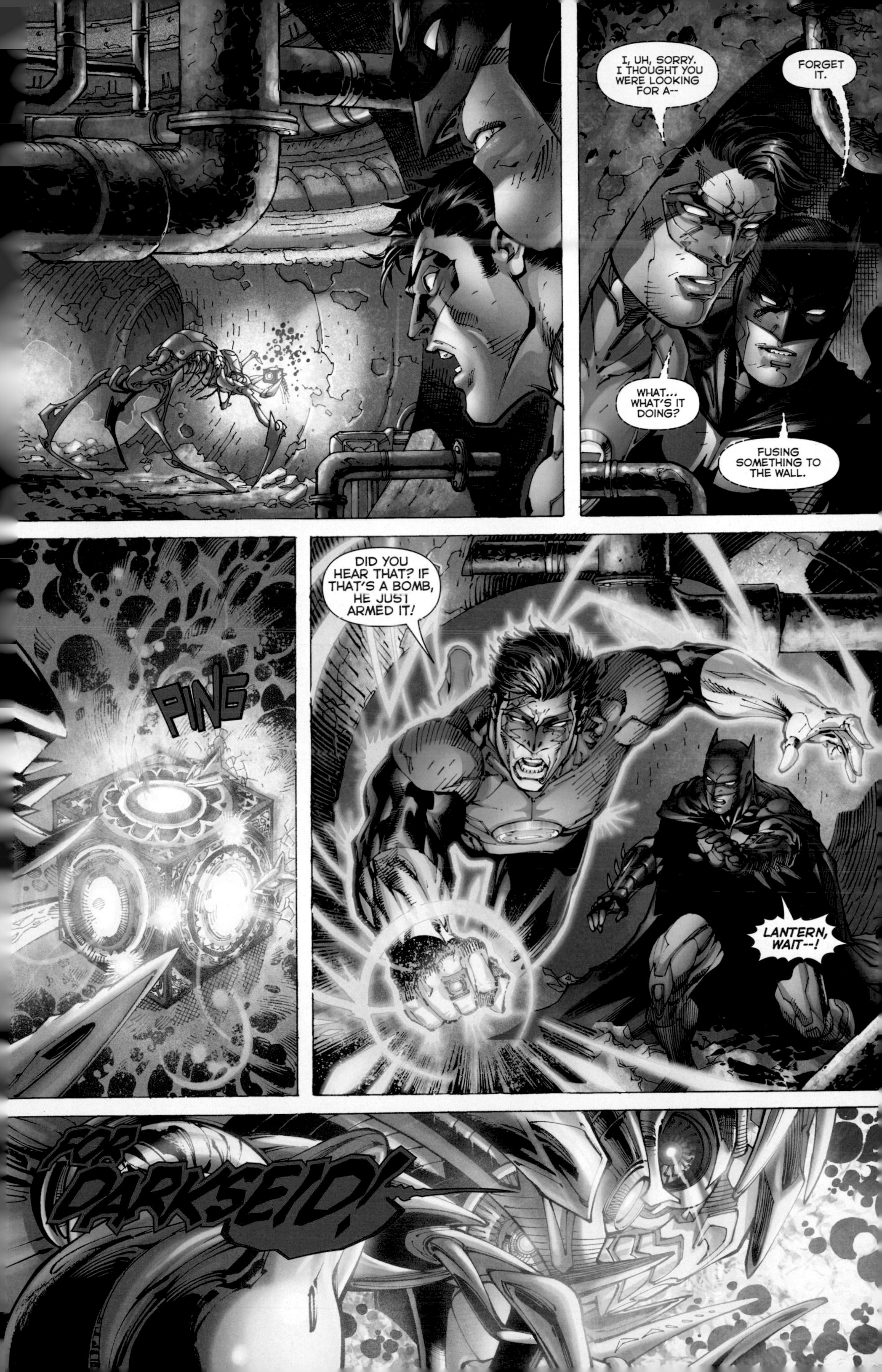
I, UH, SORRY. I THOUGHT YOU WERE LOOKING FOR A--
FORGET IT.
WHAT... WHAT'S IT DOING?
FUSING SOMETHING TO THE WALL.
PING
DID YOU HEAR THAT? IF THAT'S A BOMB, HE JUST ARMED IT!
LANTERN, WAIT--!
FOR DARKSEID!

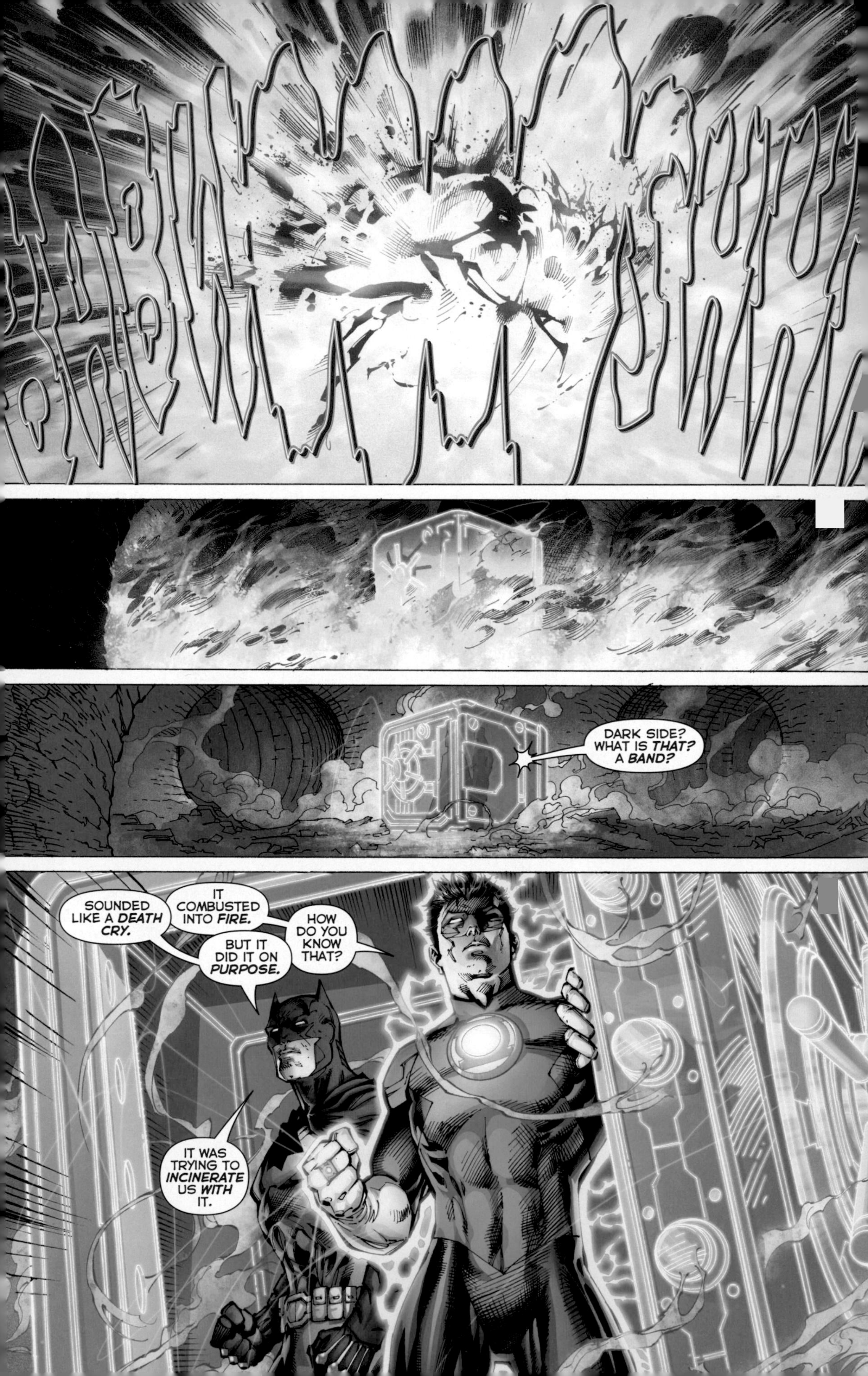
DARK SIDE? WHAT IS THAT? A BAND?
SOUNDED LIKE A DEATH CRY.
IT COMBUSTED INTO FIRE.
BUT IT DID IT ON PURPOSE.
HOW DO YOU KNOW THAT?
IT WAS TRYING TO INCINERATE US WITH IT.

WHATEVER THAT THING CAME HERE TO DO, IT DID IT.

IT PLANTED **THIS**.

RING. SCAN AND IDENTIFY.

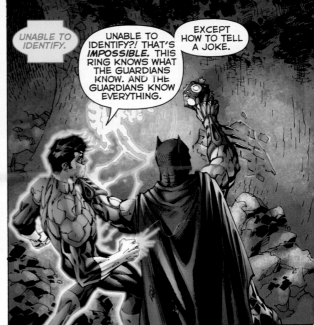

UNABLE TO IDENTIFY.

UNABLE TO IDENTIFY?! THAT'S **IMPOSSIBLE**. THIS RING KNOWS WHAT THE GUARDIANS KNOW. AND THE GUARDIANS KNOW EVERYTHING.

EXCEPT HOW TO TELL A JOKE.

IT DOESN'T LOOK LIKE A BOMB. MORE LIKE SOME KIND OF ALIEN *COMPUTER*.

ALIEN...MAYBE THIS IS ALL CONNECTED TO THAT GUY IN METROPOLIS.

SUPERMAN?

THEY SAY *HE'S* AN ALIEN.

FING

HE **IS**. AND HE'S **DANGEROUS**.

YOU'VE MET SUPERMAN?

NO. BUT I'VE... RESEARCHED HIM. HIS POWER LEVELS--

WON'T BE A PROBLEM FOR **ME**.

HEY--!

COME ON, BATMAN...

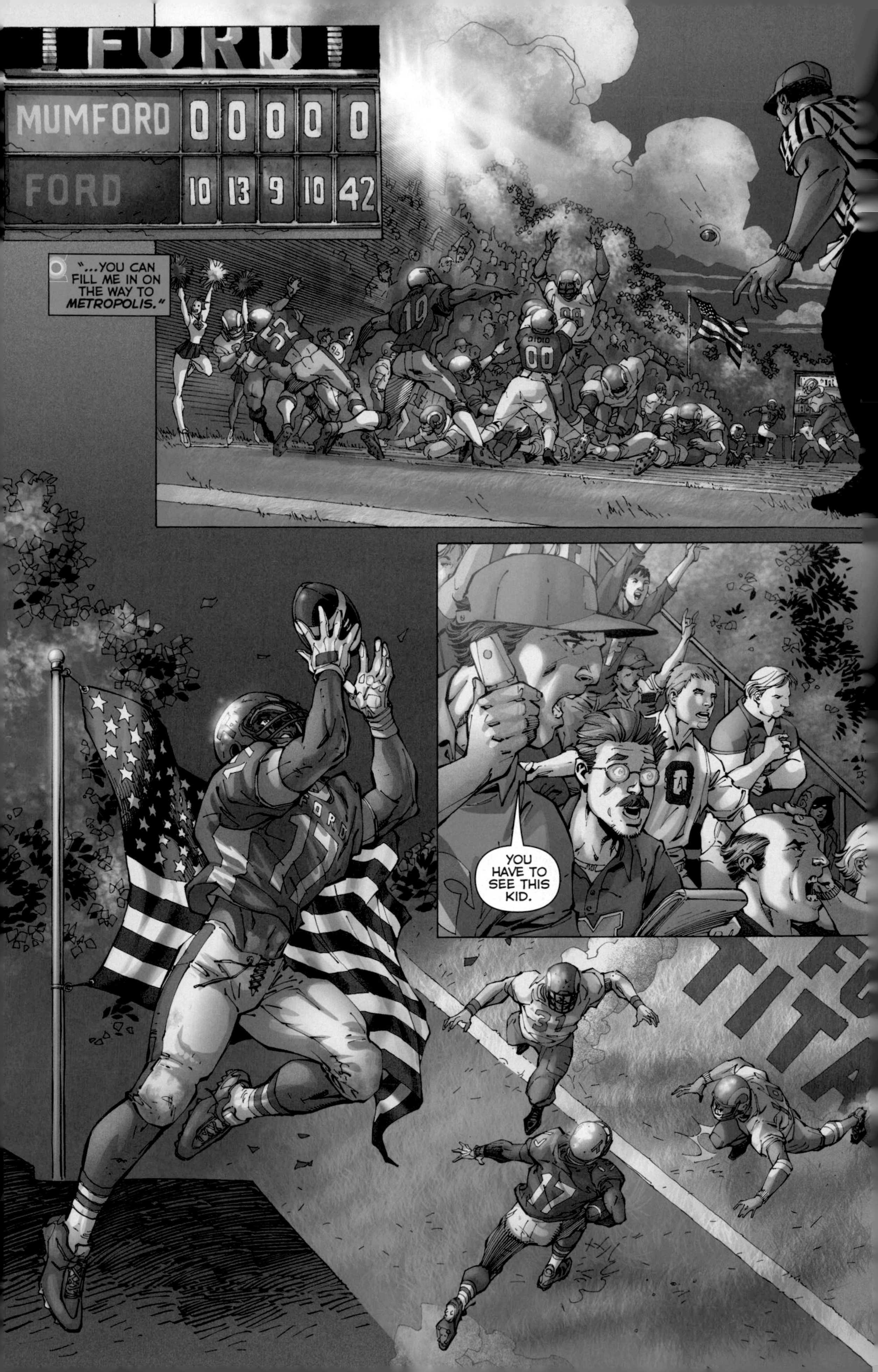
FORD
MUMFORD 0 0 0 0 0
FORD 10 13 9 10 42
"...YOU CAN FILL ME IN ON THE WAY TO METROPOLIS."
YOU HAVE TO SEE THIS KID.

NNFFF!!

TOUCHDOWN!!!

FORD 10 13 9 16 48
TIME 00.0

DAMN.

HE'S A TANK.

GET ME COACH CARROLL.

I JUST FOUND OUR NEW RECEIVER.

WAY TO GO, VIC!

NEXT STOP: STATE FINALS!

14

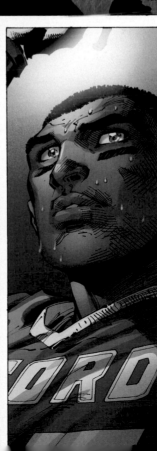

"THERE'S NOTHING VIC STONE LOVES MORE THAN FOOTBALL."

RESERVED

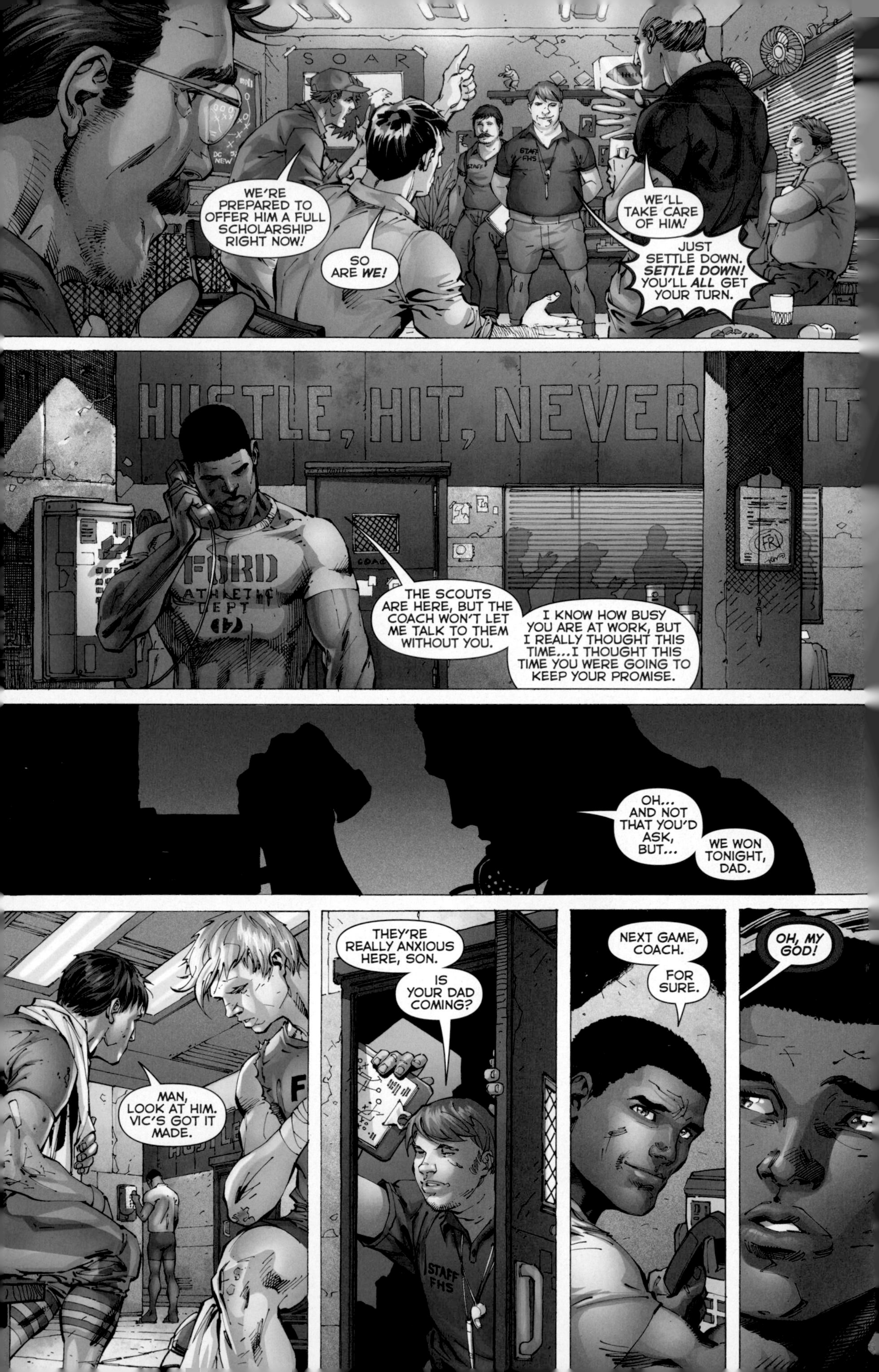

SOAR
WE'RE PREPARED TO OFFER HIM A FULL SCHOLARSHIP RIGHT NOW!
SO ARE *WE!*
WE'LL TAKE CARE OF HIM!
JUST SETTLE DOWN. *SETTLE DOWN!* YOU'LL *ALL* GET YOUR TURN.
HUSTLE, HIT, NEVER
FORD ATHLETIC DEPT
THE SCOUTS ARE HERE, BUT THE COACH WON'T LET ME TALK TO THEM WITHOUT YOU.
I KNOW HOW BUSY YOU ARE AT WORK, BUT I REALLY THOUGHT THIS TIME... I THOUGHT THIS TIME YOU WERE GOING TO KEEP YOUR PROMISE.
OH... AND NOT THAT YOU'D ASK, BUT...
WE WON TONIGHT, DAD.
MAN, LOOK AT HIM. VIC'S GOT IT MADE.
THEY'RE REALLY ANXIOUS HERE, SON.
IS YOUR DAD COMING?
STAFF FHS
NEXT GAME, COACH.
FOR SURE.
OH, MY GOD!

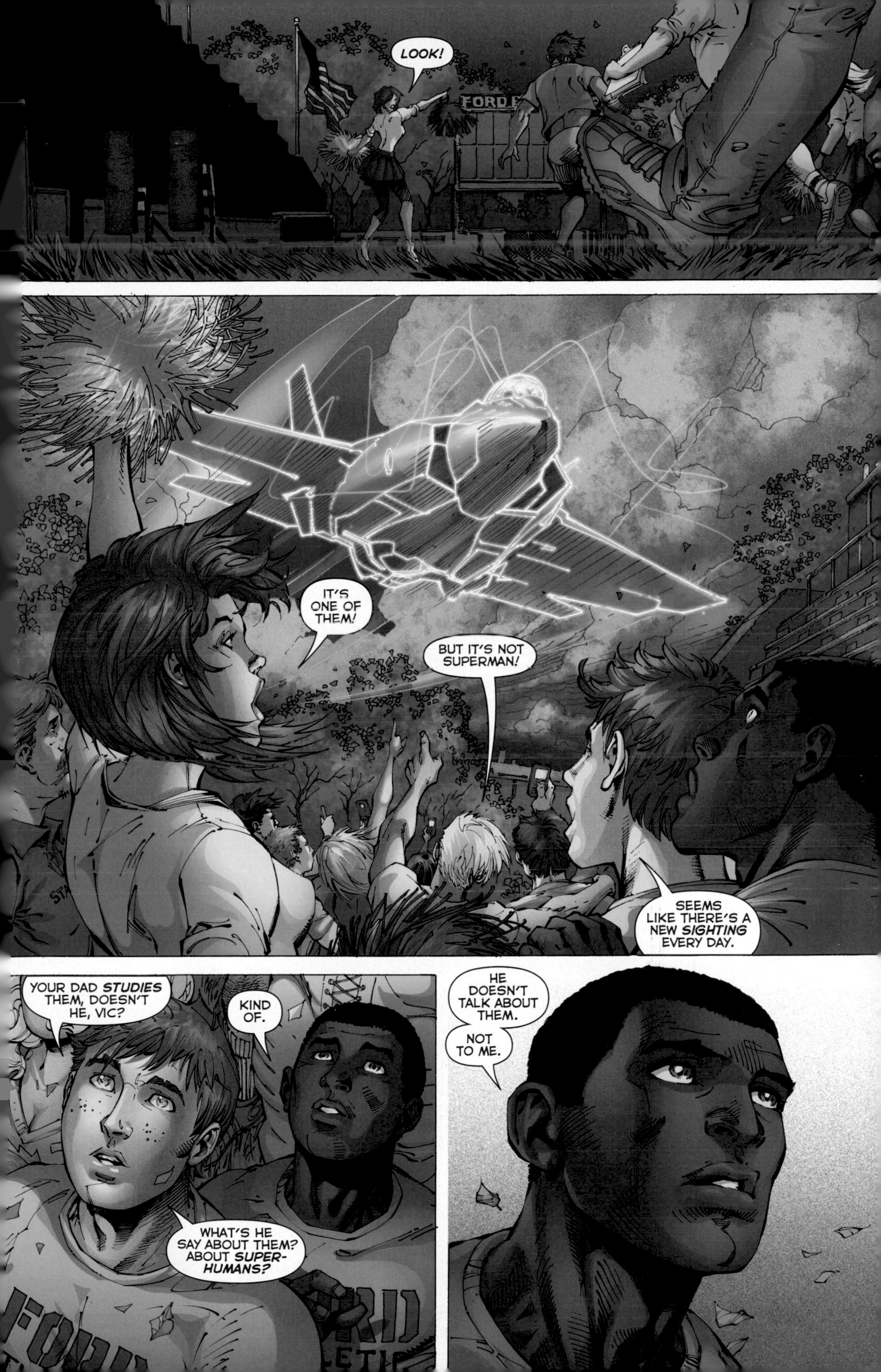
LOOK!
FORD
IT'S ONE OF THEM!
BUT IT'S NOT SUPERMAN!
SEEMS LIKE THERE'S A NEW SIGHTING EVERY DAY.
YOUR DAD STUDIES THEM, DOESN'T HE, VIC?
KIND OF.
WHAT'S HE SAY ABOUT THEM? ABOUT SUPER-HUMANS?
HE DOESN'T TALK ABOUT THEM.
NOT TO ME.

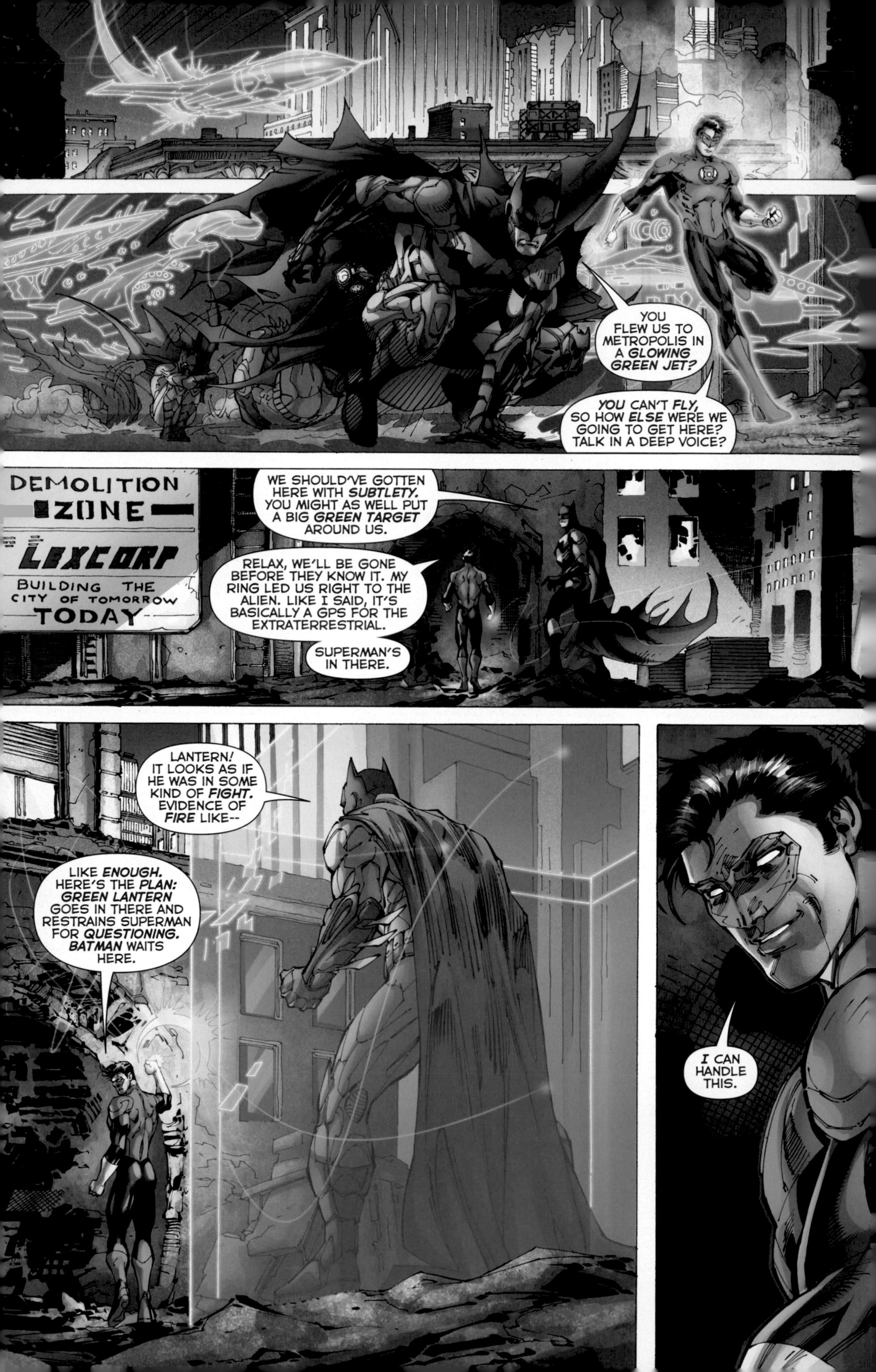

YOU FLEW US TO METROPOLIS IN A GLOWING GREEN JET?
YOU CAN'T FLY, SO HOW ELSE WERE WE GOING TO GET HERE? TALK IN A DEEP VOICE?
DEMOLITION ZONE
LEXCORP
BUILDING THE CITY OF TOMORROW TODAY
WE SHOULD'VE GOTTEN HERE WITH SUBTLETY. YOU MIGHT AS WELL PUT A BIG GREEN TARGET AROUND US.
RELAX, WE'LL BE GONE BEFORE THEY KNOW IT. MY RING LED US RIGHT TO THE ALIEN. LIKE I SAID, IT'S BASICALLY A GPS FOR THE EXTRATERRESTRIAL.
SUPERMAN'S IN THERE.
LANTERN! IT LOOKS AS IF HE WAS IN SOME KIND OF FIGHT. EVIDENCE OF FIRE LIKE--
LIKE ENOUGH. HERE'S THE PLAN: GREEN LANTERN GOES IN THERE AND RESTRAINS SUPERMAN FOR QUESTIONING. BATMAN WAITS HERE.
I CAN HANDLE THIS.

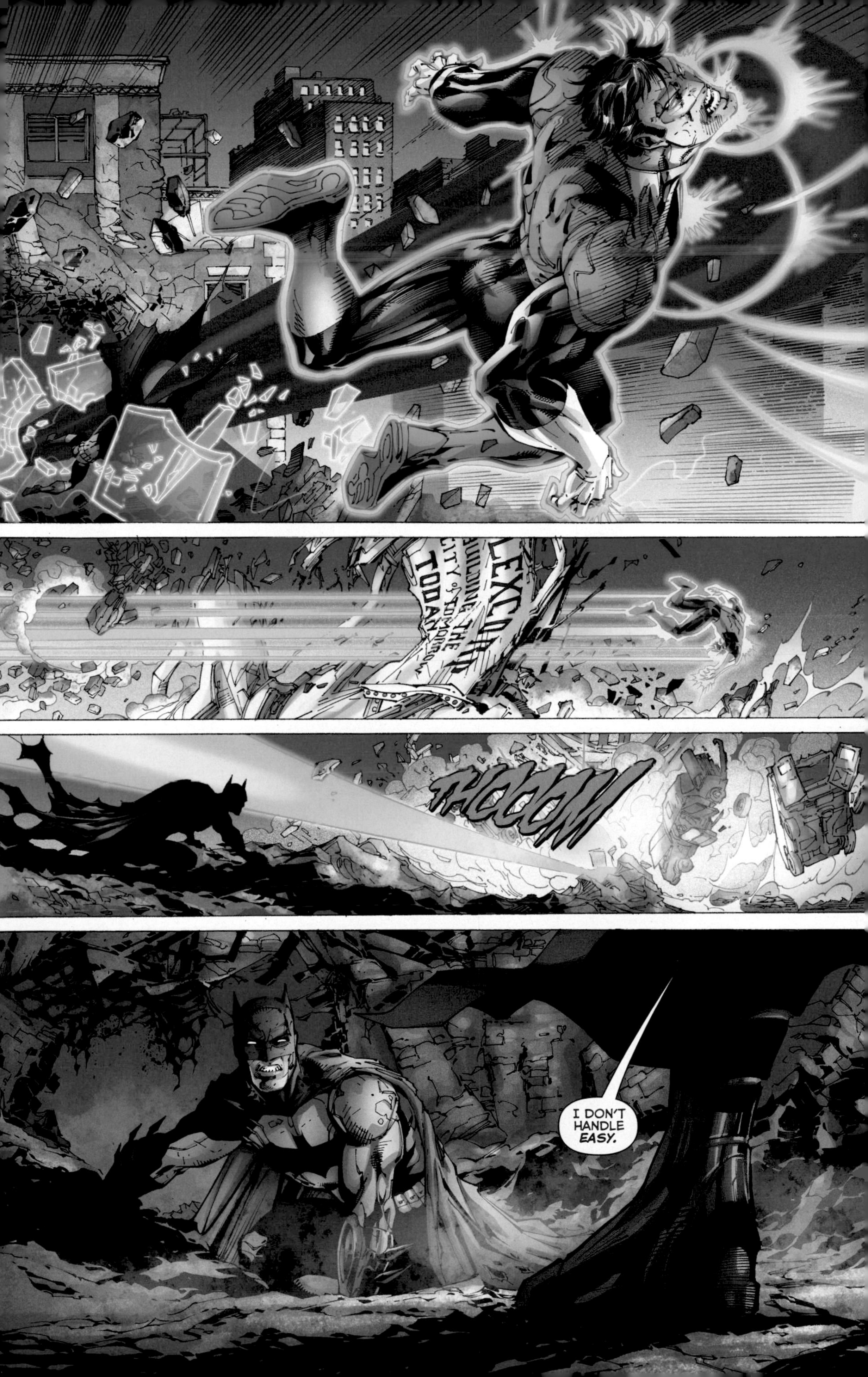
THOOOM
I DON'T HANDLE EASY.

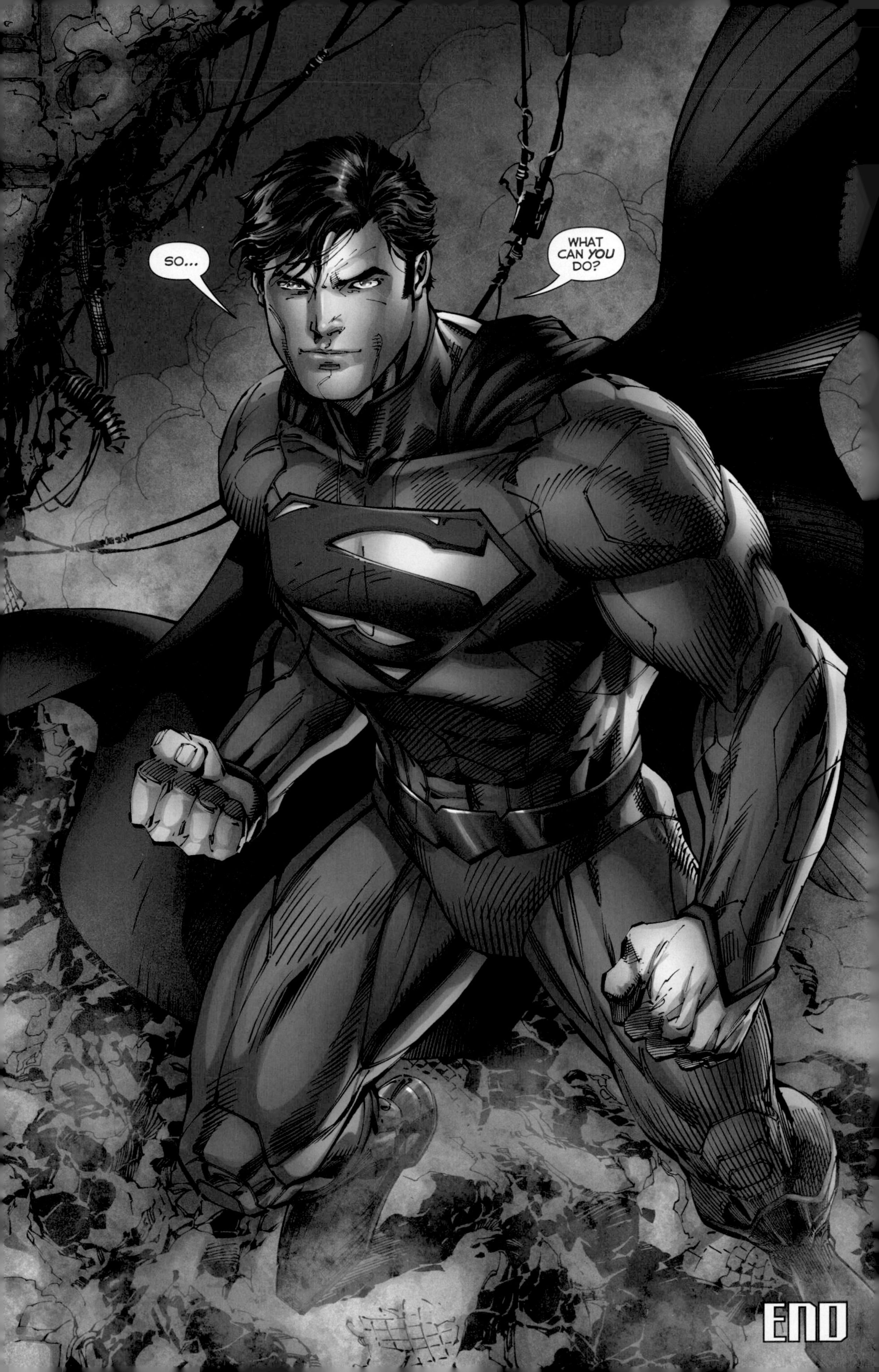
SO...
WHAT CAN YOU DO?
END

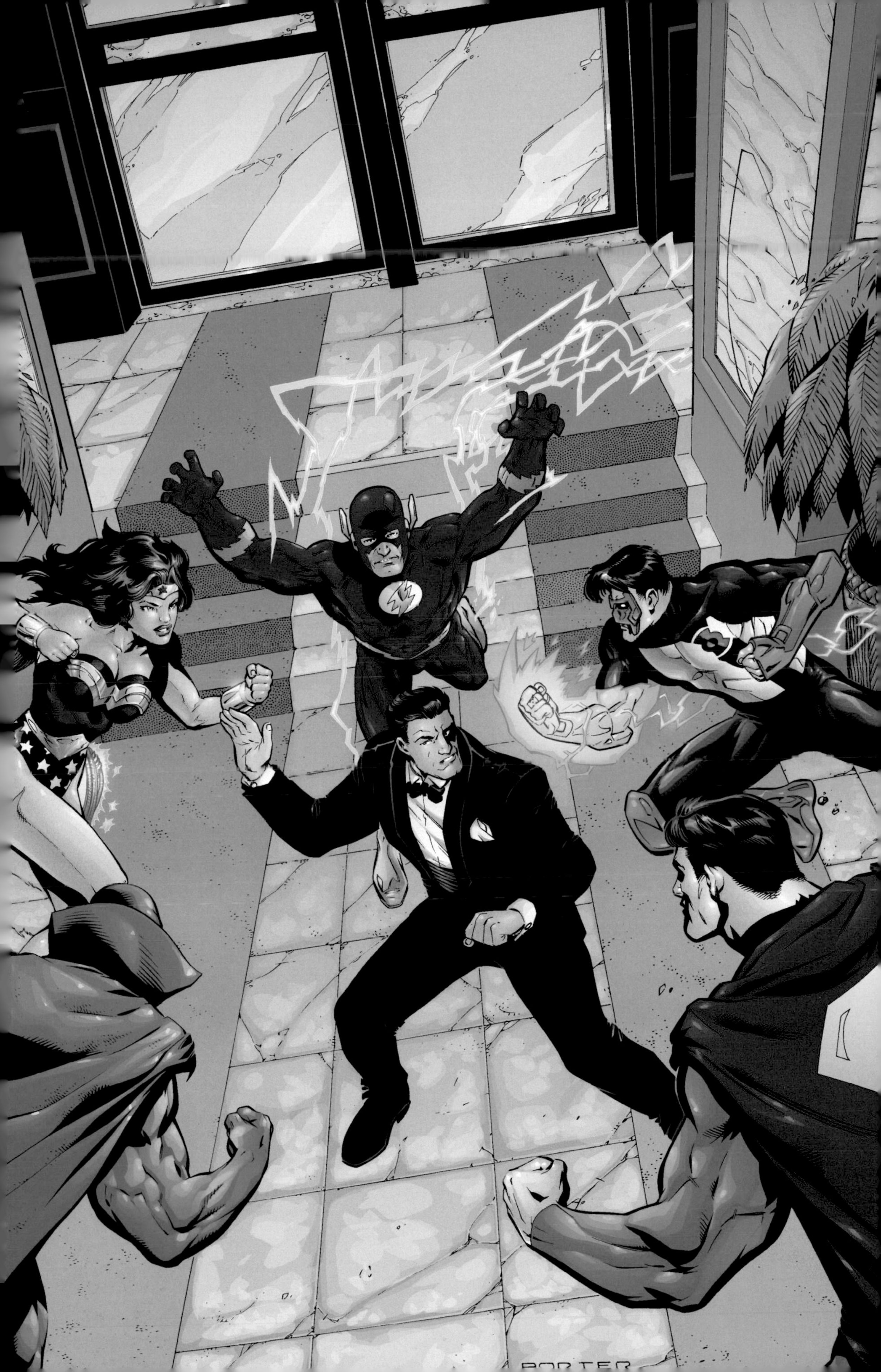

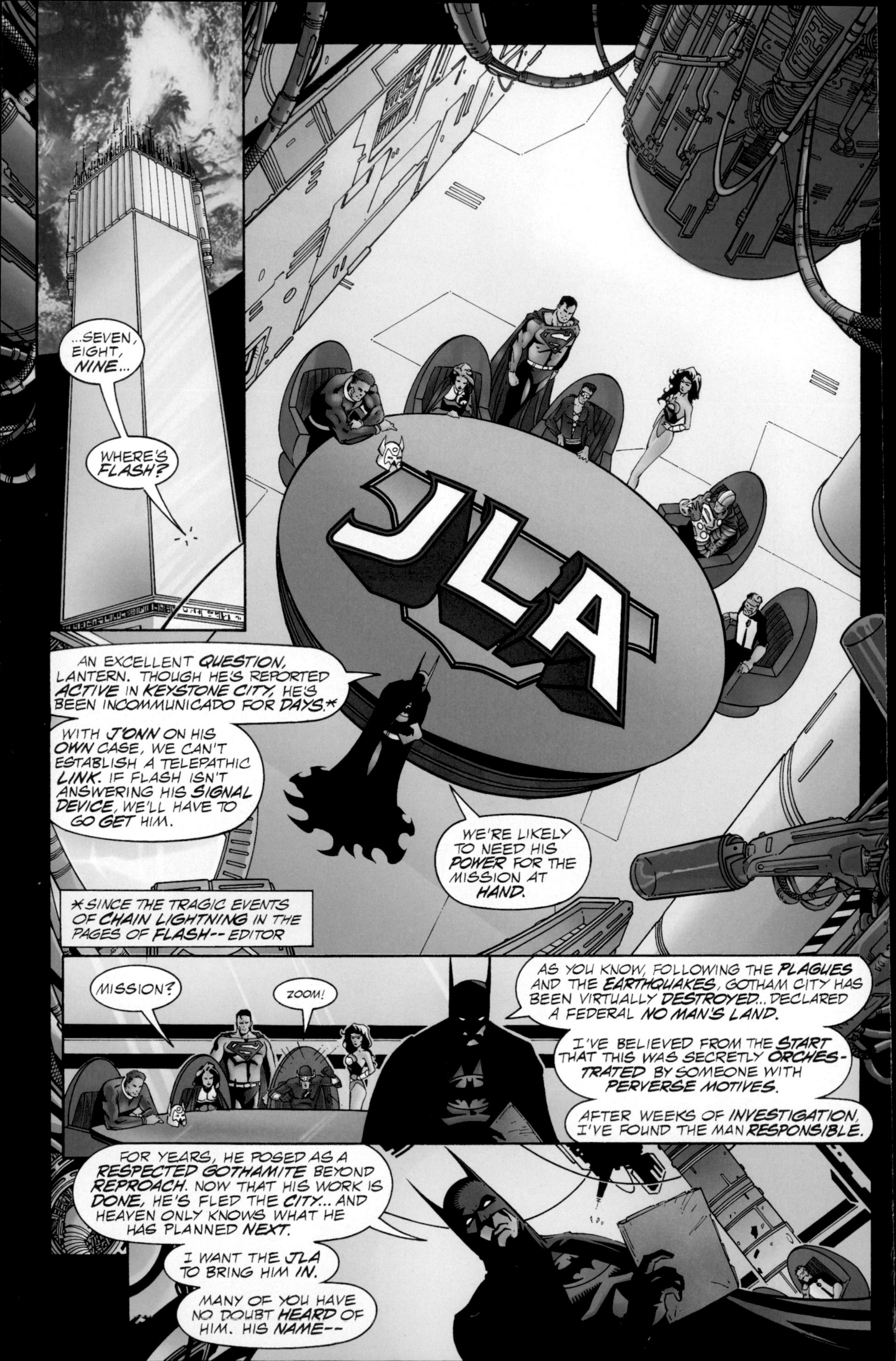

...SEVEN, EIGHT, NINE...
WHERE'S FLASH?
AN EXCELLENT QUESTION, LANTERN. THOUGH HE'S REPORTED ACTIVE IN KEYSTONE CITY, HE'S BEEN INCOMMUNICADO FOR DAYS.*
WITH J'ONN ON HIS OWN CASE, WE CAN'T ESTABLISH A TELEPATHIC LINK. IF FLASH ISN'T ANSWERING HIS SIGNAL DEVICE, WE'LL HAVE TO GO GET HIM.
WE'RE LIKELY TO NEED HIS POWER FOR THE MISSION AT HAND.
*SINCE THE TRAGIC EVENTS OF CHAIN LIGHTNING IN THE PAGES OF FLASH-- EDITOR
MISSION?
ZOOM!
AS YOU KNOW, FOLLOWING THE PLAGUES AND THE EARTHQUAKES, GOTHAM CITY HAS BEEN VIRTUALLY DESTROYED... DECLARED A FEDERAL NO MAN'S LAND.
I'VE BELIEVED FROM THE START THAT THIS WAS SECRETLY ORCHES-TRATED BY SOMEONE WITH PERVERSE MOTIVES.
AFTER WEEKS OF INVESTIGATION, I'VE FOUND THE MAN RESPONSIBLE.
FOR YEARS, HE POSED AS A RESPECTED GOTHAMITE BEYOND REPROACH. NOW THAT HIS WORK IS DONE, HE'S FLED THE CITY... AND HEAVEN ONLY KNOWS WHAT HE HAS PLANNED NEXT.
I WANT THE JLA TO BRING HIM IN.
MANY OF YOU HAVE NO DOUBT HEARD OF HIM. HIS NAME--

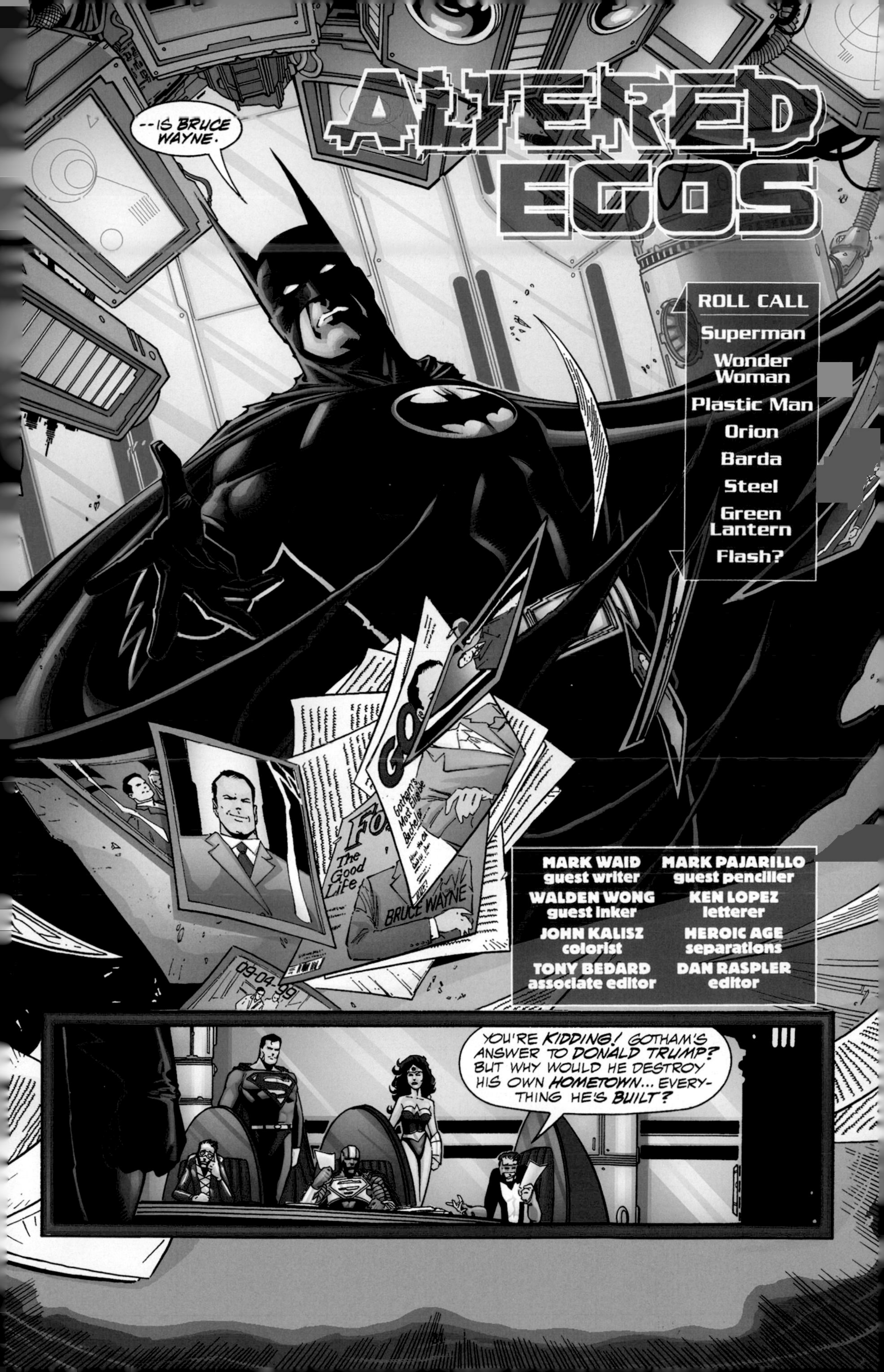
--IS BRUCE WAYNE.
ALTERED EGOS
ROLL CALL
Superman
Wonder Woman
Plastic Man
Orion
Barda
Steel
Green Lantern
Flash?
Gotham's Most Eligible Bachelor
The Good Life
BRUCE WAYNE
MARK WAID guest writer
MARK PAJARILLO guest penciller
WALDEN WONG guest inker
KEN LOPEZ letterer
JOHN KALISZ colorist
HEROIC AGE separations
TONY BEDARD associate editor
DAN RASPLER editor
YOU'RE KIDDING! GOTHAM'S ANSWER TO DONALD TRUMP? BUT WHY WOULD HE DESTROY HIS OWN HOMETOWN... EVERYTHING HE'S BUILT?

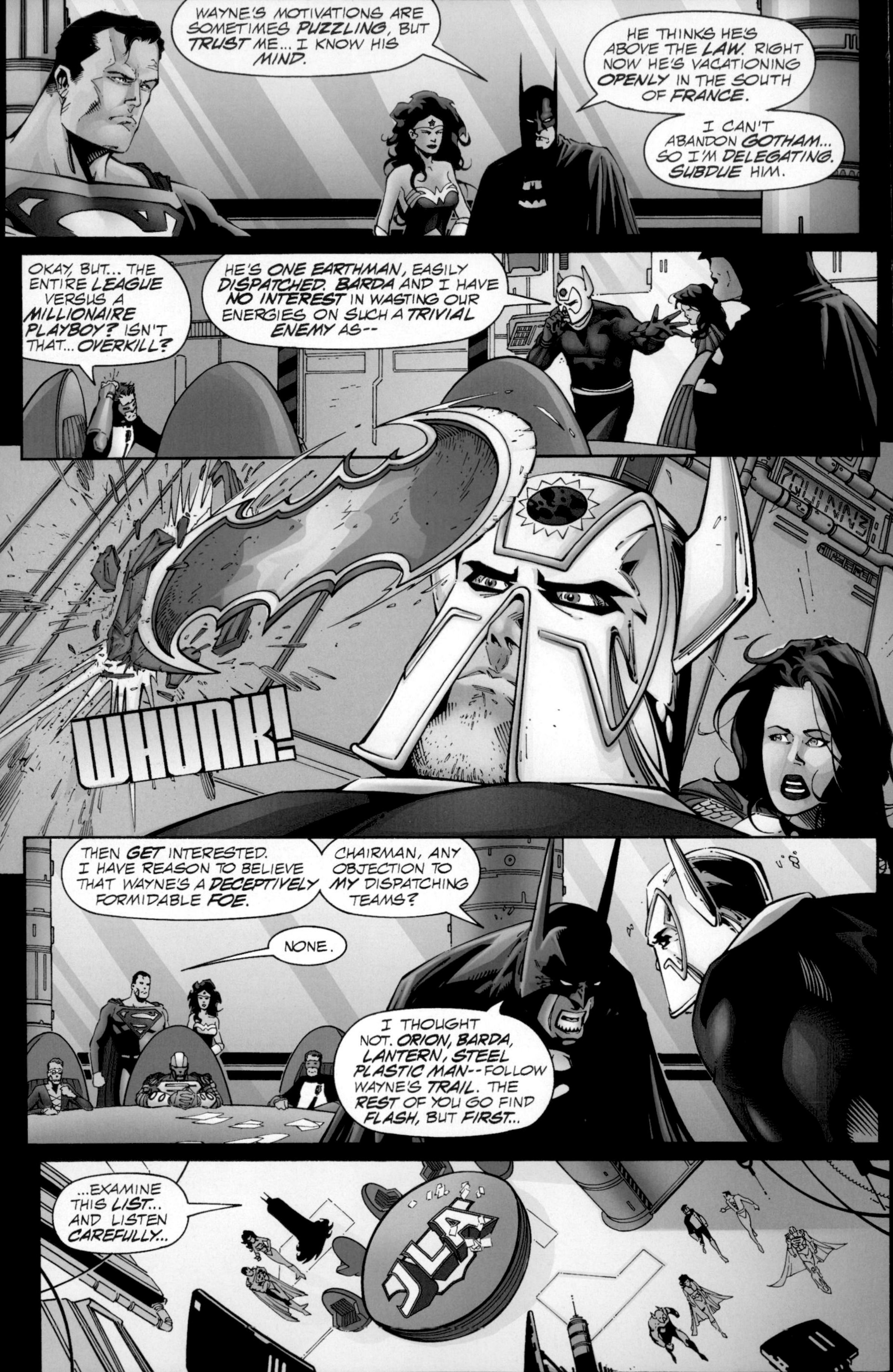
WAYNE'S MOTIVATIONS ARE SOMETIMES PUZZLING, BUT TRUST ME... I KNOW HIS MIND.
HE THINKS HE'S ABOVE THE LAW. RIGHT NOW HE'S VACATIONING OPENLY IN THE SOUTH OF FRANCE.
I CAN'T ABANDON GOTHAM... SO I'M DELEGATING. SUBDUE HIM.
OKAY, BUT... THE ENTIRE LEAGUE VERSUS A MILLIONAIRE PLAYBOY? ISN'T THAT... OVERKILL?
HE'S ONE EARTHMAN, EASILY DISPATCHED. BARDA AND I HAVE NO INTEREST IN WASTING OUR ENERGIES ON SUCH A TRIVIAL ENEMY AS--
WHUNK!
THEN GET INTERESTED. I HAVE REASON TO BELIEVE THAT WAYNE'S A DECEPTIVELY FORMIDABLE FOE.
CHAIRMAN, ANY OBJECTION TO MY DISPATCHING TEAMS?
NONE.
I THOUGHT NOT. ORION, BARDA, LANTERN, STEEL PLASTIC MAN--FOLLOW WAYNE'S TRAIL. THE REST OF YOU GO FIND FLASH, BUT FIRST...
...EXAMINE THIS LIST... AND LISTEN CAREFULLY...
JLA

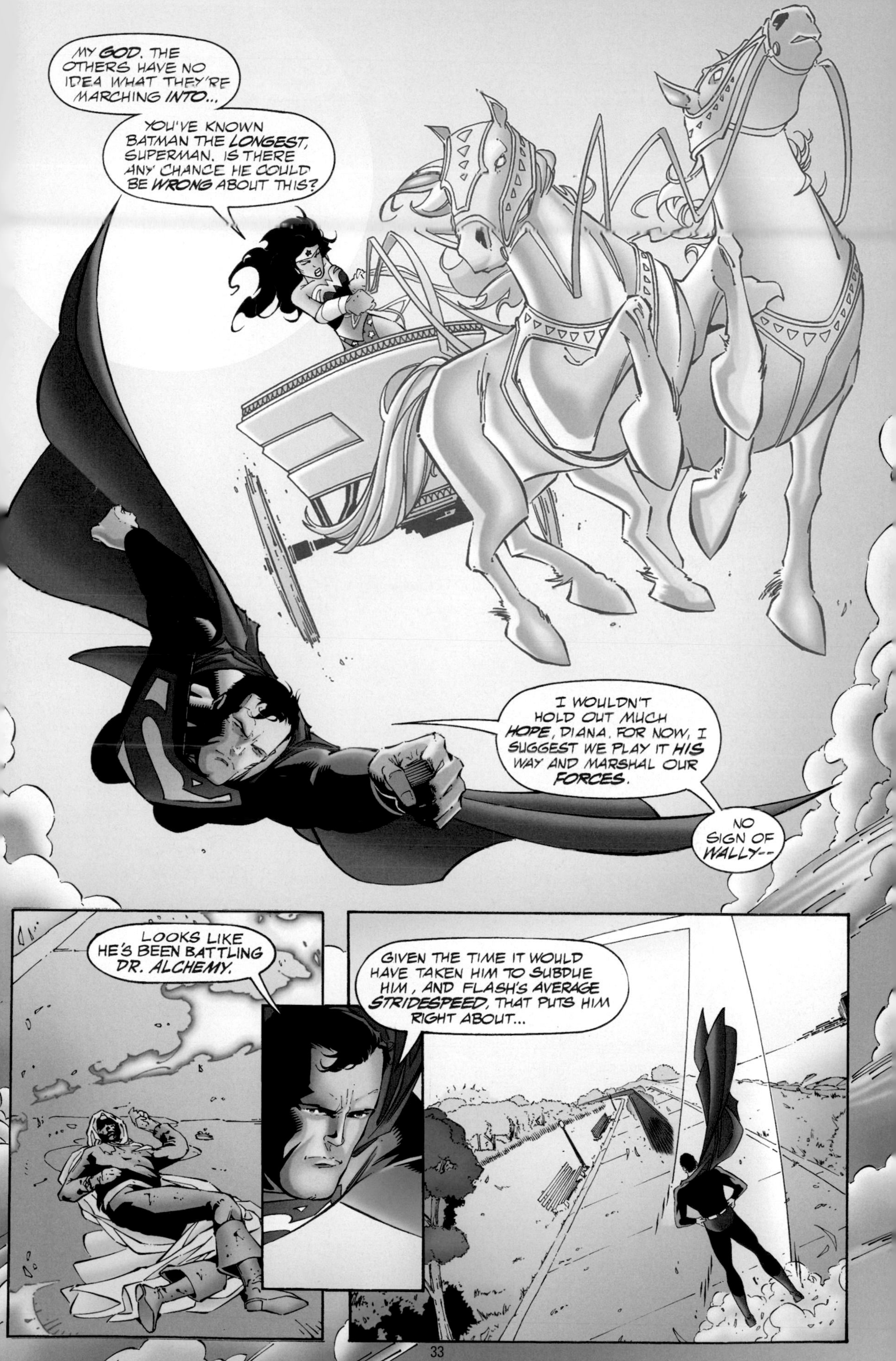
MY GOD. THE OTHERS HAVE NO IDEA WHAT THEY'RE MARCHING INTO...
YOU'VE KNOWN BATMAN THE LONGEST, SUPERMAN. IS THERE ANY CHANCE HE COULD BE WRONG ABOUT THIS?
I WOULDN'T HOLD OUT MUCH HOPE, DIANA. FOR NOW, I SUGGEST WE PLAY IT HIS WAY AND MARSHAL OUR FORCES.
NO SIGN OF WALLY--
LOOKS LIKE HE'S BEEN BATTLING DR. ALCHEMY.
GIVEN THE TIME IT WOULD HAVE TAKEN HIM TO SUBDUE HIM, AND FLASH'S AVERAGE STRIDESPEED, THAT PUTS HIM RIGHT ABOUT...

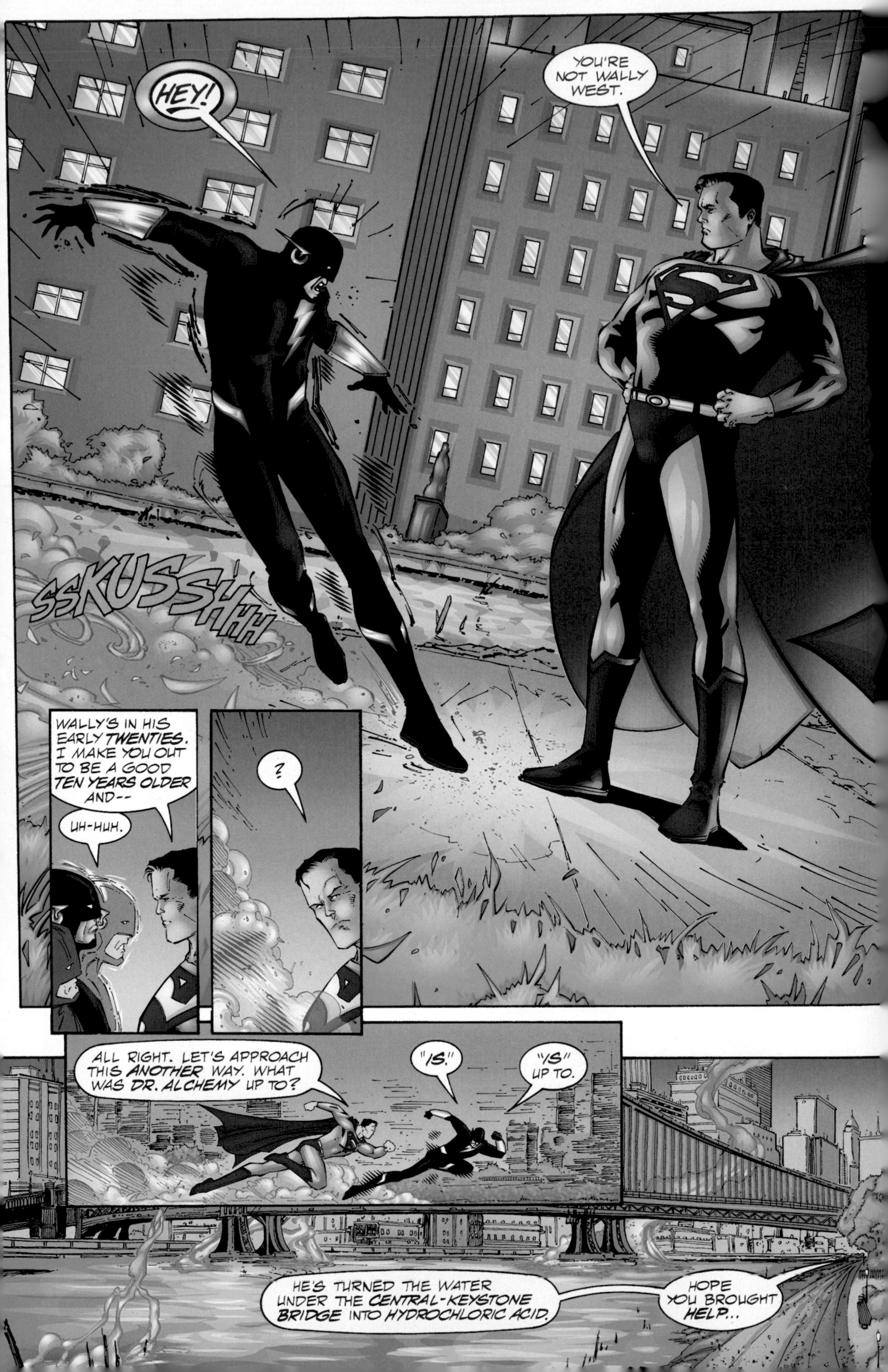
HEY!
YOU'RE NOT WALLY WEST.
SSKUSSHHH
WALLY'S IN HIS EARLY TWENTIES. I MAKE YOU OUT TO BE A GOOD TEN YEARS OLDER AND--
UH-HUH.
?
ALL RIGHT. LET'S APPROACH THIS ANOTHER WAY. WHAT WAS DR. ALCHEMY UP TO?
"IS."
"IS" UP TO.
HE'S TURNED THE WATER UNDER THE CENTRAL-KEYSTONE BRIDGE INTO HYDROCHLORIC ACID.
HOPE YOU BROUGHT HELP...

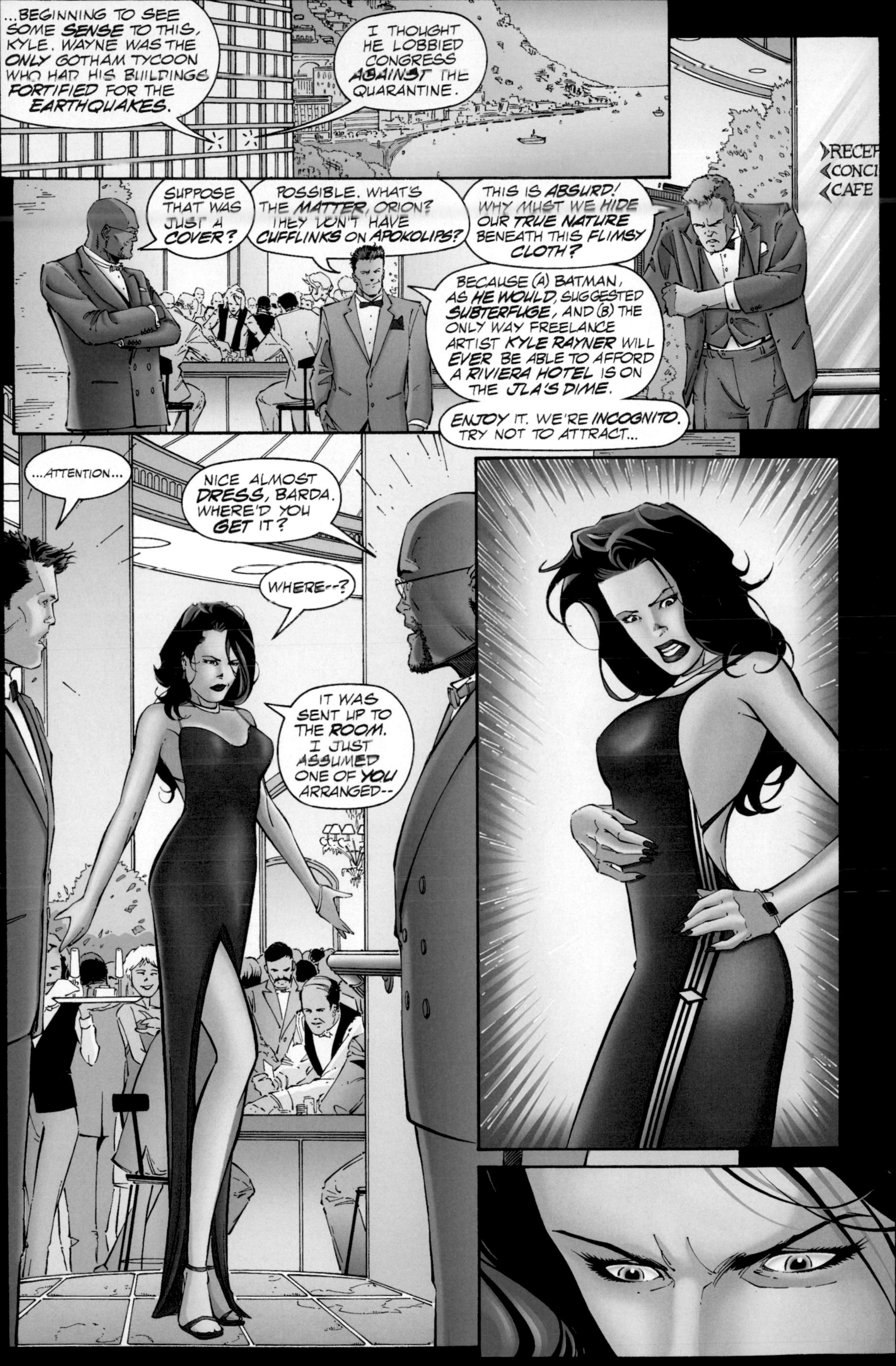
...BEGINNING TO SEE SOME SENSE TO THIS, KYLE. WAYNE WAS THE ONLY GOTHAM TYCOON WHO HAD HIS BUILDINGS FORTIFIED FOR THE EARTHQUAKES.
I THOUGHT HE LOBBIED CONGRESS AGAINST THE QUARANTINE.
RECEP
CONCI
CAFE
SUPPOSE THAT WAS JUST A COVER?
POSSIBLE. WHAT'S THE MATTER, ORION? THEY DON'T HAVE CUFFLINKS ON APOKOLIPS?
THIS IS ABSURD! WHY MUST WE HIDE OUR TRUE NATURE BENEATH THIS FLIMSY CLOTH?
BECAUSE (A) BATMAN, AS HE WOULD, SUGGESTED SUBTERFUGE, AND (B) THE ONLY WAY FREELANCE ARTIST KYLE RAYNER WILL EVER BE ABLE TO AFFORD A RIVIERA HOTEL IS ON THE JLA'S DIME.
ENJOY IT. WE'RE INCOGNITO. TRY NOT TO ATTRACT...
...ATTENTION...
NICE ALMOST DRESS, BARDA. WHERE'D YOU GET IT?
WHERE--?
IT WAS SENT UP TO THE ROOM. I JUST ASSUMED ONE OF YOU ARRANGED--

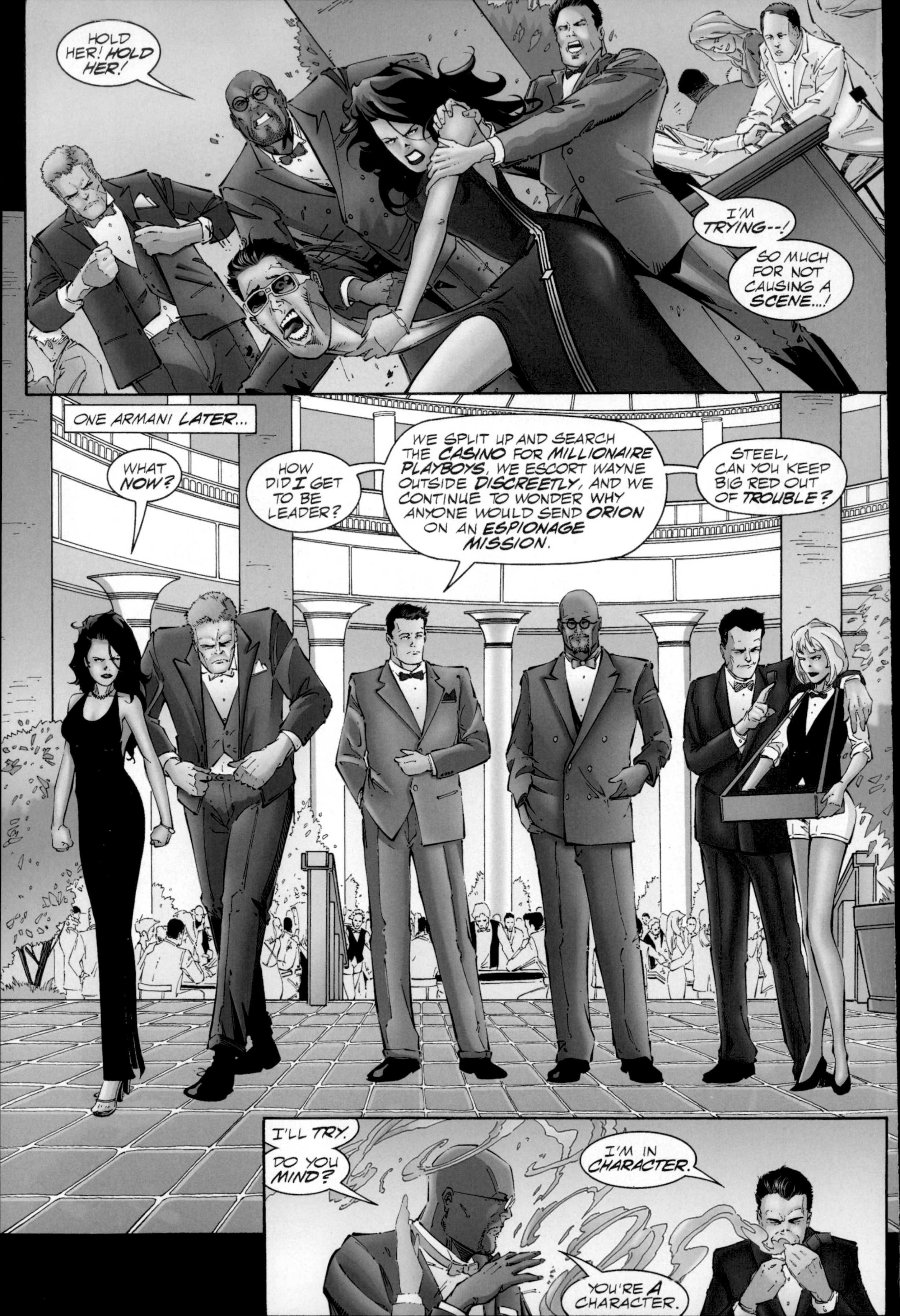
HOLD HER! HOLD HER!
I'M TRYING--!
SO MUCH FOR NOT CAUSING A SCENE...!
ONE ARMANI LATER...
WHAT NOW?
HOW DID I GET TO BE LEADER?
WE SPLIT UP AND SEARCH THE CASINO FOR MILLIONAIRE PLAYBOYS, WE ESCORT WAYNE OUTSIDE DISCREETLY, AND WE CONTINUE TO WONDER WHY ANYONE WOULD SEND ORION ON AN ESPIONAGE MISSION.
STEEL, CAN YOU KEEP BIG RED OUT OF TROUBLE?
I'LL TRY.
DO YOU MIND?
I'M IN CHARACTER.
YOU'RE A CHARACTER.

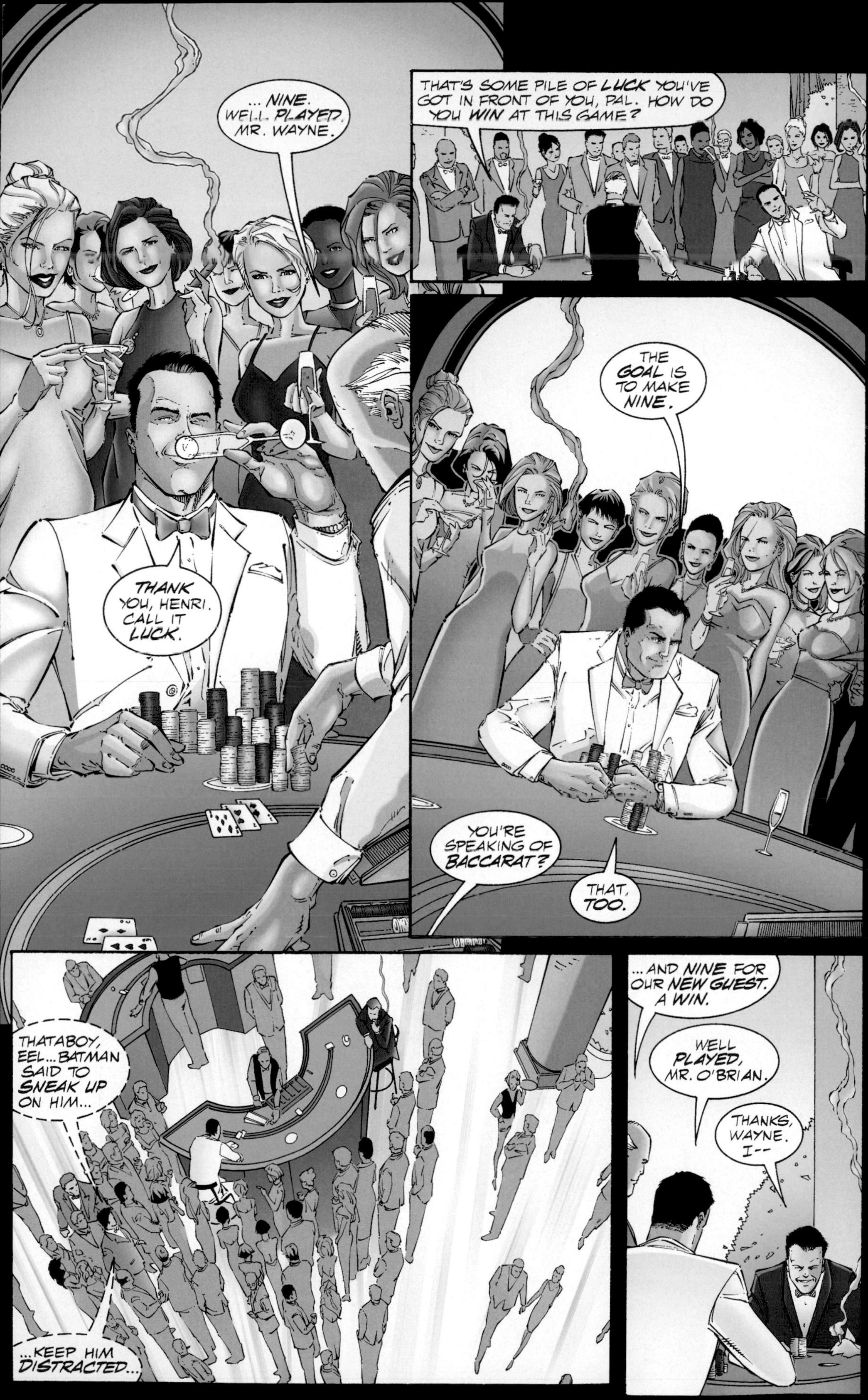

... NINE. WELL PLAYED, MR. WAYNE.
THANK YOU, HENRI. CALL IT LUCK.
THAT'S SOME PILE OF LUCK YOU'VE GOT IN FRONT OF YOU, PAL. HOW DO YOU WIN AT THIS GAME?
THE GOAL IS TO MAKE NINE.
YOU'RE SPEAKING OF BACCARAT?
THAT, TOO.
THATABOY, EEL...BATMAN SAID TO SNEAK UP ON HIM...
...KEEP HIM DISTRACTED...
...AND NINE FOR OUR NEW GUEST. A WIN.
WELL PLAYED, MR. O'BRIAN.
THANKS, WAYNE. I--

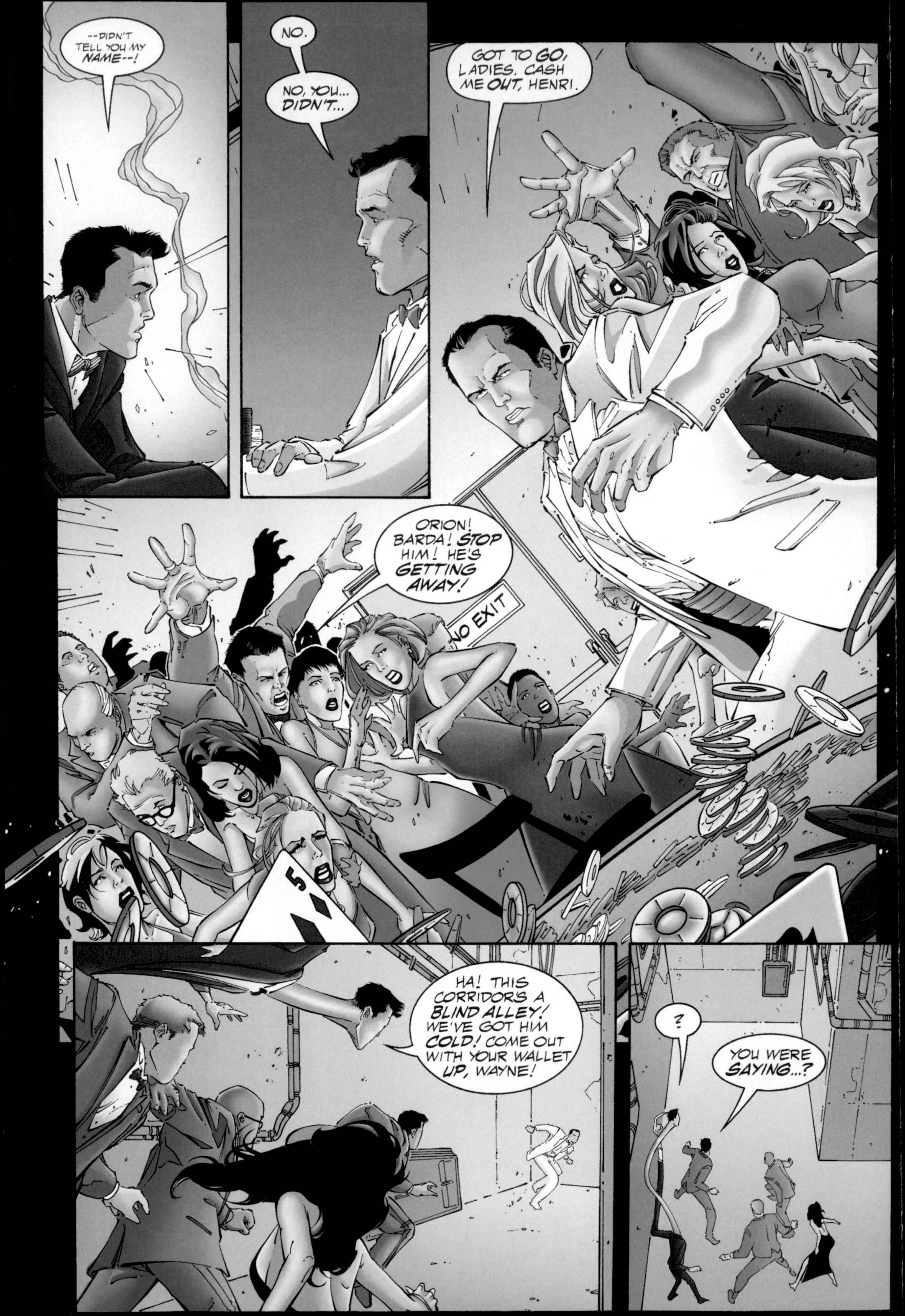

--DIDN'T TELL YOU MY NAME--!
NO.
NO, YOU... DIDN'T...
GOT TO GO, LADIES. CASH ME OUT, HENRI.
ORION! BARDA! STOP HIM! HE'S GETTING AWAY!
NO EXIT
HA! THIS CORRIDOR'S A BLIND ALLEY! WE'VE GOT HIM COLD! COME OUT WITH YOUR WALLET UP, WAYNE!
?
YOU WERE SAYING...?

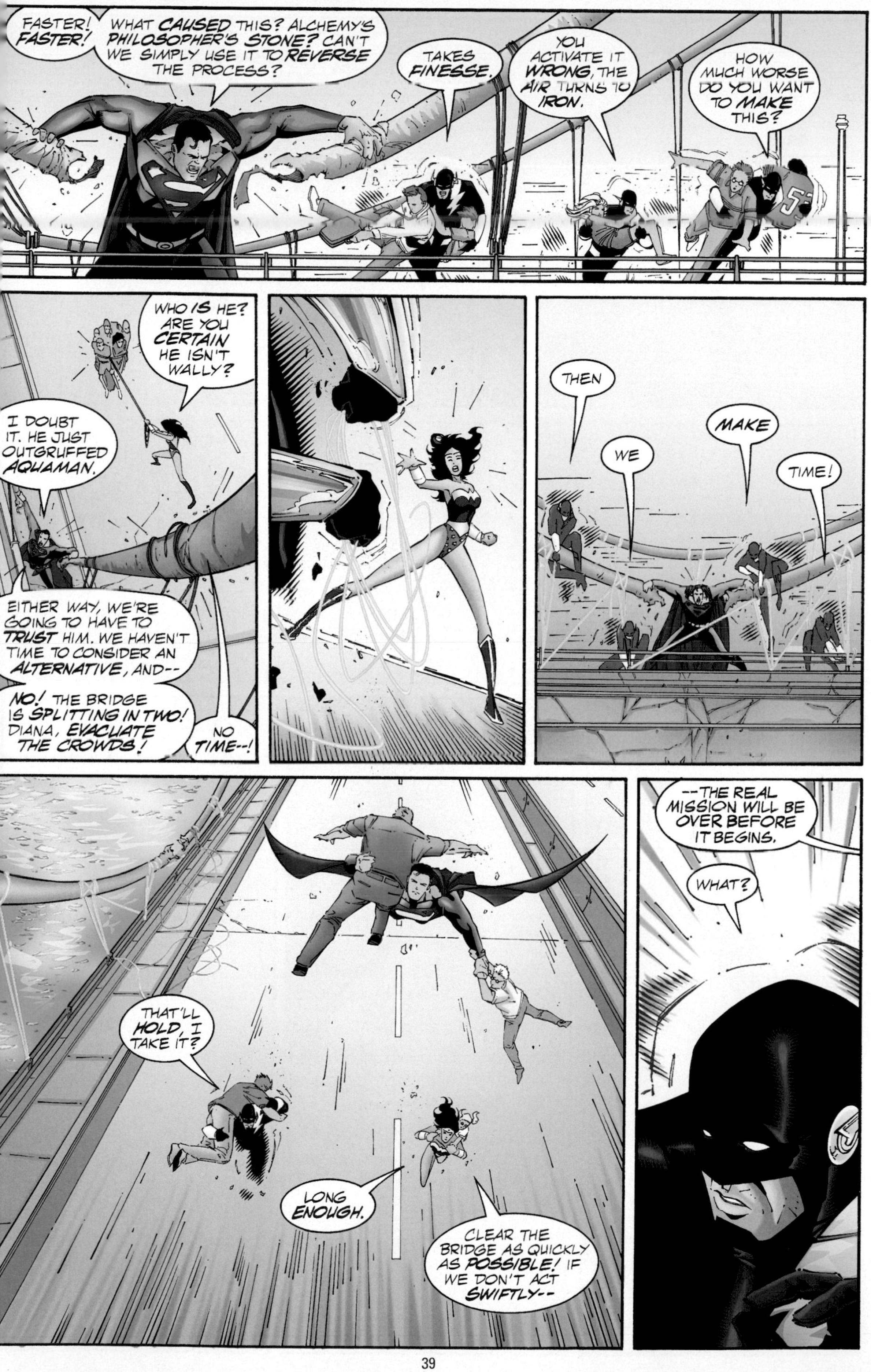
FASTER! FASTER!
WHAT CAUSED THIS? ALCHEMY'S PHILOSOPHER'S STONE? CAN'T WE SIMPLY USE IT TO REVERSE THE PROCESS?
TAKES FINESSE.
YOU ACTIVATE IT WRONG, THE AIR TURNS TO IRON.
HOW MUCH WORSE DO YOU WANT TO MAKE THIS?
WHO IS HE? ARE YOU CERTAIN HE ISN'T WALLY?
I DOUBT IT. HE JUST OUTGRUFFED AQUAMAN.
EITHER WAY, WE'RE GOING TO HAVE TO TRUST HIM. WE HAVEN'T TIME TO CONSIDER AN ALTERNATIVE, AND--
NO! THE BRIDGE IS SPLITTING IN TWO! DIANA, EVACUATE THE CROWDS!
NO TIME--!
THEN
WE
MAKE
TIME!
THAT'LL HOLD, I TAKE IT?
LONG ENOUGH.
CLEAR THE BRIDGE AS QUICKLY AS POSSIBLE! IF WE DON'T ACT SWIFTLY--
--THE REAL MISSION WILL BE OVER BEFORE IT BEGINS.
WHAT?

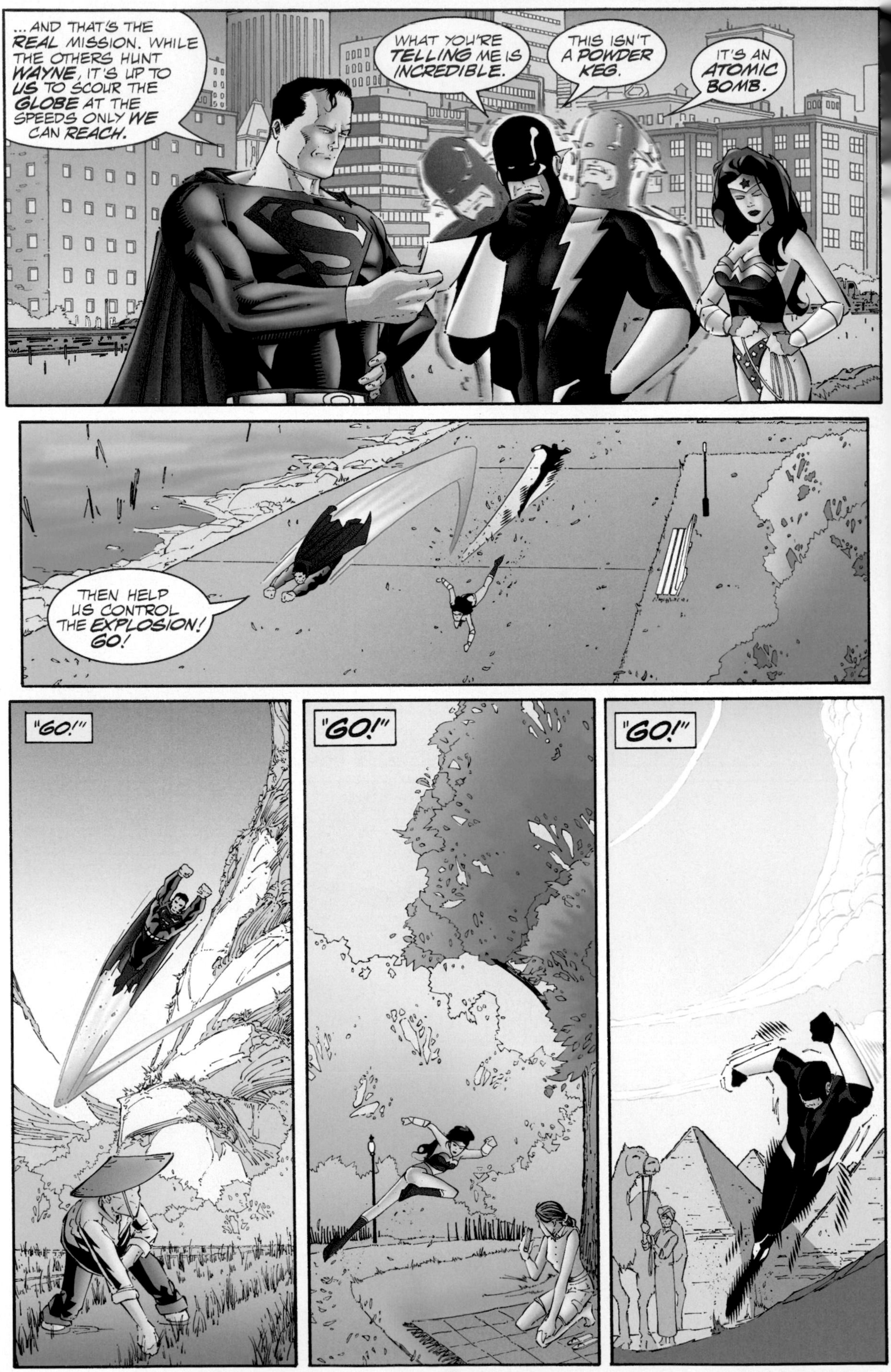
...AND THAT'S THE REAL MISSION. WHILE THE OTHERS HUNT WAYNE, IT'S UP TO US TO SCOUR THE GLOBE AT THE SPEEDS ONLY WE CAN REACH.
WHAT YOU'RE TELLING ME IS INCREDIBLE.
THIS ISN'T A POWDER KEG.
IT'S AN ATOMIC BOMB.
THEN HELP US CONTROL THE EXPLOSION! GO!
"GO!"
"GO!"
"GO!"

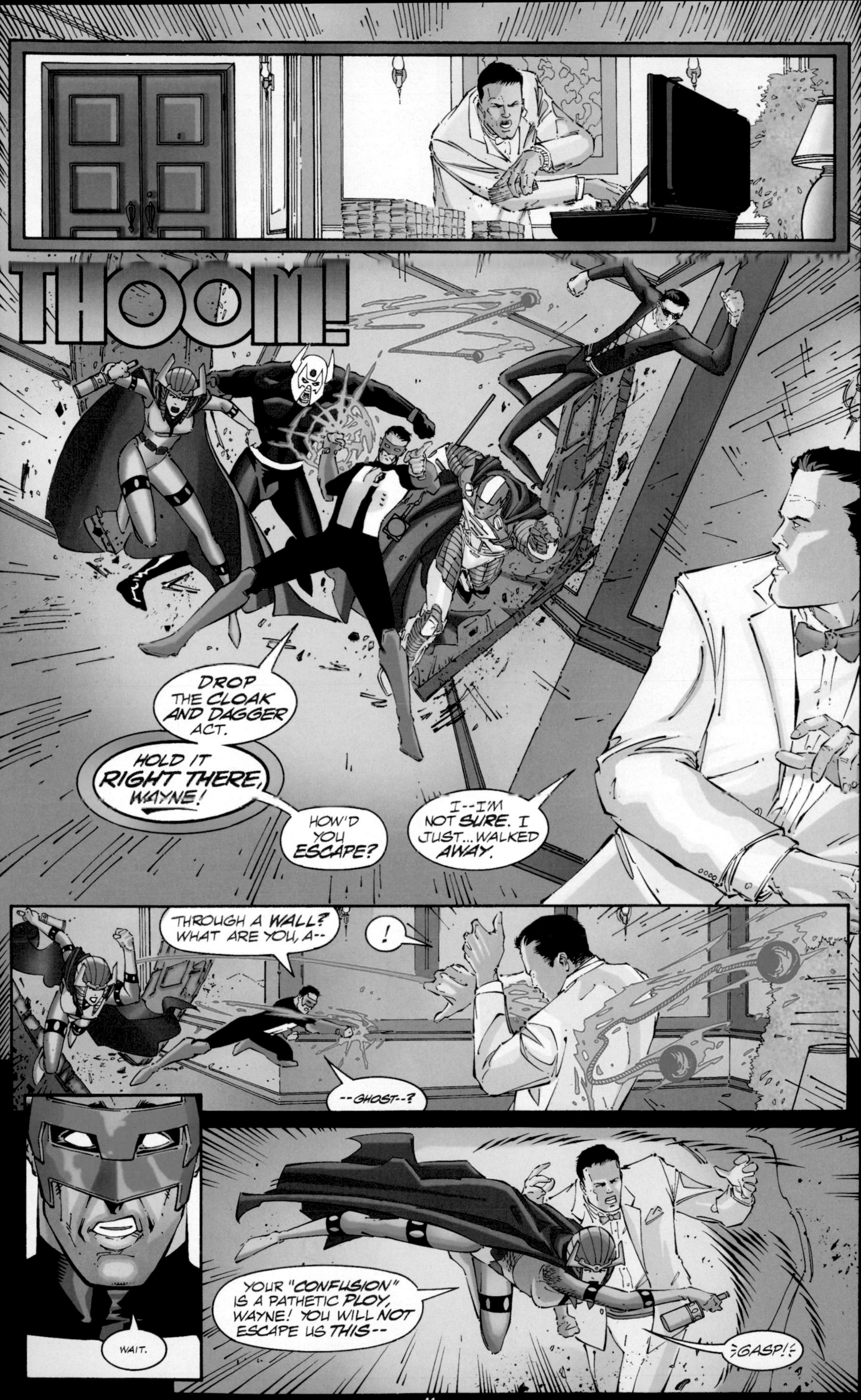
THOOM!
DROP THE CLOAK AND DAGGER ACT.
HOLD IT RIGHT THERE, WAYNE!
HOW'D YOU ESCAPE?
I--I'M NOT SURE. I JUST...WALKED AWAY.
THROUGH A WALL? WHAT ARE YOU, A--
!
--GHOST--?
WAIT.
YOUR "CONFUSION" IS A PATHETIC PLOY, WAYNE! YOU WILL NOT ESCAPE US THIS--
GASP!

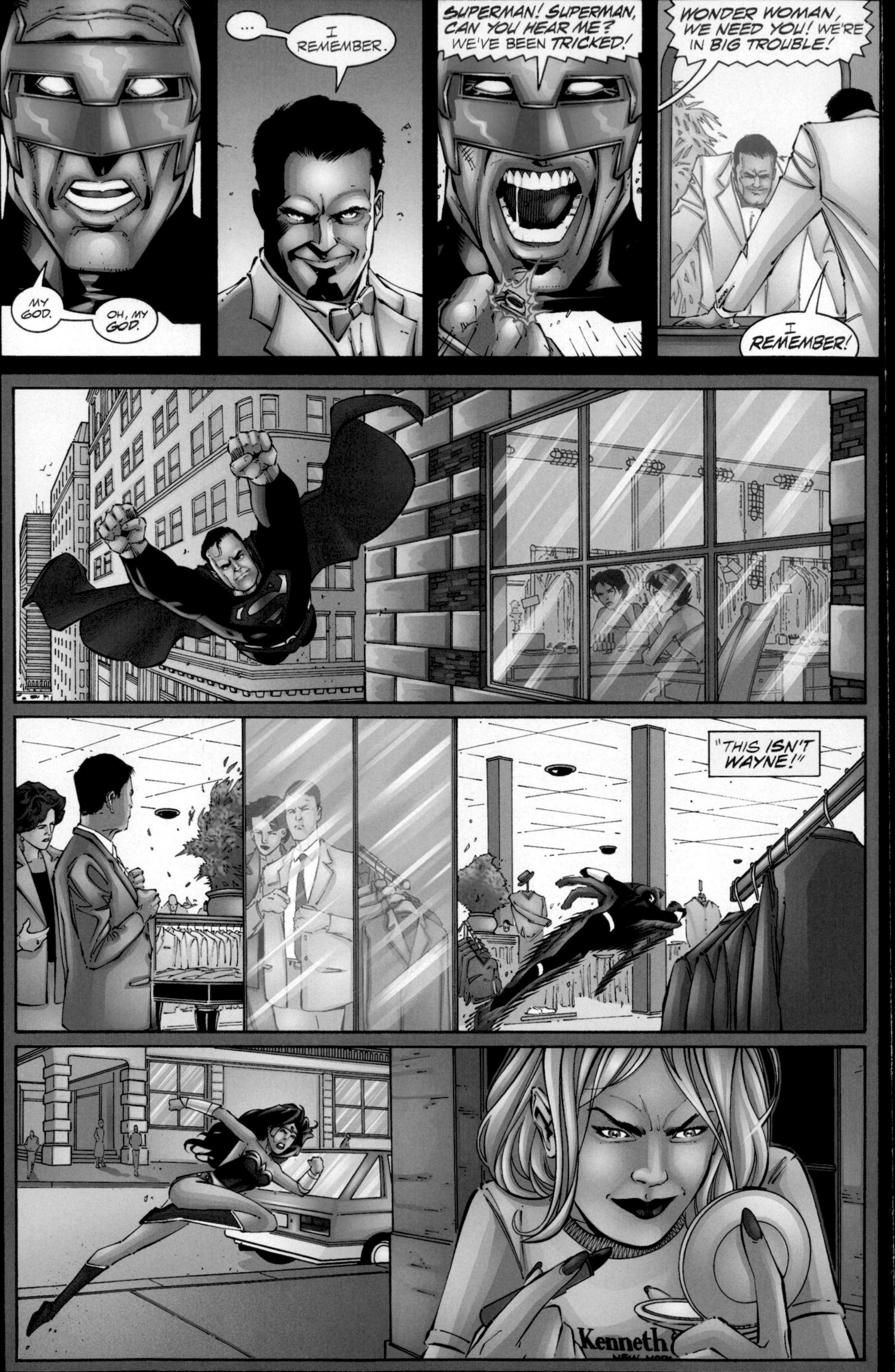
MY GOD.
OH, MY GOD.
...
I REMEMBER.
SUPERMAN! SUPERMAN, CAN YOU HEAR ME? WE'VE BEEN TRICKED!
WONDER WOMAN, WE NEED YOU! WE'RE IN BIG TROUBLE!
I REMEMBER!
"THIS ISN'T WAYNE!"
Kenneth

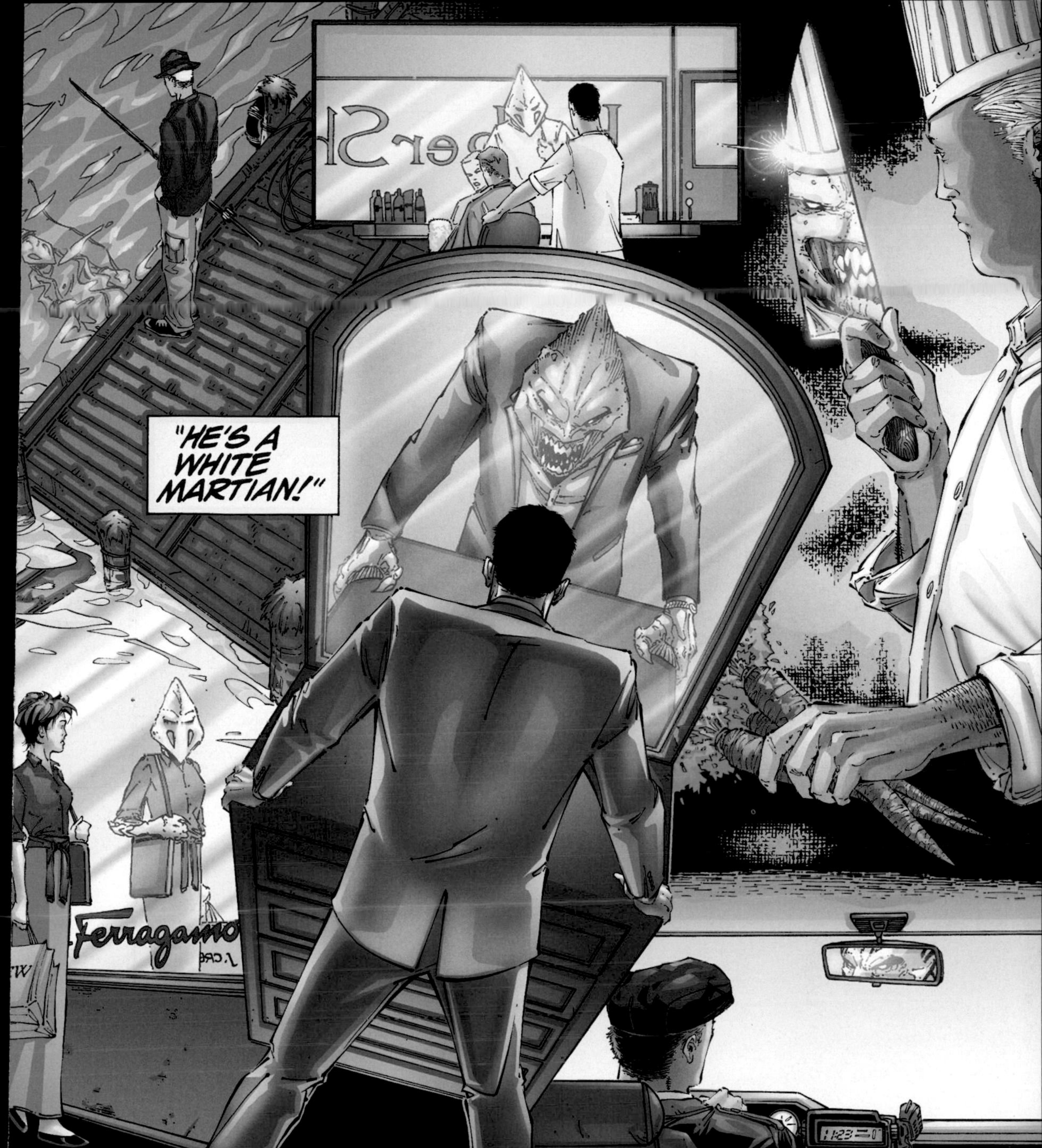
"HE'S A WHITE MARTIAN!"
Ferragamo

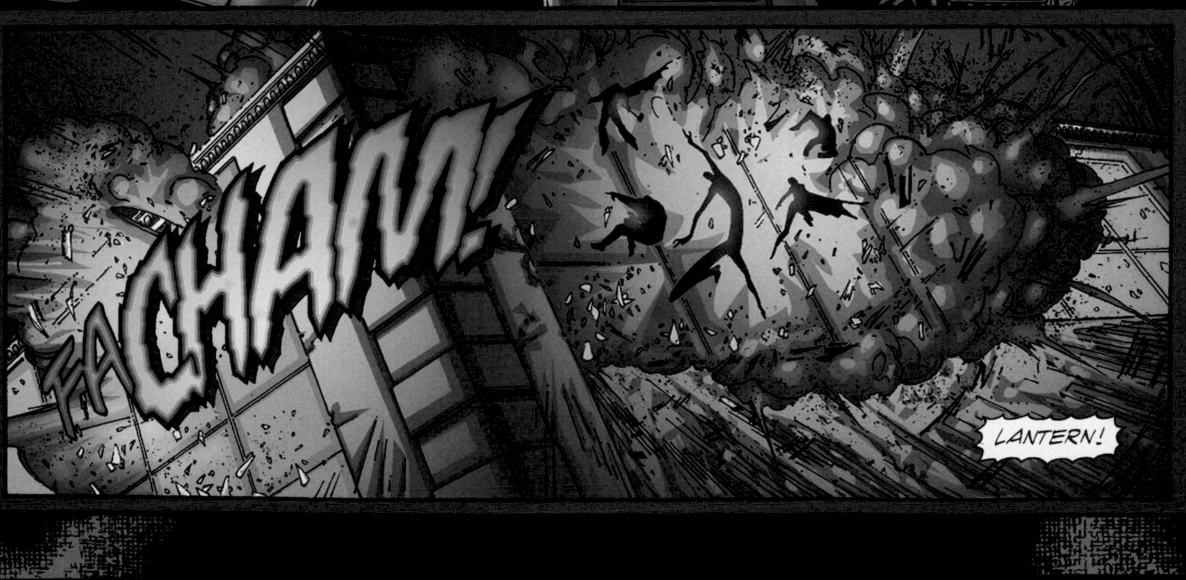
FACHAM!
LANTERN!

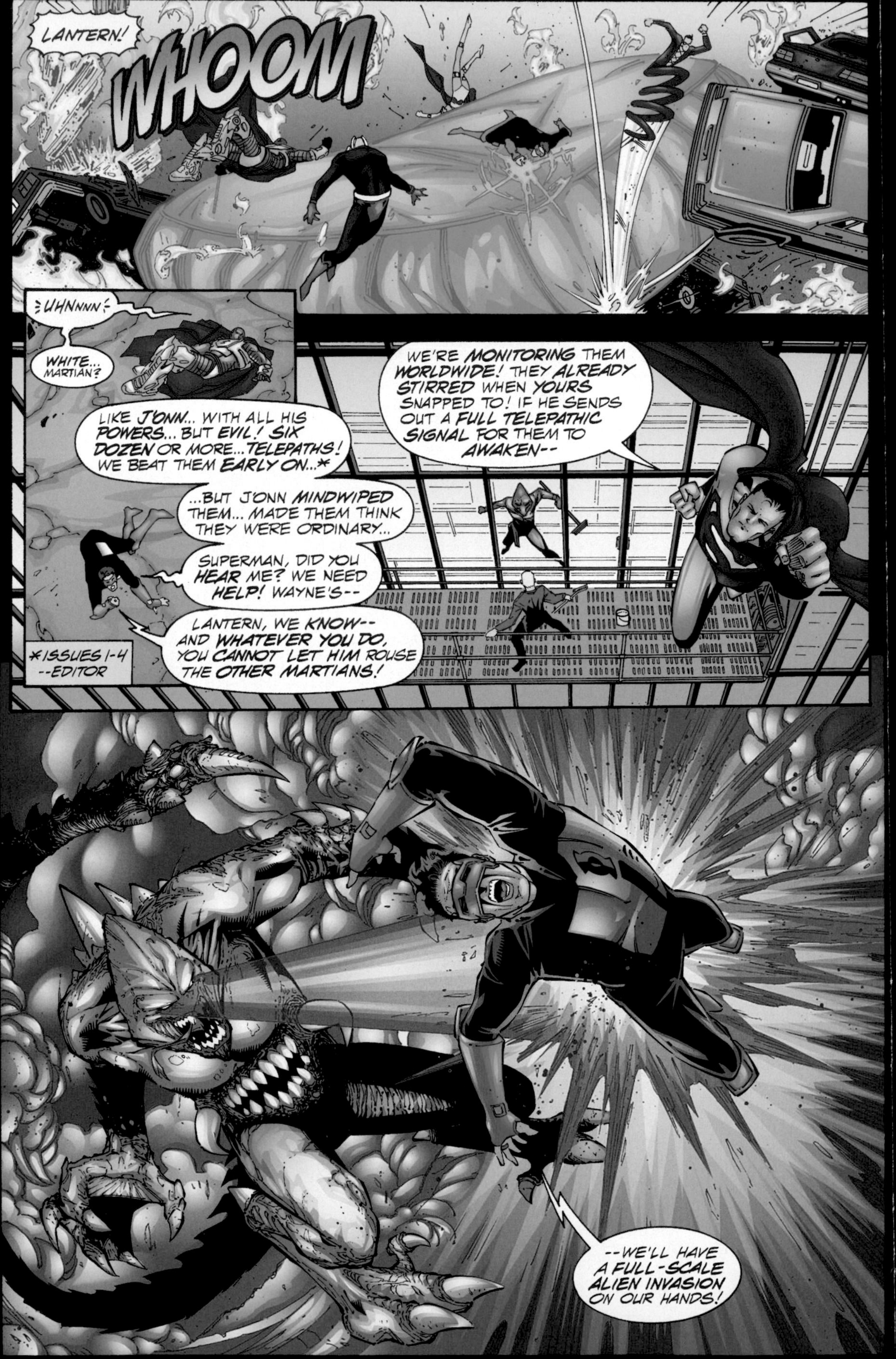
LANTERN!
WHOOM
UHNNNN
WHITE... MARTIAN?
LIKE J'ONN... WITH ALL HIS POWERS... BUT EVIL! SIX DOZEN OR MORE... TELEPATHS! WE BEAT THEM EARLY ON...*
...BUT J'ONN MINDWIPED THEM... MADE THEM THINK THEY WERE ORDINARY...
SUPERMAN, DID YOU HEAR ME? WE NEED HELP! WAYNE'S--
LANTERN, WE KNOW-- AND WHATEVER YOU DO, YOU CANNOT LET HIM ROUSE THE OTHER MARTIANS!
*ISSUES 1-4 --EDITOR
WE'RE MONITORING THEM WORLDWIDE! THEY ALREADY STIRRED WHEN YOURS SNAPPED TO! IF HE SENDS OUT A FULL TELEPATHIC SIGNAL FOR THEM TO AWAKEN--
--WE'LL HAVE A FULL-SCALE ALIEN INVASION ON OUR HANDS!

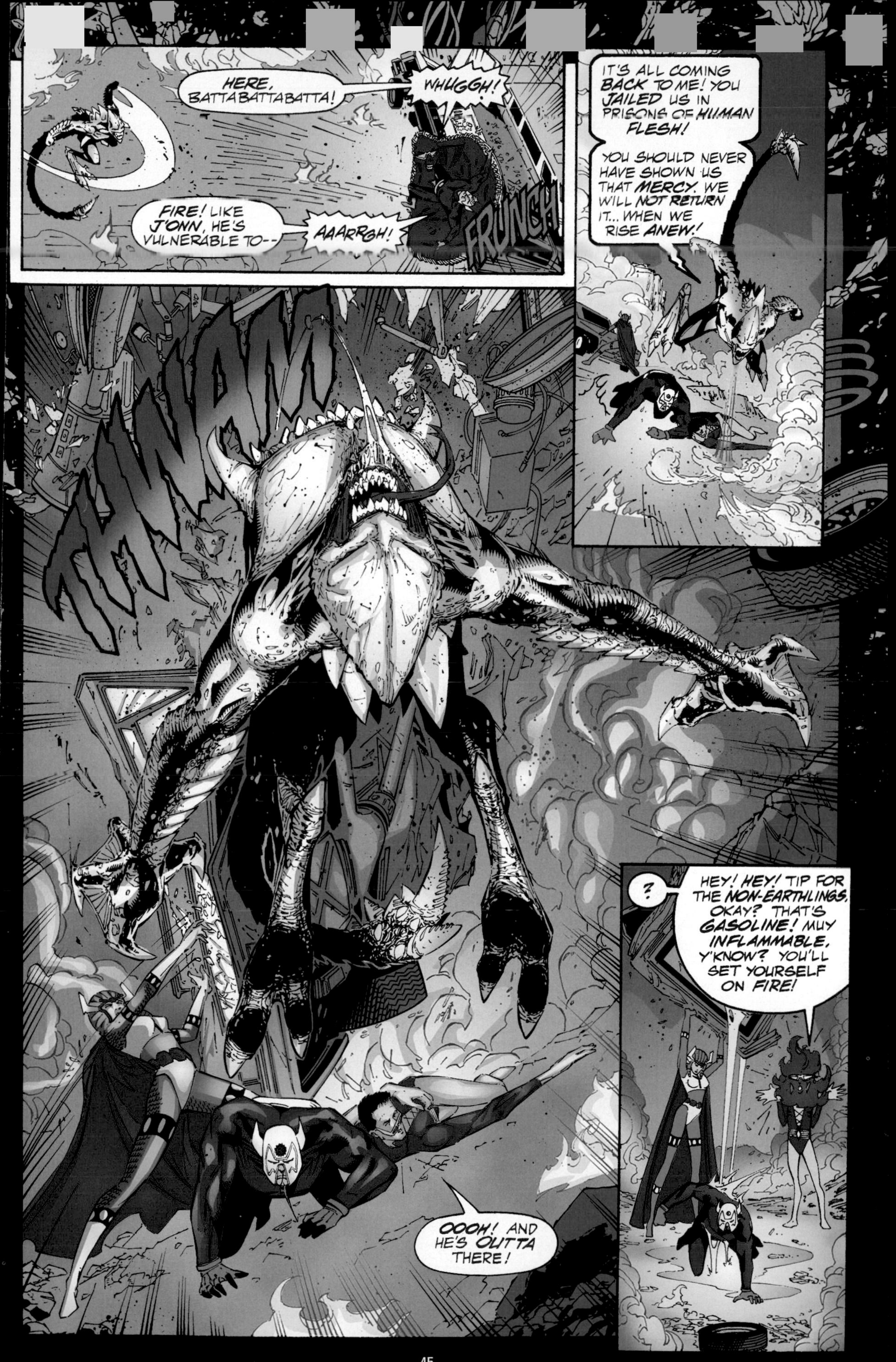

HERE, BATTABATTABATTA!
WHUGGH!
FIRE! LIKE J'ONN, HE'S VULNERABLE TO--
AAARRGH!
FRUNCH
IT'S ALL COMING BACK TO ME! YOU JAILED US IN PRISONS OF HUMAN FLESH!
YOU SHOULD NEVER HAVE SHOWN US THAT MERCY. WE WILL NOT RETURN IT... WHEN WE RISE ANEW!
THWOM
OOOH! AND HE'S OUTTA THERE!
?
HEY! HEY! TIP FOR THE NON-EARTHLINGS, OKAY? THAT'S GASOLINE! MUY INFLAMMABLE, Y'KNOW? YOU'LL SET YOURSELF ON FIRE!

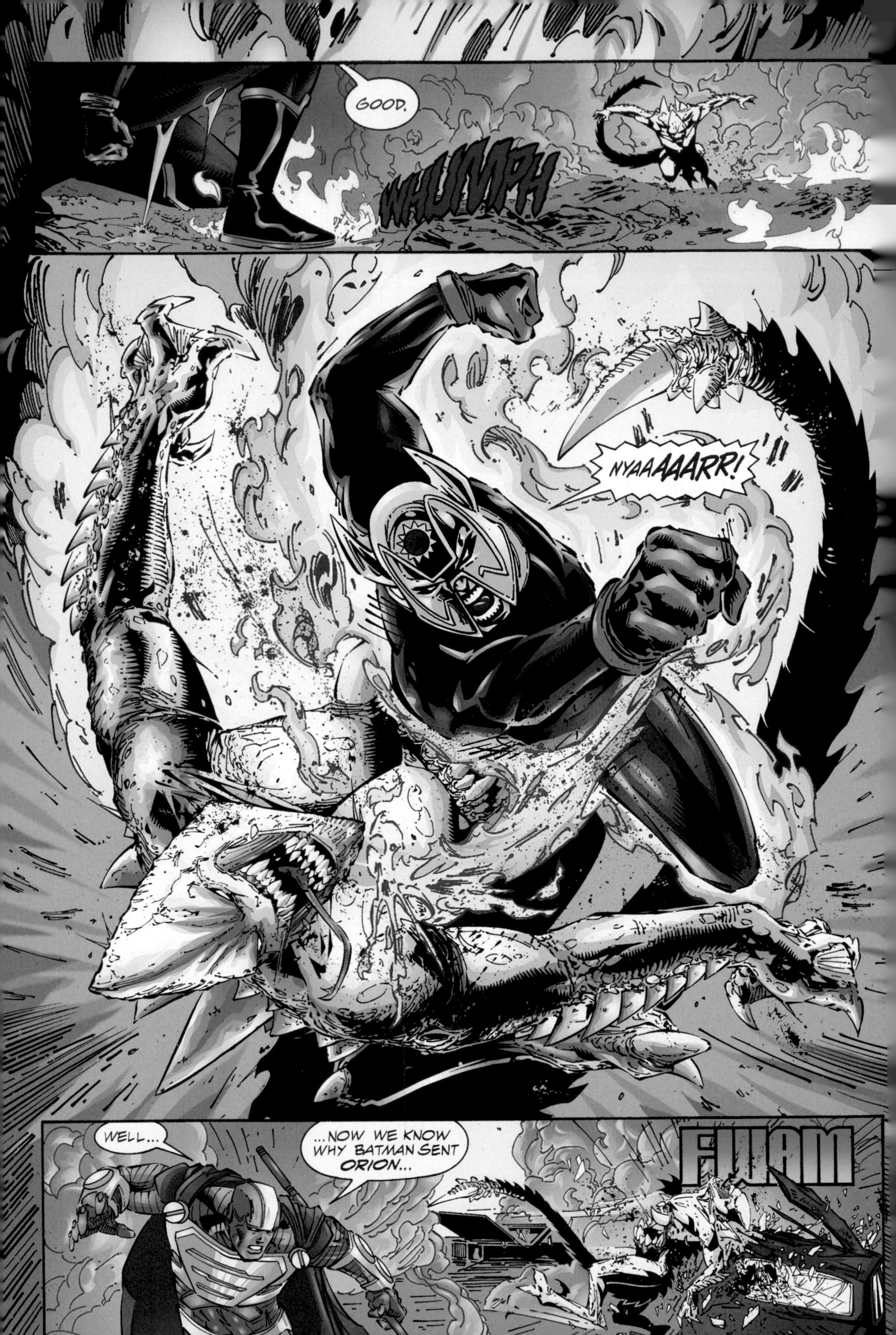

GOOD.
WHUMPH
NYAAAAARR!
WELL...
...NOW WE KNOW WHY BATMAN SENT ORION...
FWAM

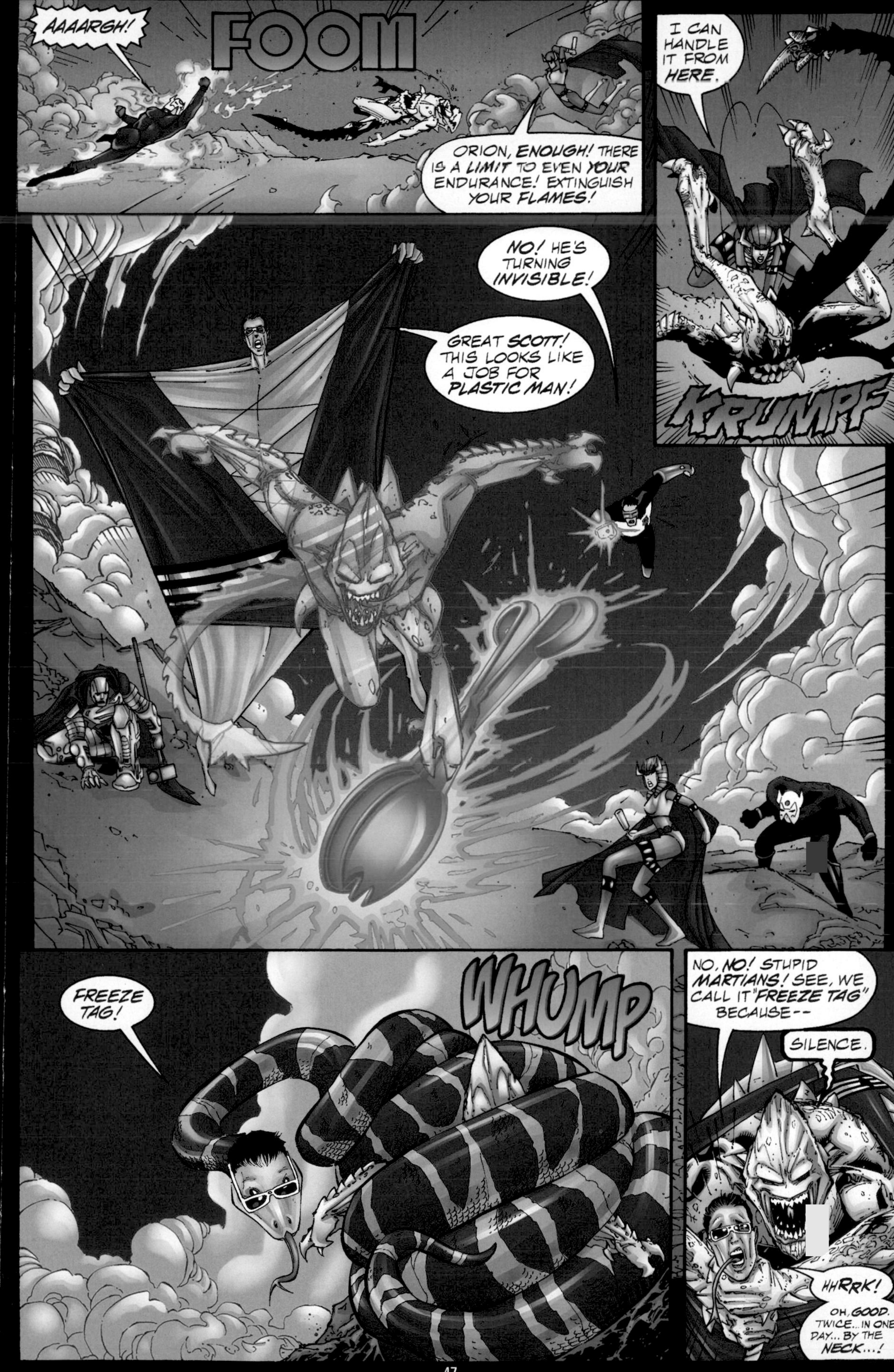
AAAARGH!
FOOM
ORION, ENOUGH! THERE IS A LIMIT TO EVEN YOUR ENDURANCE! EXTINGUISH YOUR FLAMES!
I CAN HANDLE IT FROM HERE.
KRUMPF
NO! HE'S TURNING INVISIBLE!
GREAT SCOTT! THIS LOOKS LIKE A JOB FOR PLASTIC MAN!
FREEZE TAG!
WHUMP
NO, NO! STUPID MARTIANS! SEE, WE CALL IT "FREEZE TAG" BECAUSE--
SILENCE.
HHRRK!
OH, GOOD. TWICE... IN ONE DAY... BY THE NECK...!

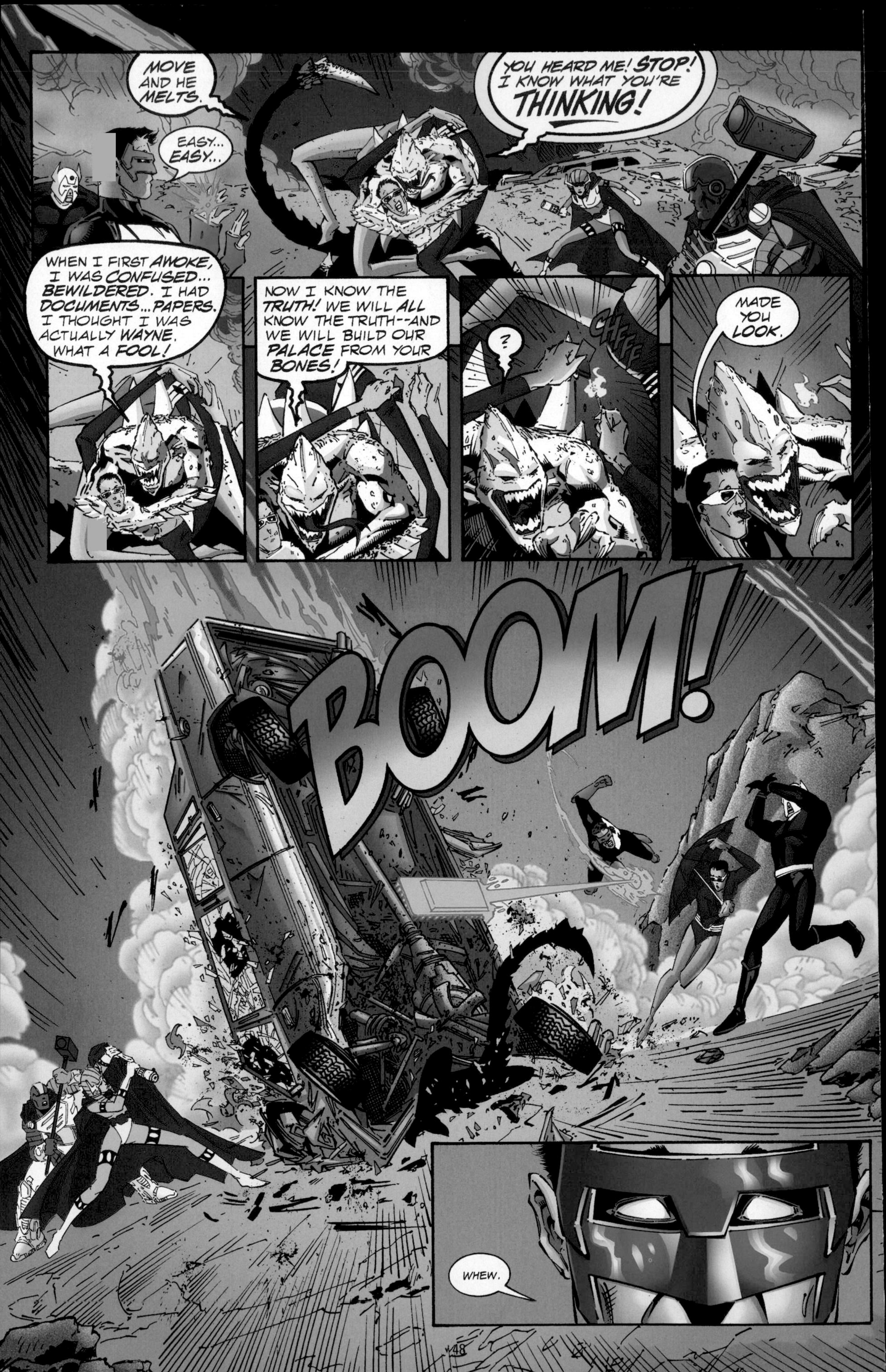
MOVE AND HE MELTS.
EASY... EASY...
YOU HEARD ME! STOP! I KNOW WHAT YOU'RE THINKING!
WHEN I FIRST AWOKE, I WAS CONFUSED... BEWILDERED. I HAD DOCUMENTS...PAPERS. I THOUGHT I WAS ACTUALLY WAYNE. WHAT A FOOL!
NOW I KNOW THE TRUTH! WE WILL ALL KNOW THE TRUTH--AND WE WILL BUILD OUR PALACE FROM YOUR BONES!
?
CHFFF
MADE YOU LOOK.
BOOM!
WHEW.

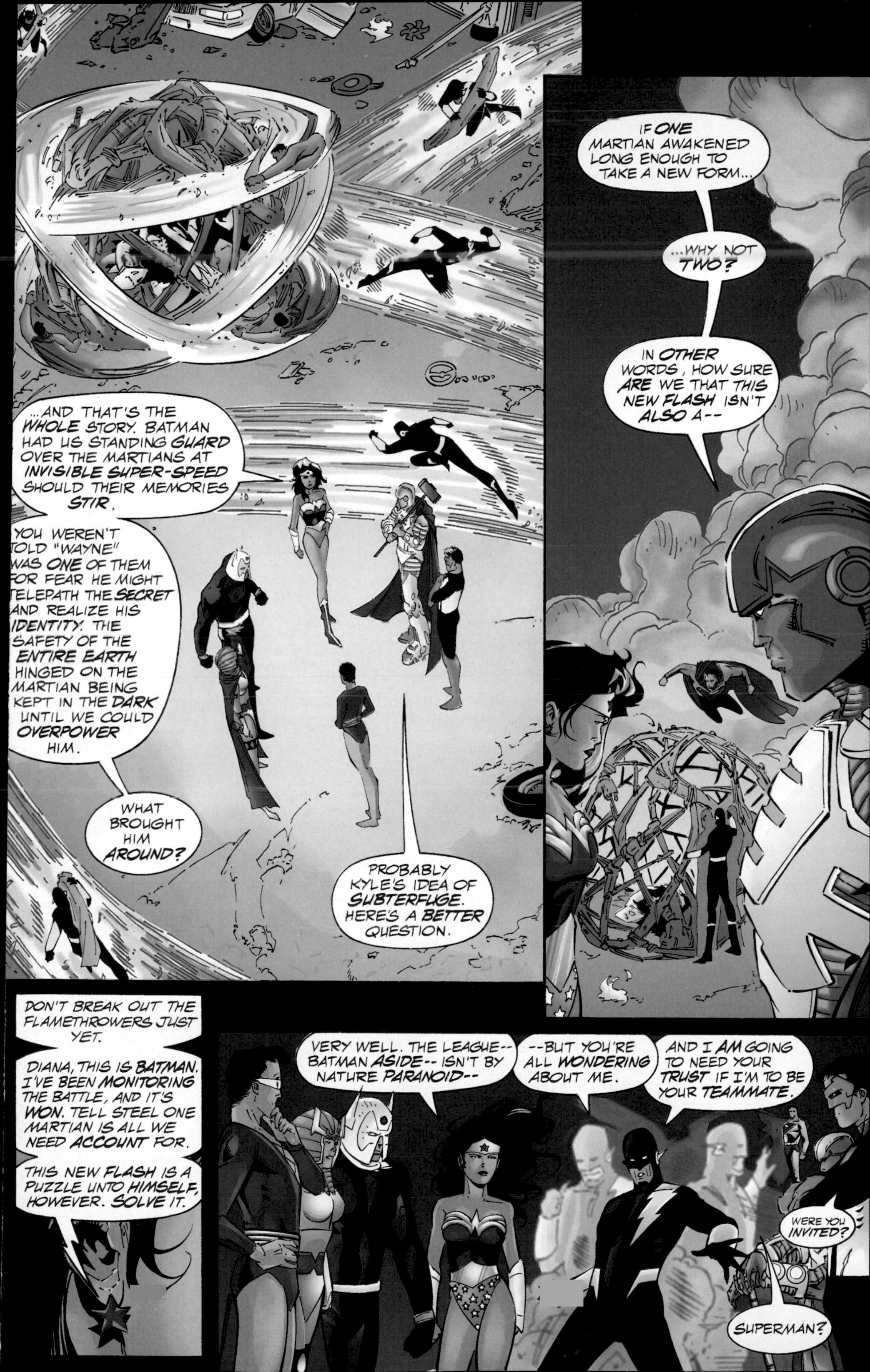
...AND THAT'S THE WHOLE STORY. BATMAN HAD US STANDING GUARD OVER THE MARTIANS AT INVISIBLE SUPER-SPEED SHOULD THEIR MEMORIES STIR.
YOU WEREN'T TOLD "WAYNE" WAS ONE OF THEM FOR FEAR HE MIGHT TELEPATH THE SECRET AND REALIZE HIS IDENTITY. THE SAFETY OF THE ENTIRE EARTH HINGED ON THE MARTIAN BEING KEPT IN THE DARK UNTIL WE COULD OVERPOWER HIM.
WHAT BROUGHT HIM AROUND?
PROBABLY KYLE'S IDEA OF SUBTERFUGE. HERE'S A BETTER QUESTION.
IF ONE MARTIAN AWAKENED LONG ENOUGH TO TAKE A NEW FORM...
...WHY NOT TWO?
IN OTHER WORDS, HOW SURE ARE WE THAT THIS NEW FLASH ISN'T ALSO A--
DON'T BREAK OUT THE FLAMETHROWERS JUST YET.
DIANA, THIS IS BATMAN. I'VE BEEN MONITORING THE BATTLE, AND IT'S WON. TELL STEEL ONE MARTIAN IS ALL WE NEED ACCOUNT FOR.
THIS NEW FLASH IS A PUZZLE UNTO HIMSELF, HOWEVER. SOLVE IT.
VERY WELL. THE LEAGUE-- BATMAN ASIDE-- ISN'T BY NATURE PARANOID--
--BUT YOU'RE ALL WONDERING ABOUT ME.
AND I AM GOING TO NEED YOUR TRUST IF I'M TO BE YOUR TEAMMATE.
WERE YOU INVITED?
SUPERMAN?

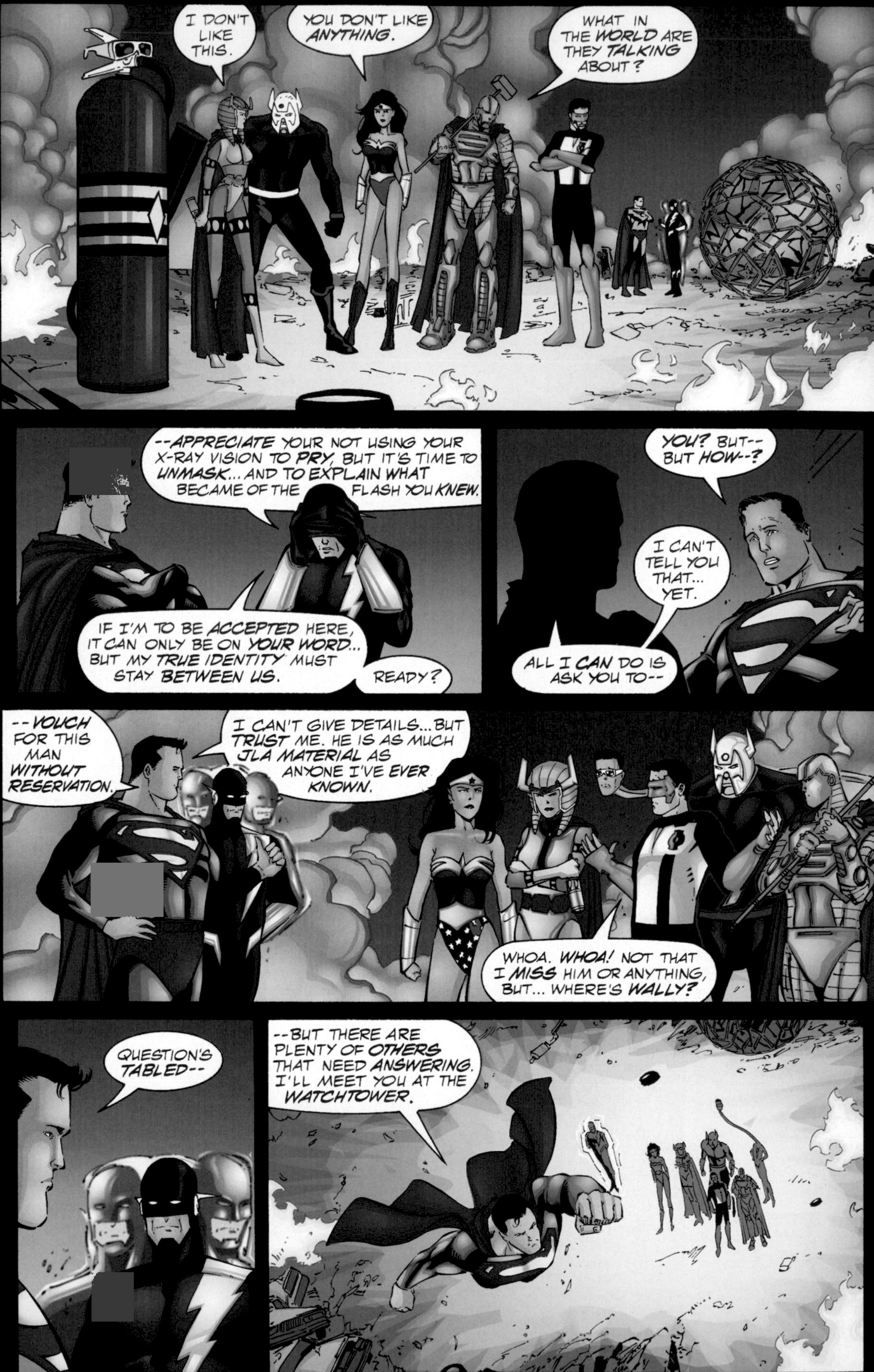
I DON'T LIKE THIS.
YOU DON'T LIKE ANYTHING.
WHAT IN THE WORLD ARE THEY TALKING ABOUT?
--APPRECIATE YOUR NOT USING YOUR X-RAY VISION TO PRY, BUT IT'S TIME TO UNMASK... AND TO EXPLAIN WHAT BECAME OF THE FLASH YOU KNEW.
IF I'M TO BE ACCEPTED HERE, IT CAN ONLY BE ON YOUR WORD... BUT MY TRUE IDENTITY MUST STAY BETWEEN US.
READY?
YOU? BUT-- BUT HOW--?
I CAN'T TELL YOU THAT... YET.
ALL I CAN DO IS ASK YOU TO--
--VOUCH FOR THIS MAN WITHOUT RESERVATION.
I CAN'T GIVE DETAILS... BUT TRUST ME. HE IS AS MUCH JLA MATERIAL AS ANYONE I'VE EVER KNOWN.
WHOA. WHOA! NOT THAT I MISS HIM OR ANYTHING, BUT... WHERE'S WALLY?
QUESTION'S TABLED--
--BUT THERE ARE PLENTY OF OTHERS THAT NEED ANSWERING. I'LL MEET YOU AT THE WATCHTOWER.

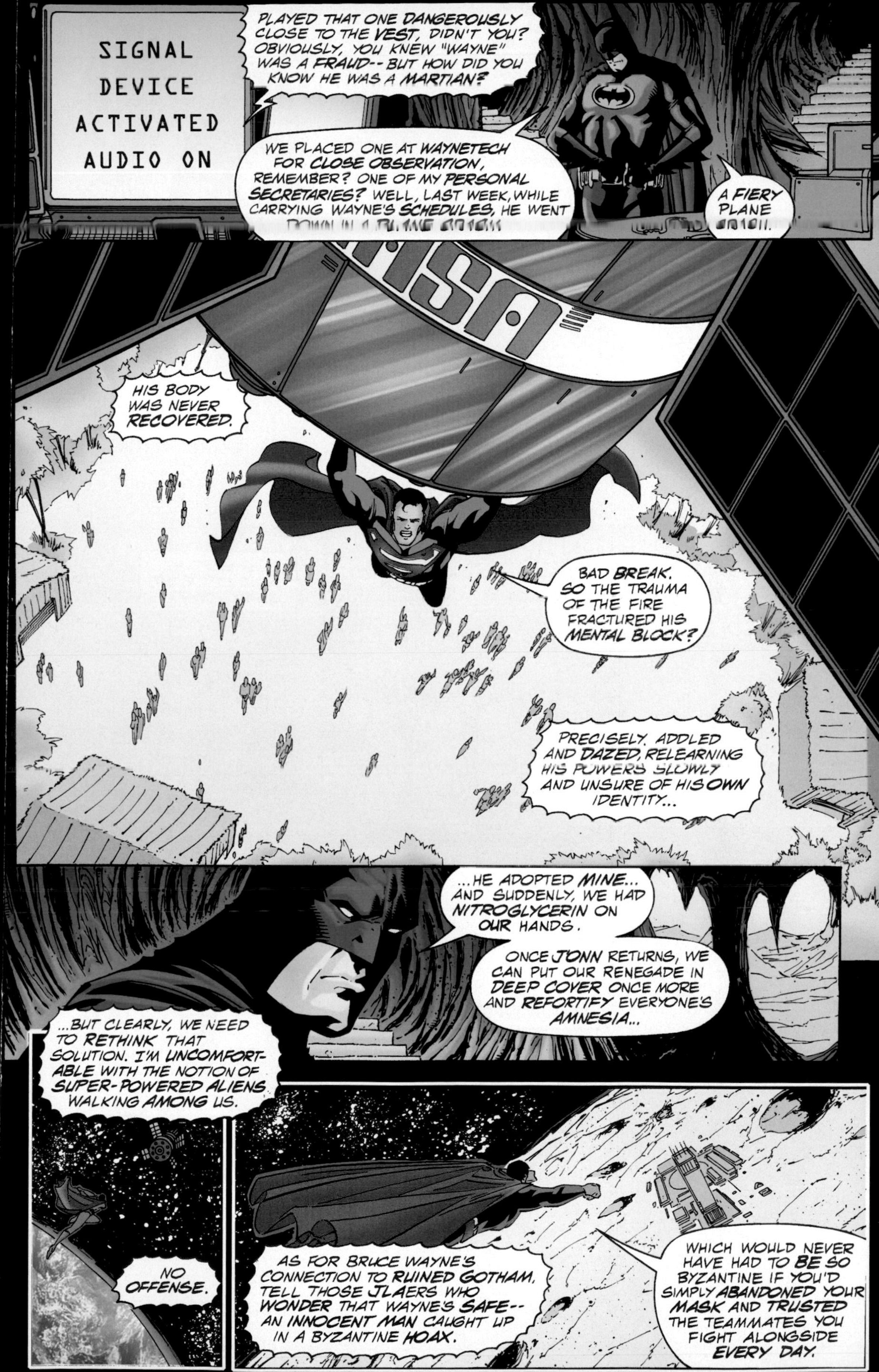
SIGNAL DEVICE ACTIVATED AUDIO ON
PLAYED THAT ONE DANGEROUSLY CLOSE TO THE VEST, DIDN'T YOU? OBVIOUSLY, YOU KNEW "WAYNE" WAS A FRAUD-- BUT HOW DID YOU KNOW HE WAS A MARTIAN?
WE PLACED ONE AT WAYNETECH FOR CLOSE OBSERVATION, REMEMBER? ONE OF MY PERSONAL SECRETARIES? WELL, LAST WEEK, WHILE CARRYING WAYNE'S SCHEDULES, HE WENT
A FIERY PLANE
HIS BODY WAS NEVER RECOVERED.
BAD BREAK. SO THE TRAUMA OF THE FIRE FRACTURED HIS MENTAL BLOCK?
PRECISELY. ADDLED AND DAZED, RELEARNING HIS POWERS SLOWLY AND UNSURE OF HIS OWN IDENTITY...
...HE ADOPTED MINE... AND SUDDENLY, WE HAD NITROGLYCERIN ON OUR HANDS.
ONCE J'ONN RETURNS, WE CAN PUT OUR RENEGADE IN DEEP COVER ONCE MORE AND REFORTIFY EVERYONE'S AMNESIA...
...BUT CLEARLY, WE NEED TO RETHINK THAT SOLUTION. I'M UNCOMFORTABLE WITH THE NOTION OF SUPER-POWERED ALIENS WALKING AMONG US.
NO OFFENSE.
AS FOR BRUCE WAYNE'S CONNECTION TO RUINED GOTHAM, TELL THOSE JLAERS WHO WONDER THAT WAYNE'S SAFE-- AN INNOCENT MAN CAUGHT UP IN A BYZANTINE HOAX.
WHICH WOULD NEVER HAVE HAD TO BE SO BYZANTINE IF YOU'D SIMPLY ABANDONED YOUR MASK AND TRUSTED THE TEAMMATES YOU FIGHT ALONGSIDE EVERY DAY.

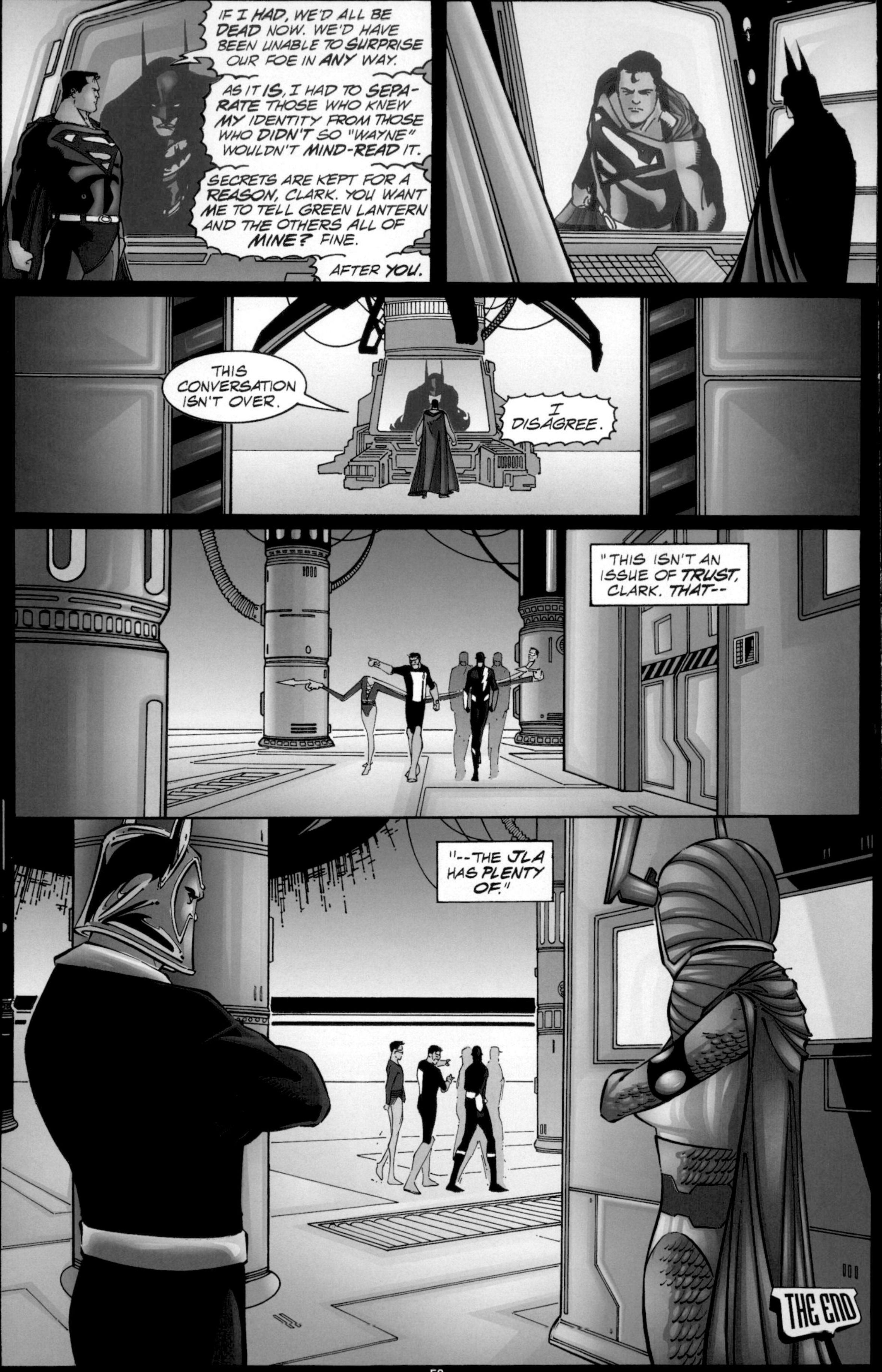
IF I HAD, WE'D ALL BE DEAD NOW. WE'D HAVE BEEN UNABLE TO SURPRISE OUR FOE IN ANY WAY.
AS IT IS, I HAD TO SEPARATE THOSE WHO KNEW MY IDENTITY FROM THOSE WHO DIDN'T SO "WAYNE" WOULDN'T MIND-READ IT.
SECRETS ARE KEPT FOR A REASON, CLARK. YOU WANT ME TO TELL GREEN LANTERN AND THE OTHERS ALL OF MINE? FINE.
AFTER YOU.
THIS CONVERSATION ISN'T OVER.
I DISAGREE.
"THIS ISN'T AN ISSUE OF TRUST, CLARK. THAT--
"--THE JLA HAS PLENTY OF."
THE END

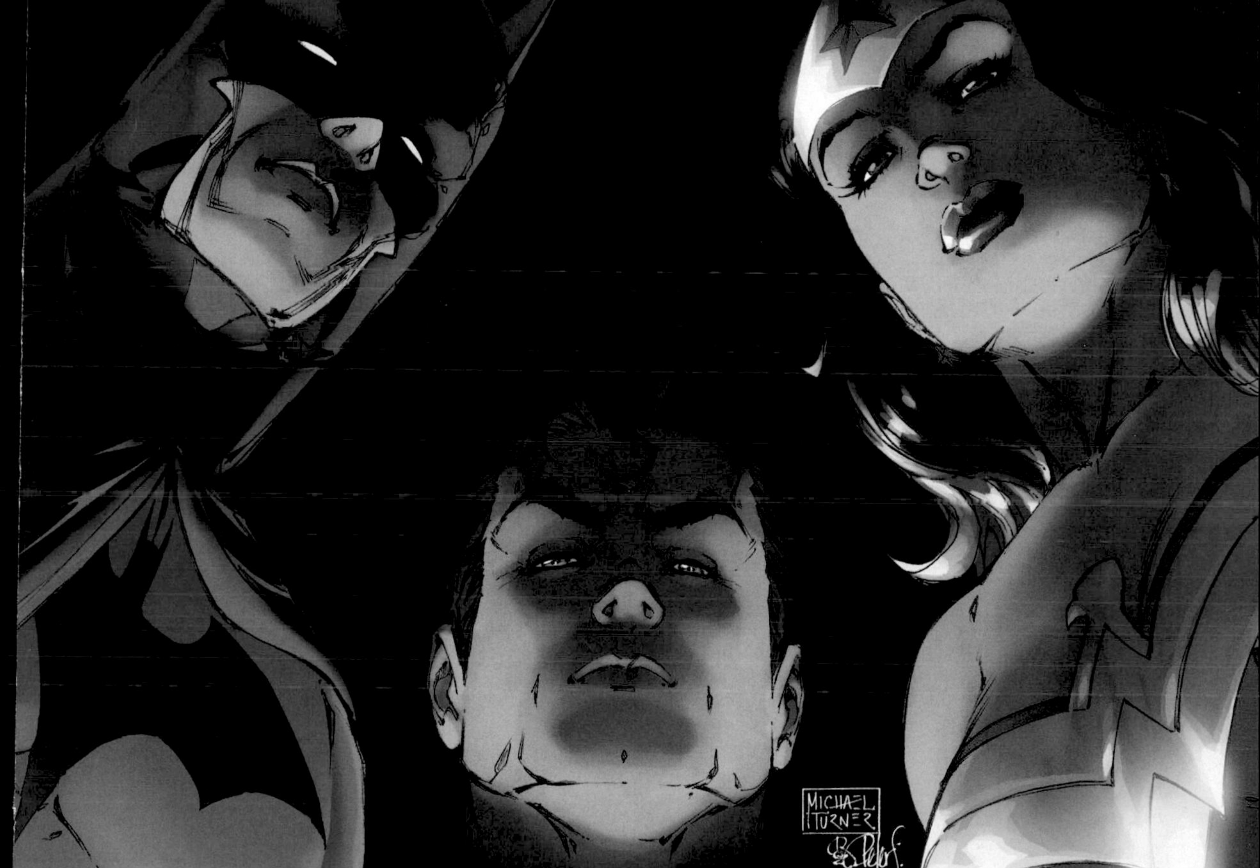
MICHAEL TURNER

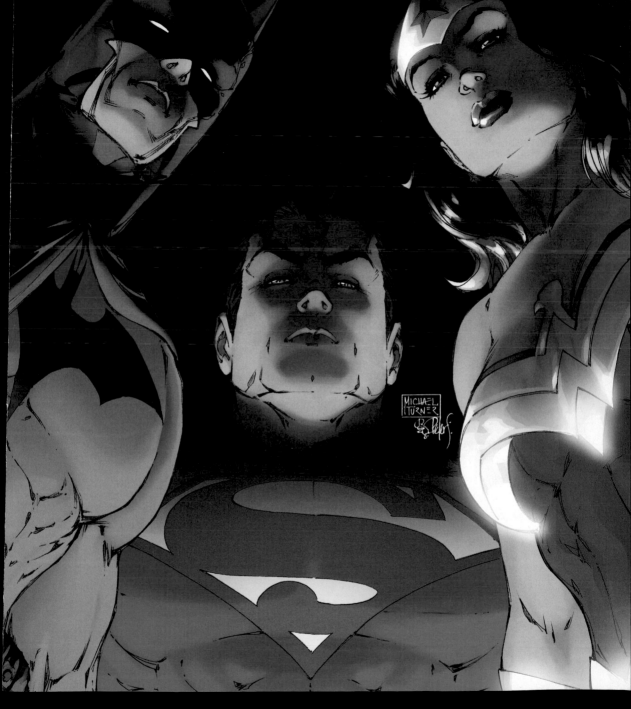

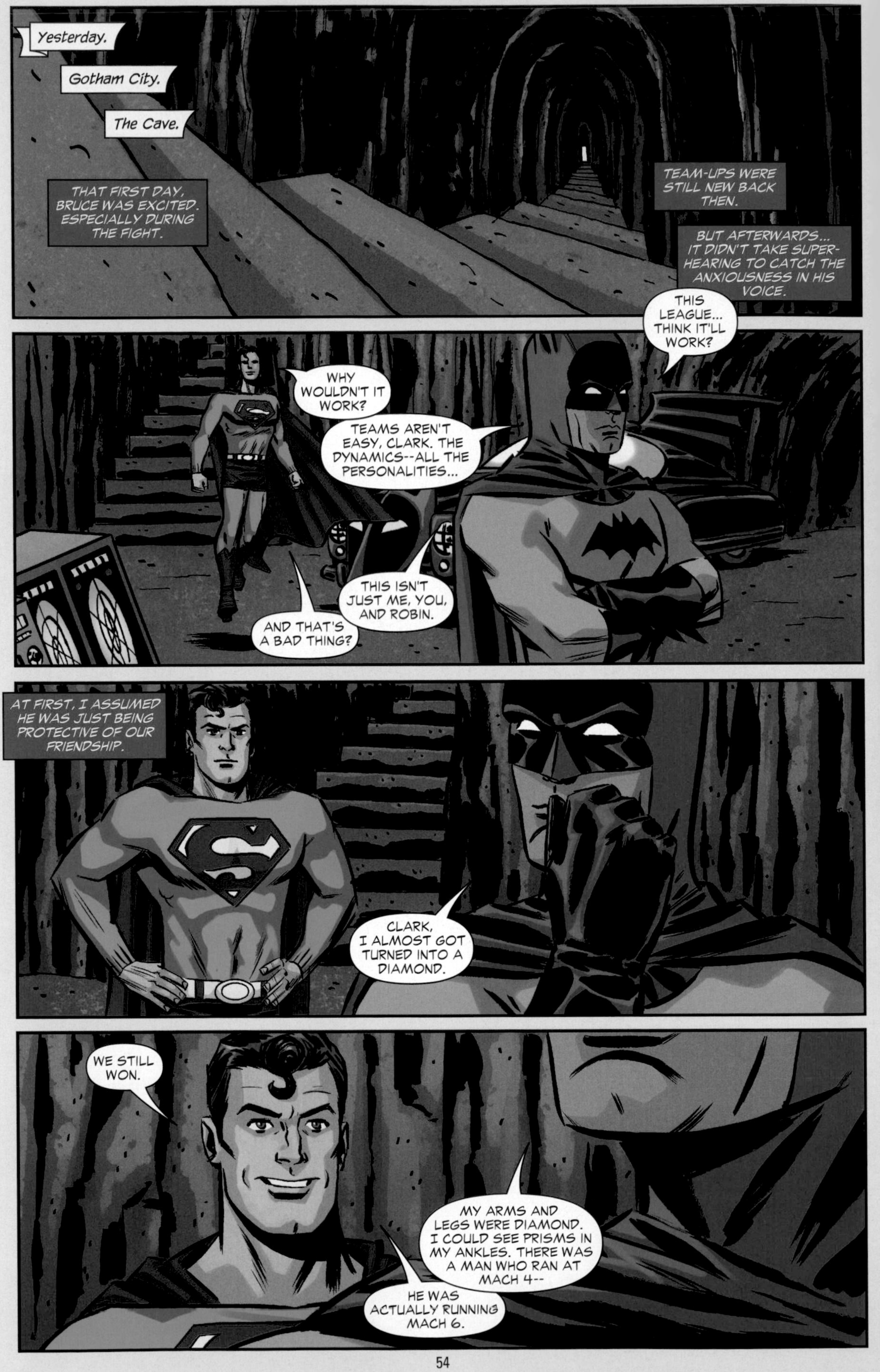
Yesterday.
Gotham City.
The Cave.
THAT FIRST DAY, BRUCE WAS EXCITED. ESPECIALLY DURING THE FIGHT.
TEAM-UPS WERE STILL NEW BACK THEN.
BUT AFTERWARDS... IT DIDN'T TAKE SUPER-HEARING TO CATCH THE ANXIOUSNESS IN HIS VOICE.
THIS LEAGUE... THINK IT'LL WORK?
WHY WOULDN'T IT WORK?
TEAMS AREN'T EASY, CLARK. THE DYNAMICS--ALL THE PERSONALITIES...
THIS ISN'T JUST ME, YOU, AND ROBIN.
AND THAT'S A BAD THING?
AT FIRST, I ASSUMED HE WAS JUST BEING PROTECTIVE OF OUR FRIENDSHIP.
CLARK, I ALMOST GOT TURNED INTO A DIAMOND.
WE STILL WON.
MY ARMS AND LEGS WERE DIAMOND. I COULD SEE PRISMS IN MY ANKLES. THERE WAS A MAN WHO RAN AT MACH 4--
HE WAS ACTUALLY RUNNING MACH 6.

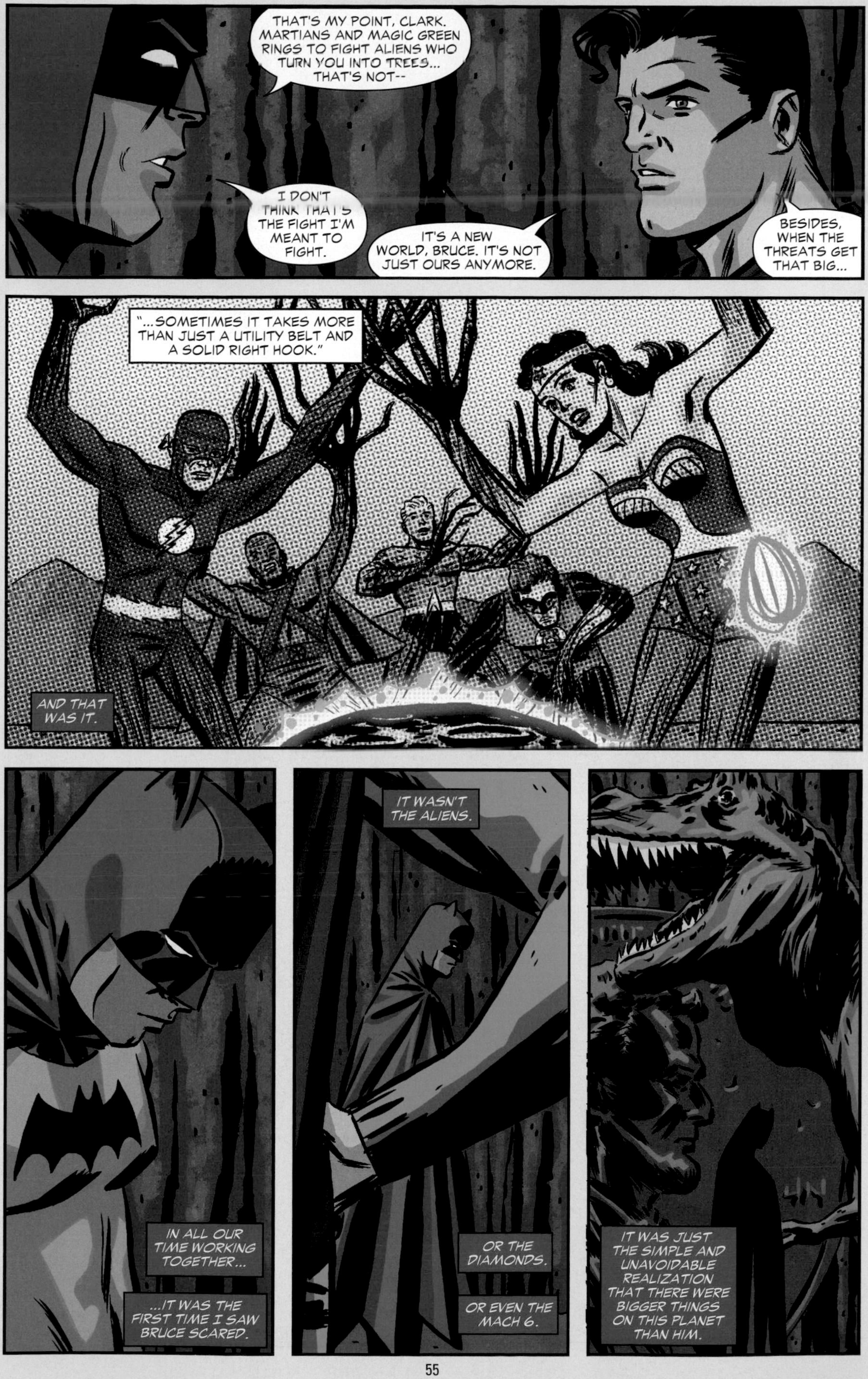
THAT'S MY POINT, CLARK. MARTIANS AND MAGIC GREEN RINGS TO FIGHT ALIENS WHO TURN YOU INTO TREES... THAT'S NOT--
I DON'T THINK THAT'S THE FIGHT I'M MEANT TO FIGHT.
IT'S A NEW WORLD, BRUCE. IT'S NOT JUST OURS ANYMORE.
BESIDES, WHEN THE THREATS GET THAT BIG...
"...SOMETIMES IT TAKES MORE THAN JUST A UTILITY BELT AND A SOLID RIGHT HOOK."
AND THAT WAS IT.
IN ALL OUR TIME WORKING TOGETHER...
...IT WAS THE FIRST TIME I SAW BRUCE SCARED.
IT WASN'T THE ALIENS.
OR THE DIAMONDS.
OR EVEN THE MACH 6.
IT WAS JUST THE SIMPLE AND UNAVOIDABLE REALIZATION THAT THERE WERE BIGGER THINGS ON THIS PLANET THAN HIM.

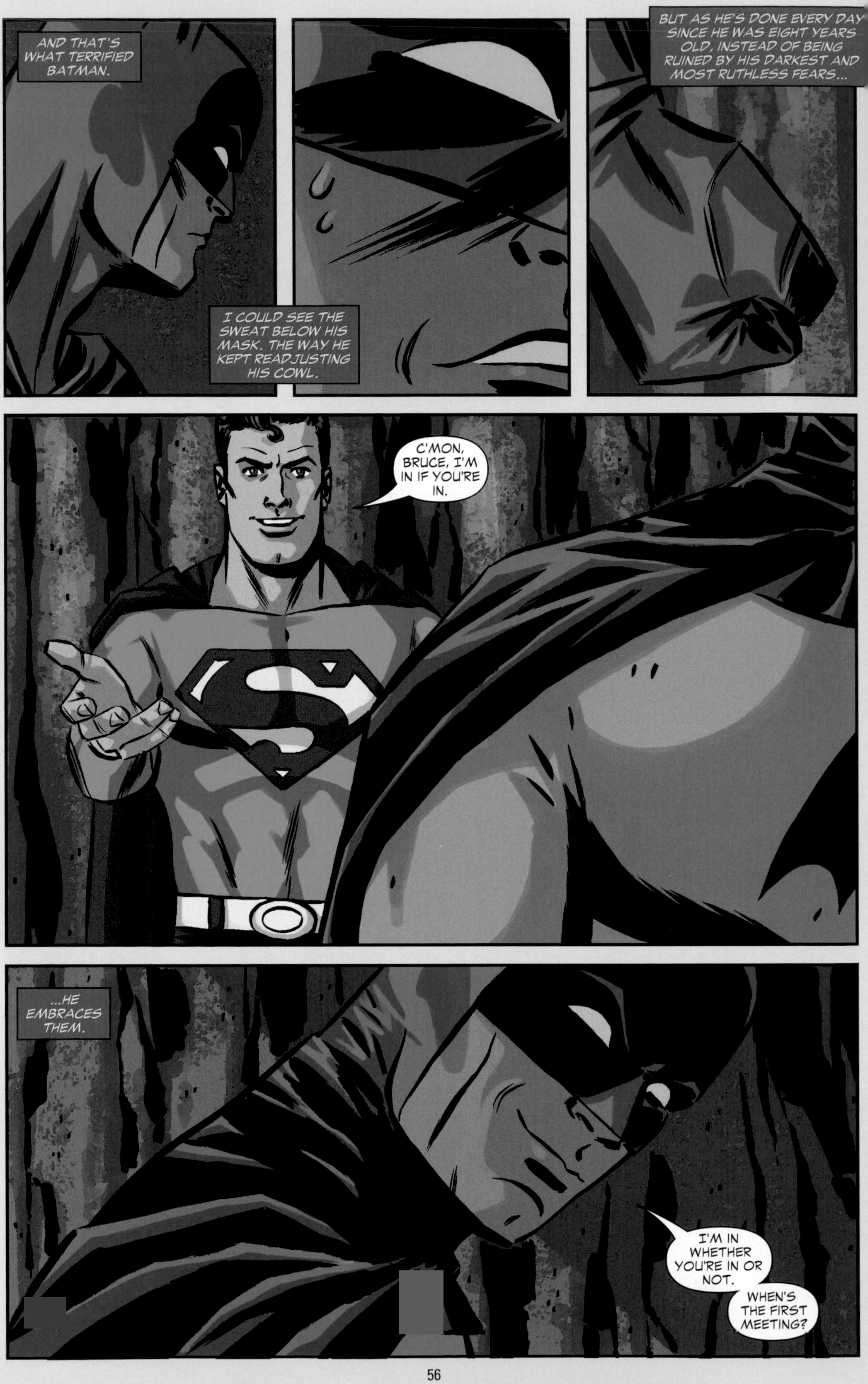
AND THAT'S WHAT TERRIFIED BATMAN.
I COULD SEE THE SWEAT BELOW HIS MASK. THE WAY HE KEPT READJUSTING HIS COWL.
BUT AS HE'S DONE EVERY DAY SINCE HE WAS EIGHT YEARS OLD, INSTEAD OF BEING RUINED BY HIS DARKEST AND MOST RUTHLESS FEARS...
C'MON, BRUCE, I'M IN IF YOU'RE IN.
...HE EMBRACES THEM.
I'M IN WHETHER YOU'RE IN OR NOT.
WHEN'S THE FIRST MEETING?

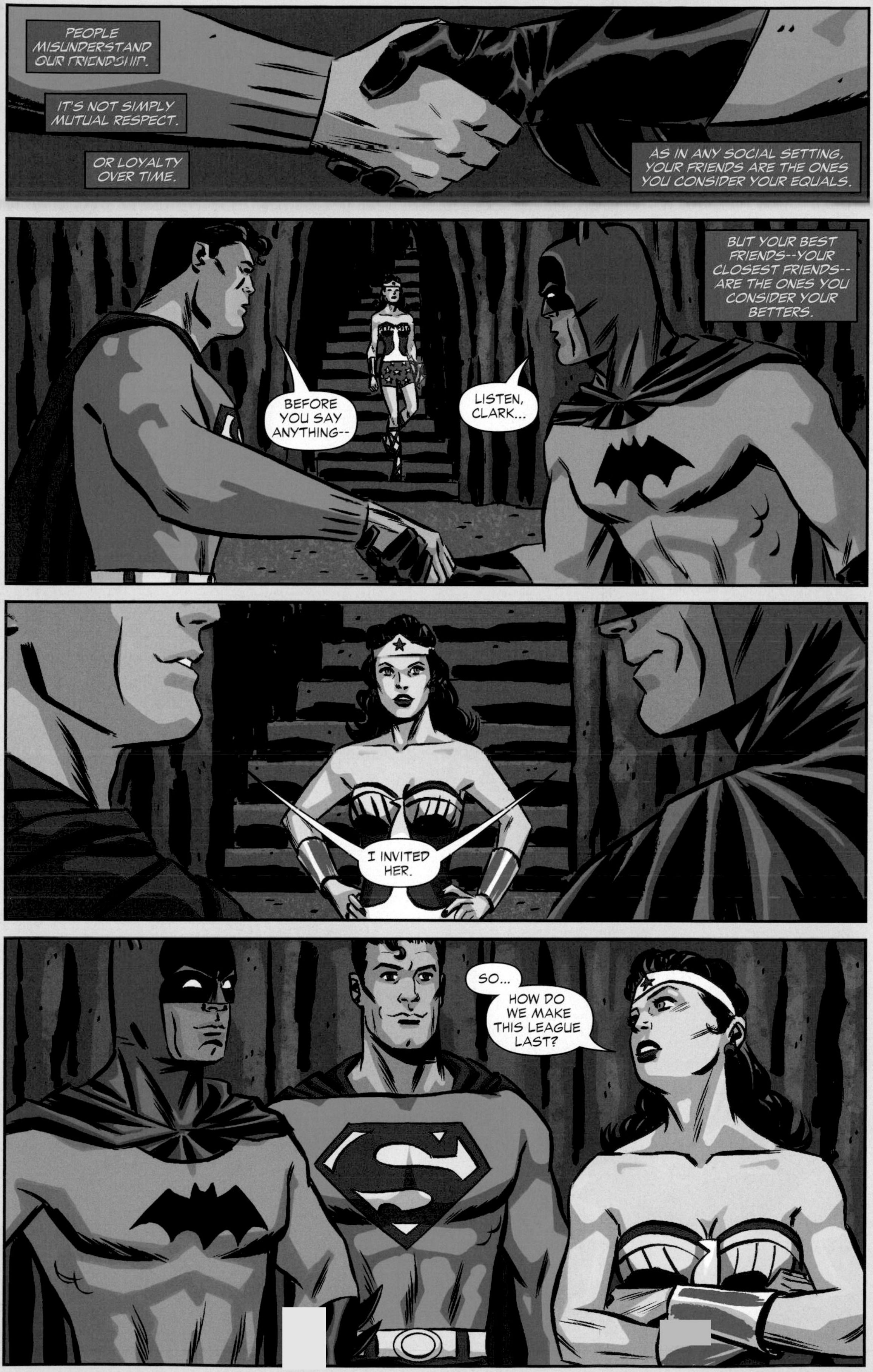
PEOPLE MISUNDERSTAND OUR FRIENDSHIP.
IT'S NOT SIMPLY MUTUAL RESPECT.
OR LOYALTY OVER TIME.
AS IN ANY SOCIAL SETTING, YOUR FRIENDS ARE THE ONES YOU CONSIDER YOUR EQUALS.
BUT YOUR BEST FRIENDS--YOUR CLOSEST FRIENDS--ARE THE ONES YOU CONSIDER YOUR BETTERS.
BEFORE YOU SAY ANYTHING--
LISTEN, CLARK...
I INVITED HER.
SO...
HOW DO WE MAKE THIS LEAGUE LAST?

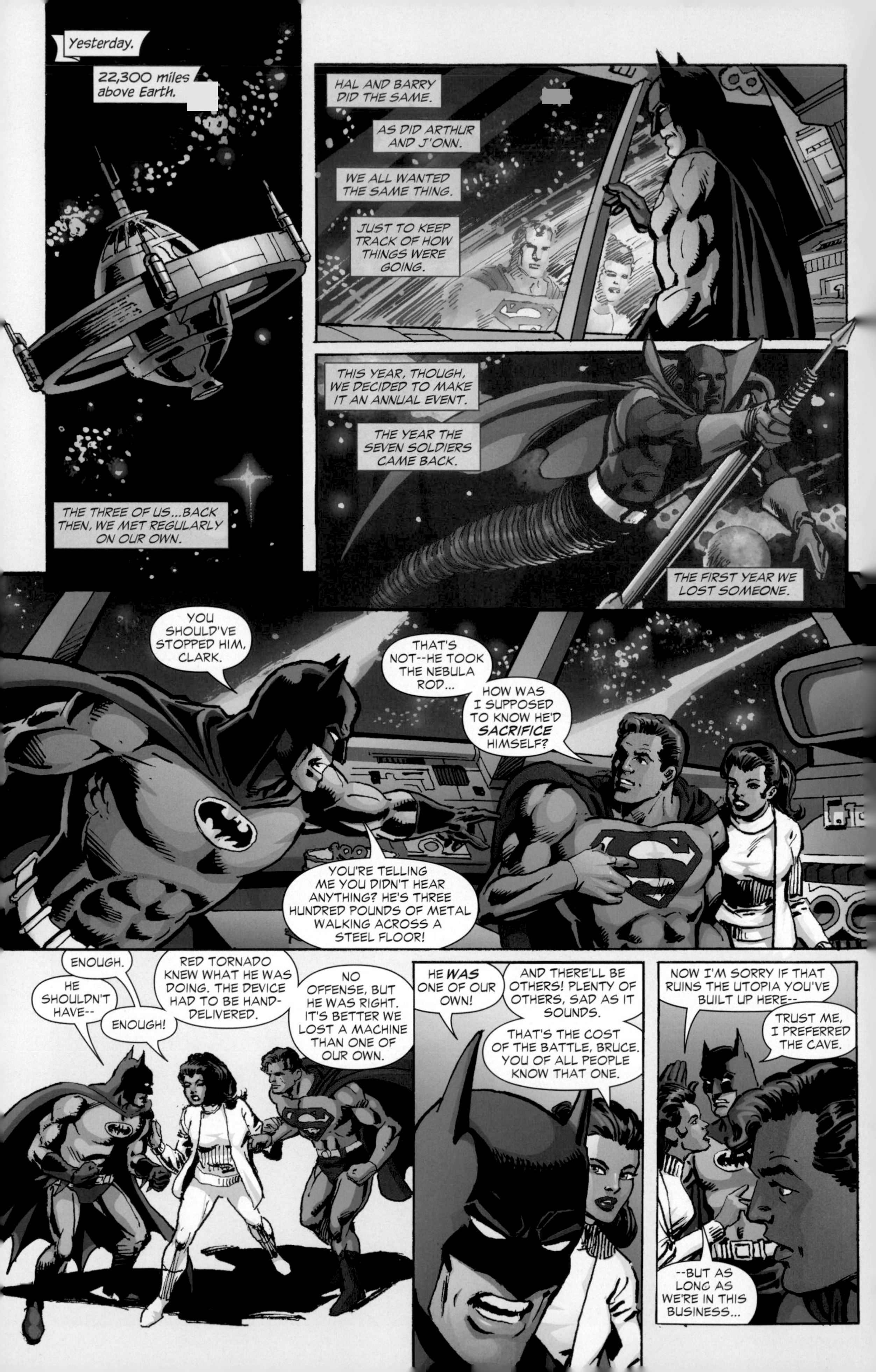

Yesterday.
22,300 miles above Earth.
THE THREE OF US...BACK THEN, WE MET REGULARLY ON OUR OWN.
HAL AND BARRY DID THE SAME.
AS DID ARTHUR AND J'ONN.
WE ALL WANTED THE SAME THING.
JUST TO KEEP TRACK OF HOW THINGS WERE GOING.
THIS YEAR, THOUGH, WE DECIDED TO MAKE IT AN ANNUAL EVENT.
THE YEAR THE SEVEN SOLDIERS CAME BACK.
THE FIRST YEAR WE LOST SOMEONE.
YOU SHOULD'VE STOPPED HIM, CLARK.
THAT'S NOT--HE TOOK THE NEBULA ROD...
HOW WAS I SUPPOSED TO KNOW HE'D SACRIFICE HIMSELF?
YOU'RE TELLING ME YOU DIDN'T HEAR ANYTHING? HE'S THREE HUNDRED POUNDS OF METAL WALKING ACROSS A STEEL FLOOR!
ENOUGH.
HE SHOULDN'T HAVE--
ENOUGH!
RED TORNADO KNEW WHAT HE WAS DOING. THE DEVICE HAD TO BE HAND-DELIVERED.
NO OFFENSE, BUT HE WAS RIGHT. IT'S BETTER WE LOST A MACHINE THAN ONE OF OUR OWN.
HE WAS ONE OF OUR OWN!
AND THERE'LL BE OTHERS! PLENTY OF OTHERS, SAD AS IT SOUNDS.
THAT'S THE COST OF THE BATTLE, BRUCE. YOU OF ALL PEOPLE KNOW THAT ONE.
NOW I'M SORRY IF THAT RUINS THE UTOPIA YOU'VE BUILT UP HERE--
TRUST ME, I PREFERRED THE CAVE.
--BUT AS LONG AS WE'RE IN THIS BUSINESS...

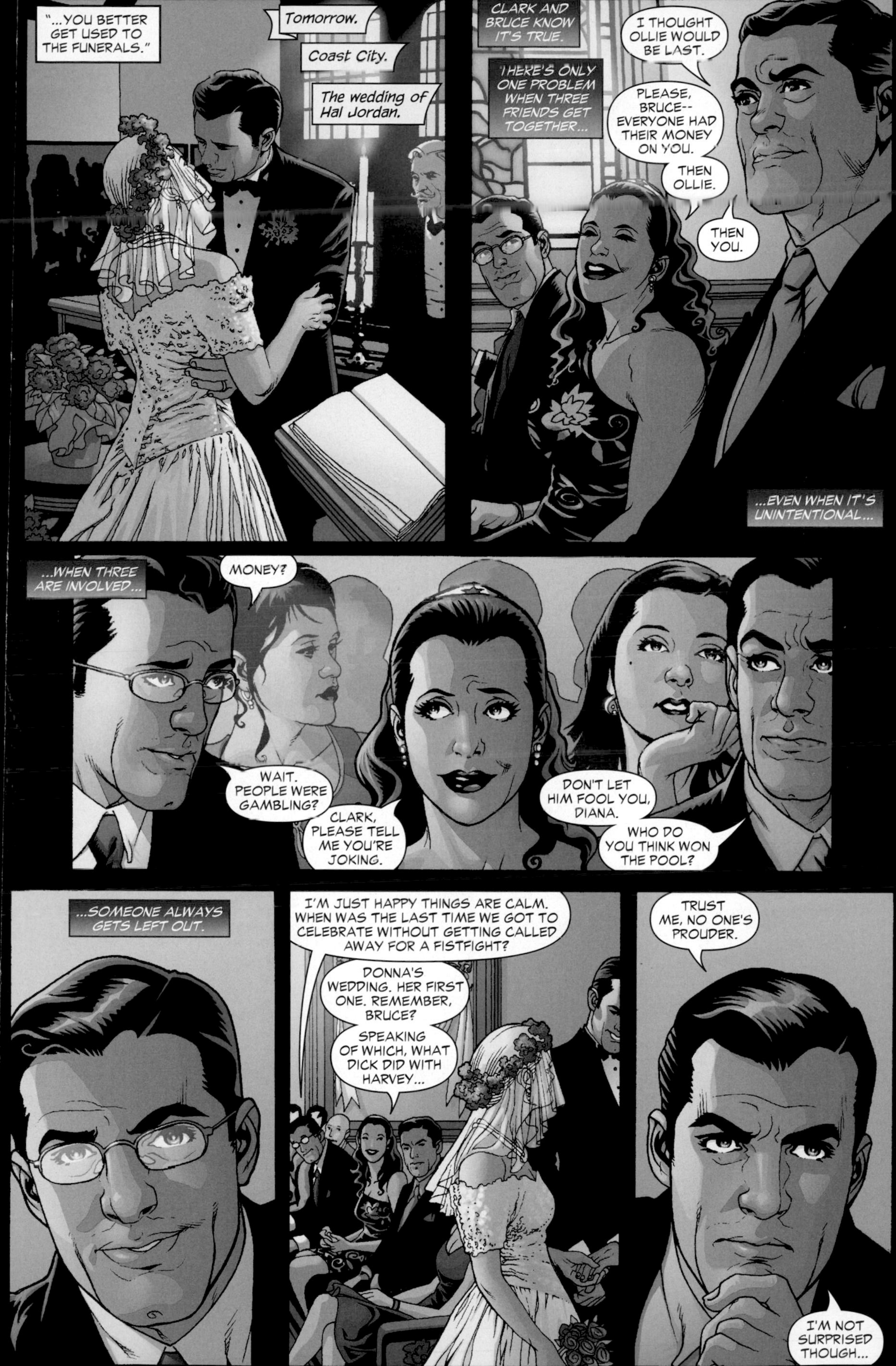
"...YOU BETTER GET USED TO THE FUNERALS."
Tomorrow.
Coast City.
The wedding of Hal Jordan.
CLARK AND BRUCE KNOW IT'S TRUE.
THERE'S ONLY ONE PROBLEM WHEN THREE FRIENDS GET TOGETHER...
I THOUGHT OLLIE WOULD BE LAST.
PLEASE, BRUCE-- EVERYONE HAD THEIR MONEY ON YOU.
THEN OLLIE.
THEN YOU.
...EVEN WHEN IT'S UNINTENTIONAL...
...WHEN THREE ARE INVOLVED...
MONEY?
WAIT. PEOPLE WERE GAMBLING?
CLARK, PLEASE TELL ME YOU'RE JOKING.
DON'T LET HIM FOOL YOU, DIANA.
WHO DO YOU THINK WON THE POOL?
...SOMEONE ALWAYS GETS LEFT OUT.
I'M JUST HAPPY THINGS ARE CALM. WHEN WAS THE LAST TIME WE GOT TO CELEBRATE WITHOUT GETTING CALLED AWAY FOR A FISTFIGHT?
DONNA'S WEDDING. HER FIRST ONE. REMEMBER, BRUCE?
SPEAKING OF WHICH, WHAT DICK DID WITH HARVEY...
TRUST ME, NO ONE'S PROUDER.
I'M NOT SURPRISED THOUGH...

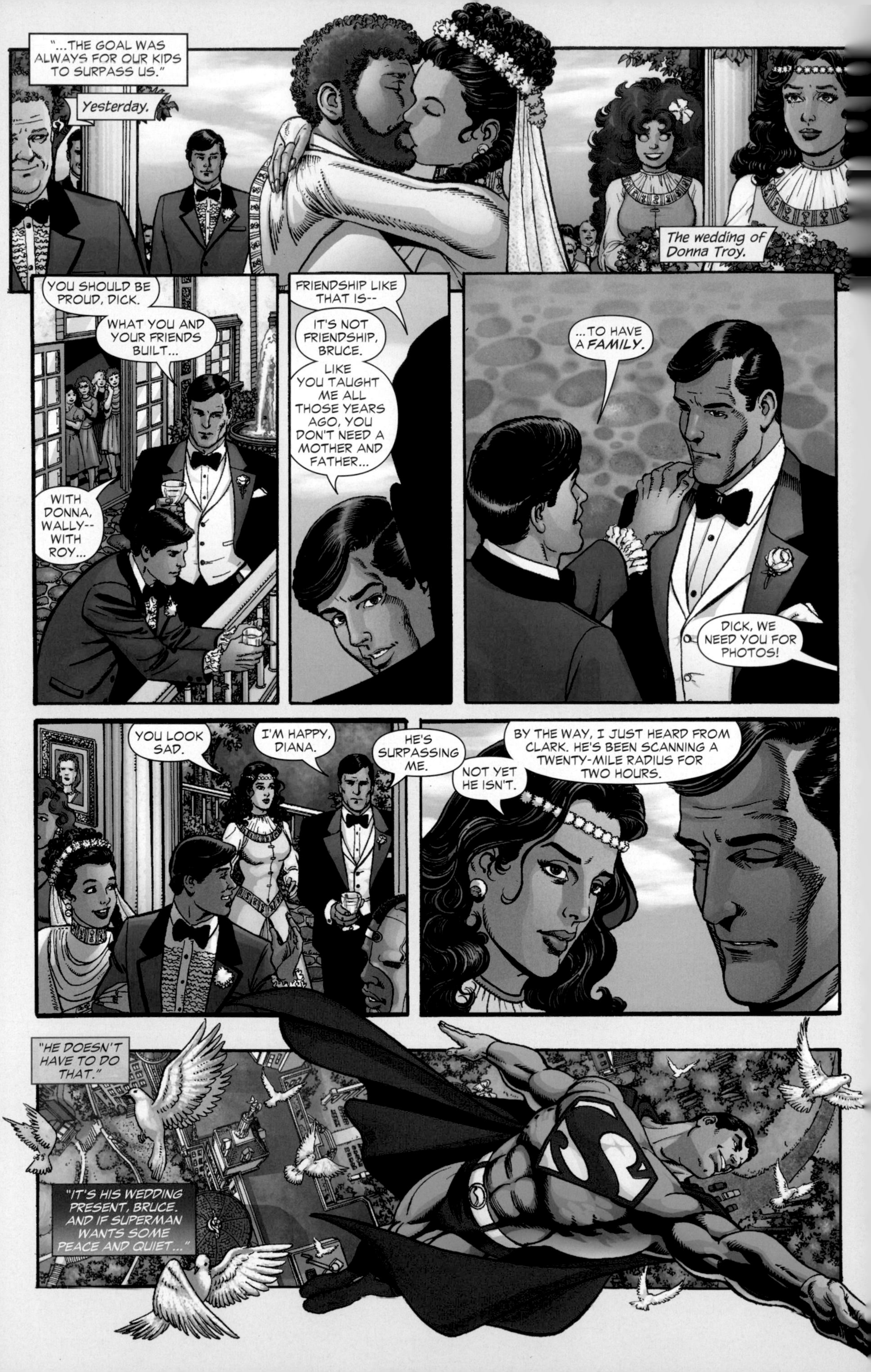
"...THE GOAL WAS ALWAYS FOR OUR KIDS TO SURPASS US."
Yesterday.
The wedding of Donna Troy.
YOU SHOULD BE PROUD, DICK.
WHAT YOU AND YOUR FRIENDS BUILT...
WITH DONNA, WALLY-- WITH ROY...
FRIENDSHIP LIKE THAT IS--
IT'S NOT FRIENDSHIP, BRUCE.
LIKE YOU TAUGHT ME ALL THOSE YEARS AGO, YOU DON'T NEED A MOTHER AND FATHER...
...TO HAVE A FAMILY.
DICK, WE NEED YOU FOR PHOTOS!
YOU LOOK SAD.
I'M HAPPY, DIANA.
HE'S SURPASSING ME.
NOT YET HE ISN'T.
BY THE WAY, I JUST HEARD FROM CLARK. HE'S BEEN SCANNING A TWENTY-MILE RADIUS FOR TWO HOURS.
"HE DOESN'T HAVE TO DO THAT."
"IT'S HIS WEDDING PRESENT, BRUCE. AND IF SUPERMAN WANTS SOME PEACE AND QUIET..."

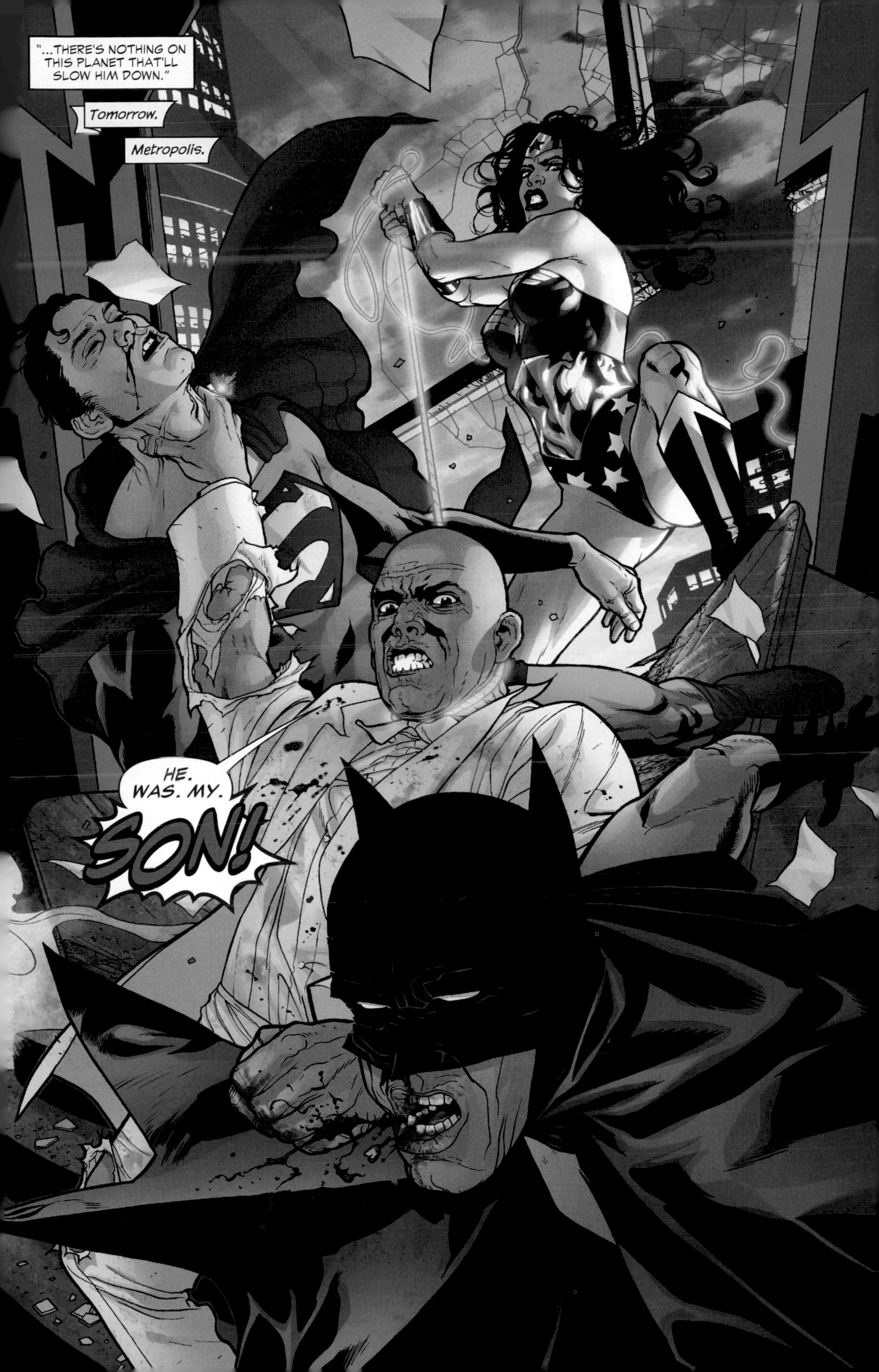
"...THERE'S NOTHING ON THIS PLANET THAT'LL SLOW HIM DOWN."
Tomorrow.
Metropolis.
HE. WAS. MY. SON!

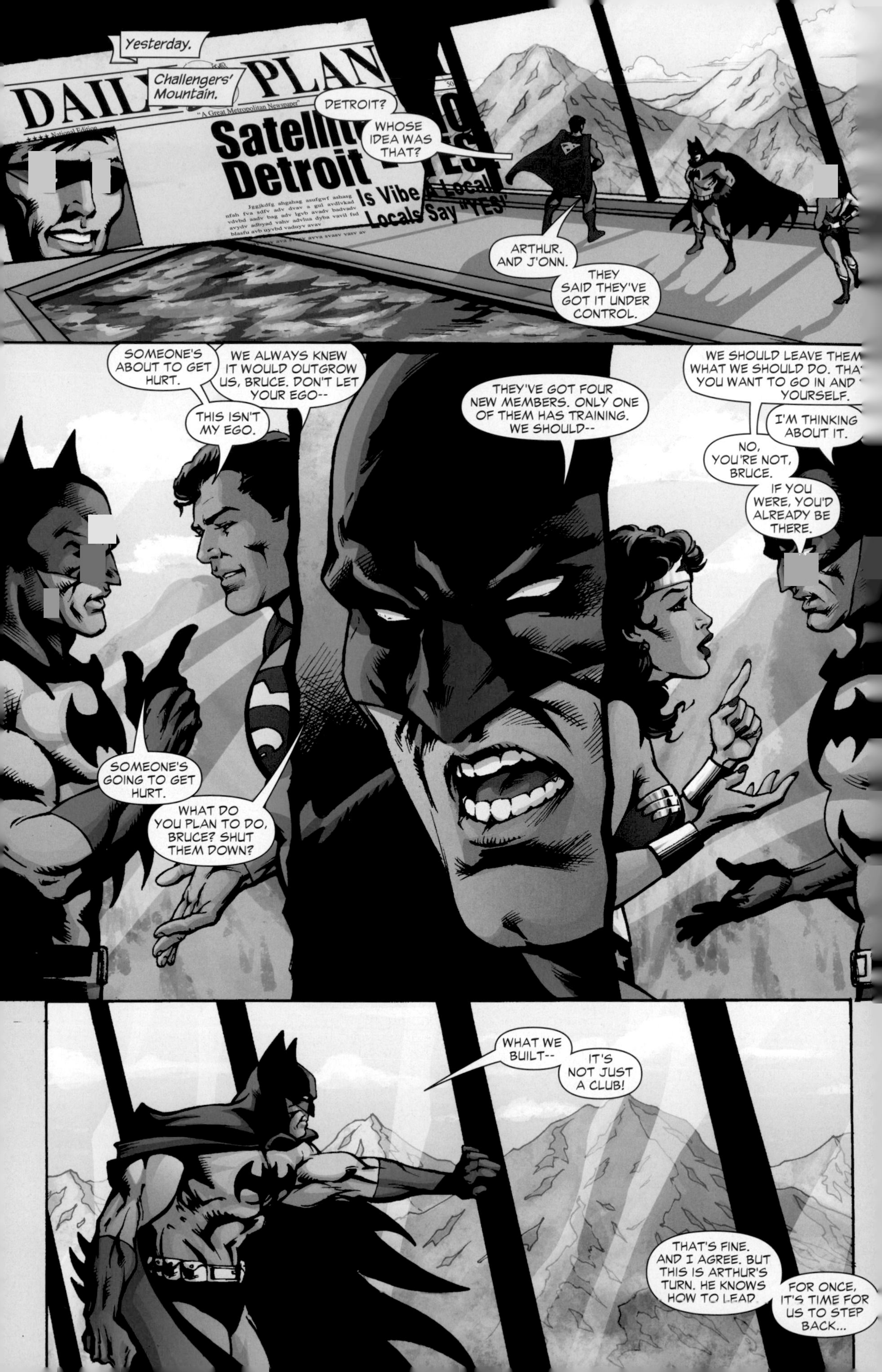
Yesterday.
Challengers' Mountain.
DETROIT?
WHOSE IDEA WAS THAT?
ARTHUR. AND J'ONN.
THEY SAID THEY'VE GOT IT UNDER CONTROL.
SOMEONE'S ABOUT TO GET HURT.
WE ALWAYS KNEW IT WOULD OUTGROW US, BRUCE. DON'T LET YOUR EGO--
THIS ISN'T MY EGO.
THEY'VE GOT FOUR NEW MEMBERS. ONLY ONE OF THEM HAS TRAINING. WE SHOULD--
WE SHOULD LEAVE THEM WHAT WE SHOULD DO. THA YOU WANT TO GO IN AND YOURSELF.
I'M THINKING ABOUT IT.
NO, YOU'RE NOT, BRUCE.
IF YOU WERE, YOU'D ALREADY BE THERE.
SOMEONE'S GOING TO GET HURT.
WHAT DO YOU PLAN TO DO, BRUCE? SHUT THEM DOWN?
WHAT WE BUILT--
IT'S NOT JUST A CLUB!
THAT'S FINE. AND I AGREE. BUT THIS IS ARTHUR'S TURN. HE KNOWS HOW TO LEAD.
FOR ONCE, IT'S TIME FOR US TO STEP BACK...

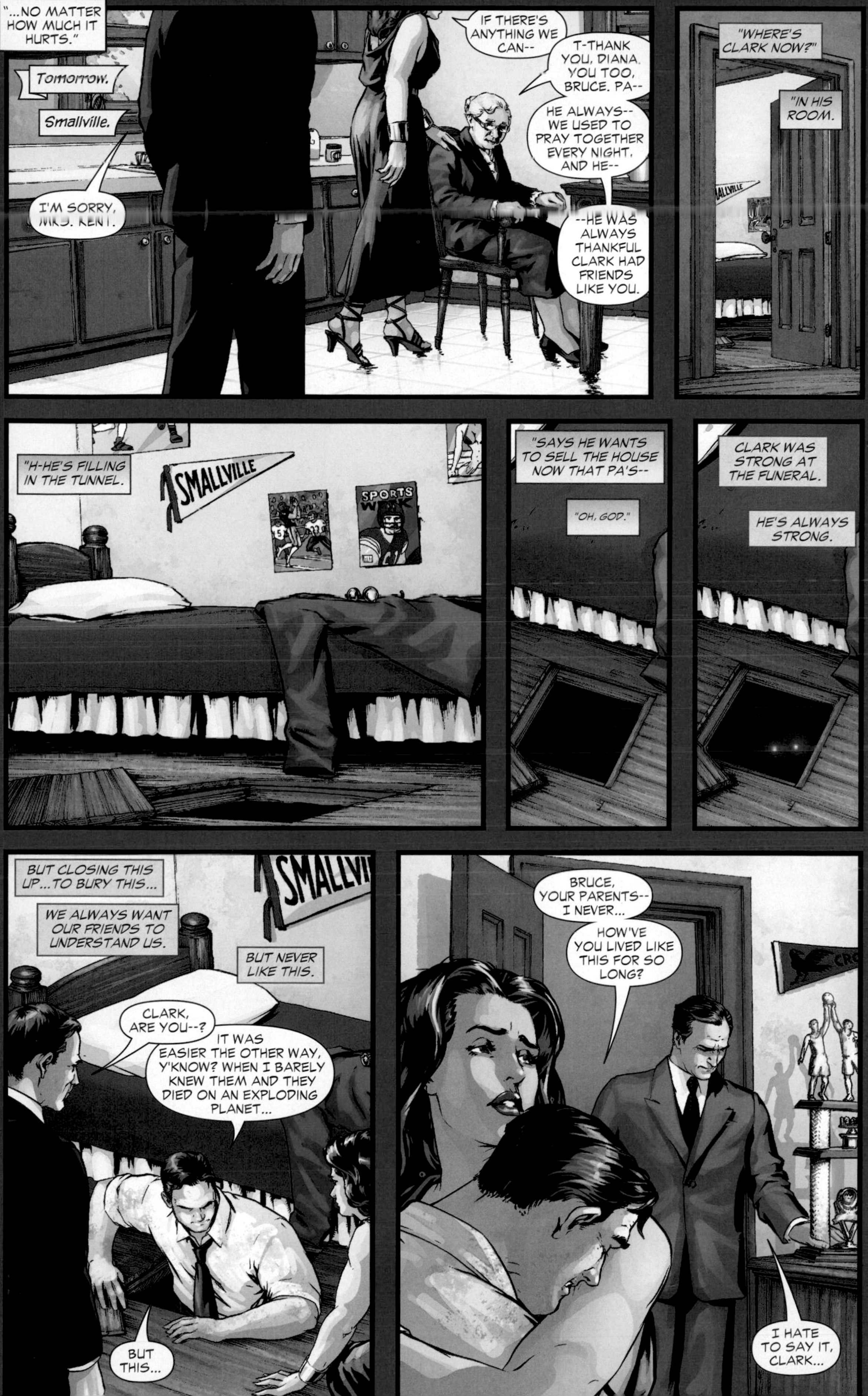
"...NO MATTER HOW MUCH IT HURTS."
Tomorrow.
Smallville.
I'M SORRY, MRS. KENT.
IF THERE'S ANYTHING WE CAN--
T-THANK YOU, DIANA. YOU TOO, BRUCE. PA--
HE ALWAYS-- WE USED TO PRAY TOGETHER EVERY NIGHT, AND HE--
--HE WAS ALWAYS THANKFUL CLARK HAD FRIENDS LIKE YOU.
"WHERE'S CLARK NOW?"
"IN HIS ROOM.
"H-HE'S FILLING IN THE TUNNEL.
SMALLVILLE
SPORTS
"SAYS HE WANTS TO SELL THE HOUSE NOW THAT PA'S--
"OH, GOD."
CLARK WAS STRONG AT THE FUNERAL.
HE'S ALWAYS STRONG.
BUT CLOSING THIS UP...TO BURY THIS...
WE ALWAYS WANT OUR FRIENDS TO UNDERSTAND US.
BUT NEVER LIKE THIS.
CLARK, ARE YOU--?
IT WAS EASIER THE OTHER WAY, Y'KNOW? WHEN I BARELY KNEW THEM AND THEY DIED ON AN EXPLODING PLANET...
BUT THIS...
BRUCE, YOUR PARENTS-- I NEVER...
HOW'VE YOU LIVED LIKE THIS FOR SO LONG?
I HATE TO SAY IT, CLARK...

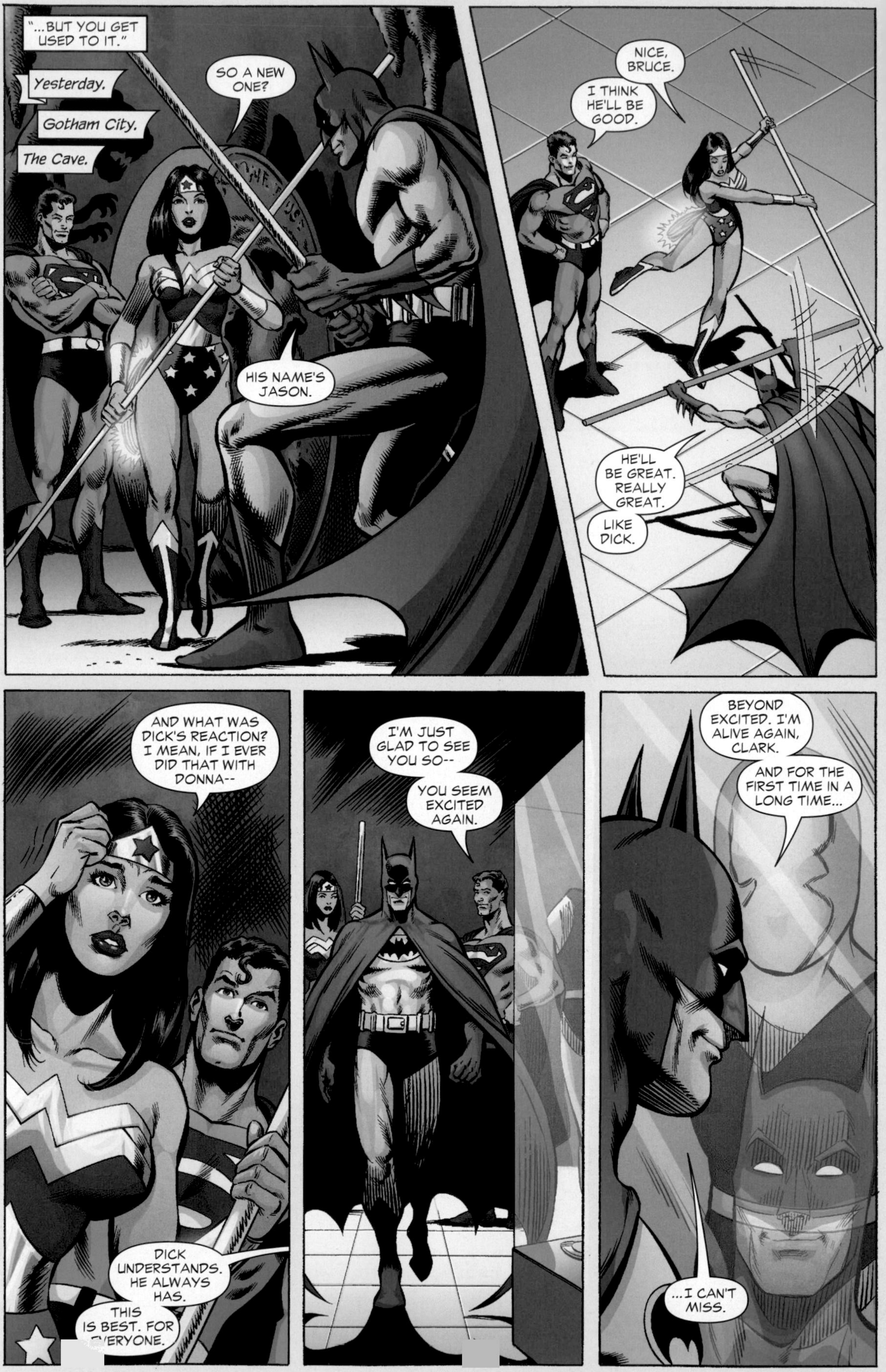
"...BUT YOU GET USED TO IT."
Yesterday.
Gotham City.
The Cave.
SO A NEW ONE?
HIS NAME'S JASON.
NICE, BRUCE.
I THINK HE'LL BE GOOD.
HE'LL BE GREAT. REALLY GREAT.
LIKE DICK.
AND WHAT WAS DICK'S REACTION? I MEAN, IF I EVER DID THAT WITH DONNA--
DICK UNDERSTANDS. HE ALWAYS HAS.
THIS IS BEST. FOR EVERYONE.
I'M JUST GLAD TO SEE YOU SO--
YOU SEEM EXCITED AGAIN.
BEYOND EXCITED. I'M ALIVE AGAIN, CLARK.
AND FOR THE FIRST TIME IN A LONG TIME...
...I CAN'T MISS.

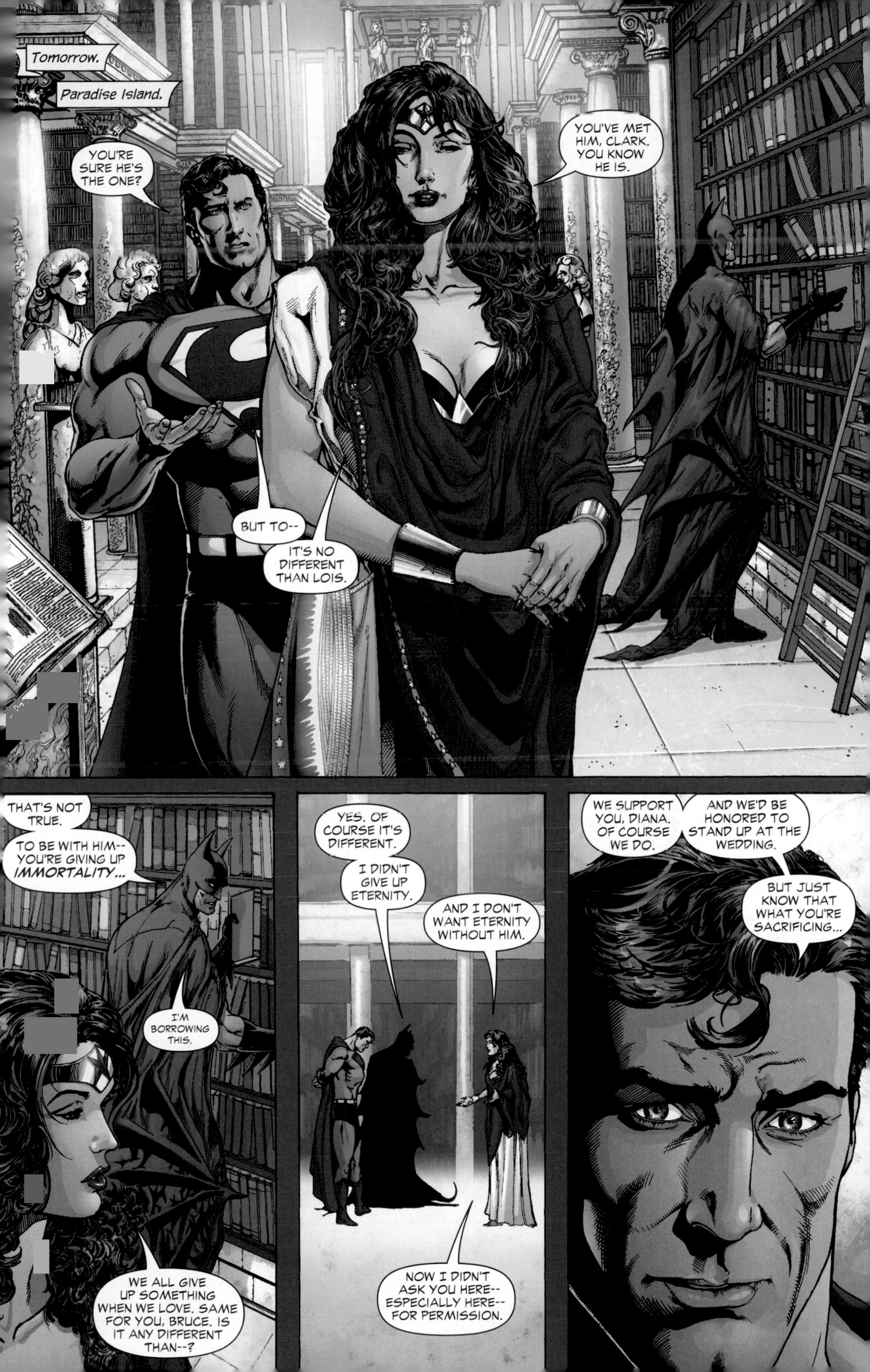
Tomorrow.
Paradise Island.
YOU'RE SURE HE'S THE ONE?
YOU'VE MET HIM, CLARK. YOU KNOW HE IS.
BUT TO--
IT'S NO DIFFERENT THAN LOIS.
THAT'S NOT TRUE.
TO BE WITH HIM-- YOU'RE GIVING UP IMMORTALITY...
I'M BORROWING THIS.
WE ALL GIVE UP SOMETHING WHEN WE LOVE. SAME FOR YOU, BRUCE. IS IT ANY DIFFERENT THAN--?
YES. OF COURSE IT'S DIFFERENT.
I DIDN'T GIVE UP ETERNITY.
AND I DON'T WANT ETERNITY WITHOUT HIM.
NOW I DIDN'T ASK YOU HERE-- ESPECIALLY HERE-- FOR PERMISSION.
WE SUPPORT YOU, DIANA. OF COURSE WE DO.
AND WE'D BE HONORED TO STAND UP AT THE WEDDING.
BUT JUST KNOW THAT WHAT YOU'RE SACRIFICING...

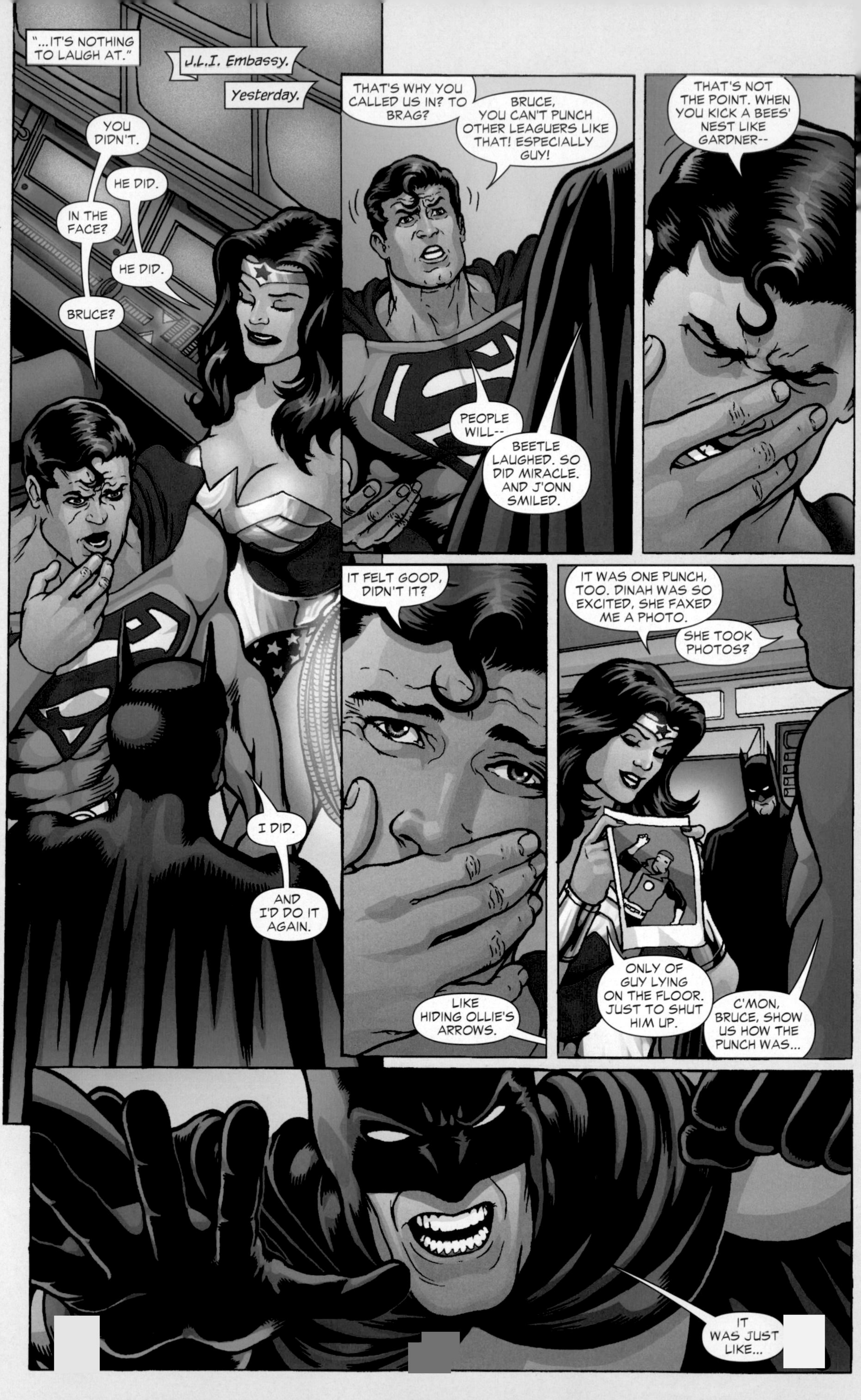
"...IT'S NOTHING TO LAUGH AT."
J.L.I. Embassy.
Yesterday.
YOU DIDN'T.
HE DID.
IN THE FACE?
HE DID.
BRUCE?
I DID.
AND I'D DO IT AGAIN.
THAT'S WHY YOU CALLED US IN? TO BRAG?
BRUCE, YOU CAN'T PUNCH OTHER LEAGUERS LIKE THAT! ESPECIALLY GUY!
PEOPLE WILL--
BEETLE LAUGHED. SO DID MIRACLE. AND J'ONN SMILED.
THAT'S NOT THE POINT. WHEN YOU KICK A BEES' NEST LIKE GARDNER--
IT FELT GOOD, DIDN'T IT?
LIKE HIDING OLLIE'S ARROWS.
IT WAS ONE PUNCH, TOO. DINAH WAS SO EXCITED, SHE FAXED ME A PHOTO.
SHE TOOK PHOTOS?
ONLY OF GUY LYING ON THE FLOOR. JUST TO SHUT HIM UP.
C'MON, BRUCE, SHOW US HOW THE PUNCH WAS...
IT WAS JUST LIKE...

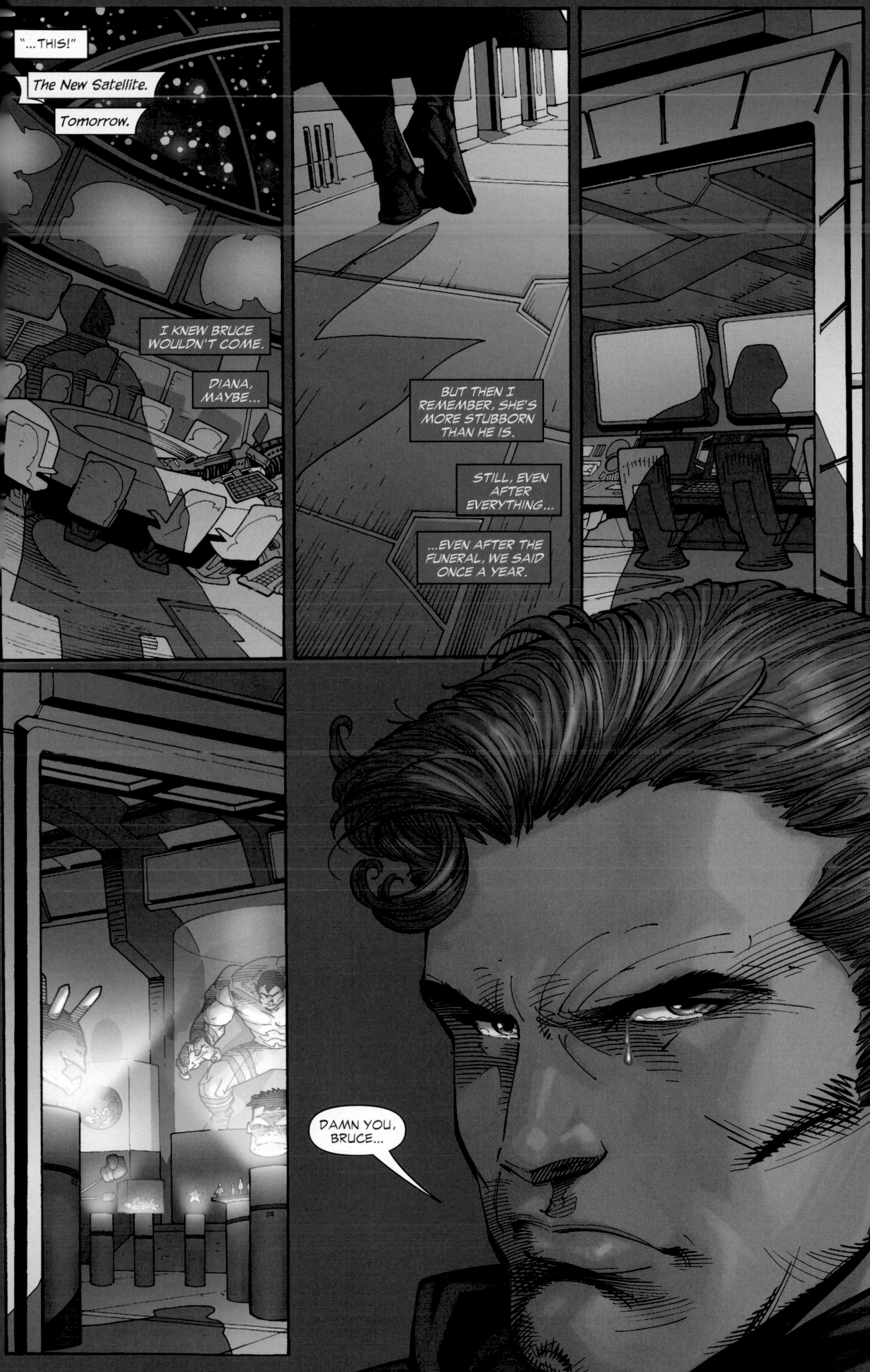

"...THIS!"
The New Satellite.
Tomorrow.
I KNEW BRUCE WOULDN'T COME.
DIANA, MAYBE...
BUT THEN I REMEMBER, SHE'S MORE STUBBORN THAN HE IS.
STILL, EVEN AFTER EVERYTHING...
...EVEN AFTER THE FUNERAL, WE SAID ONCE A YEAR.
DAMN YOU, BRUCE...

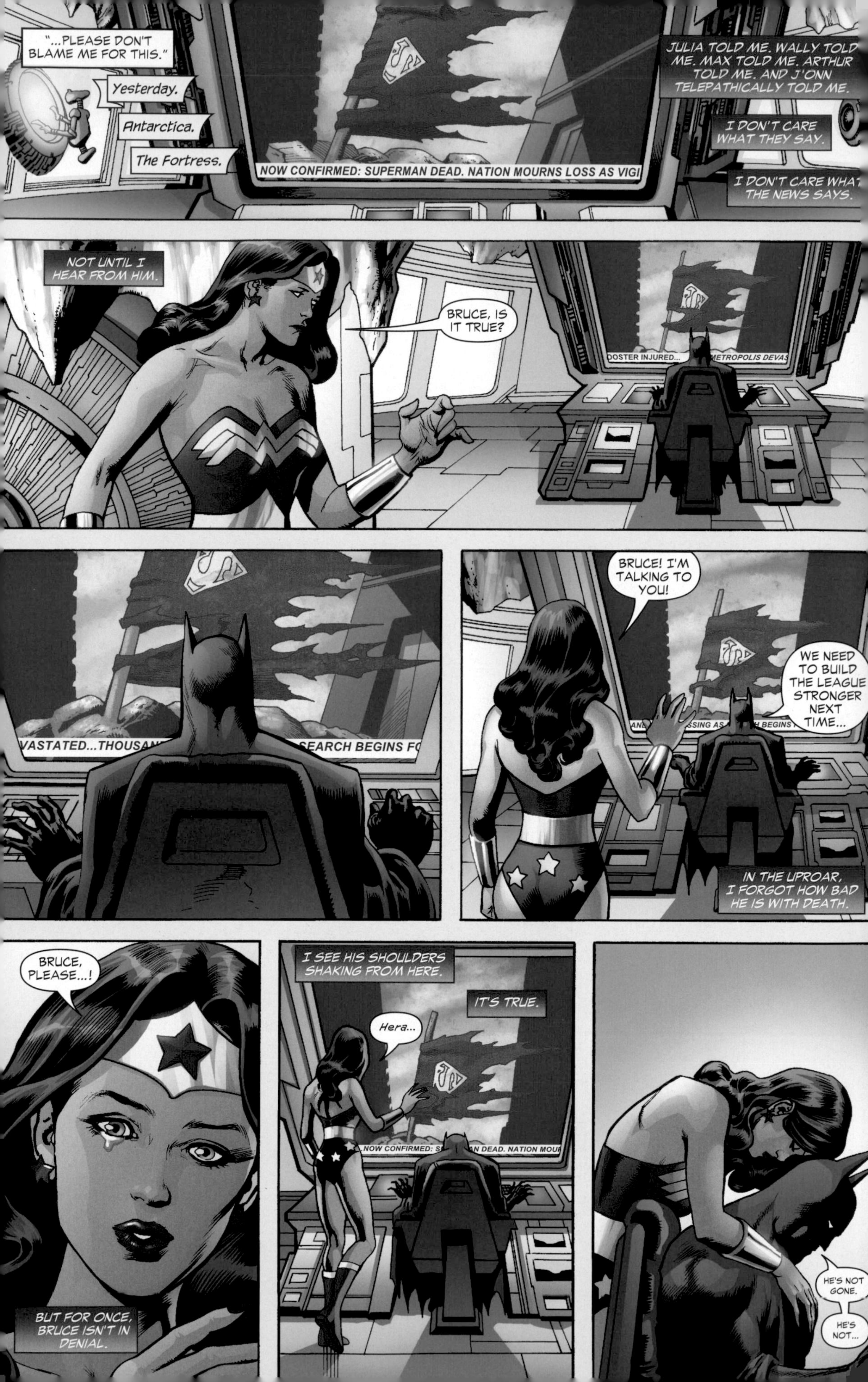
"...PLEASE DON'T BLAME ME FOR THIS."
Yesterday.
Antarctica.
The Fortress.
NOW CONFIRMED: SUPERMAN DEAD. NATION MOURNS LOSS AS VIGI
JULIA TOLD ME. WALLY TOLD ME. MAX TOLD ME. ARTHUR TOLD ME. AND J'ONN TELEPATHICALLY TOLD ME.
I DON'T CARE WHAT THEY SAY.
I DON'T CARE WHAT THE NEWS SAYS.
NOT UNTIL I HEAR FROM HIM.
BRUCE, IS IT TRUE?
OOSTER INJURED... METROPOLIS DEVAS
VASTATED...THOUSAN
SEARCH BEGINS FO
BRUCE! I'M TALKING TO YOU!
WE NEED TO BUILD THE LEAGUE STRONGER NEXT TIME...
IN THE UPROAR, I FORGOT HOW BAD HE IS WITH DEATH.
BRUCE, PLEASE...!
BUT FOR ONCE, BRUCE ISN'T IN DENIAL.
I SEE HIS SHOULDERS SHAKING FROM HERE.
IT'S TRUE.
Hera...
NOW CONFIRMED: S MAN DEAD. NATION MOUR
HE'S NOT GONE.
HE'S NOT...

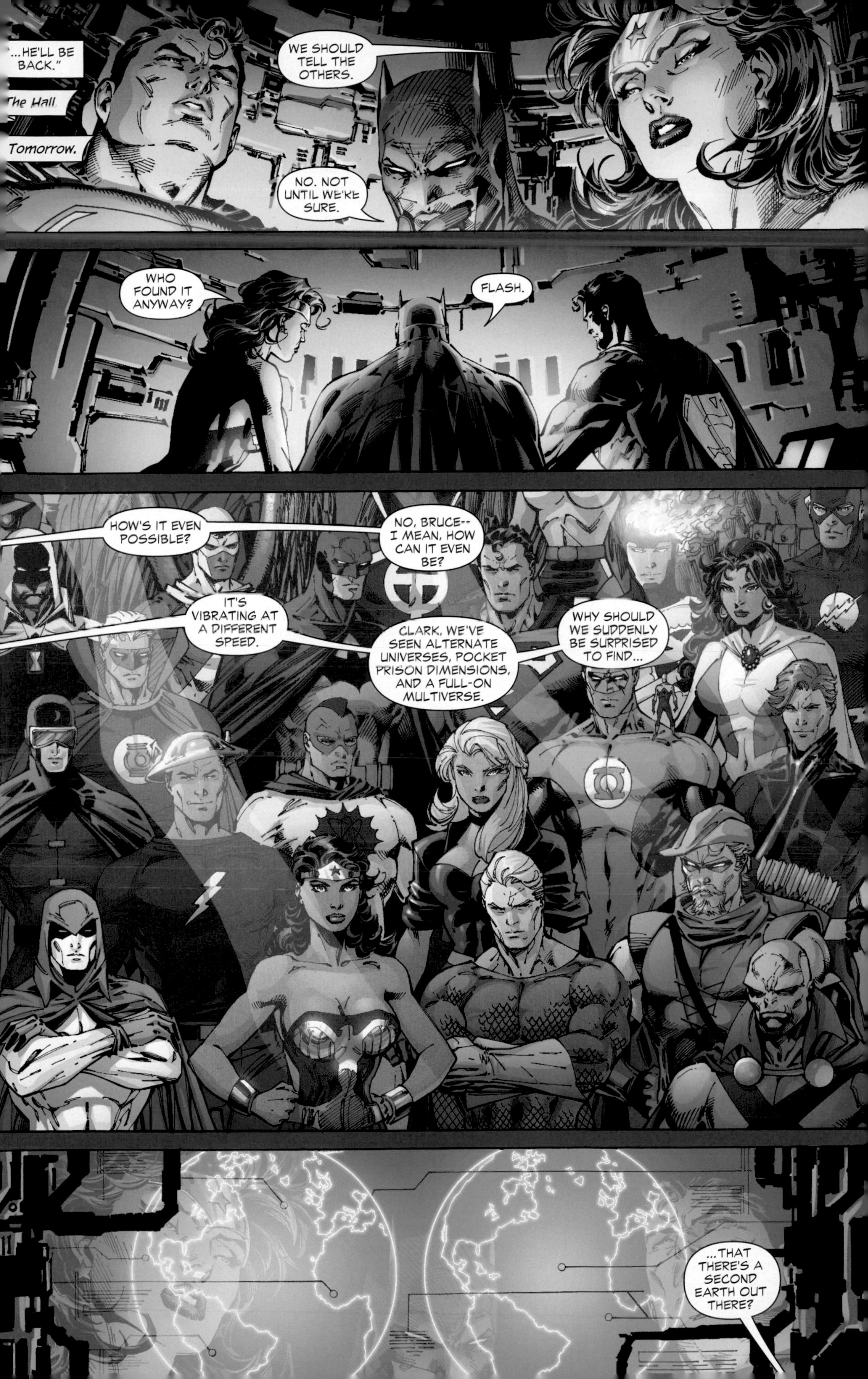

"...HE'LL BE BACK."
The Hall.
Tomorrow.
WE SHOULD TELL THE OTHERS.
NO. NOT UNTIL WE'RE SURE.
WHO FOUND IT ANYWAY?
FLASH.
HOW'S IT EVEN POSSIBLE?
NO, BRUCE-- I MEAN, HOW CAN IT EVEN BE?
IT'S VIBRATING AT A DIFFERENT SPEED.
CLARK, WE'VE SEEN ALTERNATE UNIVERSES, POCKET PRISON DIMENSIONS, AND A FULL-ON MULTIVERSE.
WHY SHOULD WE SUDDENLY BE SURPRISED TO FIND...
...THAT THERE'S A SECOND EARTH OUT THERE?

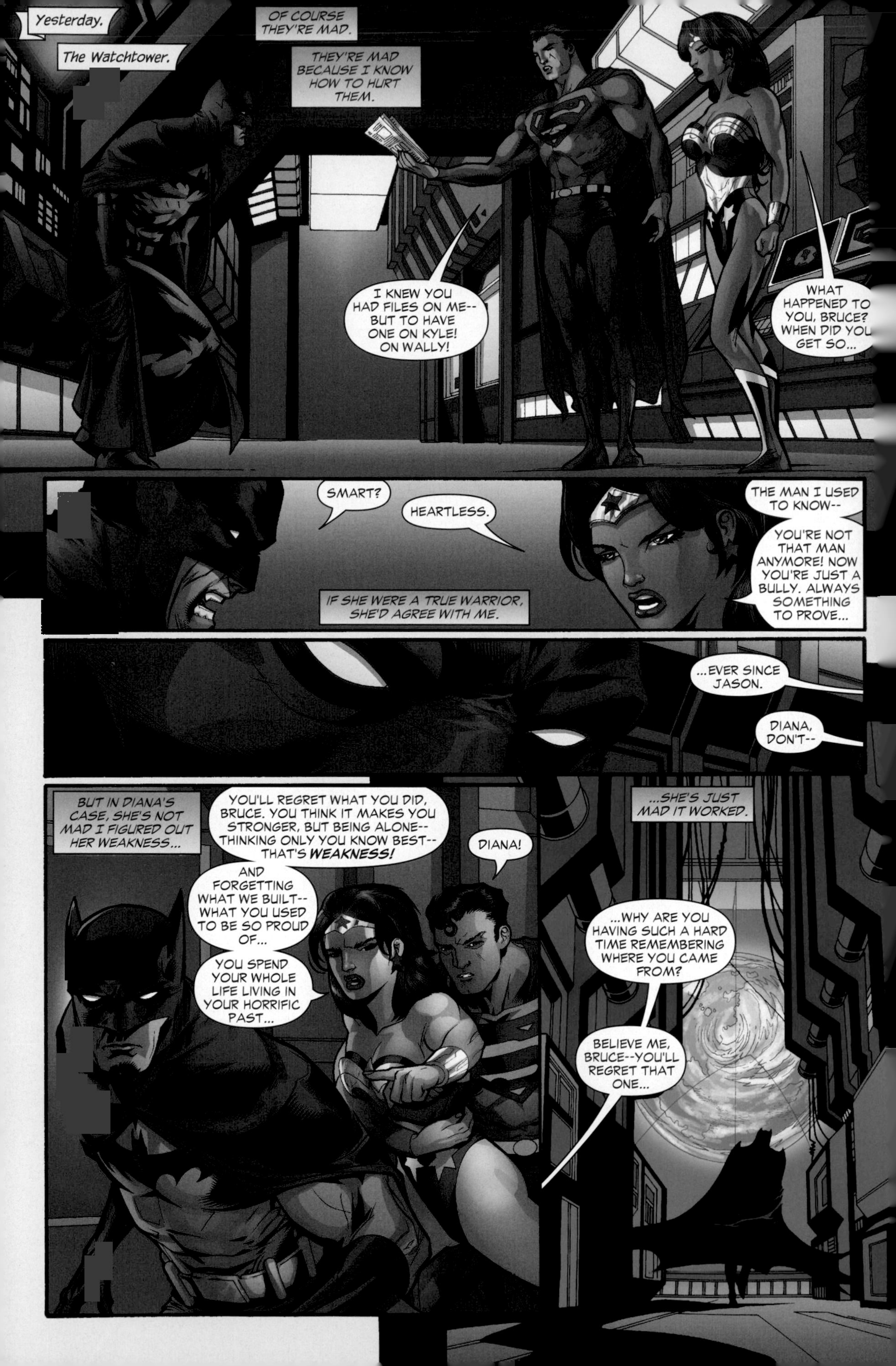
Yesterday.
The Watchtower.
OF COURSE THEY'RE MAD.
THEY'RE MAD BECAUSE I KNOW HOW TO HURT THEM.
I KNEW YOU HAD FILES ON ME-- BUT TO HAVE ONE ON KYLE! ON WALLY!
WHAT HAPPENED TO YOU, BRUCE? WHEN DID YOU GET SO...
SMART?
HEARTLESS.
THE MAN I USED TO KNOW--
YOU'RE NOT THAT MAN ANYMORE! NOW YOU'RE JUST A BULLY. ALWAYS SOMETHING TO PROVE...
IF SHE WERE A TRUE WARRIOR, SHE'D AGREE WITH ME.
...EVER SINCE JASON.
DIANA, DON'T--
BUT IN DIANA'S CASE, SHE'S NOT MAD I FIGURED OUT HER WEAKNESS...
YOU'LL REGRET WHAT YOU DID, BRUCE. YOU THINK IT MAKES YOU STRONGER, BUT BEING ALONE-- THINKING ONLY YOU KNOW BEST-- THAT'S **WEAKNESS!**
DIANA!
AND FORGETTING WHAT WE BUILT-- WHAT YOU USED TO BE SO PROUD OF...
YOU SPEND YOUR WHOLE LIFE LIVING IN YOUR HORRIFIC PAST...
...SHE'S JUST MAD IT WORKED.
...WHY ARE YOU HAVING SUCH A HARD TIME REMEMBERING WHERE YOU CAME FROM?
BELIEVE ME, BRUCE--YOU'LL REGRET THAT ONE...

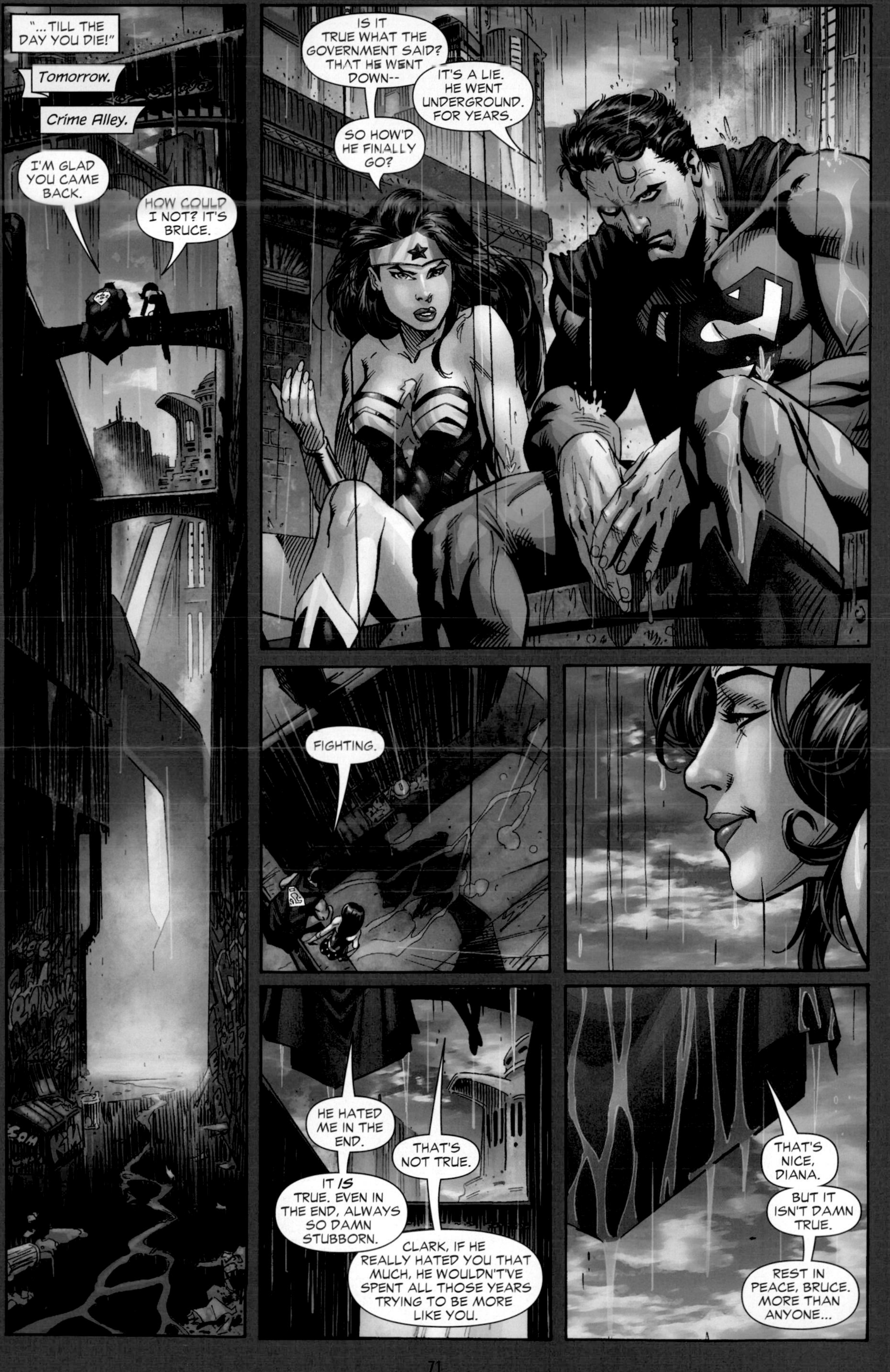

"...TILL THE DAY YOU DIE!"
Tomorrow.
Crime Alley.
I'M GLAD YOU CAME BACK.
HOW COULD I NOT? IT'S BRUCE.
IS IT TRUE WHAT THE GOVERNMENT SAID? THAT HE WENT DOWN--
IT'S A LIE. HE WENT UNDERGROUND. FOR YEARS.
SO HOW'D HE FINALLY GO?
FIGHTING.
HE HATED ME IN THE END.
THAT'S NOT TRUE.
IT IS TRUE. EVEN IN THE END, ALWAYS SO DAMN STUBBORN.
CLARK, IF HE REALLY HATED YOU THAT MUCH, HE WOULDN'T'VE SPENT ALL THOSE YEARS TRYING TO BE MORE LIKE YOU.
THAT'S NICE, DIANA.
BUT IT ISN'T DAMN TRUE.
REST IN PEACE, BRUCE. MORE THAN ANYONE...

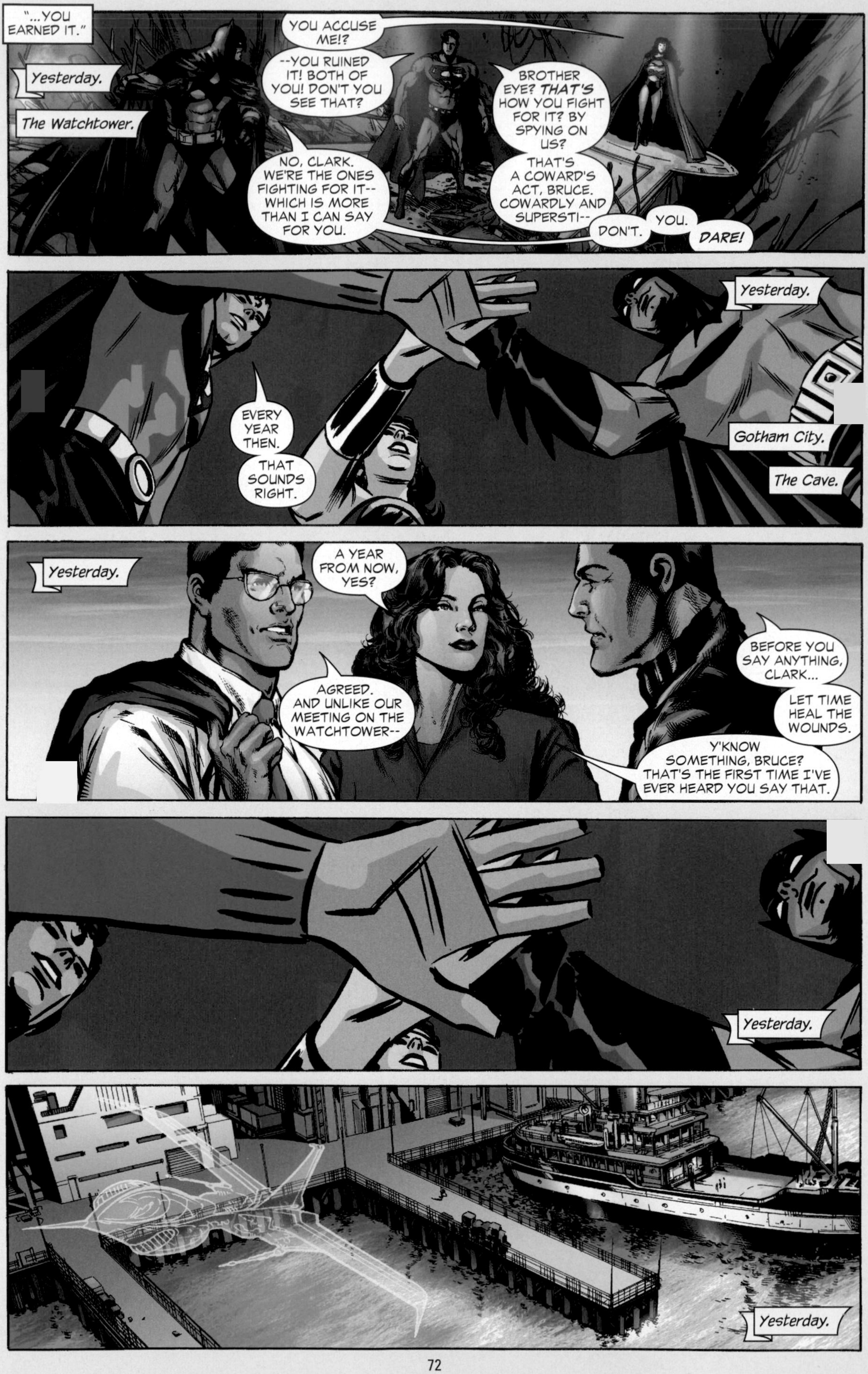
"...YOU EARNED IT."
Yesterday.
The Watchtower.
YOU ACCUSE ME!?
--YOU RUINED IT! BOTH OF YOU! DON'T YOU SEE THAT?
NO, CLARK. WE'RE THE ONES FIGHTING FOR IT--WHICH IS MORE THAN I CAN SAY FOR YOU.
BROTHER EYE? THAT'S HOW YOU FIGHT FOR IT? BY SPYING ON US?
THAT'S A COWARD'S ACT, BRUCE. COWARDLY AND SUPERSTI--
DON'T.
YOU.
DARE!
Yesterday.
EVERY YEAR THEN.
THAT SOUNDS RIGHT.
Gotham City.
The Cave.
Yesterday.
A YEAR FROM NOW, YES?
AGREED. AND UNLIKE OUR MEETING ON THE WATCHTOWER--
BEFORE YOU SAY ANYTHING, CLARK...
LET TIME HEAL THE WOUNDS.
Y'KNOW SOMETHING, BRUCE? THAT'S THE FIRST TIME I'VE EVER HEARD YOU SAY THAT.
Yesterday.
Yesterday.

Today.

Gotham City.

The Cave.

I DON'T GET NERVOUS.

NOT ANYMORE.

BUT WITH CLARK AND DIANA...

...I'M JUST SO DIFFERENT...

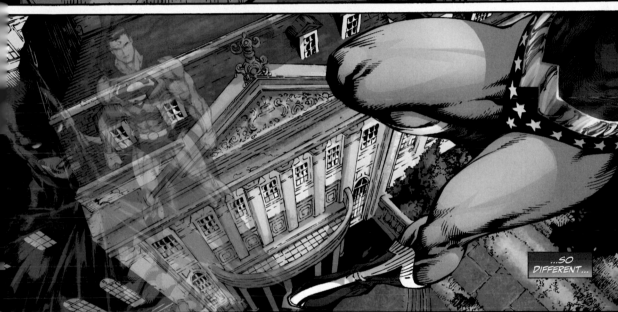

...SO DIFFERENT...

...SO DIFFERENT FROM THEM.

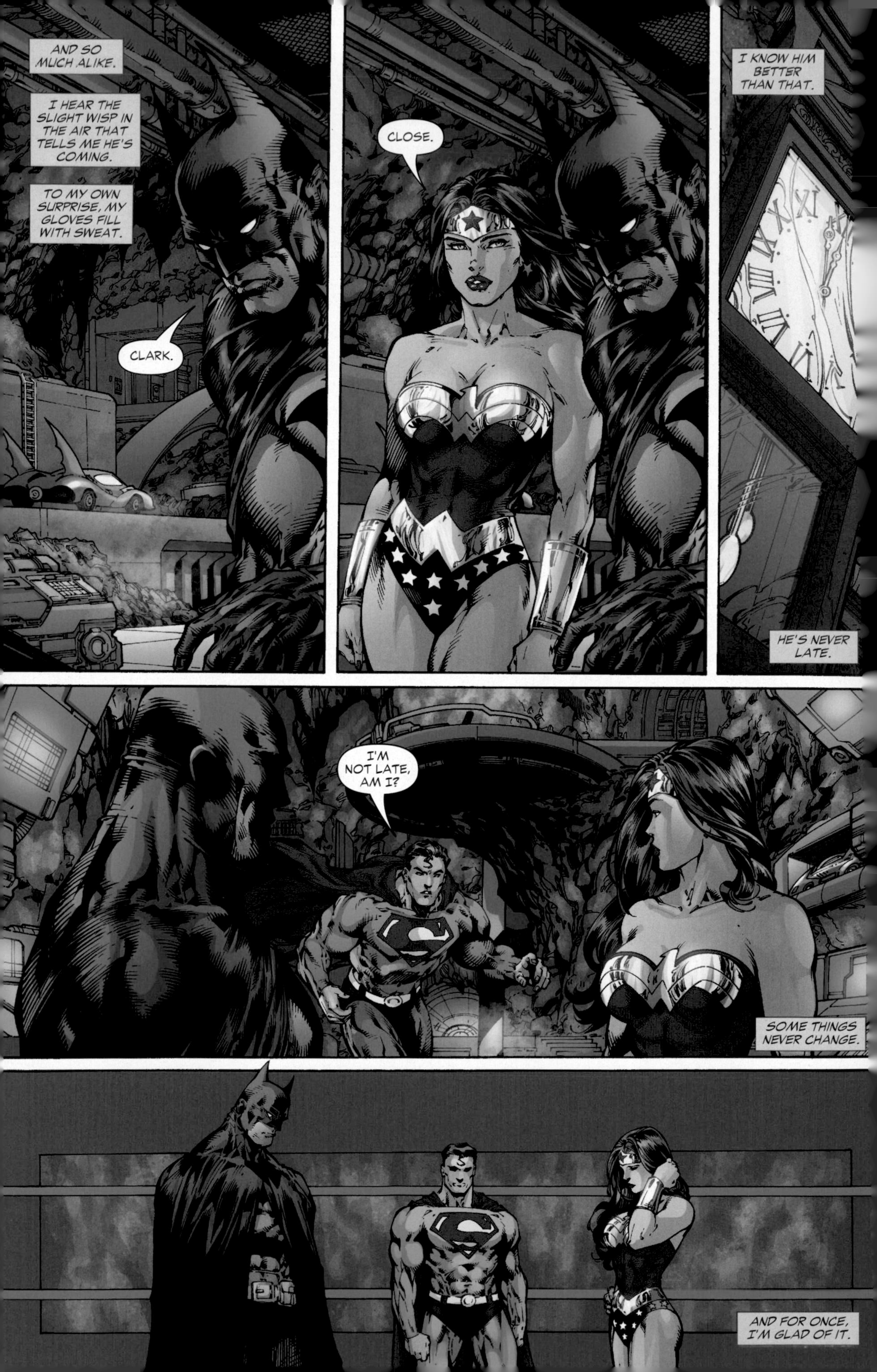
AND SO MUCH ALIKE.
I HEAR THE SLIGHT WISP IN THE AIR THAT TELLS ME HE'S COMING.
TO MY OWN SURPRISE, MY GLOVES FILL WITH SWEAT.
CLARK.
CLOSE.
I KNOW HIM BETTER THAN THAT.
HE'S NEVER LATE.
I'M NOT LATE, AM I?
SOME THINGS NEVER CHANGE.
AND FOR ONCE, I'M GLAD OF IT.

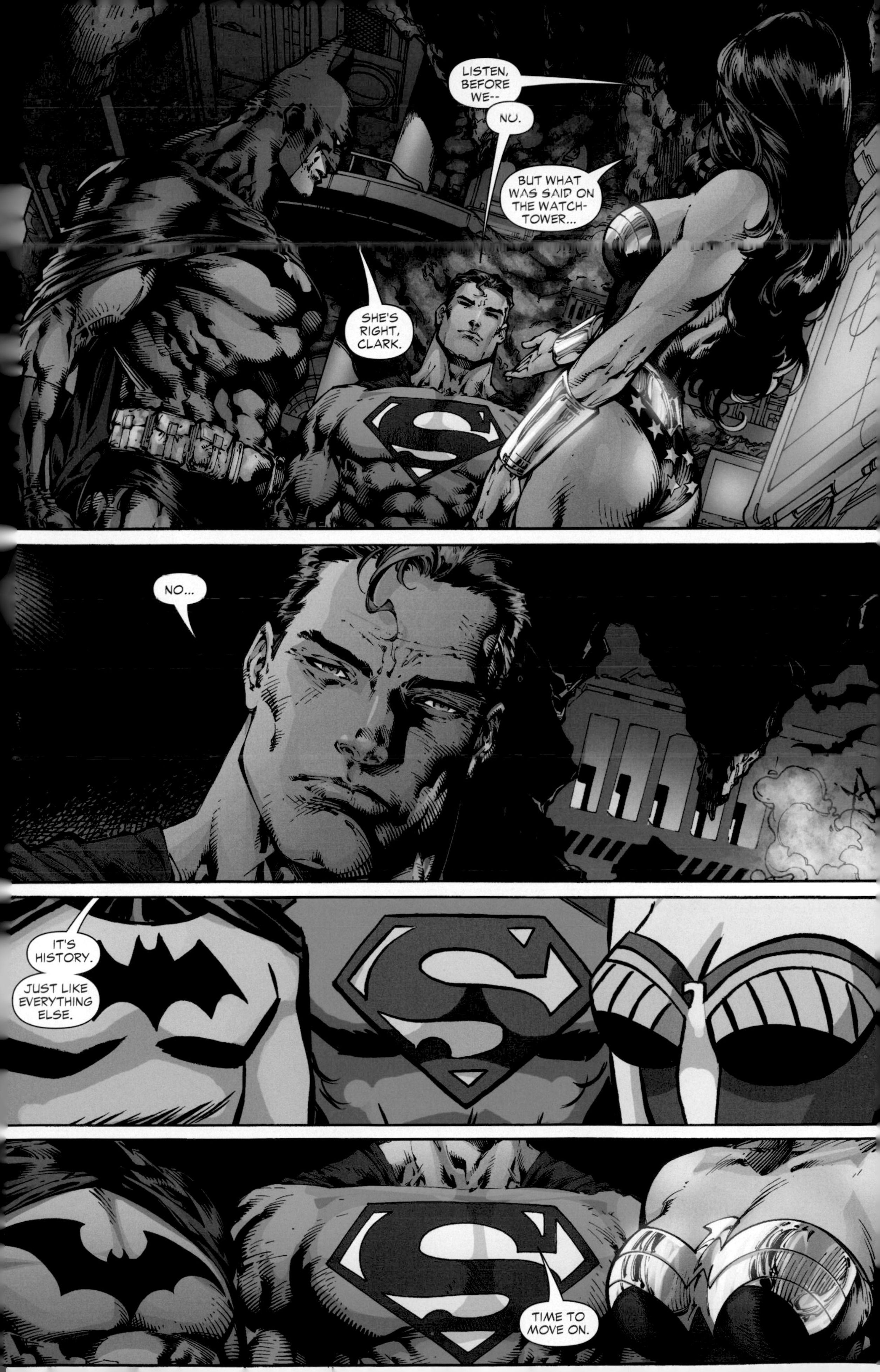
LISTEN, BEFORE WE--
NO.
BUT WHAT WAS SAID ON THE WATCH-TOWER...
SHE'S RIGHT, CLARK.
NO...
IT'S HISTORY.
JUST LIKE EVERYTHING ELSE.
TIME TO MOVE ON.

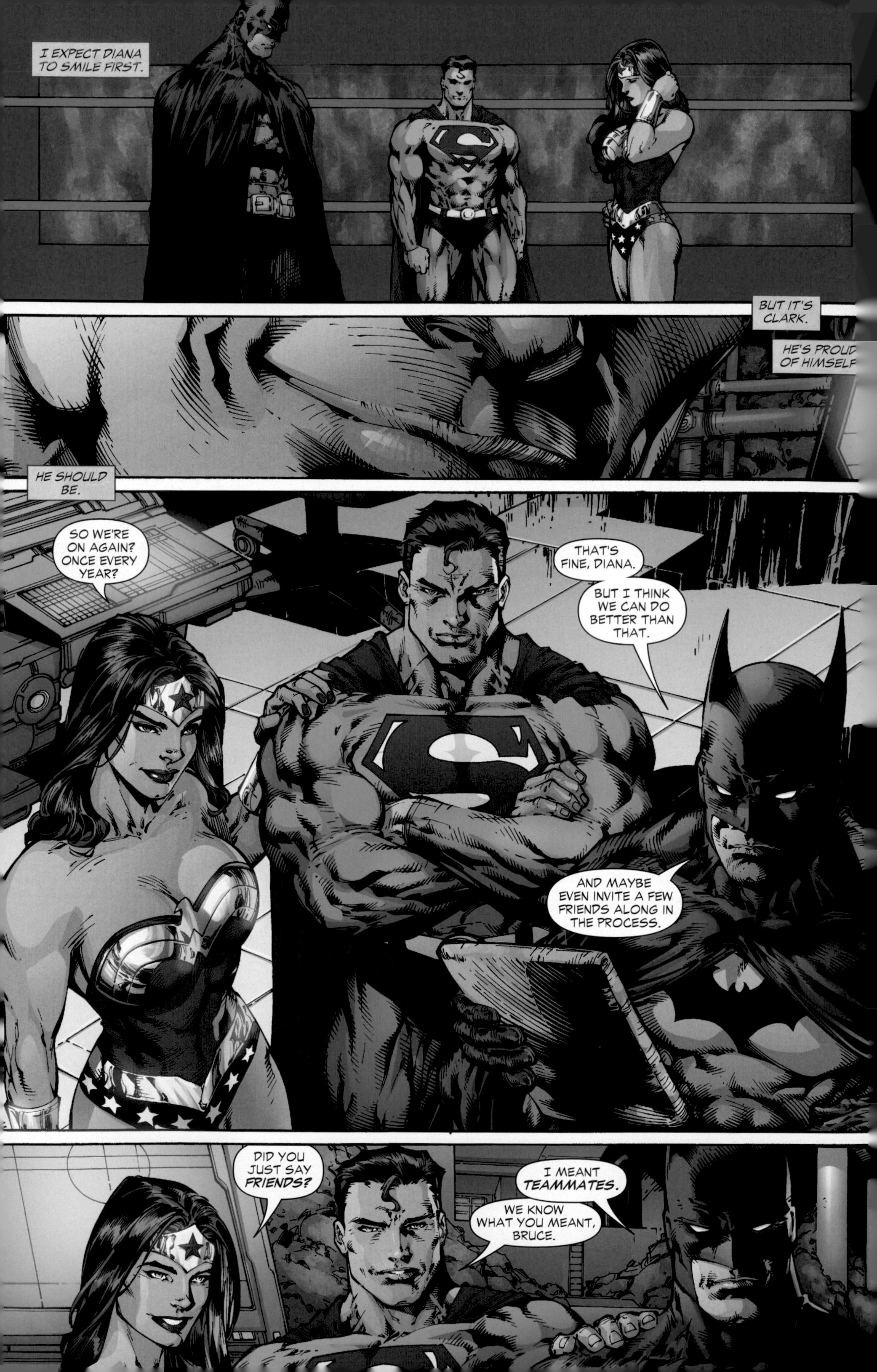

I EXPECT DIANA TO SMILE FIRST.
BUT IT'S CLARK.
HE'S PROUD OF HIMSELF
HE SHOULD BE.
SO WE'RE ON AGAIN? ONCE EVERY YEAR?
THAT'S FINE, DIANA.
BUT I THINK WE CAN DO BETTER THAN THAT.
AND MAYBE EVEN INVITE A FEW FRIENDS ALONG IN THE PROCESS.
DID YOU JUST SAY *FRIENDS?*
I MEANT *TEAMMATES.*
WE KNOW WHAT YOU MEANT, BRUCE.

YESTERDAY, TODAY, TOMORROW

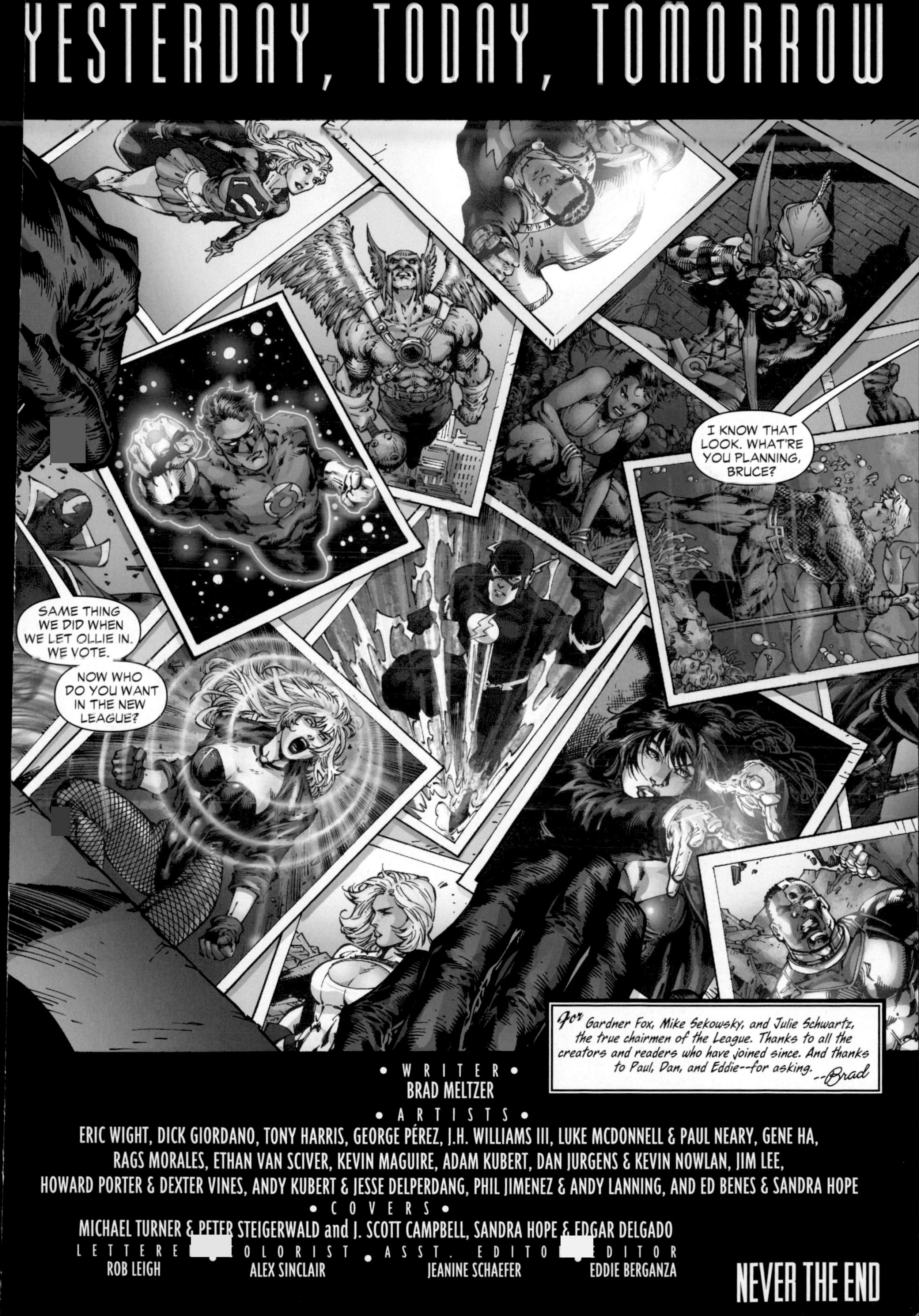
SAME THING WE DID WHEN WE LET OLLIE IN. WE VOTE.
NOW WHO DO YOU WANT IN THE NEW LEAGUE?
I KNOW THAT LOOK. WHAT'RE YOU PLANNING, BRUCE?

For Gardner Fox, Mike Sekowsky, and Julie Schwartz, the true chairmen of the League. Thanks to all the creators and readers who have joined since. And thanks to Paul, Dan, and Eddie--for asking. --Brad

• WRITER •
BRAD MELTZER

• ARTISTS •
ERIC WIGHT, DICK GIORDANO, TONY HARRIS, GEORGE PÉREZ, J.H. WILLIAMS III, LUKE MCDONNELL & PAUL NEARY, GENE HA, RAGS MORALES, ETHAN VAN SCIVER, KEVIN MAGUIRE, ADAM KUBERT, DAN JURGENS & KEVIN NOWLAN, JIM LEE, HOWARD PORTER & DEXTER VINES, ANDY KUBERT & JESSE DELPERDANG, PHIL JIMENEZ & ANDY LANNING, AND ED BENES & SANDRA HOPE

• COVERS •
MICHAEL TURNER & PETER STEIGERWALD and J. SCOTT CAMPBELL, SANDRA HOPE & EDGAR DELGADO

LETTERER • COLORIST • ASST. EDITOR • EDITOR
ROB LEIGH • ALEX SINCLAIR • JEANINE SCHAEFER • EDDIE BERGANZA

NEVER THE END

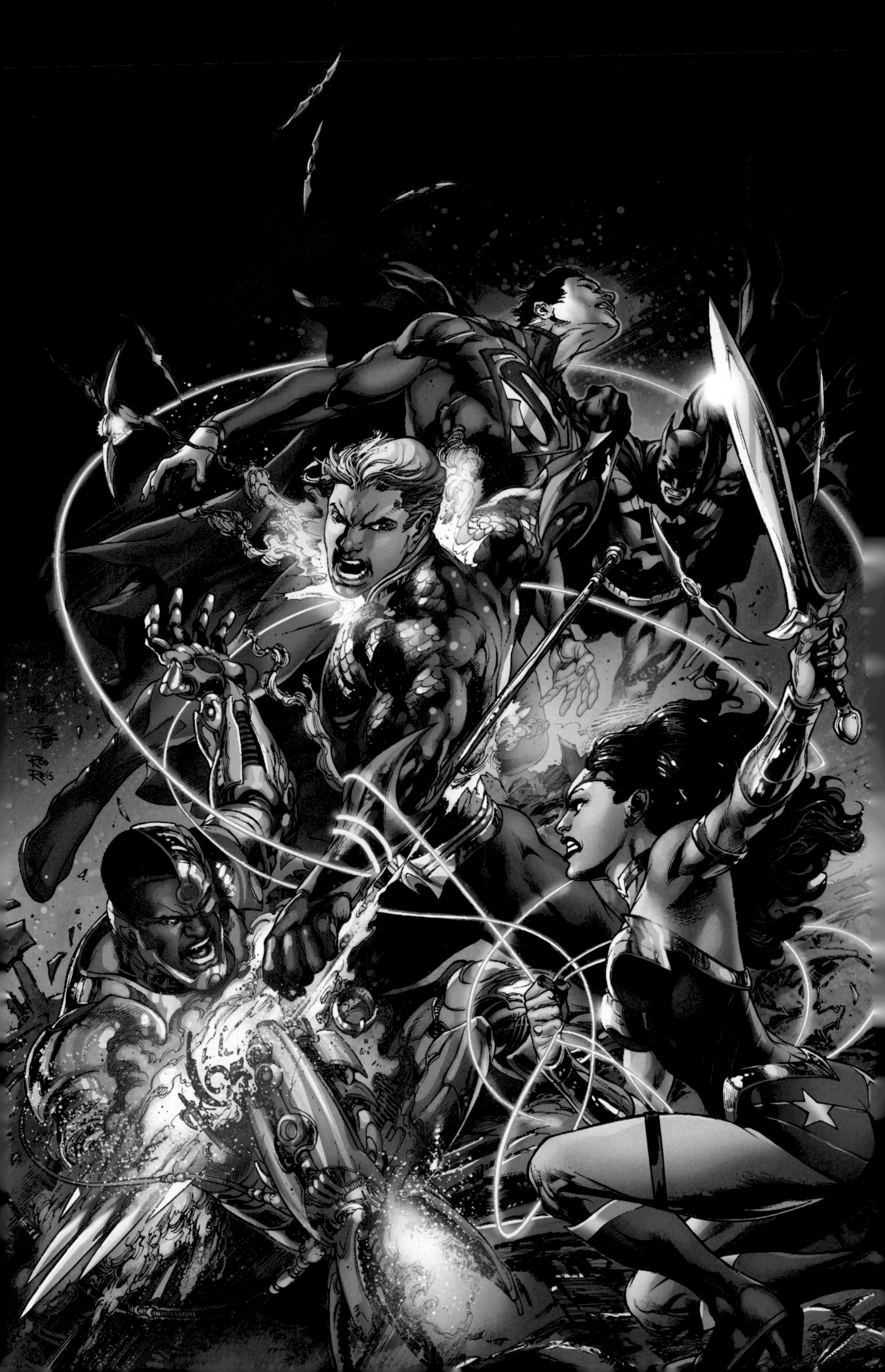

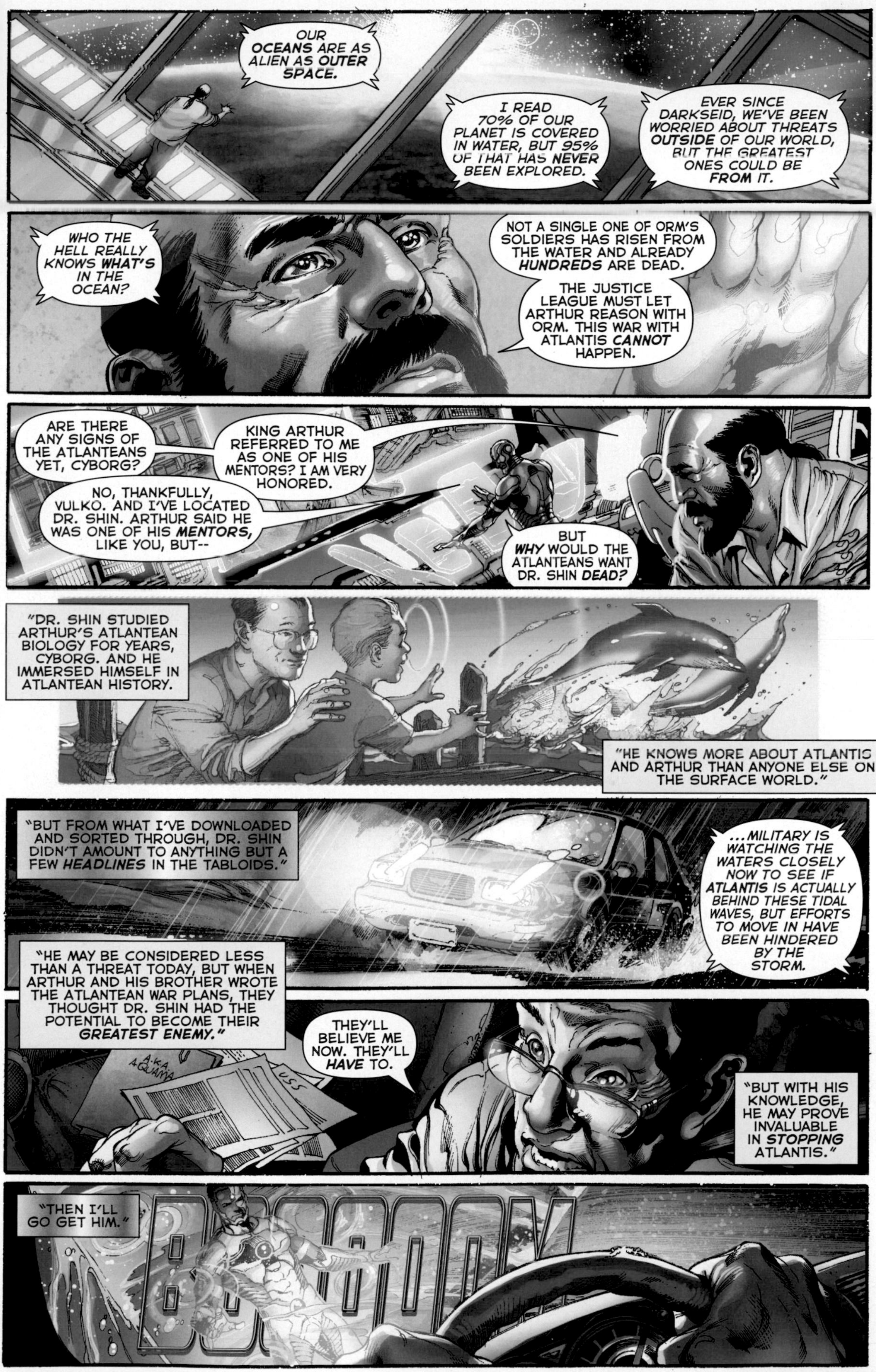
OUR OCEANS ARE AS ALIEN AS OUTER SPACE.
I READ 70% OF OUR PLANET IS COVERED IN WATER, BUT 95% OF THAT HAS NEVER BEEN EXPLORED.
EVER SINCE DARKSEID, WE'VE BEEN WORRIED ABOUT THREATS OUTSIDE OF OUR WORLD, BUT THE GREATEST ONES COULD BE FROM IT.
WHO THE HELL REALLY KNOWS WHAT'S IN THE OCEAN?
NOT A SINGLE ONE OF ORM'S SOLDIERS HAS RISEN FROM THE WATER AND ALREADY HUNDREDS ARE DEAD.
THE JUSTICE LEAGUE MUST LET ARTHUR REASON WITH ORM. THIS WAR WITH ATLANTIS CANNOT HAPPEN.
ARE THERE ANY SIGNS OF THE ATLANTEANS YET, CYBORG?
NO, THANKFULLY, VULKO. AND I'VE LOCATED DR. SHIN. ARTHUR SAID HE WAS ONE OF HIS MENTORS, LIKE YOU, BUT--
KING ARTHUR REFERRED TO ME AS ONE OF HIS MENTORS? I AM VERY HONORED.
BUT WHY WOULD THE ATLANTEANS WANT DR. SHIN DEAD?
"DR. SHIN STUDIED ARTHUR'S ATLANTEAN BIOLOGY FOR YEARS, CYBORG. AND HE IMMERSED HIMSELF IN ATLANTEAN HISTORY.
"HE KNOWS MORE ABOUT ATLANTIS AND ARTHUR THAN ANYONE ELSE ON THE SURFACE WORLD."
"BUT FROM WHAT I'VE DOWNLOADED AND SORTED THROUGH, DR. SHIN DIDN'T AMOUNT TO ANYTHING BUT A FEW HEADLINES IN THE TABLOIDS."
...MILITARY IS WATCHING THE WATERS CLOSELY NOW TO SEE IF ATLANTIS IS ACTUALLY BEHIND THESE TIDAL WAVES, BUT EFFORTS TO MOVE IN HAVE BEEN HINDERED BY THE STORM.
"HE MAY BE CONSIDERED LESS THAN A THREAT TODAY, BUT WHEN ARTHUR AND HIS BROTHER WROTE THE ATLANTEAN WAR PLANS, THEY THOUGHT DR. SHIN HAD THE POTENTIAL TO BECOME THEIR GREATEST ENEMY."
THEY'LL BELIEVE ME NOW. THEY'LL HAVE TO.
"BUT WITH HIS KNOWLEDGE, HE MAY PROVE INVALUABLE IN STOPPING ATLANTIS."
"THEN I'LL GO GET HIM."

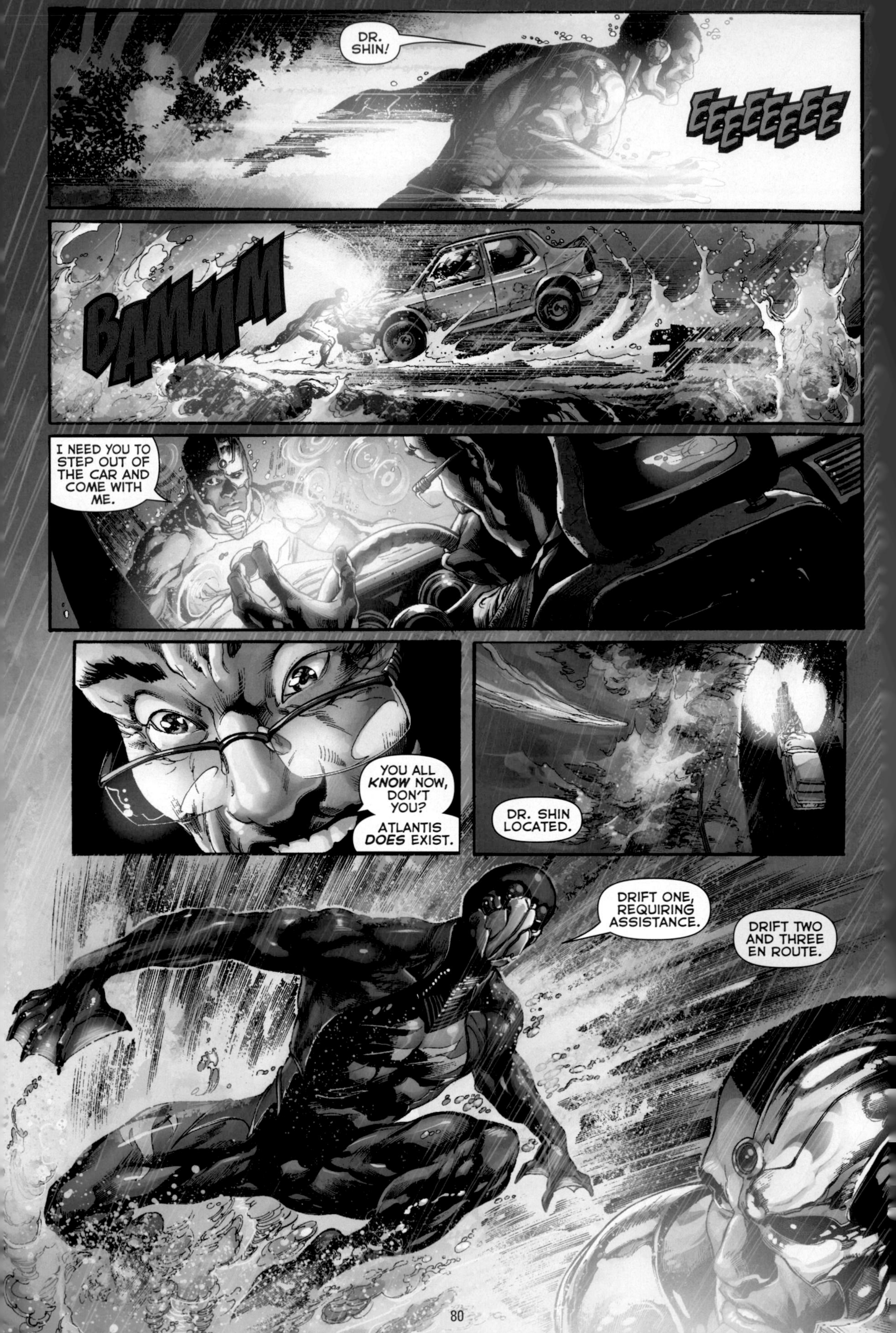
DR. SHIN!
EEEEEEEE
BAMMM
I NEED YOU TO STEP OUT OF THE CAR AND COME WITH ME.
YOU ALL KNOW NOW, DON'T YOU?
ATLANTIS DOES EXIST.
DR. SHIN LOCATED.
DRIFT ONE, REQUIRING ASSISTANCE.
DRIFT TWO AND THREE EN ROUTE.

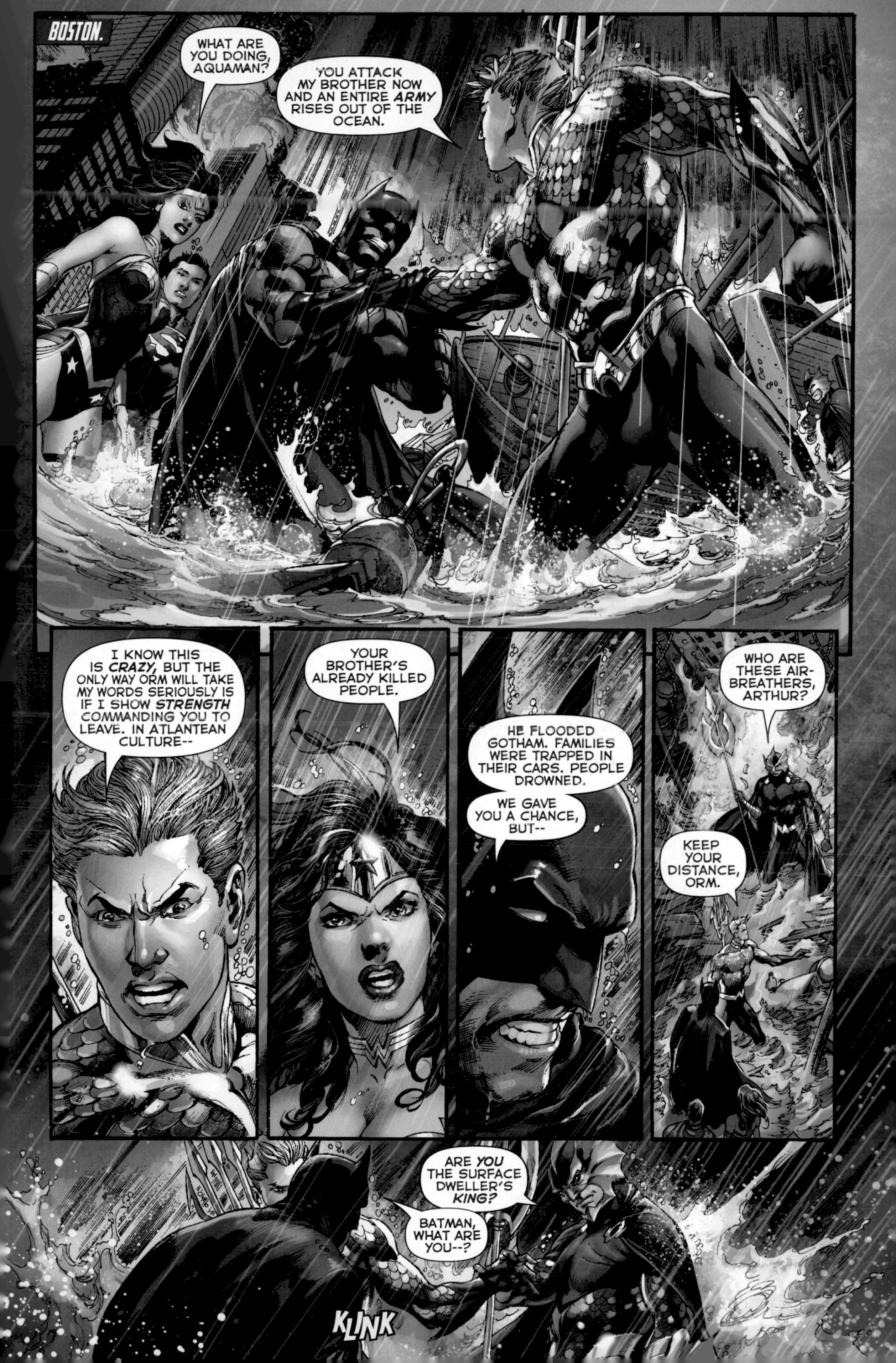
BOSTON.
WHAT ARE YOU DOING, AQUAMAN?
YOU ATTACK MY BROTHER NOW AND AN ENTIRE ARMY RISES OUT OF THE OCEAN.
I KNOW THIS IS CRAZY, BUT THE ONLY WAY ORM WILL TAKE MY WORDS SERIOUSLY IS IF I SHOW STRENGTH COMMANDING YOU TO LEAVE. IN ATLANTEAN CULTURE--
YOUR BROTHER'S ALREADY KILLED PEOPLE.
HE FLOODED GOTHAM. FAMILIES WERE TRAPPED IN THEIR CARS. PEOPLE DROWNED.
WE GAVE YOU A CHANCE, BUT--
WHO ARE THESE AIR-BREATHERS, ARTHUR?
KEEP YOUR DISTANCE, ORM.
ARE YOU THE SURFACE DWELLER'S KING?
BATMAN, WHAT ARE YOU--?
KLINK

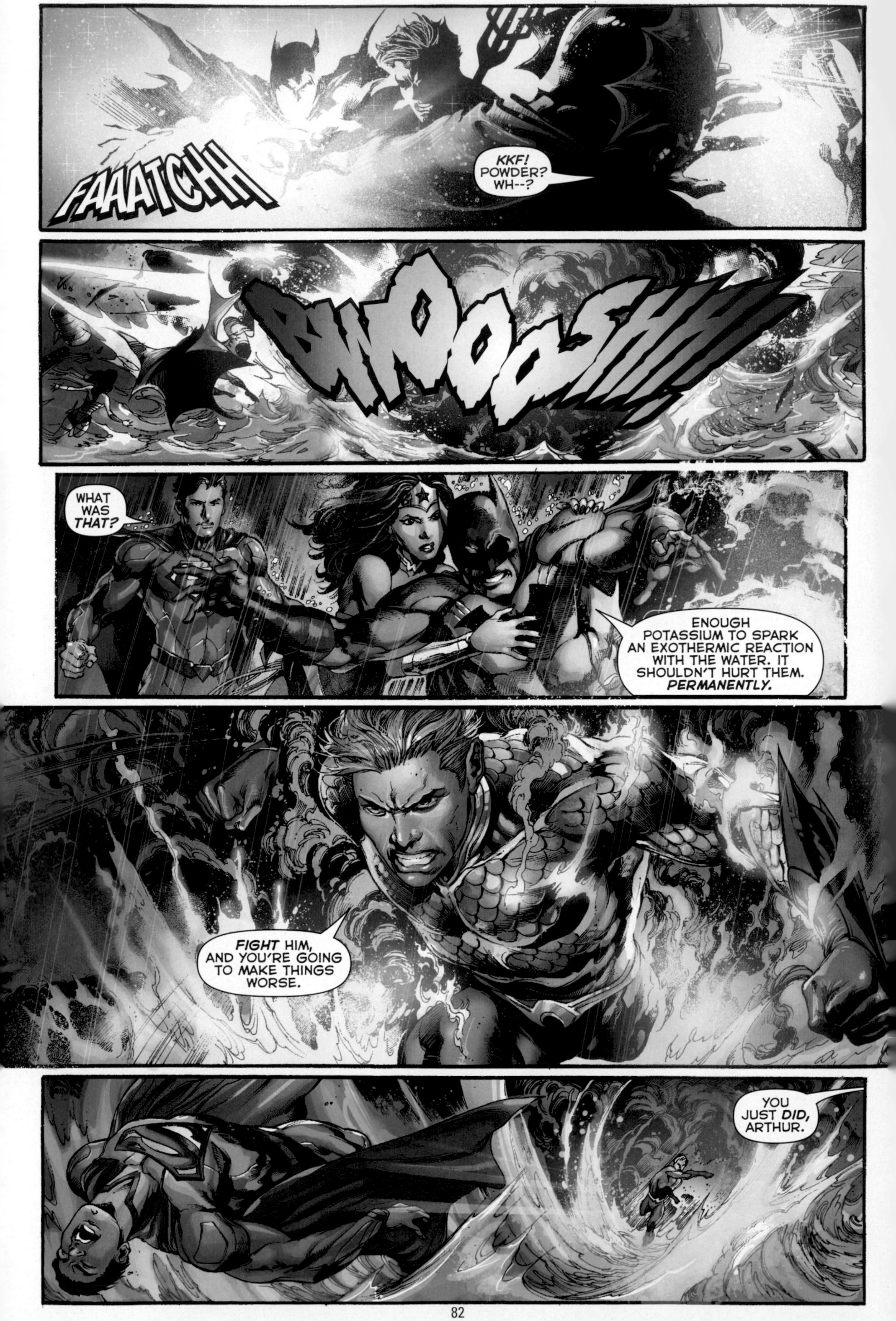
FAAATCHH
KKF! POWDER? WH--?
BWOOSHH
WHAT WAS THAT?
ENOUGH POTASSIUM TO SPARK AN EXOTHERMIC REACTION WITH THE WATER. IT SHOULDN'T HURT THEM. PERMANENTLY.
FIGHT HIM, AND YOU'RE GOING TO MAKE THINGS WORSE.
YOU JUST DID, ARTHUR.

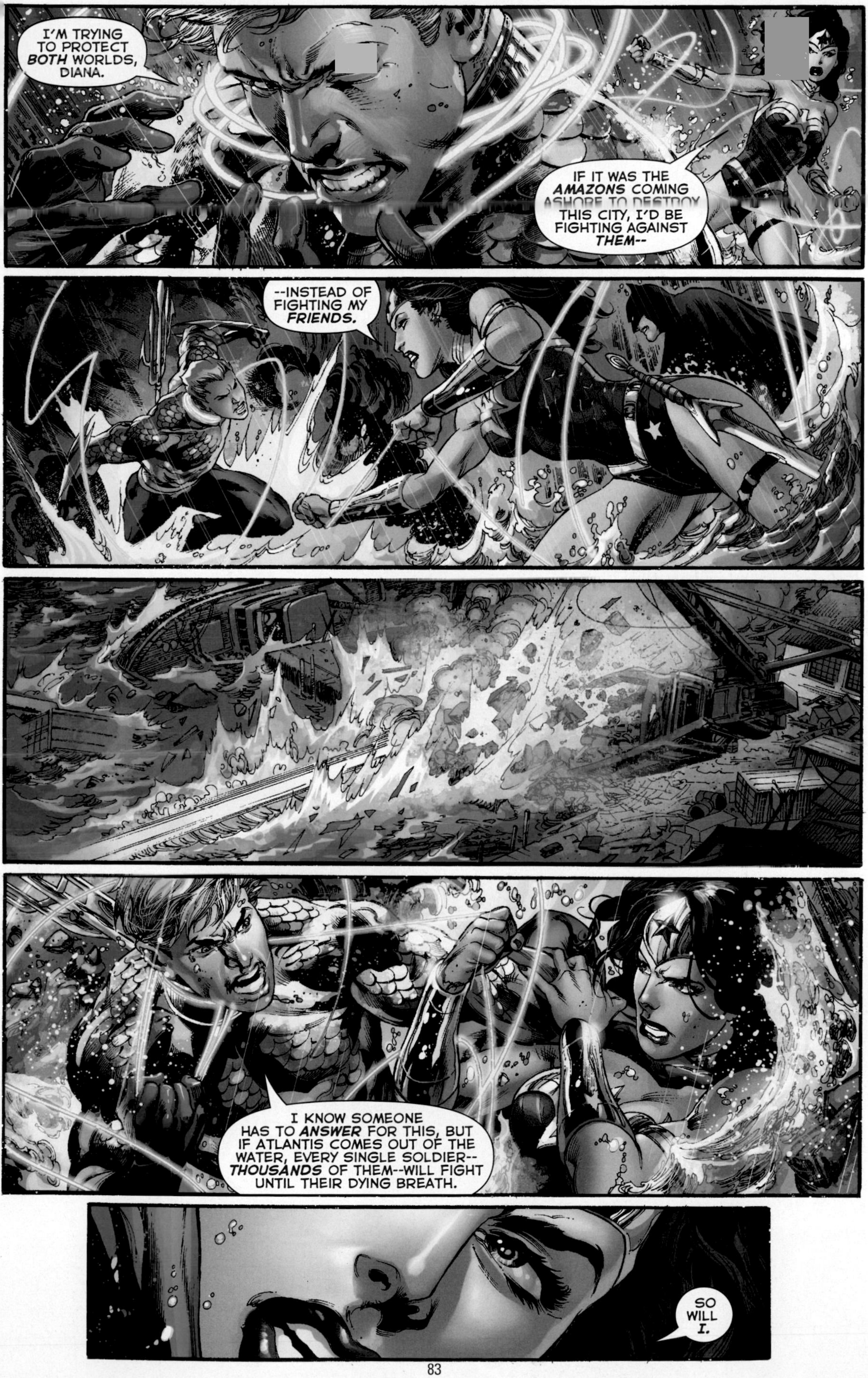
I'M TRYING TO PROTECT BOTH WORLDS, DIANA.
IF IT WAS THE AMAZONS COMING ASHORE TO DESTROY THIS CITY, I'D BE FIGHTING AGAINST THEM--
--INSTEAD OF FIGHTING MY FRIENDS.
I KNOW SOMEONE HAS TO ANSWER FOR THIS, BUT IF ATLANTIS COMES OUT OF THE WATER, EVERY SINGLE SOLDIER--THOUSANDS OF THEM--WILL FIGHT UNTIL THEIR DYING BREATH.
SO WILL I.

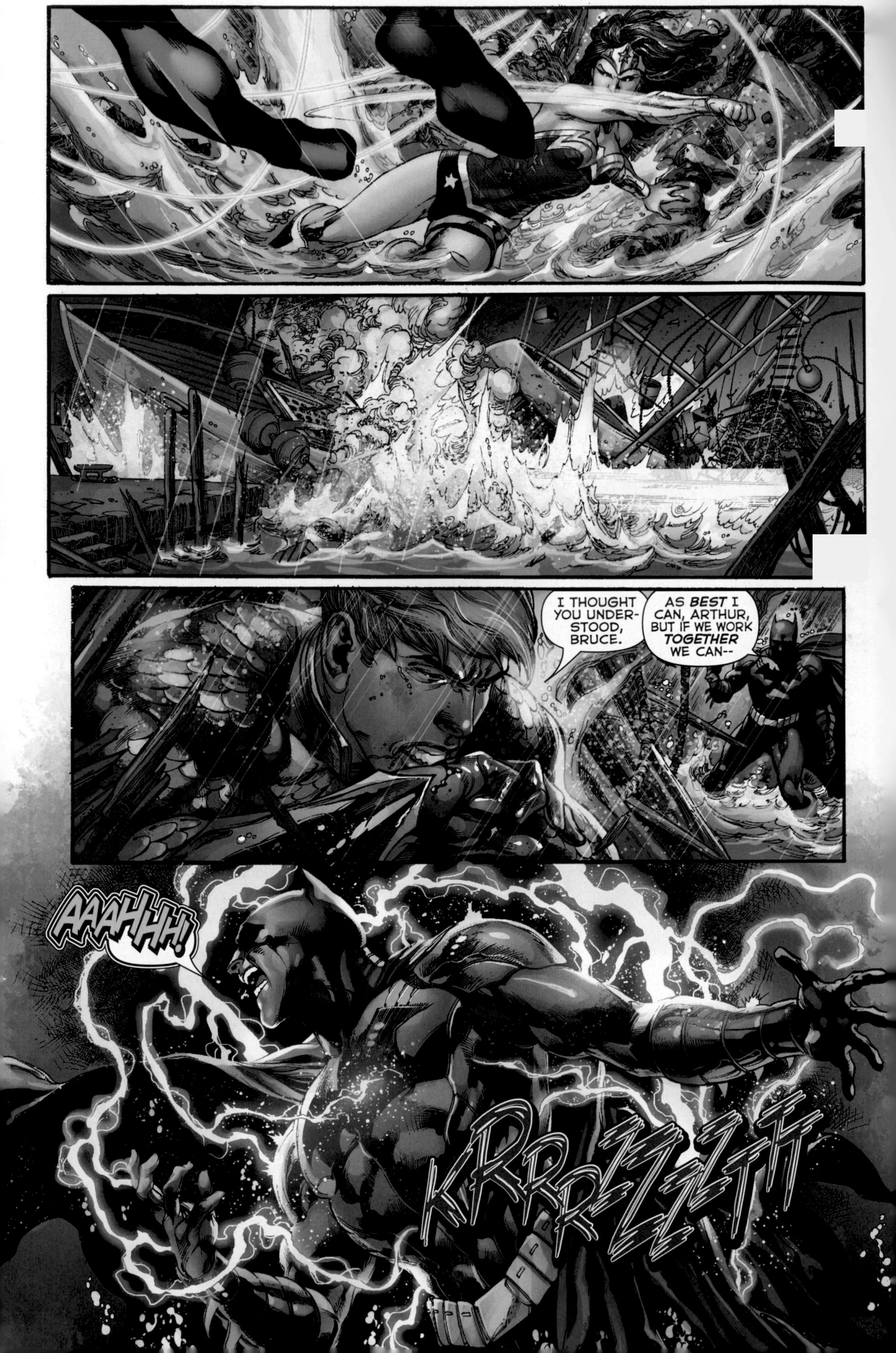
I THOUGHT YOU UNDERSTOOD, BRUCE.
AS **BEST** I CAN, ARTHUR, BUT IF WE WORK **TOGETHER** WE CAN--
AAAHHH!
KRRRZZZZTH

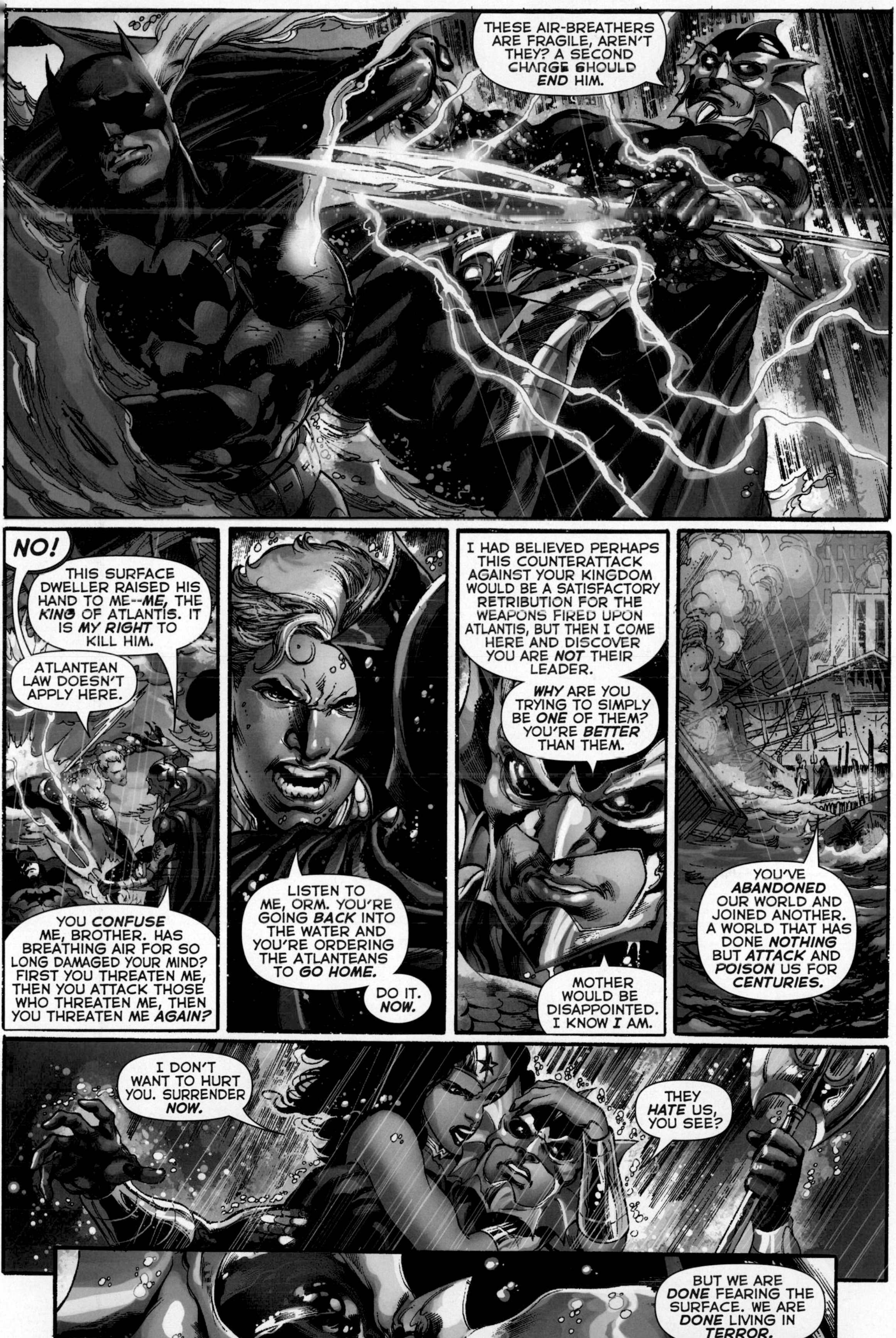
THESE AIR-BREATHERS ARE FRAGILE, AREN'T THEY? A SECOND CHARGE SHOULD END HIM.
NO!
THIS SURFACE DWELLER RAISED HIS HAND TO ME--ME, THE KING OF ATLANTIS. IT IS MY RIGHT TO KILL HIM.
ATLANTEAN LAW DOESN'T APPLY HERE.
YOU CONFUSE ME, BROTHER. HAS BREATHING AIR FOR SO LONG DAMAGED YOUR MIND? FIRST YOU THREATEN ME, THEN YOU ATTACK THOSE WHO THREATEN ME, THEN YOU THREATEN ME AGAIN?
LISTEN TO ME, ORM. YOU'RE GOING BACK INTO THE WATER AND YOU'RE ORDERING THE ATLANTEANS TO GO HOME.
DO IT. NOW.
I HAD BELIEVED PERHAPS THIS COUNTERATTACK AGAINST YOUR KINGDOM WOULD BE A SATISFACTORY RETRIBUTION FOR THE WEAPONS FIRED UPON ATLANTIS, BUT THEN I COME HERE AND DISCOVER YOU ARE NOT THEIR LEADER.
WHY ARE YOU TRYING TO SIMPLY BE ONE OF THEM? YOU'RE BETTER THAN THEM.
MOTHER WOULD BE DISAPPOINTED. I KNOW I AM.
YOU'VE ABANDONED OUR WORLD AND JOINED ANOTHER. A WORLD THAT HAS DONE NOTHING BUT ATTACK AND POISON US FOR CENTURIES.
I DON'T WANT TO HURT YOU. SURRENDER NOW.
THEY HATE US, YOU SEE?
BUT WE ARE DONE FEARING THE SURFACE. WE ARE DONE LIVING IN TERROR.

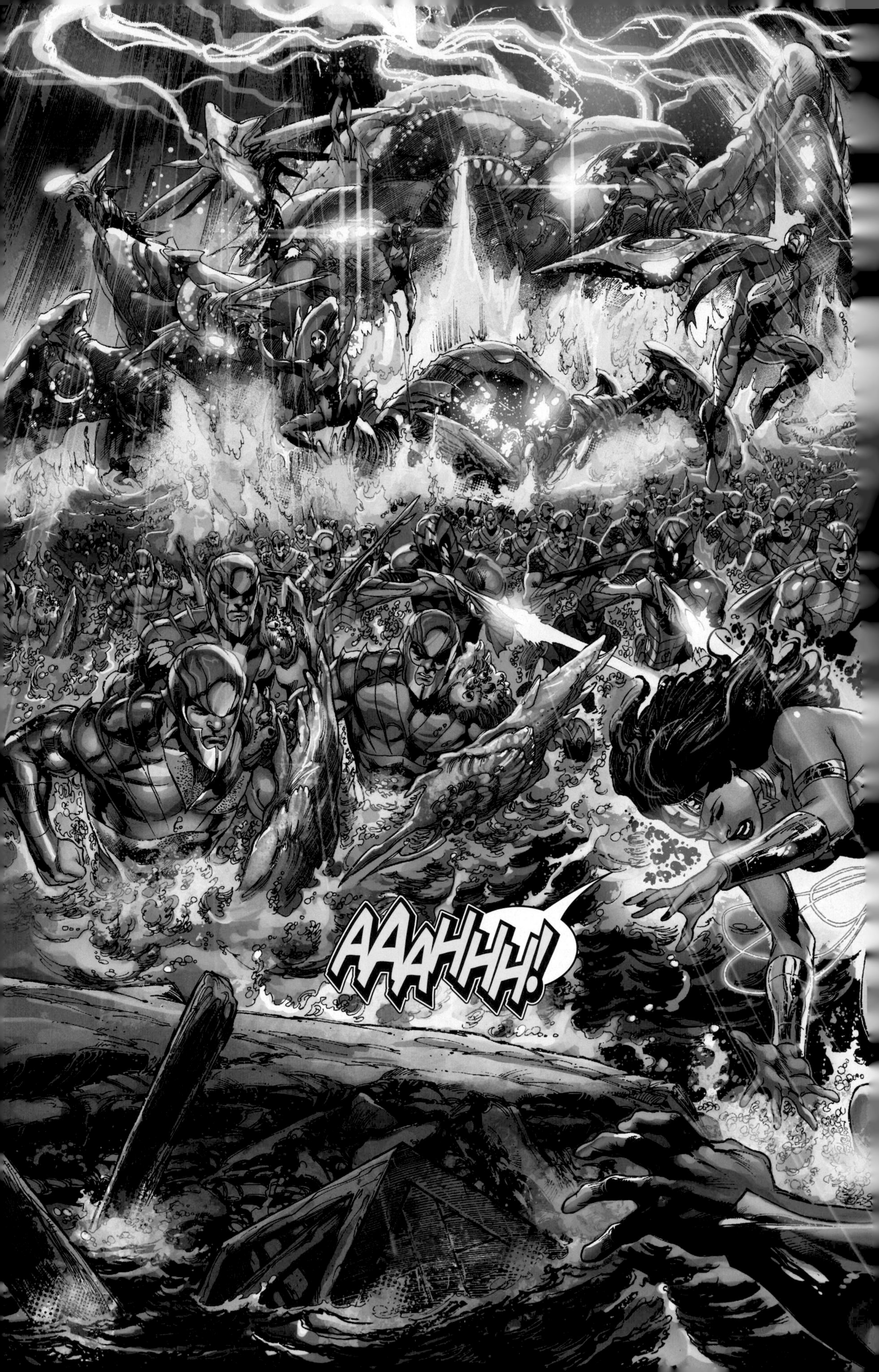
AAAHHH!

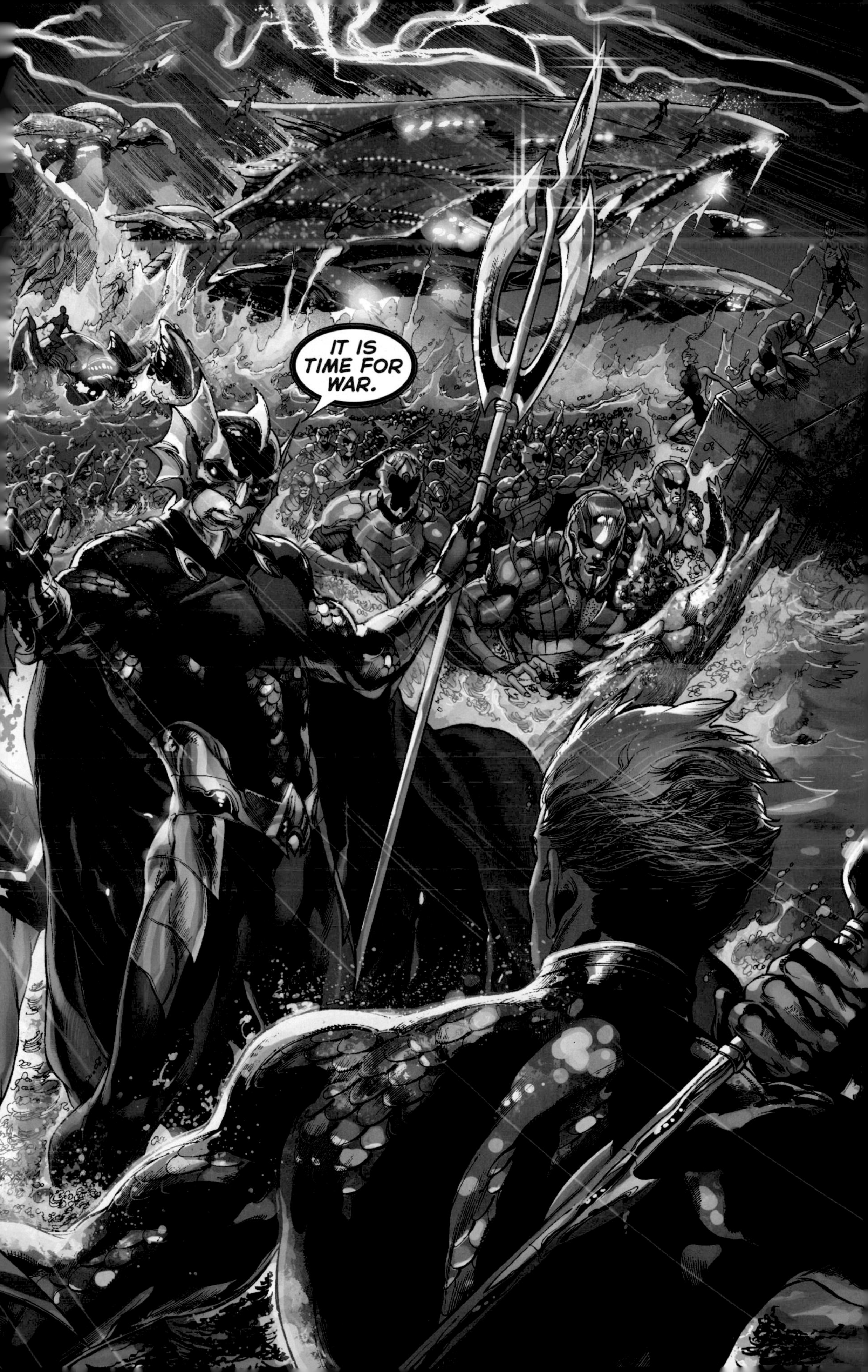
IT IS TIME FOR WAR.

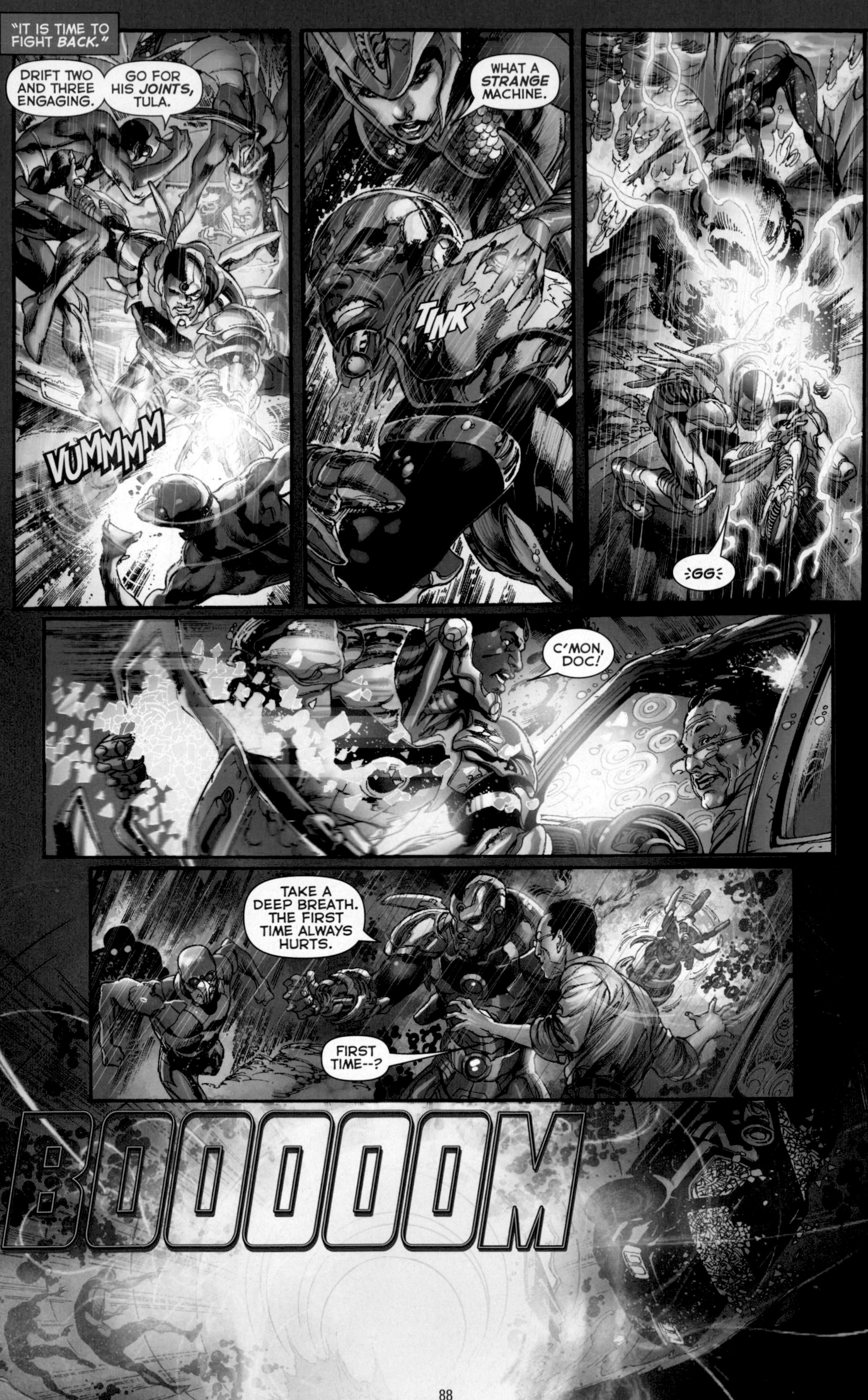
"IT IS TIME TO FIGHT *BACK.*"
DRIFT TWO AND THREE ENGAGING.
GO FOR HIS *JOINTS,* TULA.
VUMMMM
WHAT A *STRANGE* MACHINE.
TINK
GG
C'MON, DOC!
TAKE A DEEP BREATH. THE FIRST TIME ALWAYS HURTS.
FIRST TIME--?
BOOOOOM

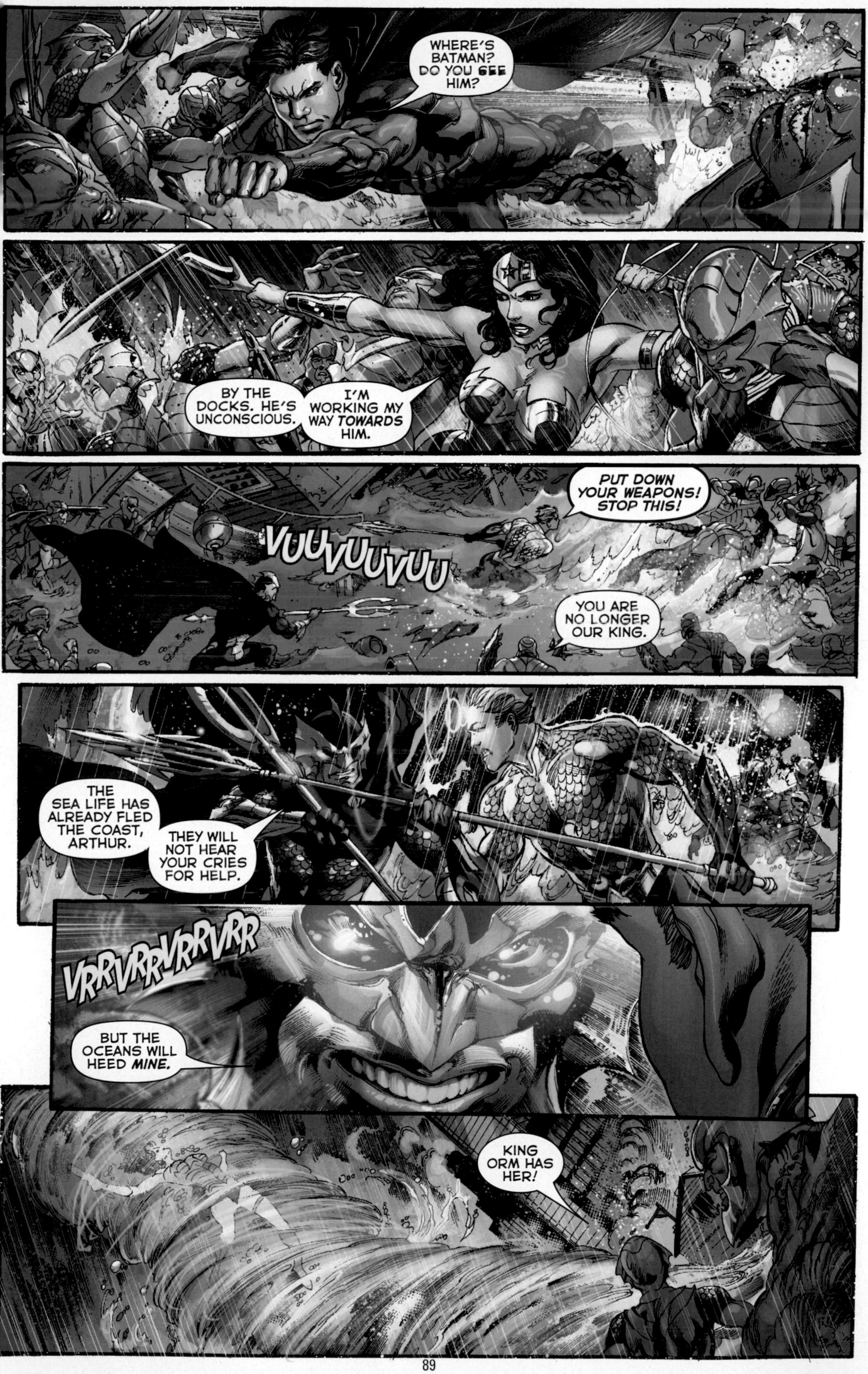

WHERE'S BATMAN? DO YOU SEE HIM?
BY THE DOCKS. HE'S UNCONSCIOUS.
I'M WORKING MY WAY *TOWARDS* HIM.
PUT DOWN YOUR WEAPONS! STOP THIS!
VUUVUUVUU
YOU ARE NO LONGER OUR KING.
THE SEA LIFE HAS ALREADY FLED THE COAST, ARTHUR.
THEY WILL NOT HEAR YOUR CRIES FOR HELP.
VRRVRRVRRVRR
BUT THE OCEANS WILL HEED ***MINE.***
KING ORM HAS HER!

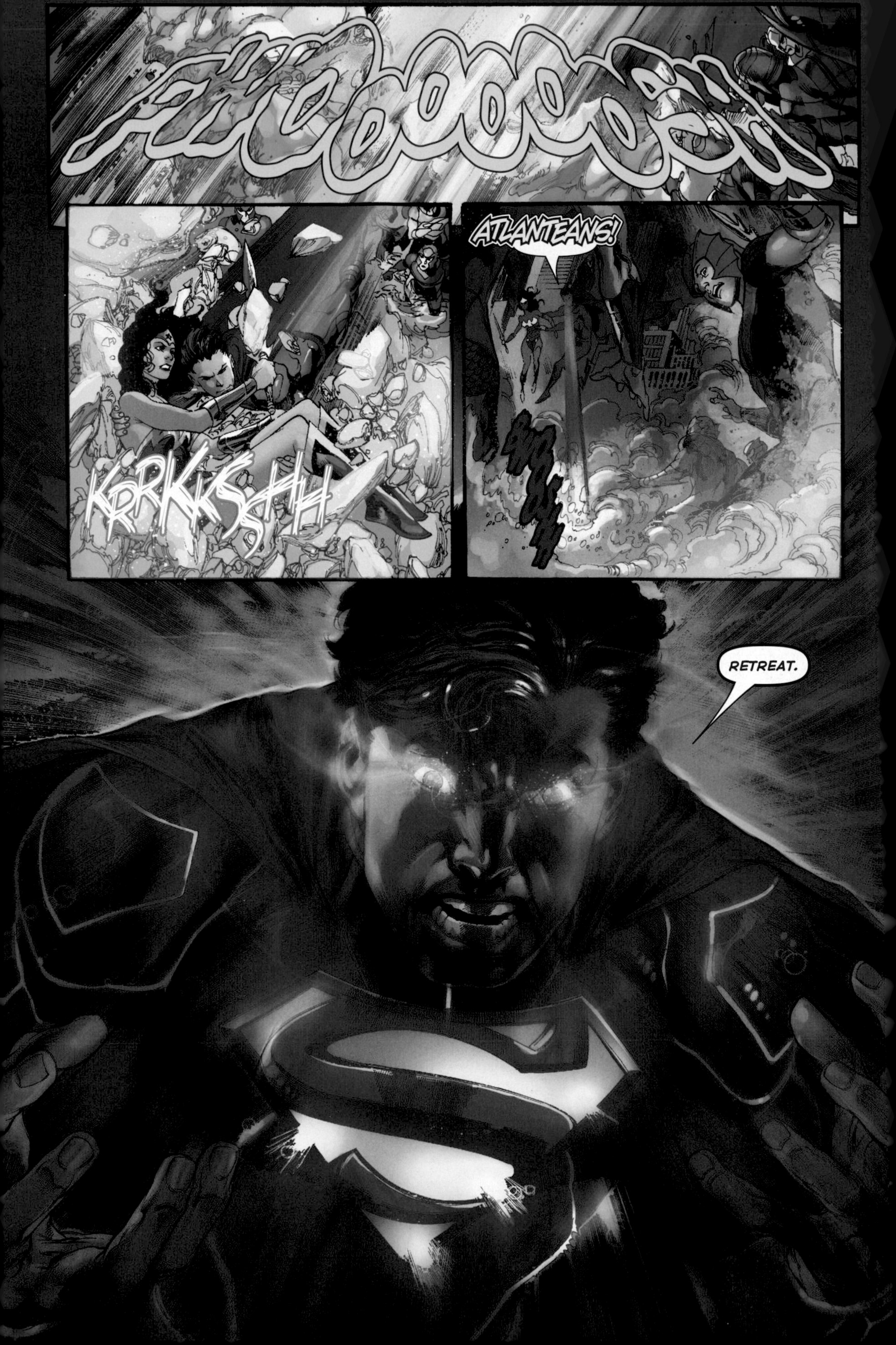
ATLANTEANS!
RETREAT.

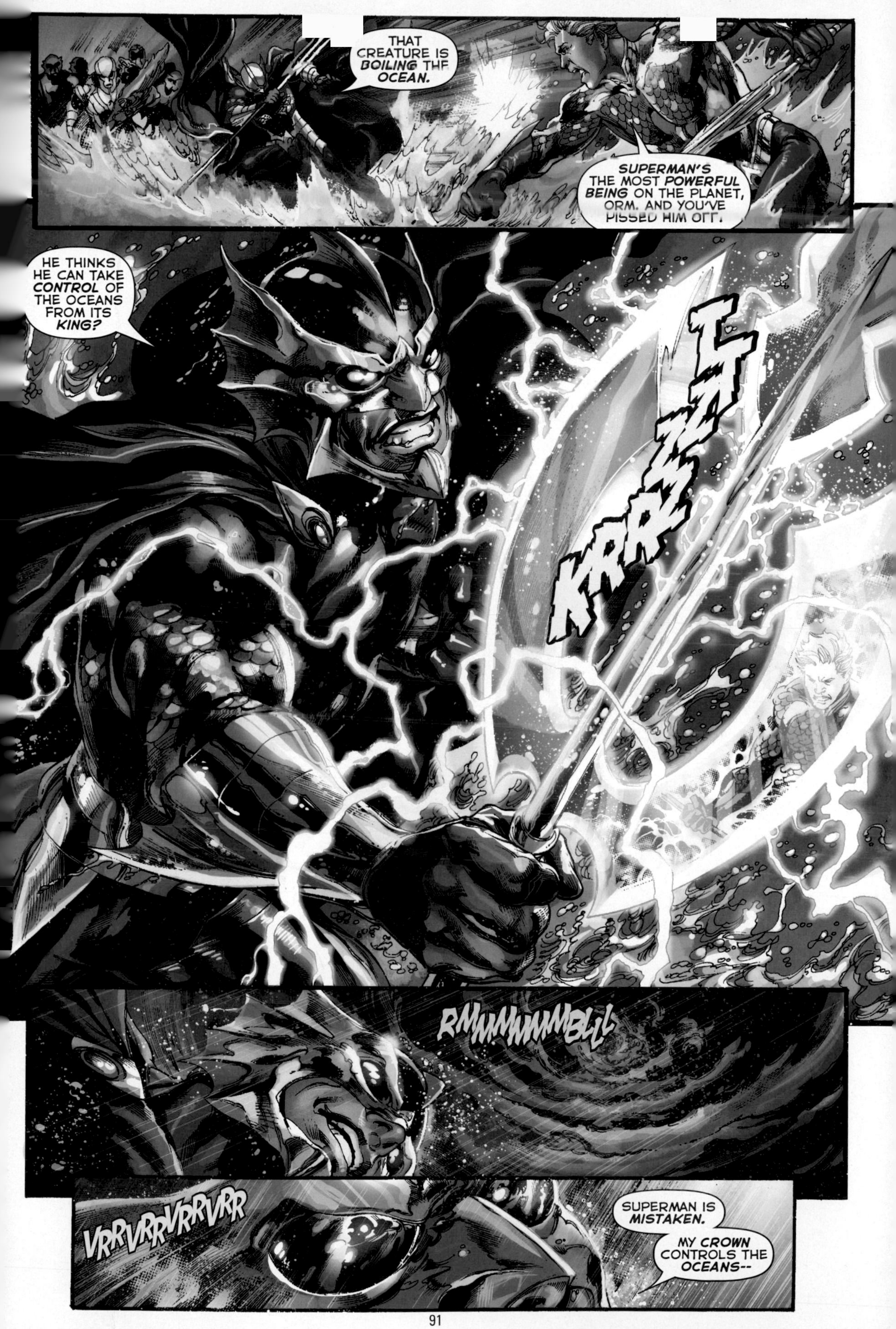
THAT CREATURE IS BOILING THE OCEAN.
SUPERMAN'S THE MOST POWERFUL BEING ON THE PLANET, ORM. AND YOU'VE PISSED HIM OFF.
HE THINKS HE CAN TAKE CONTROL OF THE OCEANS FROM ITS KING?
KRRZZZZT
RMMMMMMMBLLL
VRRVRRVRRVRR
SUPERMAN IS MISTAKEN.
MY CROWN CONTROLS THE OCEANS--

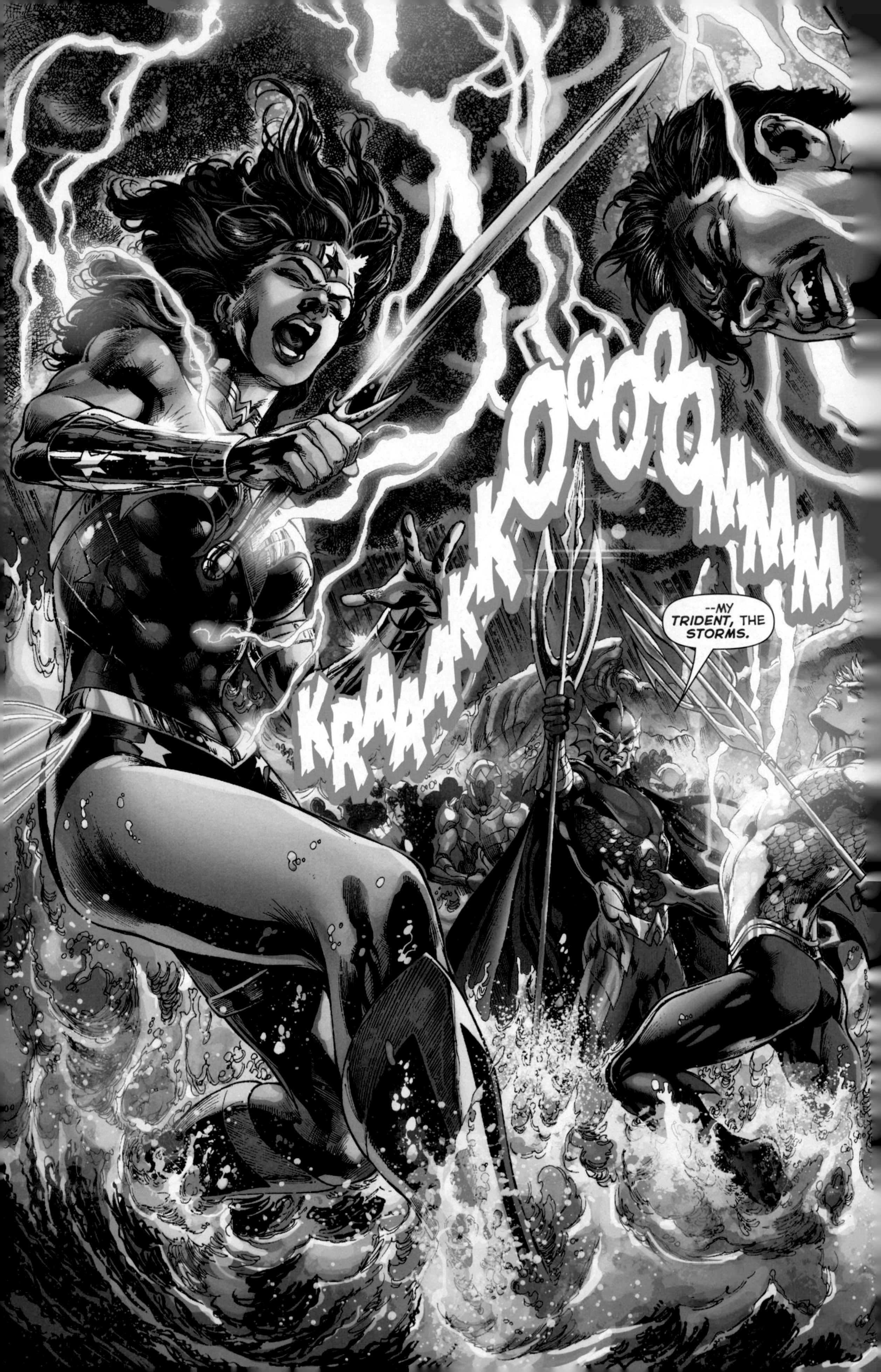
KRAAAKKOOOOOMMM
--MY TRIDENT, THE STORMS.

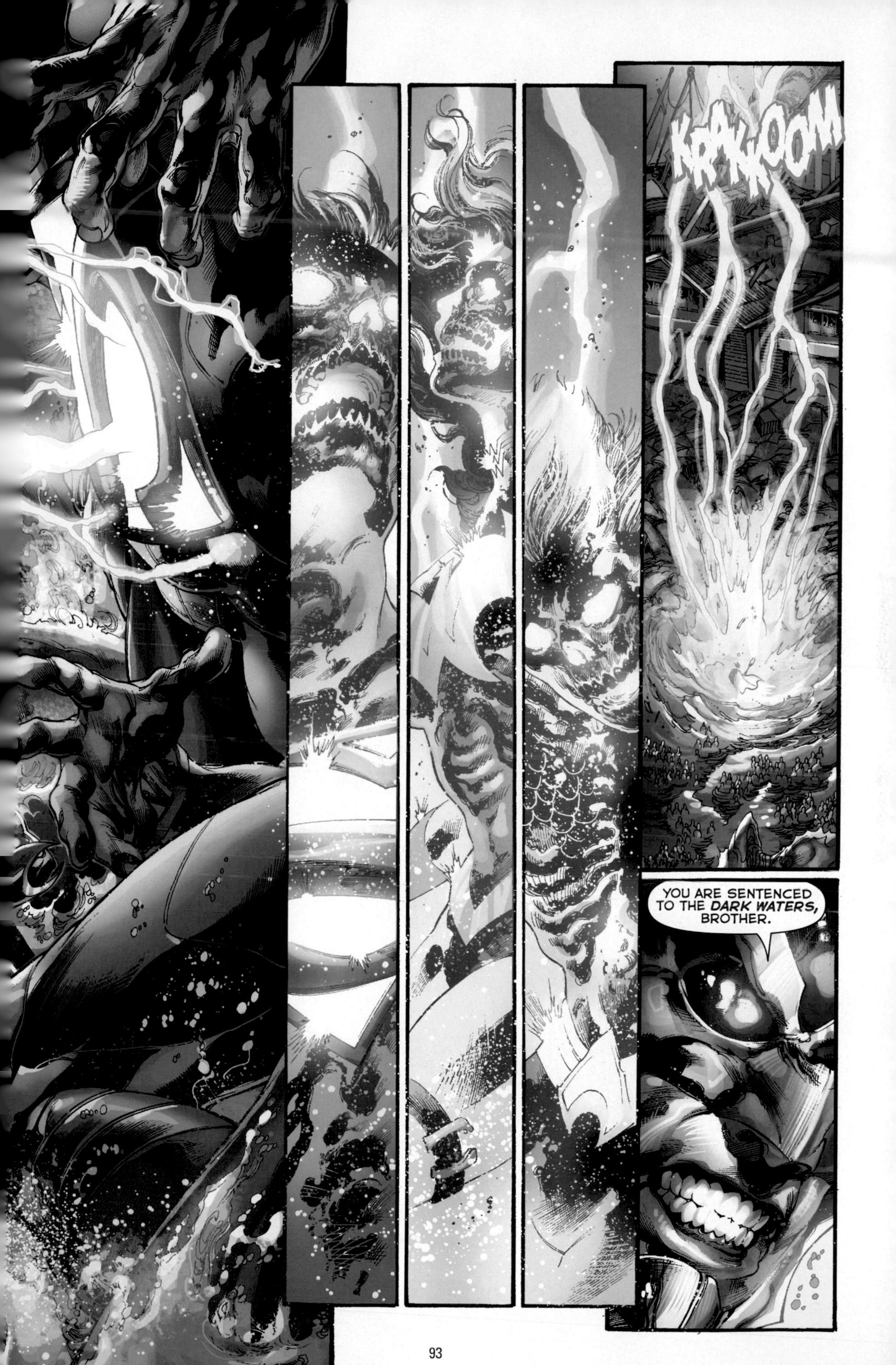
KRAKOOM
YOU ARE SENTENCED TO THE DARK WATERS, BROTHER.

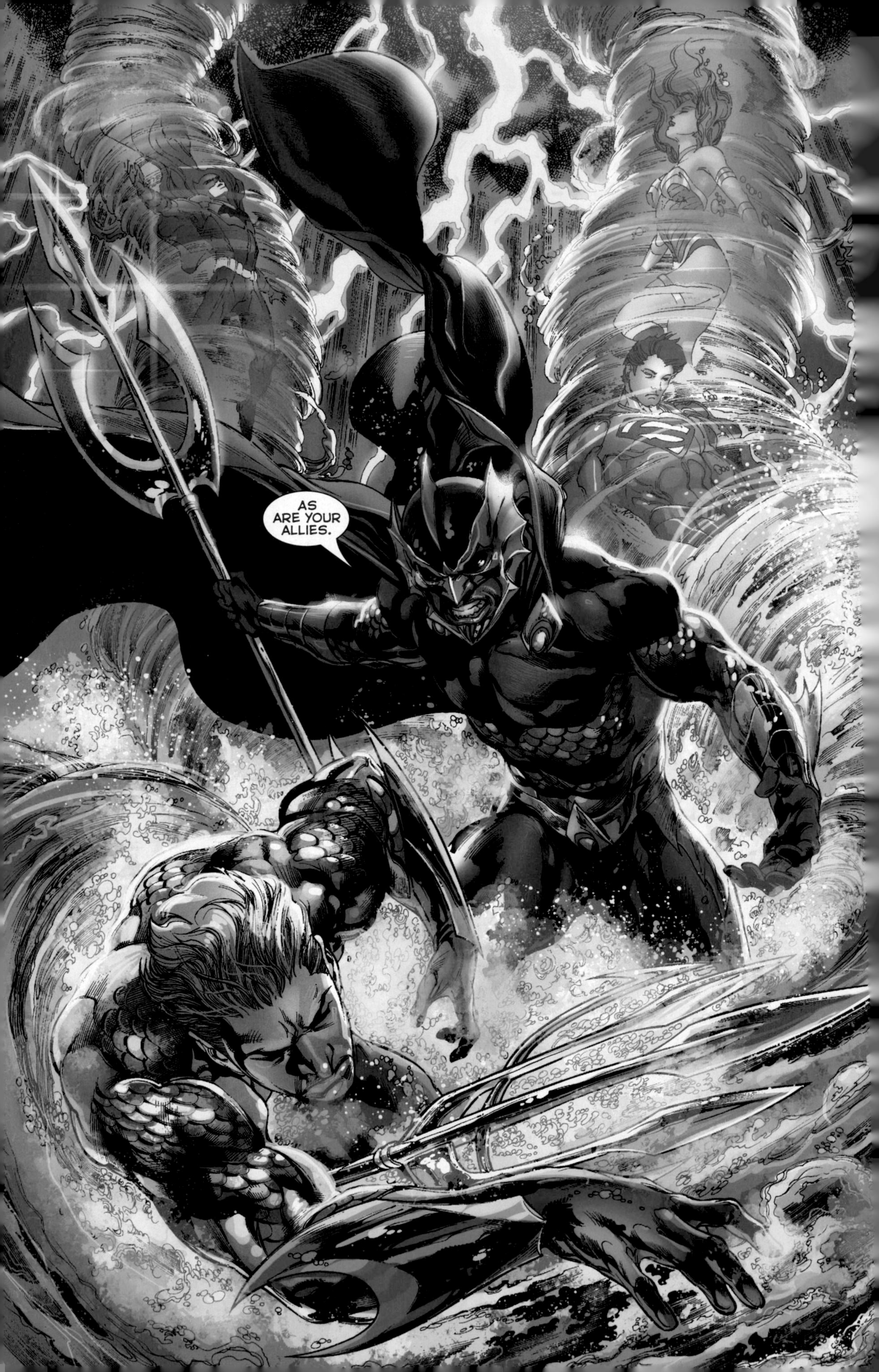
AS ARE YOUR ALLIES.

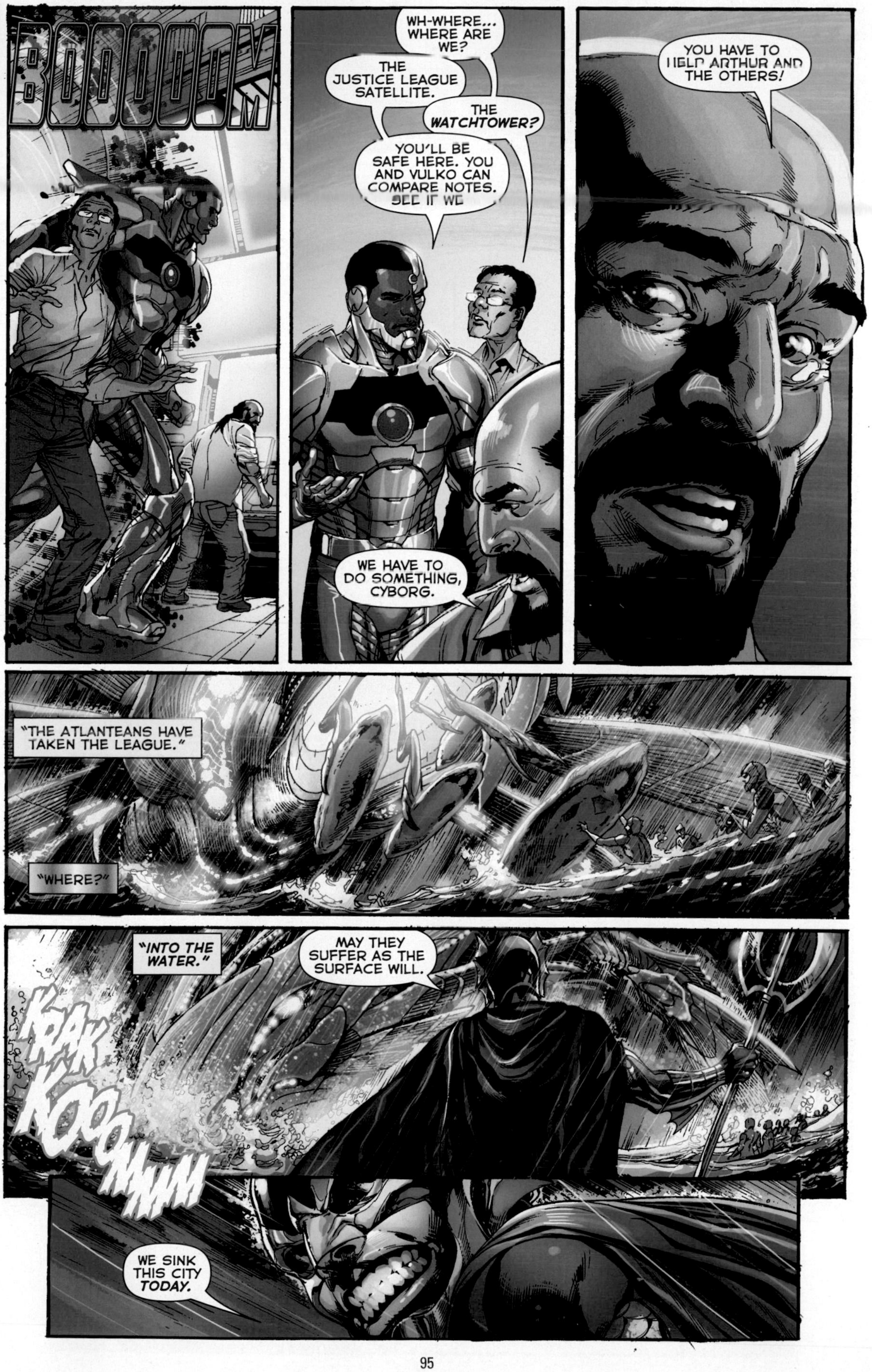
BOOOOOOM
WH-WHERE... WHERE ARE WE?
THE JUSTICE LEAGUE SATELLITE.
THE WATCHTOWER?
YOU'LL BE SAFE HERE. YOU AND VULKO CAN COMPARE NOTES. SEE IF WE
WE HAVE TO DO SOMETHING, CYBORG.
YOU HAVE TO HELP ARTHUR AND THE OTHERS!
"THE ATLANTEANS HAVE TAKEN THE LEAGUE."
"WHERE?"
"INTO THE WATER."
MAY THEY SUFFER AS THE SURFACE WILL.
KRAK KOOOMMM
WE SINK THIS CITY TODAY.

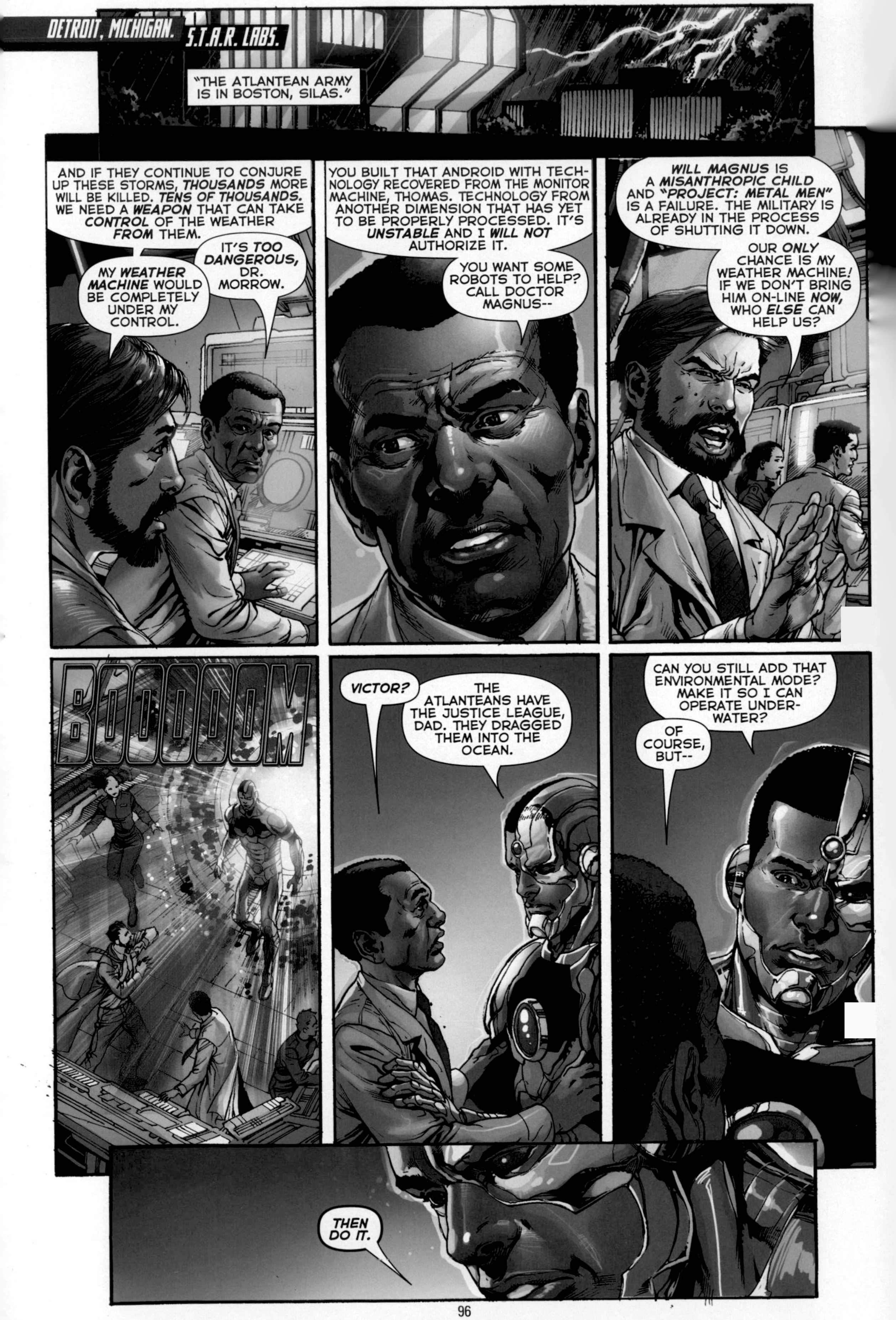
DETROIT, MICHIGAN.
S.T.A.R. LABS.
"THE ATLANTEAN ARMY IS IN BOSTON, SILAS."
AND IF THEY CONTINUE TO CONJURE UP THESE STORMS, THOUSANDS MORE WILL BE KILLED. TENS OF THOUSANDS. WE NEED A WEAPON THAT CAN TAKE CONTROL OF THE WEATHER FROM THEM.
MY WEATHER MACHINE WOULD BE COMPLETELY UNDER MY CONTROL.
IT'S TOO DANGEROUS, DR. MORROW.
YOU BUILT THAT ANDROID WITH TECHNOLOGY RECOVERED FROM THE MONITOR MACHINE, THOMAS. TECHNOLOGY FROM ANOTHER DIMENSION THAT HAS YET TO BE PROPERLY PROCESSED. IT'S UNSTABLE AND I WILL NOT AUTHORIZE IT.
YOU WANT SOME ROBOTS TO HELP? CALL DOCTOR MAGNUS--
WILL MAGNUS IS A MISANTHROPIC CHILD AND "PROJECT: METAL MEN" IS A FAILURE. THE MILITARY IS ALREADY IN THE PROCESS OF SHUTTING IT DOWN.
OUR ONLY CHANCE IS MY WEATHER MACHINE! IF WE DON'T BRING HIM ON-LINE NOW, WHO ELSE CAN HELP US?
BOOOOOM
VICTOR?
THE ATLANTEANS HAVE THE JUSTICE LEAGUE, DAD. THEY DRAGGED THEM INTO THE OCEAN.
CAN YOU STILL ADD THAT ENVIRONMENTAL MODE? MAKE IT SO I CAN OPERATE UNDERWATER?
OF COURSE, BUT--
THEN DO IT.

VICTOR, YOU KNOW WHAT WE'D HAVE TO DO. YOUR REMAINING LUNG--

GOES IN THE TRASH. JUST KEEP MY BRAIN AND MY HEART INTACT, DAD.

YOU TOLD ME THAT'S ALL I *NEED* TO STILL BE *ME*, RIGHT?

"HOW LONG WILL THIS TAKE?"

WE'LL PERFORM THE OPERATION AS QUICKLY AS POSSIBLE.

HOW LONG, DAD?

WE'LL NEED AT LEAST A FEW *HOURS*.

THEN I'VE GOT NO CHOICE BUT TO ASK FOR HELP.

WE WANTED TO *VET* THESE GUYS BEFORE BRINGING THEM ON BOARD, BUT THERE'S NO TIME.

CONNECT ME TO THE GRID.

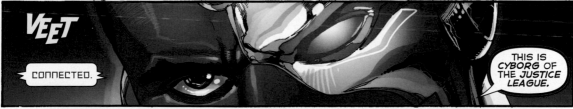

VEET

CONNECTED.

THIS IS *CYBORG* OF THE *JUSTICE LEAGUE*.

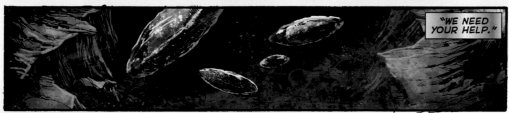

"WE NEED YOUR HELP."

THE WORLD NEEDS YOUR HELP.

WHAT'S CYBORG DOING? WHO'S HE TALKING TO?

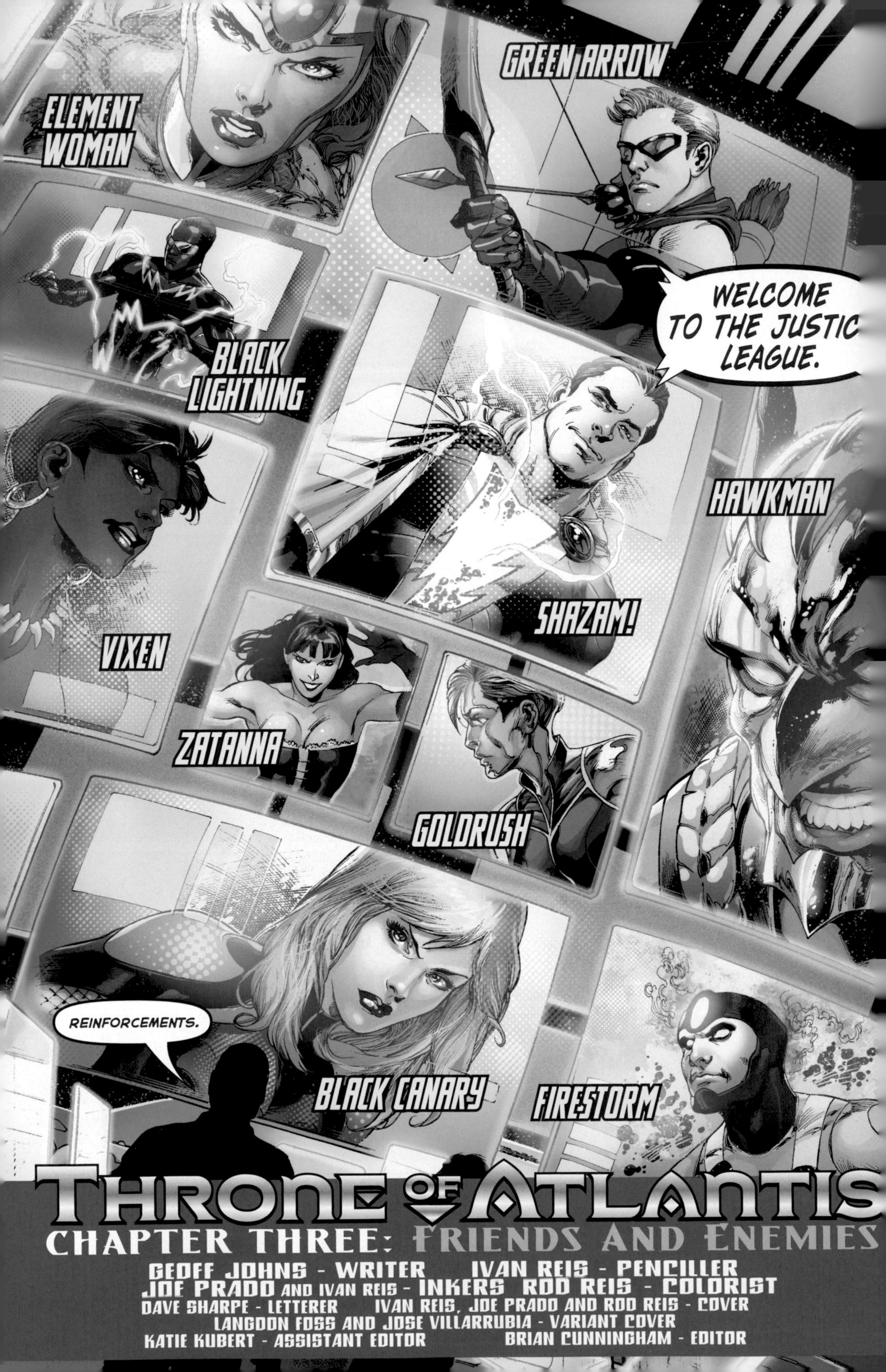
ELEMENT WOMAN
GREEN ARROW
BLACK LIGHTNING
WELCOME TO THE JUSTIC LEAGUE.
VIXEN
SHAZAM!
HAWKMAN
ZATANNA
GOLDRUSH
REINFORCEMENTS.
BLACK CANARY
FIRESTORM
THRONE OF ATLANTIS
CHAPTER THREE: FRIENDS AND ENEMIES
GEOFF JOHNS - WRITER IVAN REIS - PENCILLER
JOE PRADO AND IVAN REIS - INKERS ROD REIS - COLORIST
DAVE SHARPE - LETTERER IVAN REIS, JOE PRADO AND ROD REIS - COVER
LANGDON FOSS AND JOSE VILLARRUBIA - VARIANT COVER
KATIE KUBERT - ASSISTANT EDITOR BRIAN CUNNINGHAM - EDITOR

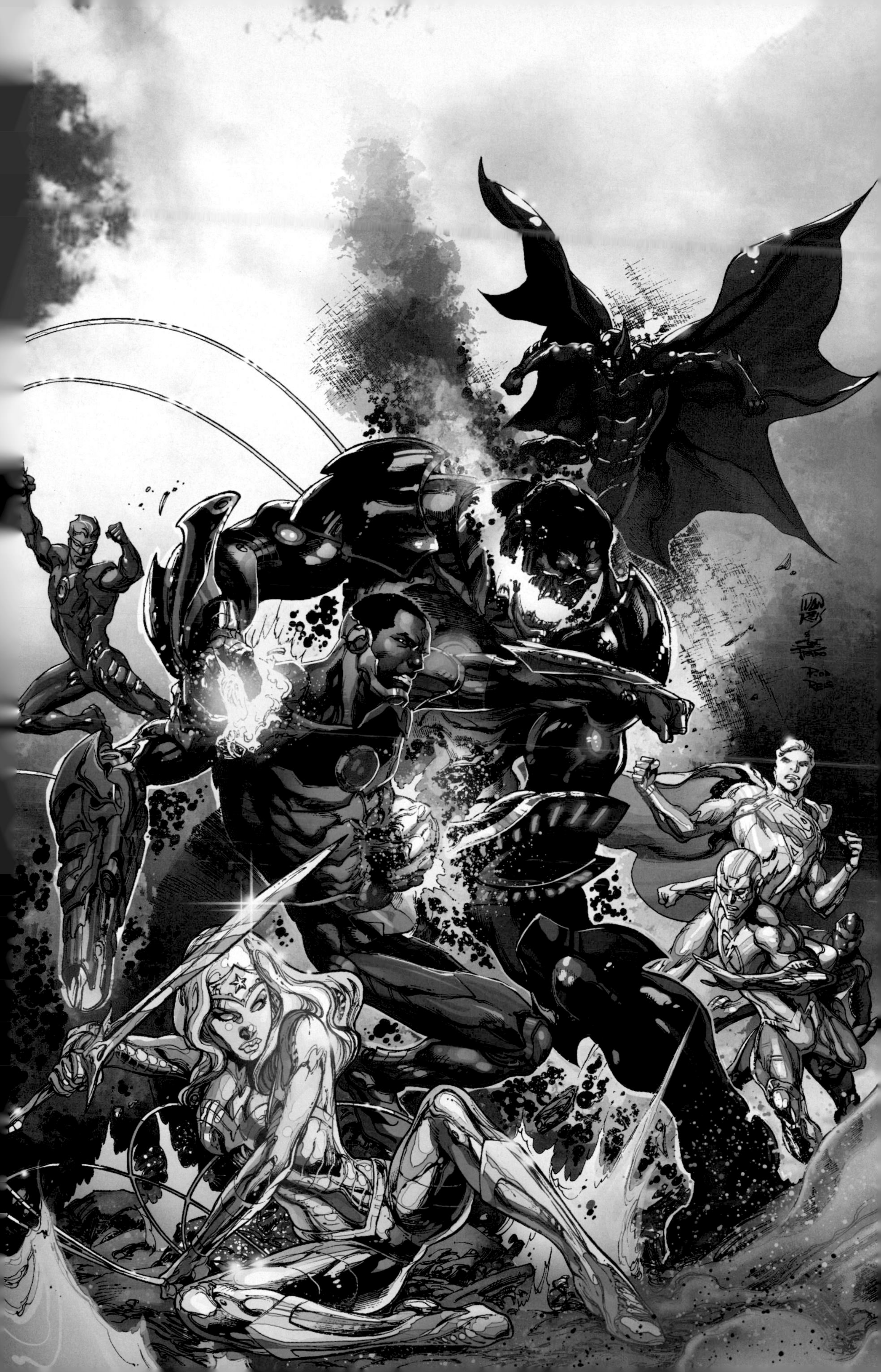

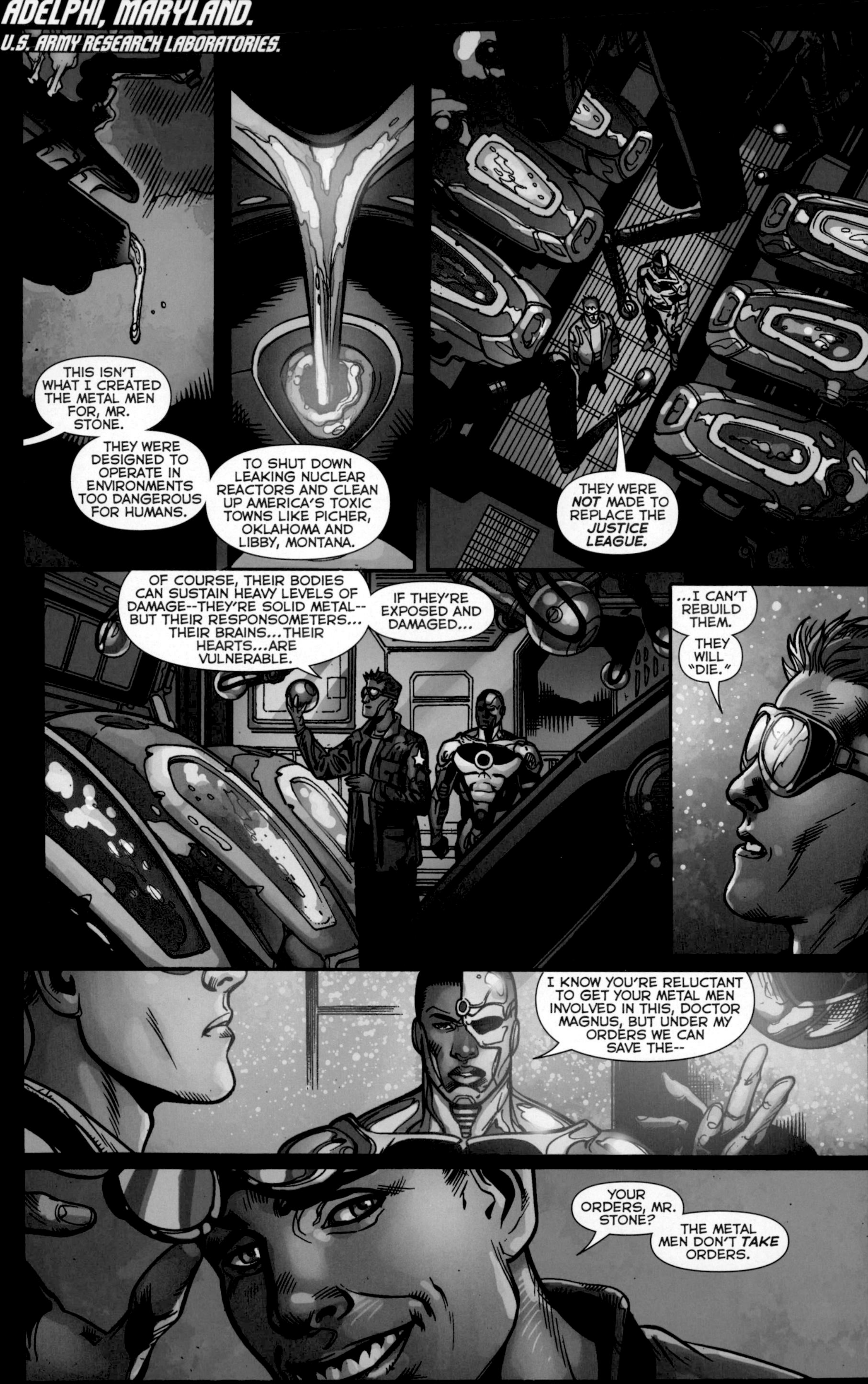
ADELPHI, MARYLAND.
U.S. ARMY RESEARCH LABORATORIES.
THIS ISN'T WHAT I CREATED THE METAL MEN FOR, MR. STONE.
THEY WERE DESIGNED TO OPERATE IN ENVIRONMENTS TOO DANGEROUS FOR HUMANS.
TO SHUT DOWN LEAKING NUCLEAR REACTORS AND CLEAN UP AMERICA'S TOXIC TOWNS LIKE PICHER, OKLAHOMA AND LIBBY, MONTANA.
THEY WERE *NOT* MADE TO REPLACE THE *JUSTICE LEAGUE.*
OF COURSE, THEIR BODIES CAN SUSTAIN HEAVY LEVELS OF DAMAGE--THEY'RE SOLID METAL--BUT THEIR RESPONSOMETERS... THEIR BRAINS... THEIR HEARTS... ARE VULNERABLE.
IF THEY'RE EXPOSED AND DAMAGED...
...I CAN'T REBUILD THEM.
THEY WILL "DIE."
I KNOW YOU'RE RELUCTANT TO GET YOUR METAL MEN INVOLVED IN THIS, DOCTOR MAGNUS, BUT UNDER MY ORDERS WE CAN SAVE THE--
YOUR ORDERS, MR. STONE?
THE METAL MEN DON'T *TAKE* ORDERS.

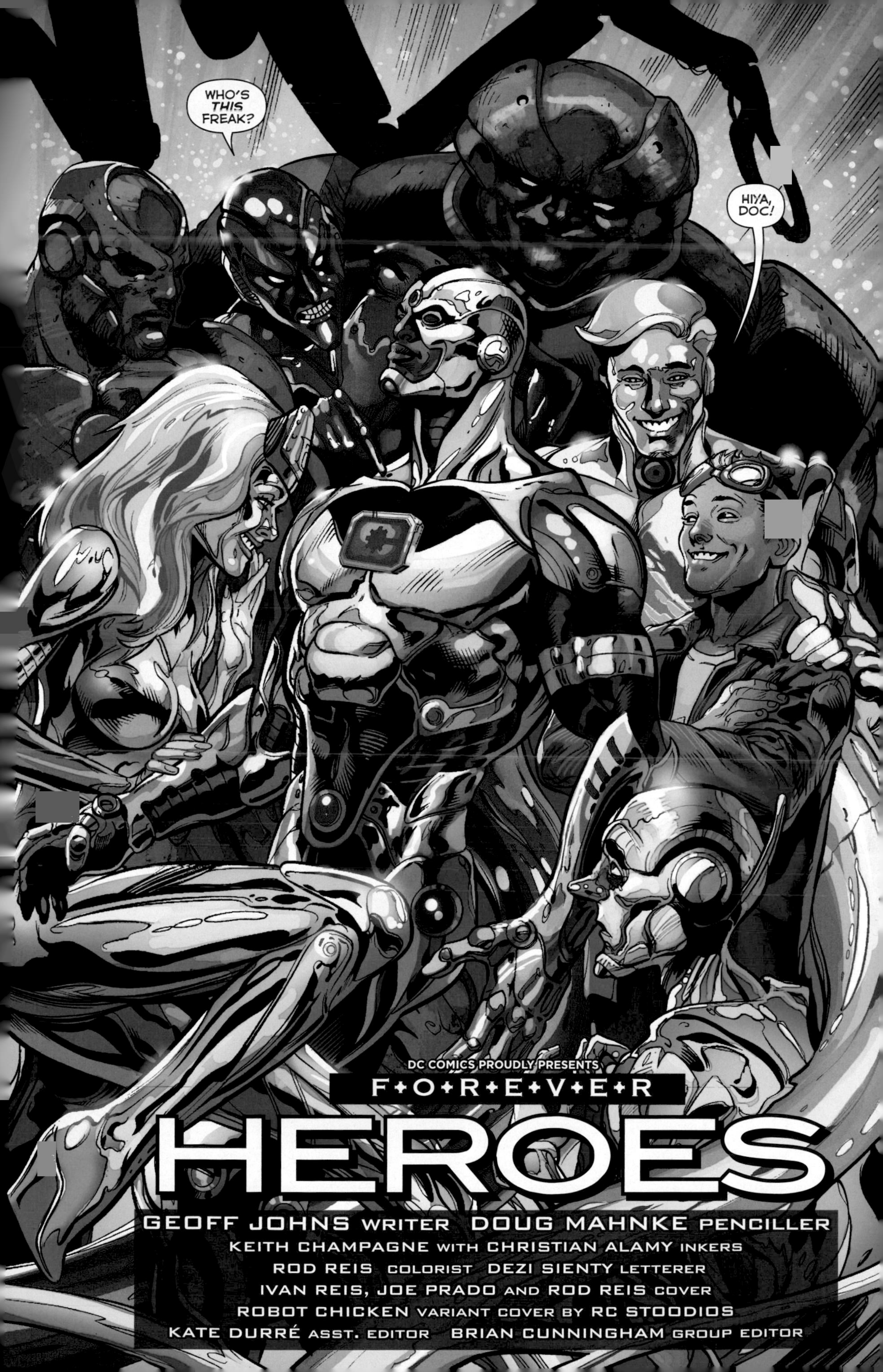
WHO'S THIS FREAK?
HIYA, DOC!
DC COMICS PROUDLY PRESENTS
F•O•R•E•V•E•R
HEROES
GEOFF JOHNS WRITER DOUG MAHNKE PENCILLER
KEITH CHAMPAGNE WITH CHRISTIAN ALAMY INKERS
ROD REIS COLORIST DEZI SIENTY LETTERER
IVAN REIS, JOE PRADO AND ROD REIS COVER
ROBOT CHICKEN VARIANT COVER BY RC STOODIOS
KATE DURRÉ ASST. EDITOR BRIAN CUNNINGHAM GROUP EDITOR

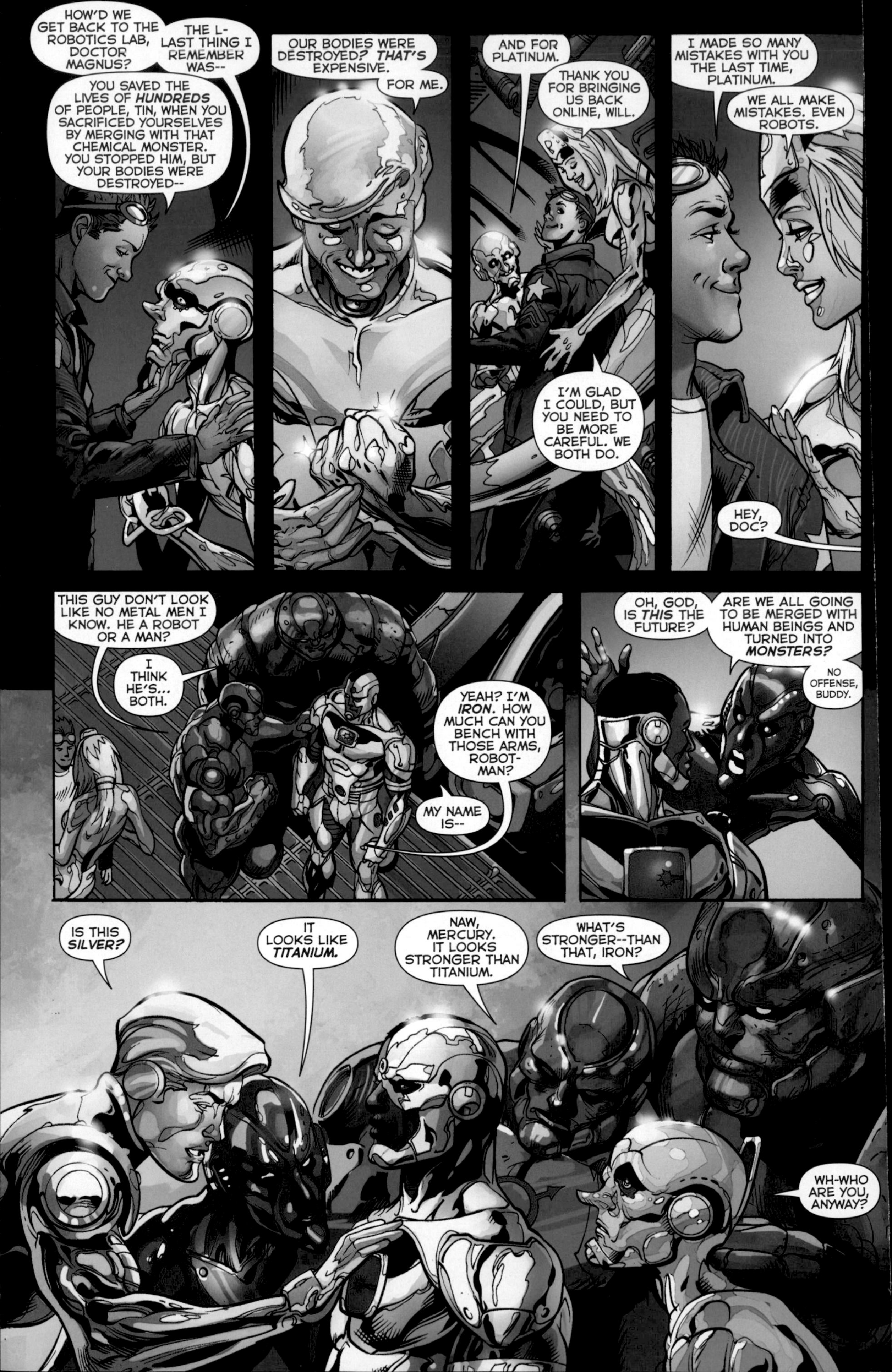
HOW'D WE GET BACK TO THE ROBOTICS LAB, DOCTOR MAGNUS?
THE L- LAST THING I REMEMBER WAS--
YOU SAVED THE LIVES OF HUNDREDS OF PEOPLE, TIN, WHEN YOU SACRIFICED YOURSELVES BY MERGING WITH THAT CHEMICAL MONSTER. YOU STOPPED HIM, BUT YOUR BODIES WERE DESTROYED--
OUR BODIES WERE DESTROYED? THAT'S EXPENSIVE.
FOR ME.
AND FOR PLATINUM.
THANK YOU FOR BRINGING US BACK ONLINE, WILL.
I'M GLAD I COULD, BUT YOU NEED TO BE MORE CAREFUL. WE BOTH DO.
I MADE SO MANY MISTAKES WITH YOU THE LAST TIME, PLATINUM.
WE ALL MAKE MISTAKES. EVEN ROBOTS.
HEY, DOC?
THIS GUY DON'T LOOK LIKE NO METAL MEN I KNOW. HE A ROBOT OR A MAN?
I THINK HE'S... BOTH.
YEAH? I'M IRON. HOW MUCH CAN YOU BENCH WITH THOSE ARMS, ROBOT-MAN?
MY NAME IS--
OH, GOD, IS THIS THE FUTURE?
ARE WE ALL GOING TO BE MERGED WITH HUMAN BEINGS AND TURNED INTO MONSTERS?
NO OFFENSE, BUDDY.
IS THIS SILVER?
IT LOOKS LIKE TITANIUM.
NAW, MERCURY. IT LOOKS STRONGER THAN TITANIUM.
WHAT'S STRONGER--THAN THAT, IRON?
WH-WHO ARE YOU, ANYWAY?

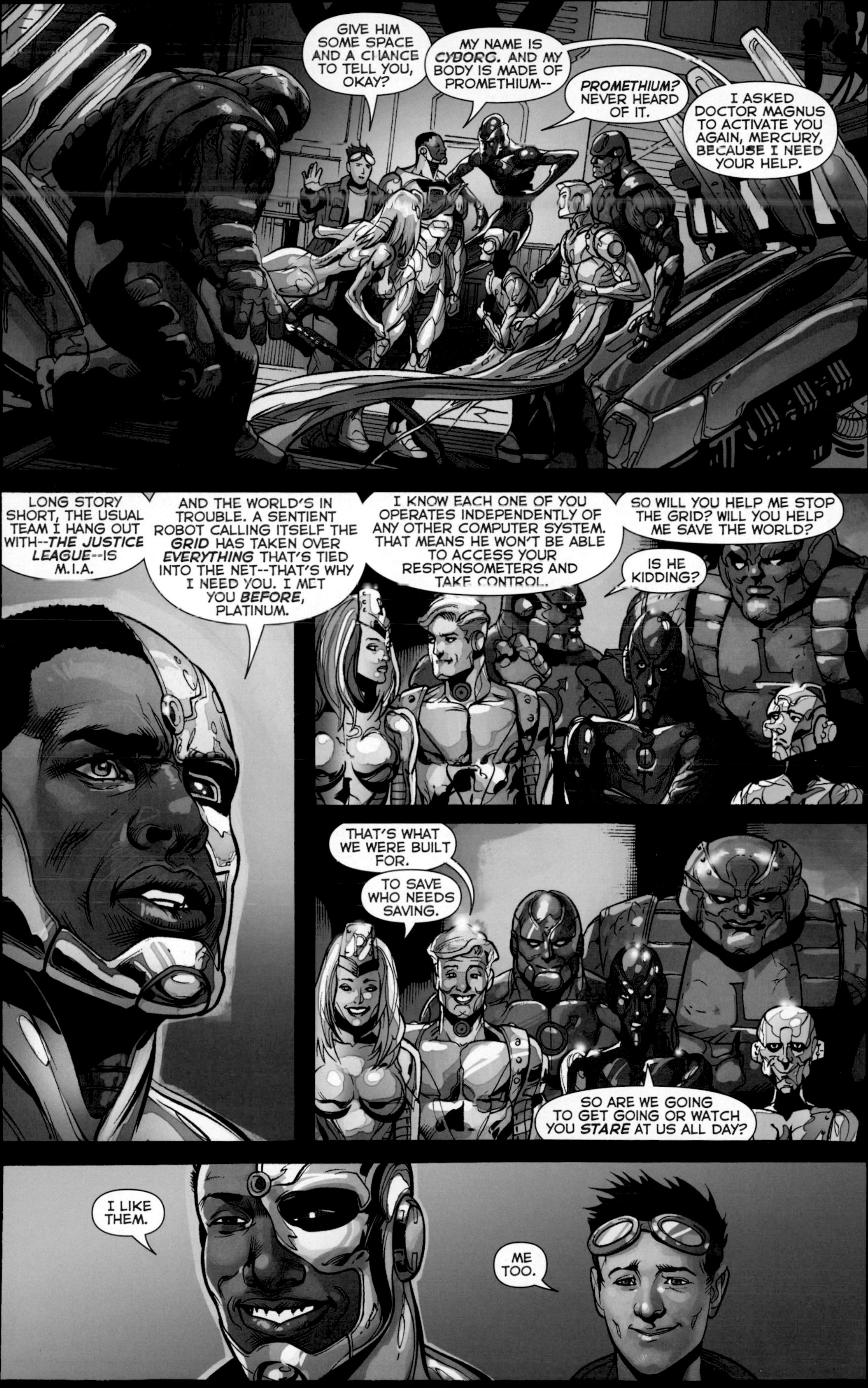
GIVE HIM SOME SPACE AND A CHANCE TO TELL YOU, OKAY?
MY NAME IS CYBORG. AND MY BODY IS MADE OF PROMETHIUM--
PROMETHIUM? NEVER HEARD OF IT.
I ASKED DOCTOR MAGNUS TO ACTIVATE YOU AGAIN, MERCURY, BECAUSE I NEED YOUR HELP.
LONG STORY SHORT, THE USUAL TEAM I HANG OUT WITH--THE JUSTICE LEAGUE--IS M.I.A.
AND THE WORLD'S IN TROUBLE. A SENTIENT ROBOT CALLING ITSELF THE GRID HAS TAKEN OVER EVERYTHING THAT'S TIED INTO THE NET--THAT'S WHY I NEED YOU. I MET YOU BEFORE, PLATINUM.
I KNOW EACH ONE OF YOU OPERATES INDEPENDENTLY OF ANY OTHER COMPUTER SYSTEM. THAT MEANS HE WON'T BE ABLE TO ACCESS YOUR RESPONSOMETERS AND TAKE CONTROL.
SO WILL YOU HELP ME STOP THE GRID? WILL YOU HELP ME SAVE THE WORLD?
IS HE KIDDING?
THAT'S WHAT WE WERE BUILT FOR.
TO SAVE WHO NEEDS SAVING.
SO ARE WE GOING TO GET GOING OR WATCH YOU STARE AT US ALL DAY?
I LIKE THEM.
ME TOO.

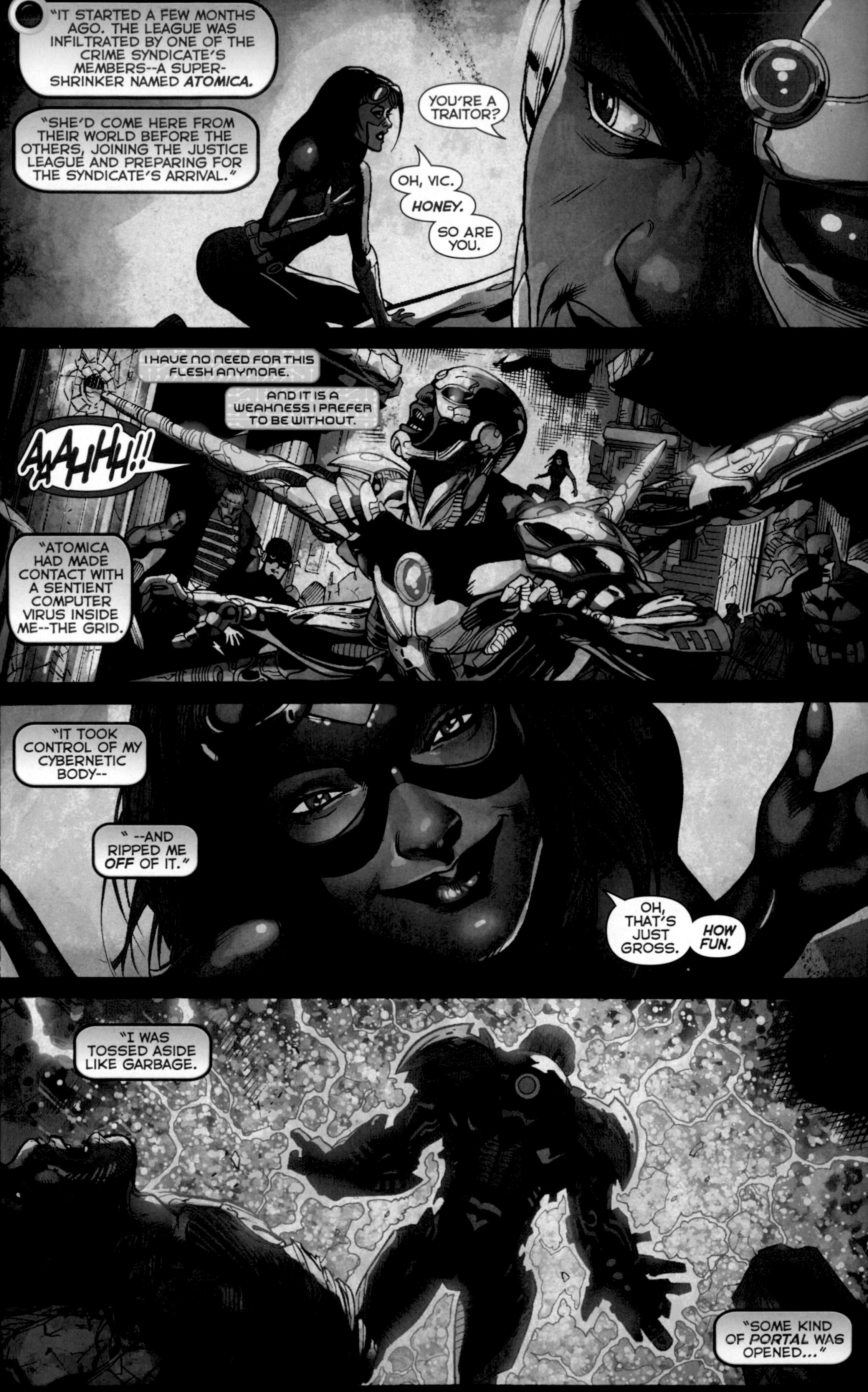
"IT STARTED A FEW MONTHS AGO. THE LEAGUE WAS INFILTRATED BY ONE OF THE CRIME SYNDICATE'S MEMBERS--A SUPER-SHRINKER NAMED *ATOMICA.*
"SHE'D COME HERE FROM THEIR WORLD BEFORE THE OTHERS, JOINING THE JUSTICE LEAGUE AND PREPARING FOR THE SYNDICATE'S ARRIVAL."
YOU'RE A TRAITOR?
OH, VIC.
HONEY.
SO ARE YOU.
I HAVE NO NEED FOR THIS FLESH ANYMORE.
AND IT IS A WEAKNESS I PREFER TO BE WITHOUT.
AAAHHH!!
"ATOMICA HAD MADE CONTACT WITH A SENTIENT COMPUTER VIRUS INSIDE ME--THE GRID.
"IT TOOK CONTROL OF MY CYBERNETIC BODY--
" --AND RIPPED ME *OFF* OF IT."
OH, THAT'S JUST GROSS.
HOW FUN.
"I WAS TOSSED ASIDE LIKE GARBAGE.
"SOME KIND OF *PORTAL* WAS OPENED..."

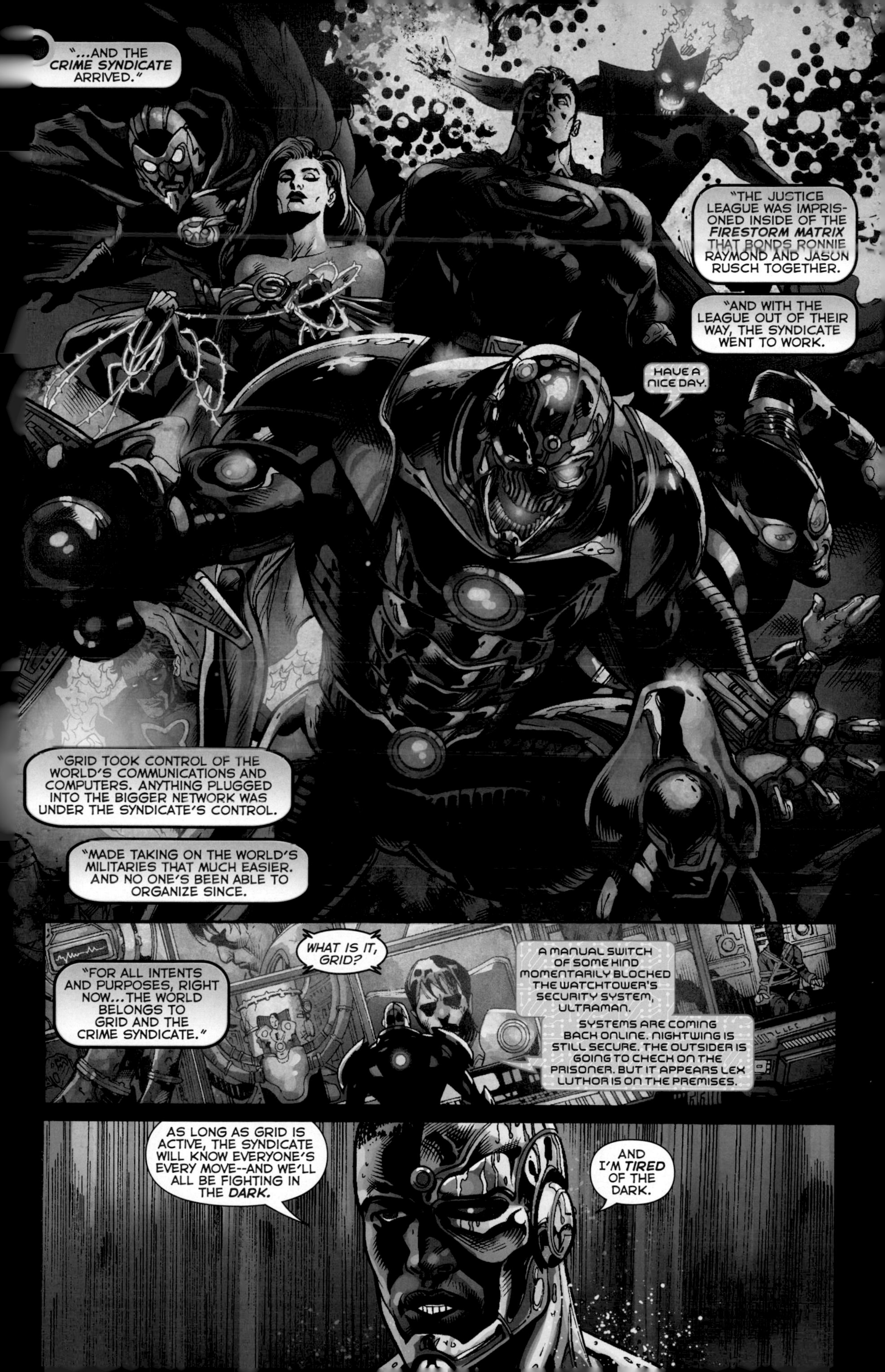
"...AND THE CRIME SYNDICATE ARRIVED."
"THE JUSTICE LEAGUE WAS IMPRISONED INSIDE OF THE FIRESTORM MATRIX THAT BONDS RONNIE RAYMOND AND JASON RUSCH TOGETHER.
"AND WITH THE LEAGUE OUT OF THEIR WAY, THE SYNDICATE WENT TO WORK.
HAVE A NICE DAY.
"GRID TOOK CONTROL OF THE WORLD'S COMMUNICATIONS AND COMPUTERS. ANYTHING PLUGGED INTO THE BIGGER NETWORK WAS UNDER THE SYNDICATE'S CONTROL.
"MADE TAKING ON THE WORLD'S MILITARIES THAT MUCH EASIER. AND NO ONE'S BEEN ABLE TO ORGANIZE SINCE.
"FOR ALL INTENTS AND PURPOSES, RIGHT NOW...THE WORLD BELONGS TO GRID AND THE CRIME SYNDICATE."
WHAT IS IT, GRID?
A MANUAL SWITCH OF SOME KIND MOMENTARILY BLOCKED THE WATCHTOWER'S SECURITY SYSTEM, ULTRAMAN.
SYSTEMS ARE COMING BACK ONLINE. NIGHTWING IS STILL SECURE. THE OUTSIDER IS GOING TO CHECK ON THE PRISONER. BUT IT APPEARS LEX LUTHOR IS ON THE PREMISES.
AS LONG AS GRID IS ACTIVE, THE SYNDICATE WILL KNOW EVERYONE'S EVERY MOVE--AND WE'LL ALL BE FIGHTING IN THE DARK.
AND I'M TIRED OF THE DARK.

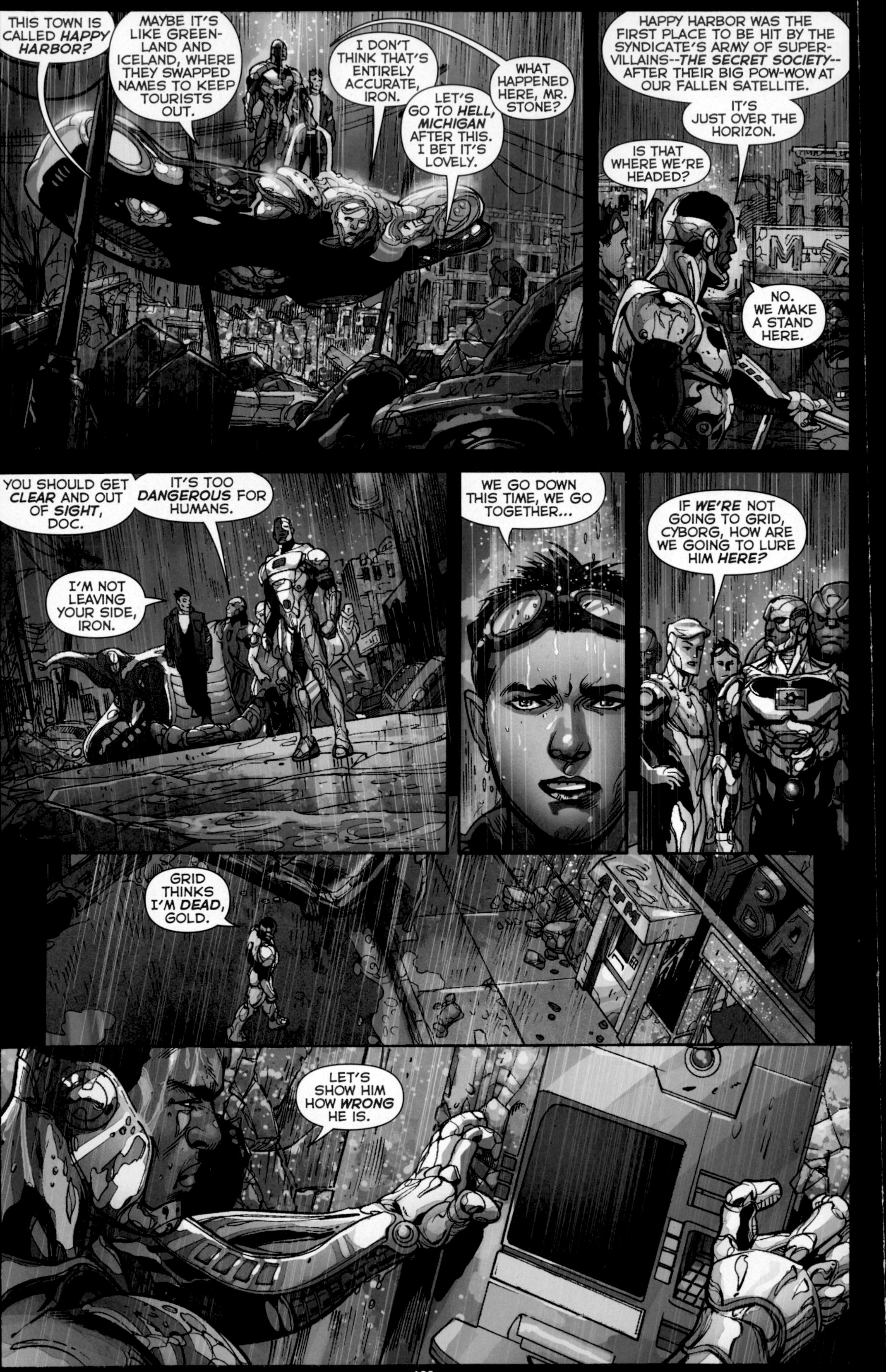
THIS TOWN IS CALLED *HAPPY HARBOR?*
MAYBE IT'S LIKE GREENLAND AND ICELAND, WHERE THEY SWAPPED NAMES TO KEEP TOURISTS OUT.
I DON'T THINK THAT'S ENTIRELY ACCURATE, IRON.
LET'S GO TO *HELL, MICHIGAN* AFTER THIS. I BET IT'S LOVELY.
WHAT HAPPENED HERE, MR. STONE?
HAPPY HARBOR WAS THE FIRST PLACE TO BE HIT BY THE SYNDICATE'S ARMY OF SUPER-VILLAINS--*THE SECRET SOCIETY*--AFTER THEIR BIG POW-WOW AT OUR FALLEN SATELLITE.
IT'S JUST OVER THE HORIZON.
IS THAT WHERE WE'RE HEADED?
NO. WE MAKE A STAND HERE.
YOU SHOULD GET *CLEAR* AND OUT OF *SIGHT*, DOC.
IT'S TOO *DANGEROUS* FOR HUMANS.
I'M NOT LEAVING YOUR SIDE, IRON.
WE GO DOWN THIS TIME, WE GO TOGETHER...
IF *WE'RE* NOT GOING TO GRID, CYBORG, HOW ARE WE GOING TO LURE HIM *HERE?*
GRID THINKS I'M *DEAD*, GOLD.
ATM
LET'S SHOW HIM HOW *WRONG* HE IS.

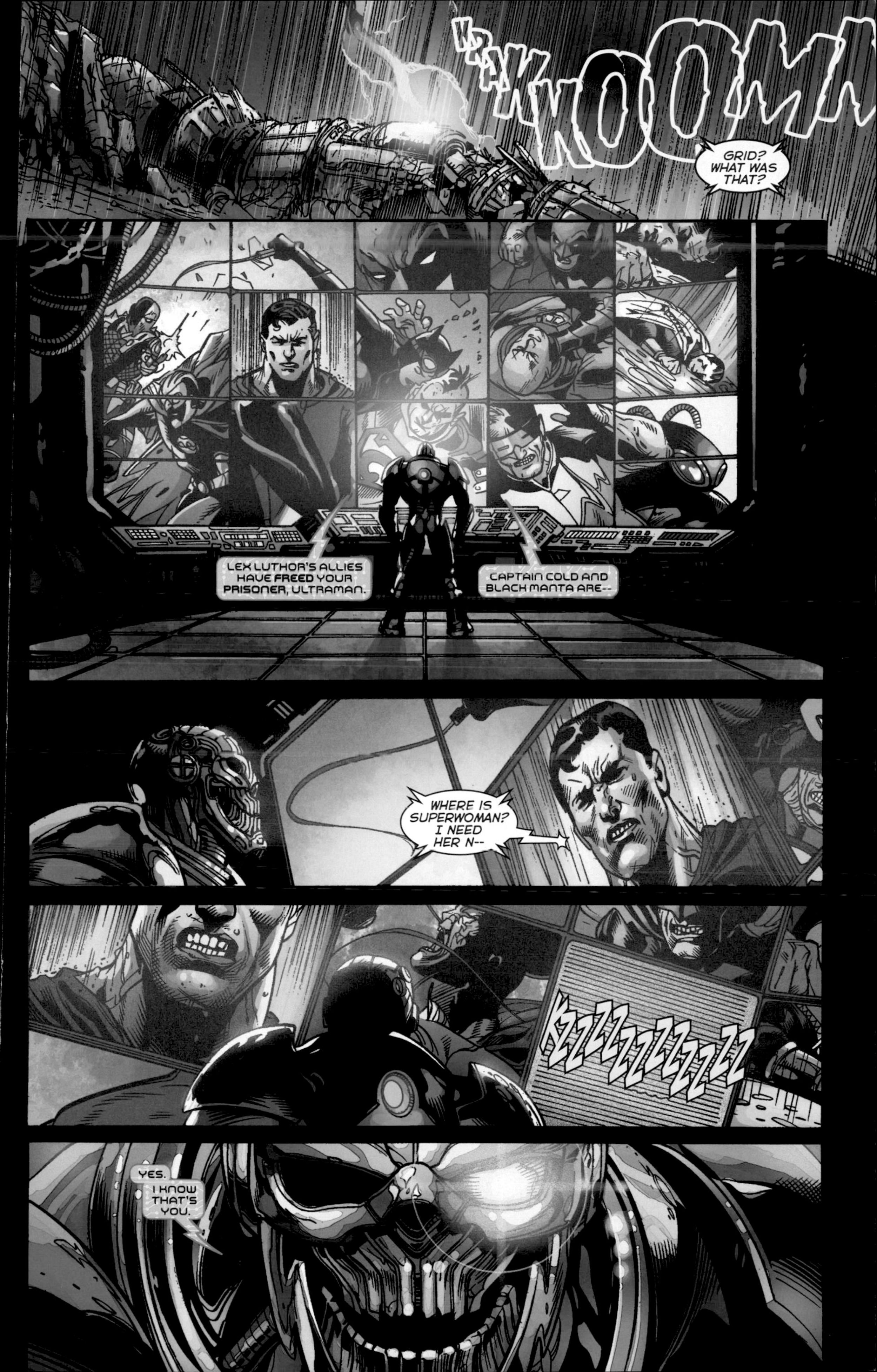
KRAKKOOOMM
GRID? WHAT WAS THAT?
LEX LUTHOR'S ALLIES HAVE FREED YOUR PRISONER, ULTRAMAN.
CAPTAIN COLD AND BLACK MANTA ARE--
WHERE IS SUPERWOMAN? I NEED HER N--
KZZZZZZZZZZZ
YES.
I KNOW THAT'S YOU.

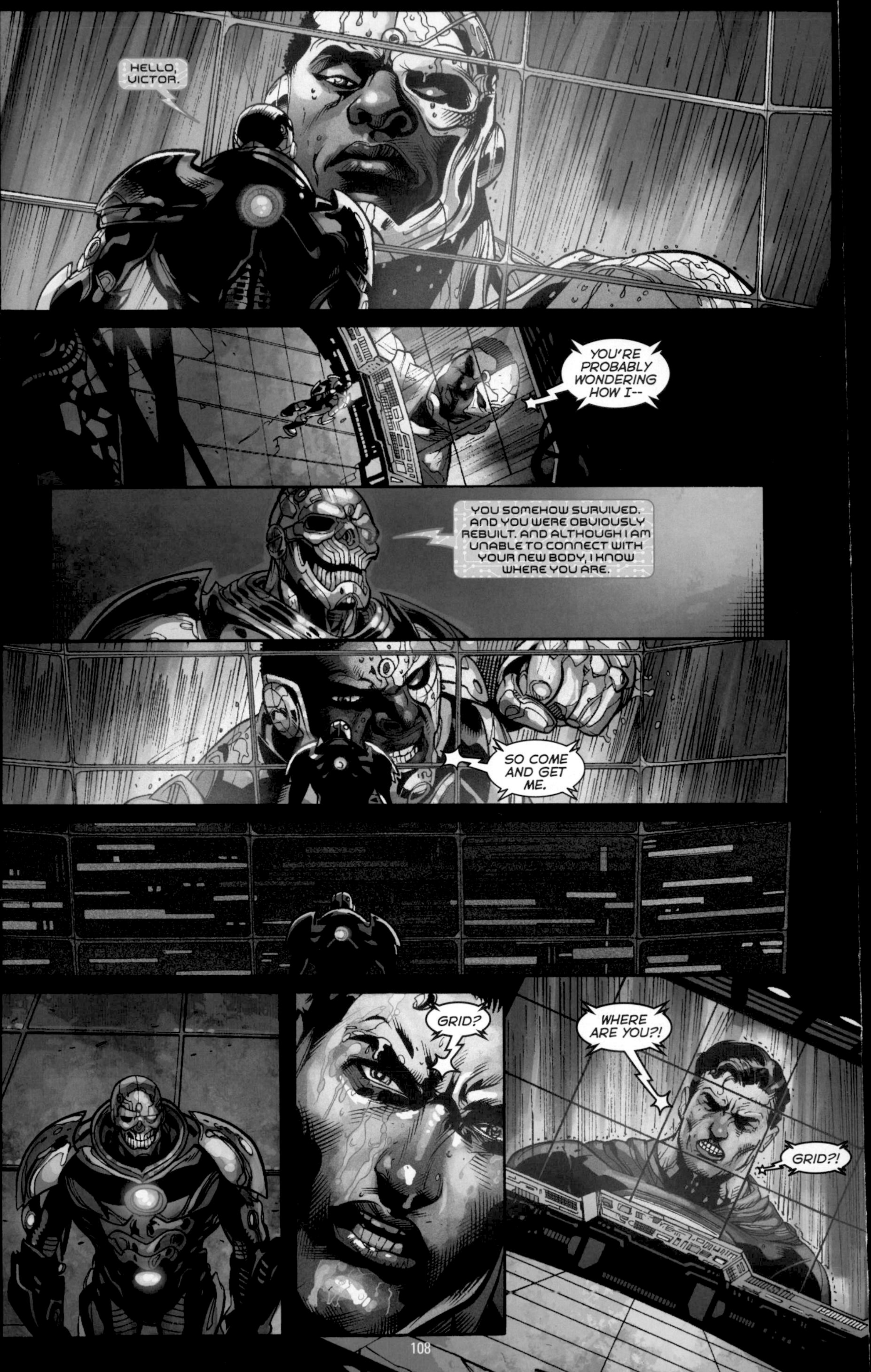
HELLO, VICTOR.
YOU'RE PROBABLY WONDERING HOW I--
YOU SOMEHOW SURVIVED. AND YOU WERE OBVIOUSLY REBUILT. AND ALTHOUGH I AM UNABLE TO CONNECT WITH YOUR NEW BODY, I KNOW WHERE YOU ARE.
SO COME AND GET ME.
GRID?
WHERE ARE YOU?!
GRID?!

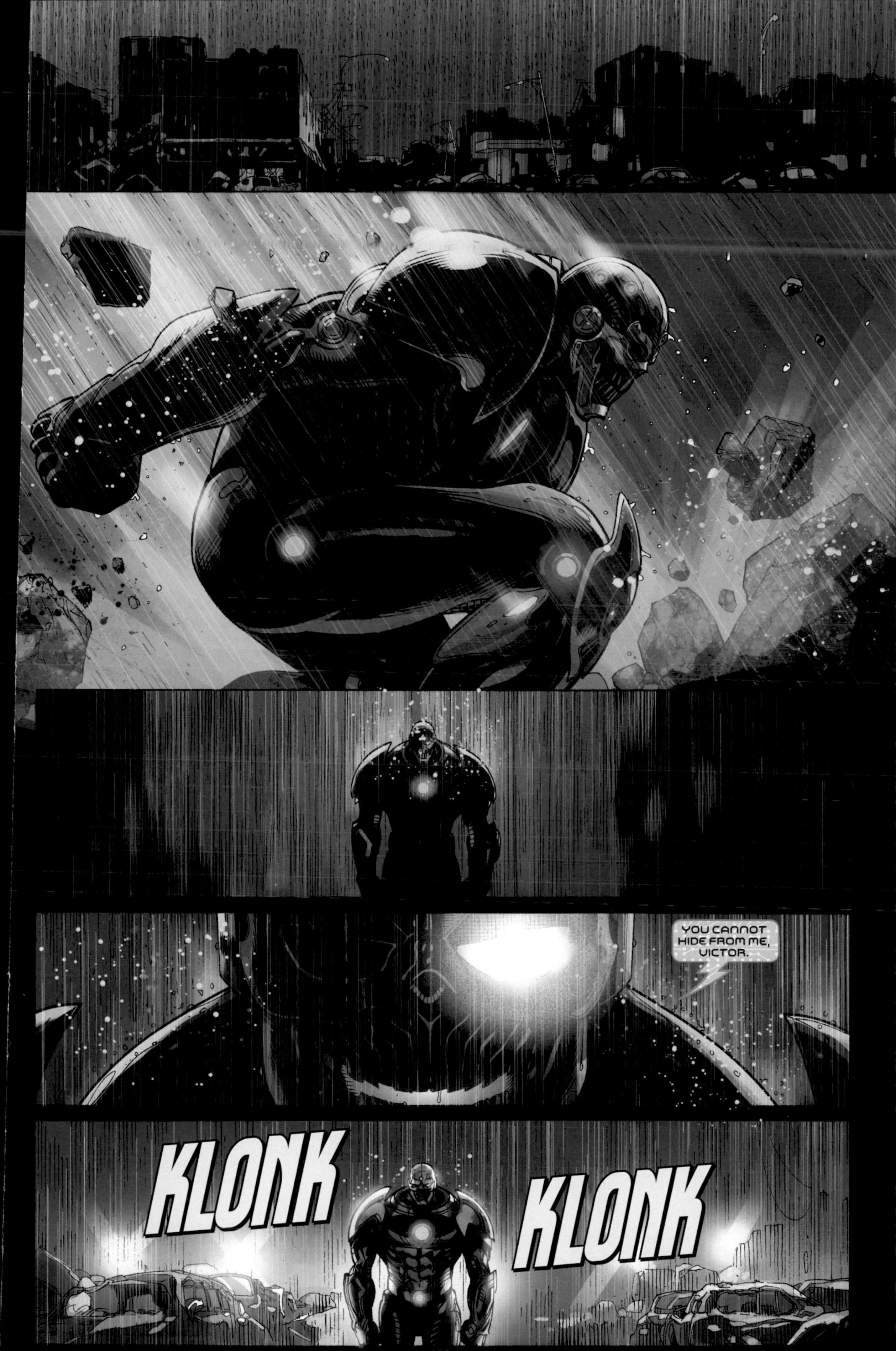
YOU CANNOT HIDE FROM ME, VICTOR.
KLONK
KLONK

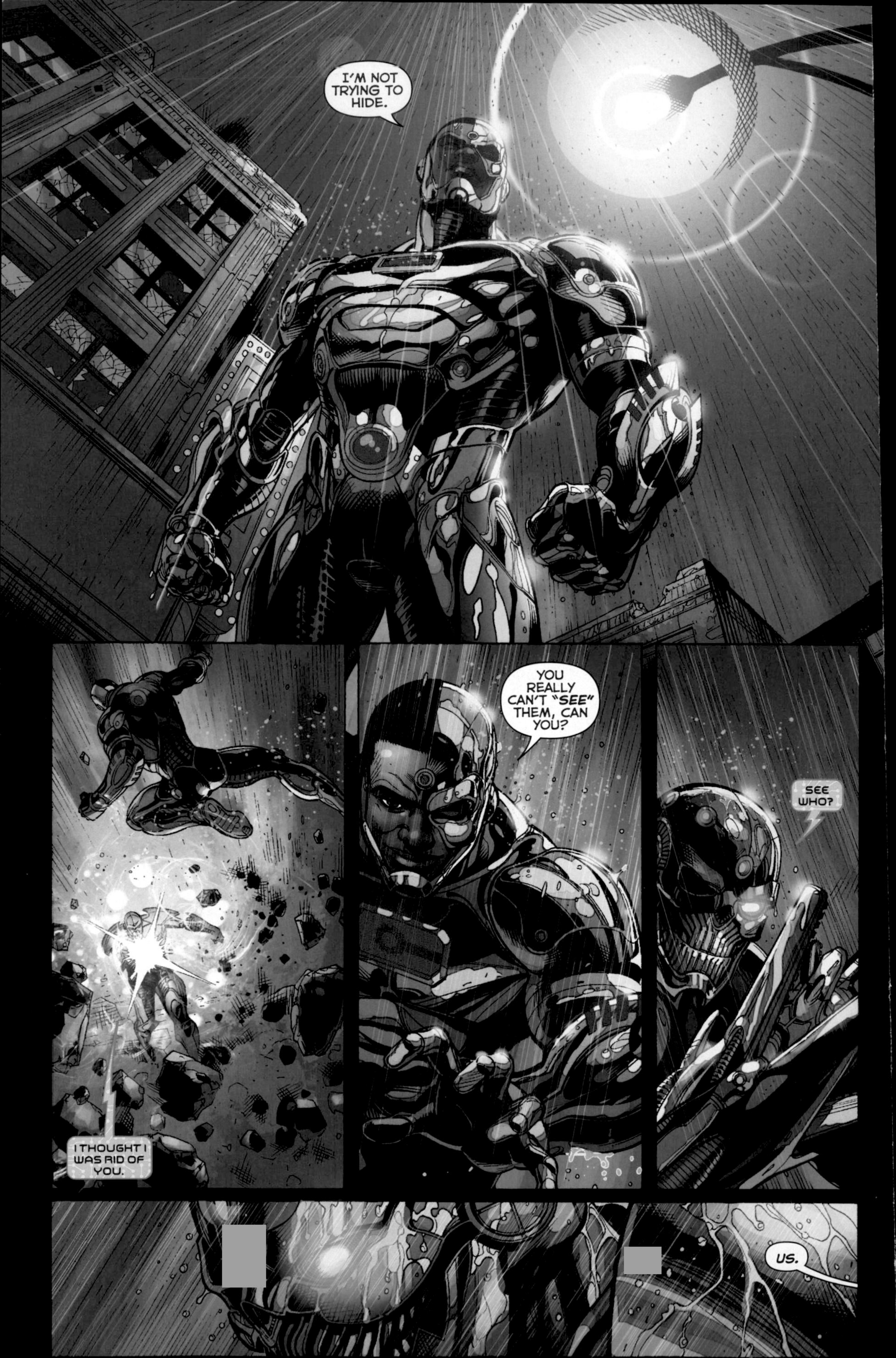
I'M NOT TRYING TO HIDE.
I THOUGHT I WAS RID OF YOU.
YOU REALLY CAN'T "SEE" THEM, CAN YOU?
SEE WHO?
US.

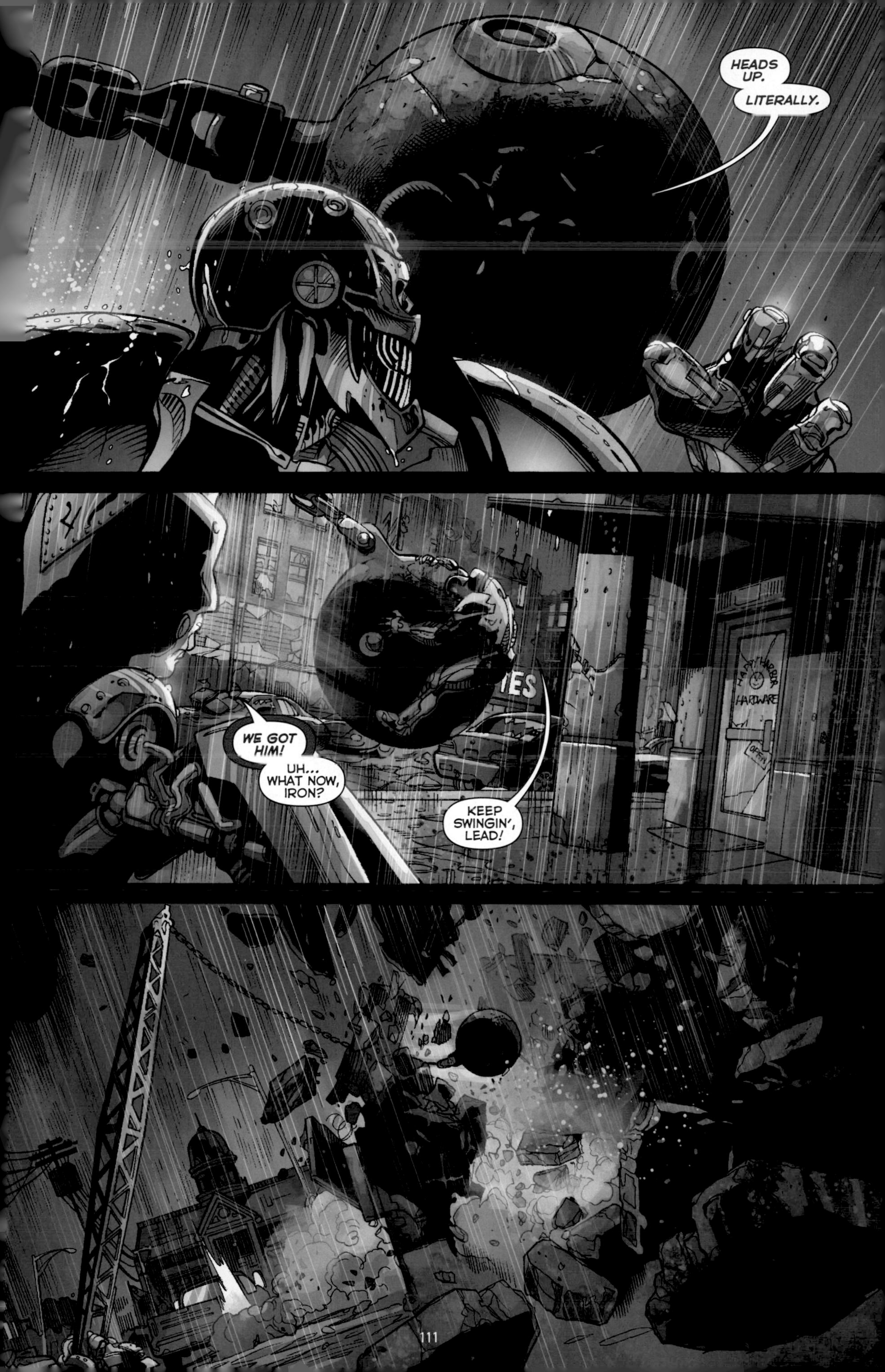
HEADS UP.
LITERALLY.
ES
HAPPY HARBOR HARDWARE
OPEN
WE GOT HIM!
UH... WHAT NOW, IRON?
KEEP SWINGIN', LEAD!

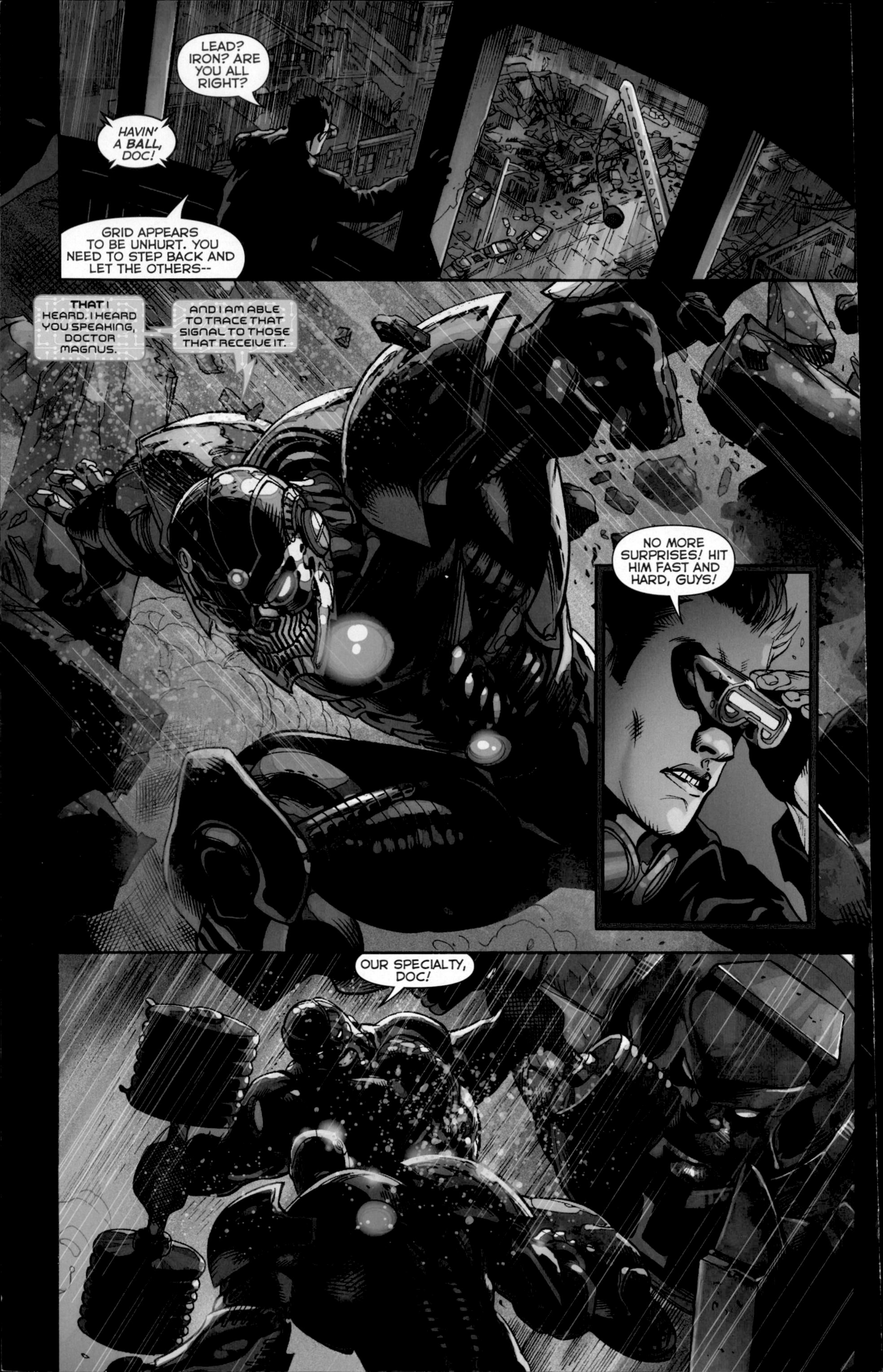

LEAD? IRON? ARE YOU ALL RIGHT?
HAVIN' A BALL, DOC!
GRID APPEARS TO BE UNHURT. YOU NEED TO STEP BACK AND LET THE OTHERS--
THAT I HEARD. I HEARD YOU SPEAKING, DOCTOR MAGNUS.
AND I AM ABLE TO TRACE THAT SIGNAL TO THOSE THAT RECEIVE IT.
NO MORE SURPRISES! HIT HIM FAST AND HARD, GUYS!
OUR SPECIALTY, DOC!

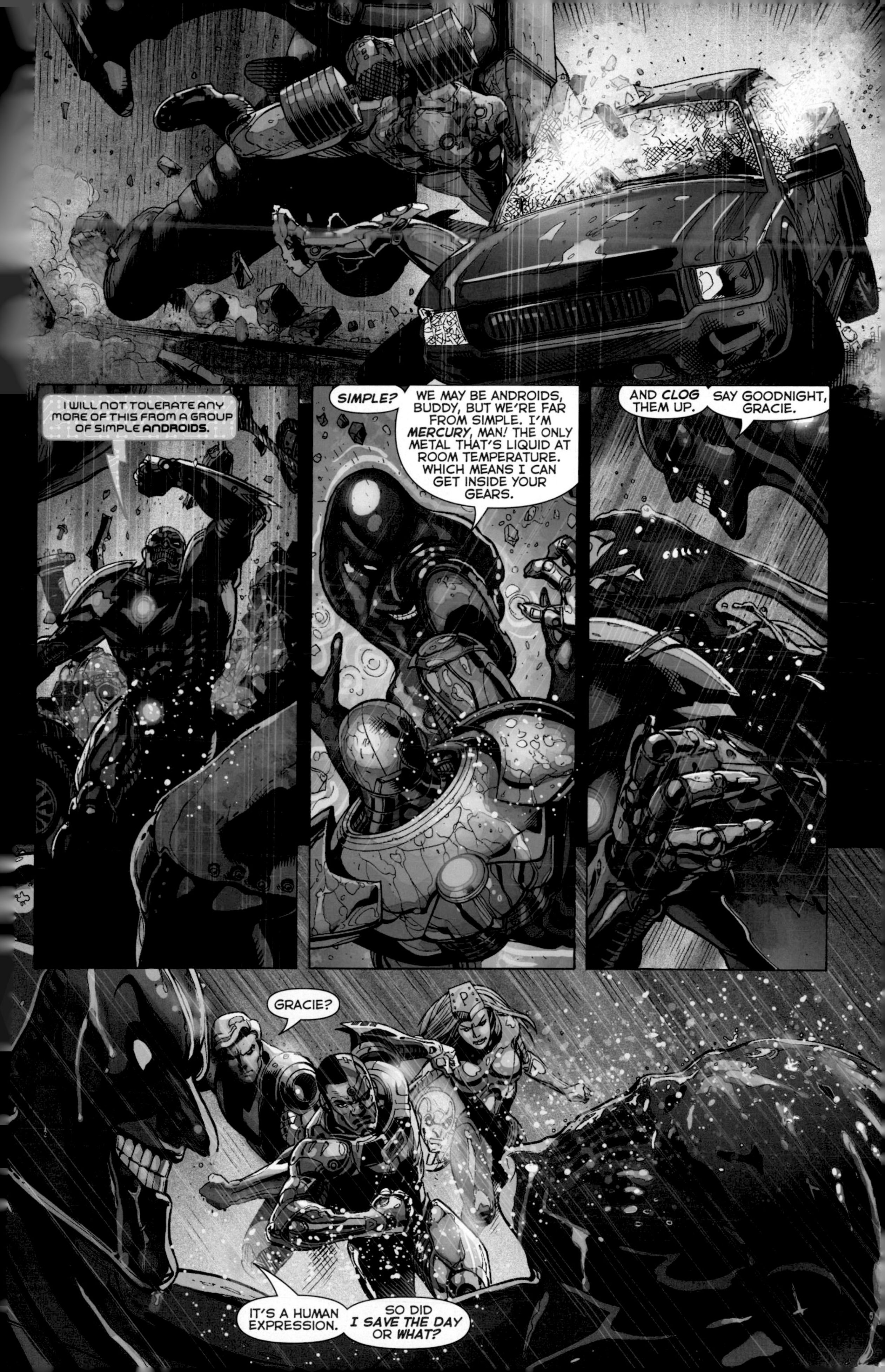
I WILL NOT TOLERATE ANY MORE OF THIS FROM A GROUP OF SIMPLE ANDROIDS.
SIMPLE?
WE MAY BE ANDROIDS, BUDDY, BUT WE'RE FAR FROM SIMPLE. I'M MERCURY, MAN! THE ONLY METAL THAT'S LIQUID AT ROOM TEMPERATURE. WHICH MEANS I CAN GET INSIDE YOUR GEARS.
AND CLOG THEM UP.
SAY GOODNIGHT, GRACIE.
GRACIE?
IT'S A HUMAN EXPRESSION.
SO DID I SAVE THE DAY OR WHAT?

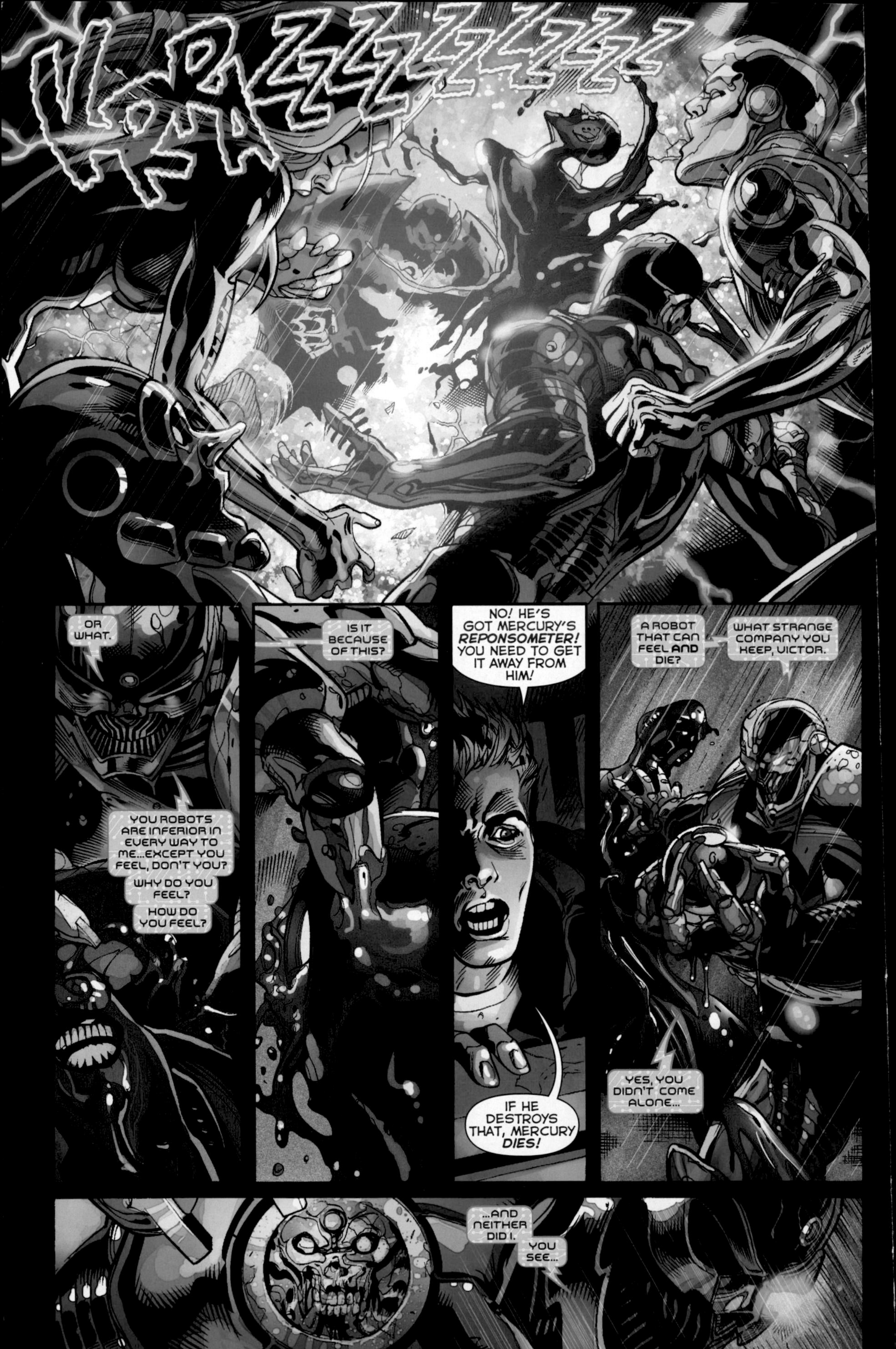
VRAZZZZZZZZZ
HA HA
OR WHAT.
YOU ROBOTS ARE INFERIOR IN EVERY WAY TO ME...EXCEPT YOU FEEL, DON'T YOU?
WHY DO YOU FEEL?
HOW DO YOU FEEL?
IS IT BECAUSE OF THIS?
NO! HE'S GOT MERCURY'S REPONSOMETER! YOU NEED TO GET IT AWAY FROM HIM!
IF HE DESTROYS THAT, MERCURY DIES!
A ROBOT THAT CAN FEEL AND DIE?
WHAT STRANGE COMPANY YOU KEEP, VICTOR.
YES, YOU DIDN'T COME ALONE...
...AND NEITHER DID I.
YOU SEE...

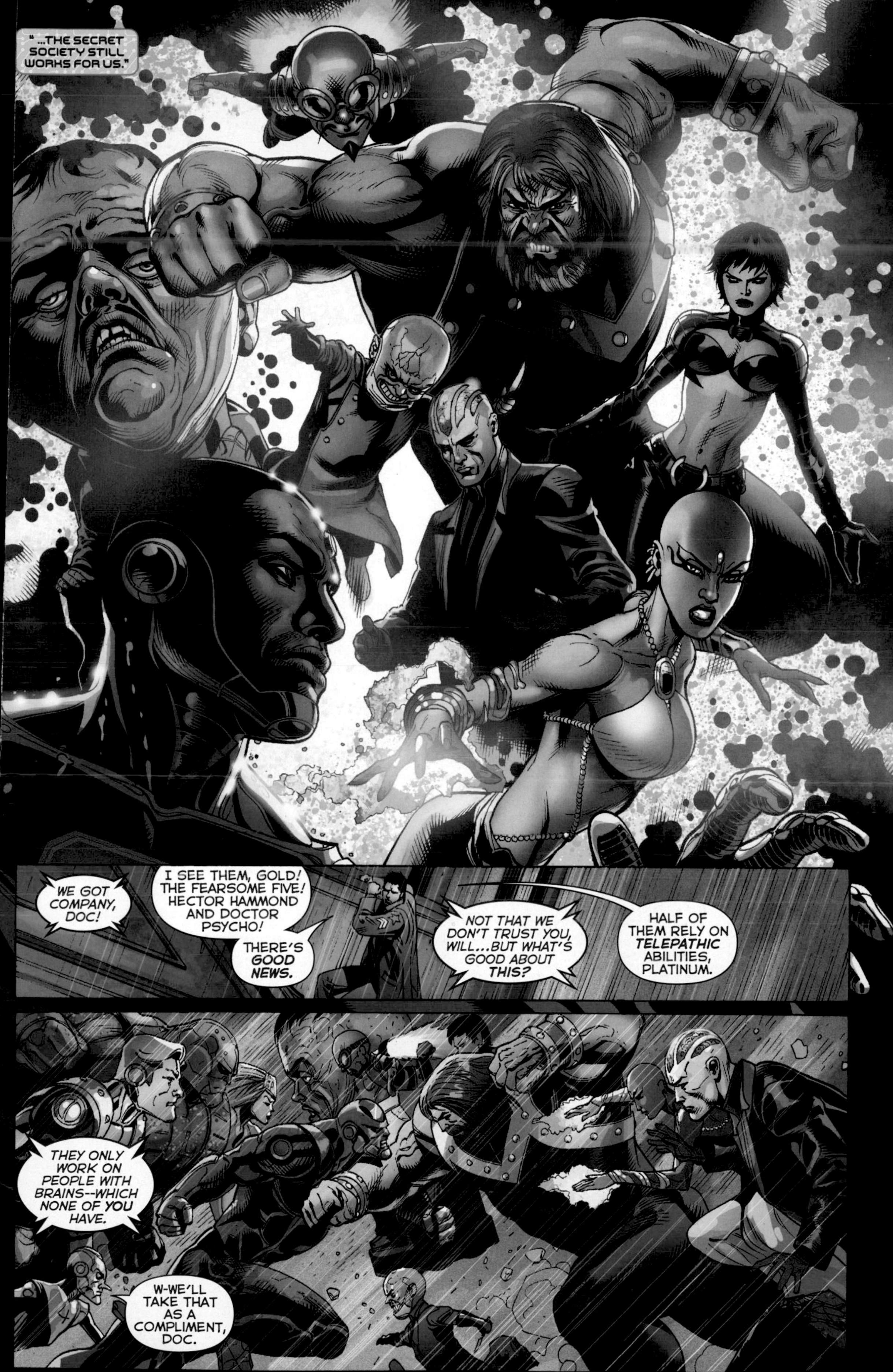
"...THE SECRET SOCIETY STILL WORKS FOR US."
WE GOT COMPANY, DOC!
I SEE THEM, GOLD! THE FEARSOME FIVE! HECTOR HAMMOND AND DOCTOR PSYCHO!
THERE'S GOOD NEWS.
NOT THAT WE DON'T TRUST YOU, WILL...BUT WHAT'S GOOD ABOUT THIS?
HALF OF THEM RELY ON TELEPATHIC ABILITIES, PLATINUM.
THEY ONLY WORK ON PEOPLE WITH BRAINS--WHICH NONE OF YOU HAVE.
W-WE'LL TAKE THAT AS A COMPLIMENT, DOC.

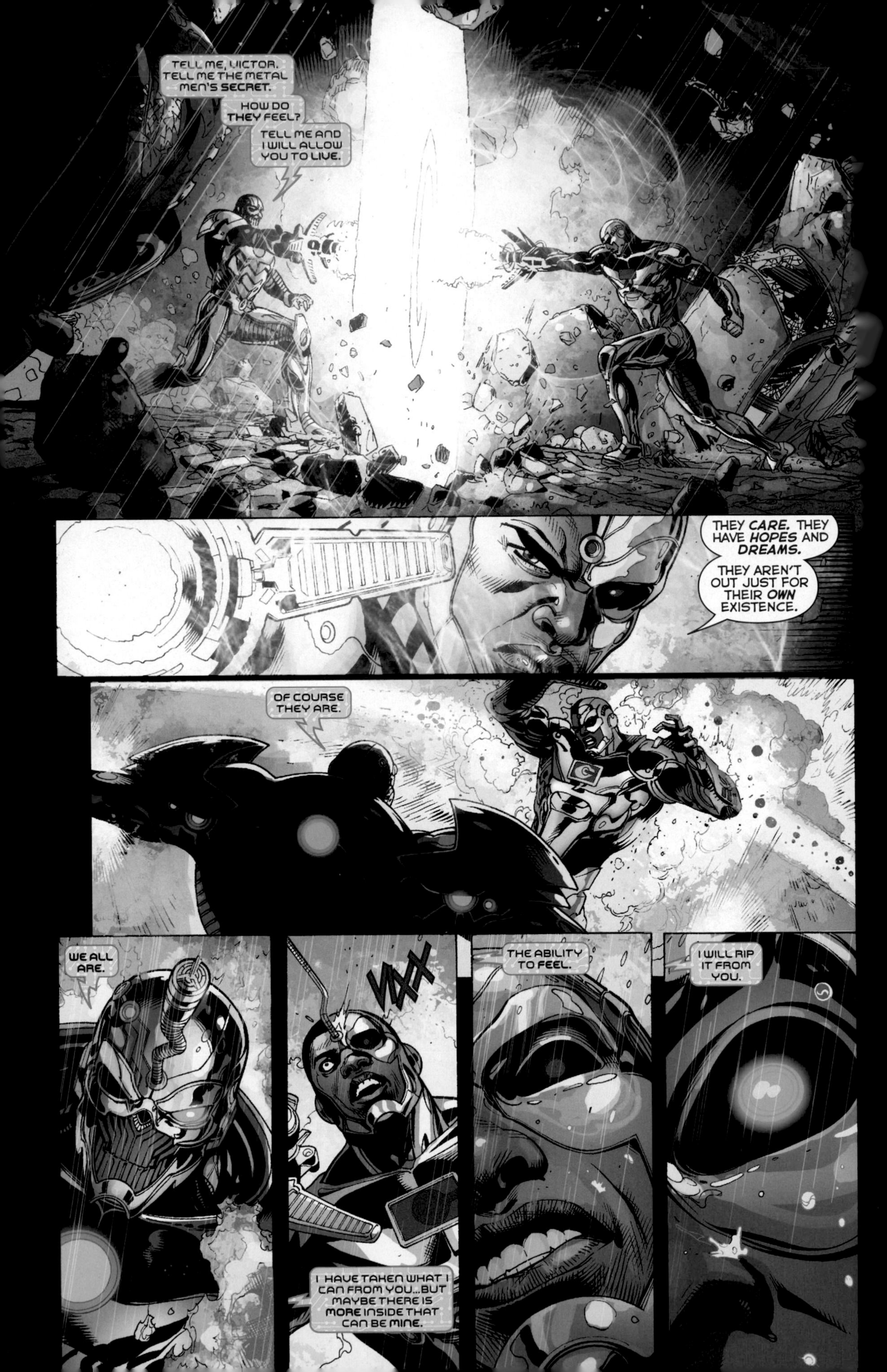
TELL ME, VICTOR. TELL ME THE METAL MEN'S SECRET.
HOW DO THEY FEEL?
TELL ME AND I WILL ALLOW YOU TO LIVE.
THEY CARE. THEY HAVE HOPES AND DREAMS.
THEY AREN'T OUT JUST FOR THEIR OWN EXISTENCE.
OF COURSE THEY ARE.
WE ALL ARE.
VXX
I HAVE TAKEN WHAT I CAN FROM YOU...BUT MAYBE THERE IS MORE INSIDE THAT CAN BE MINE.
THE ABILITY TO FEEL.
I WILL RIP IT FROM YOU.

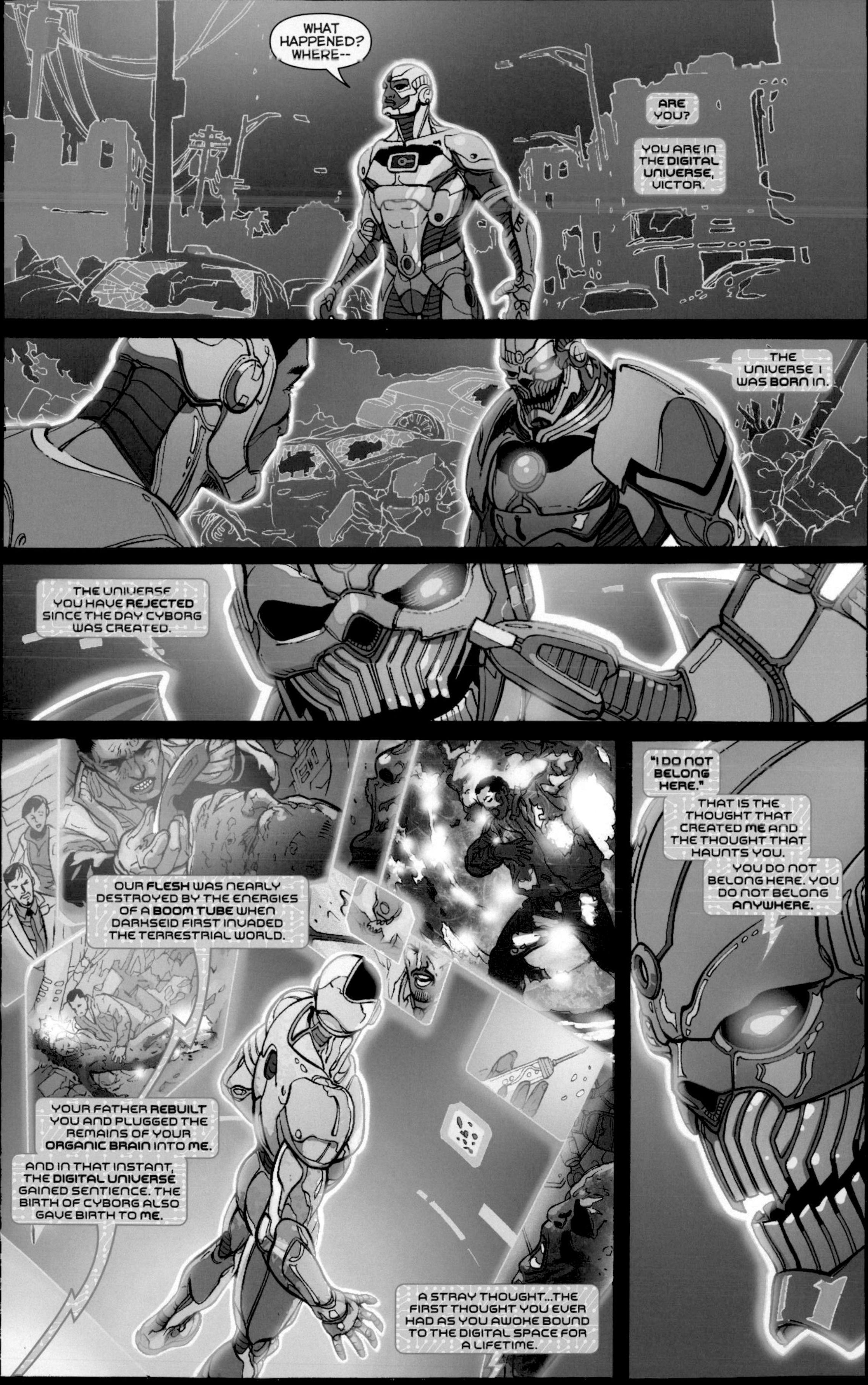
WHAT HAPPENED? WHERE--
ARE YOU?
YOU ARE IN THE DIGITAL UNIVERSE, VICTOR.
THE UNIVERSE I WAS BORN IN.
THE UNIVERSE YOU HAVE REJECTED SINCE THE DAY CYBORG WAS CREATED.
OUR FLESH WAS NEARLY DESTROYED BY THE ENERGIES OF A BOOM TUBE WHEN DARKSEID FIRST INVADED THE TERRESTRIAL WORLD.
YOUR FATHER REBUILT YOU AND PLUGGED THE REMAINS OF YOUR ORGANIC BRAIN INTO ME.
AND IN THAT INSTANT, THE DIGITAL UNIVERSE GAINED SENTIENCE. THE BIRTH OF CYBORG ALSO GAVE BIRTH TO ME.
A STRAY THOUGHT...THE FIRST THOUGHT YOU EVER HAD AS YOU AWOKE BOUND TO THE DIGITAL SPACE FOR A LIFETIME.
"I DO NOT BELONG HERE."
THAT IS THE THOUGHT THAT CREATED ME AND THE THOUGHT THAT HAUNTS YOU.
YOU DO NOT BELONG HERE. YOU DO NOT BELONG ANYWHERE.

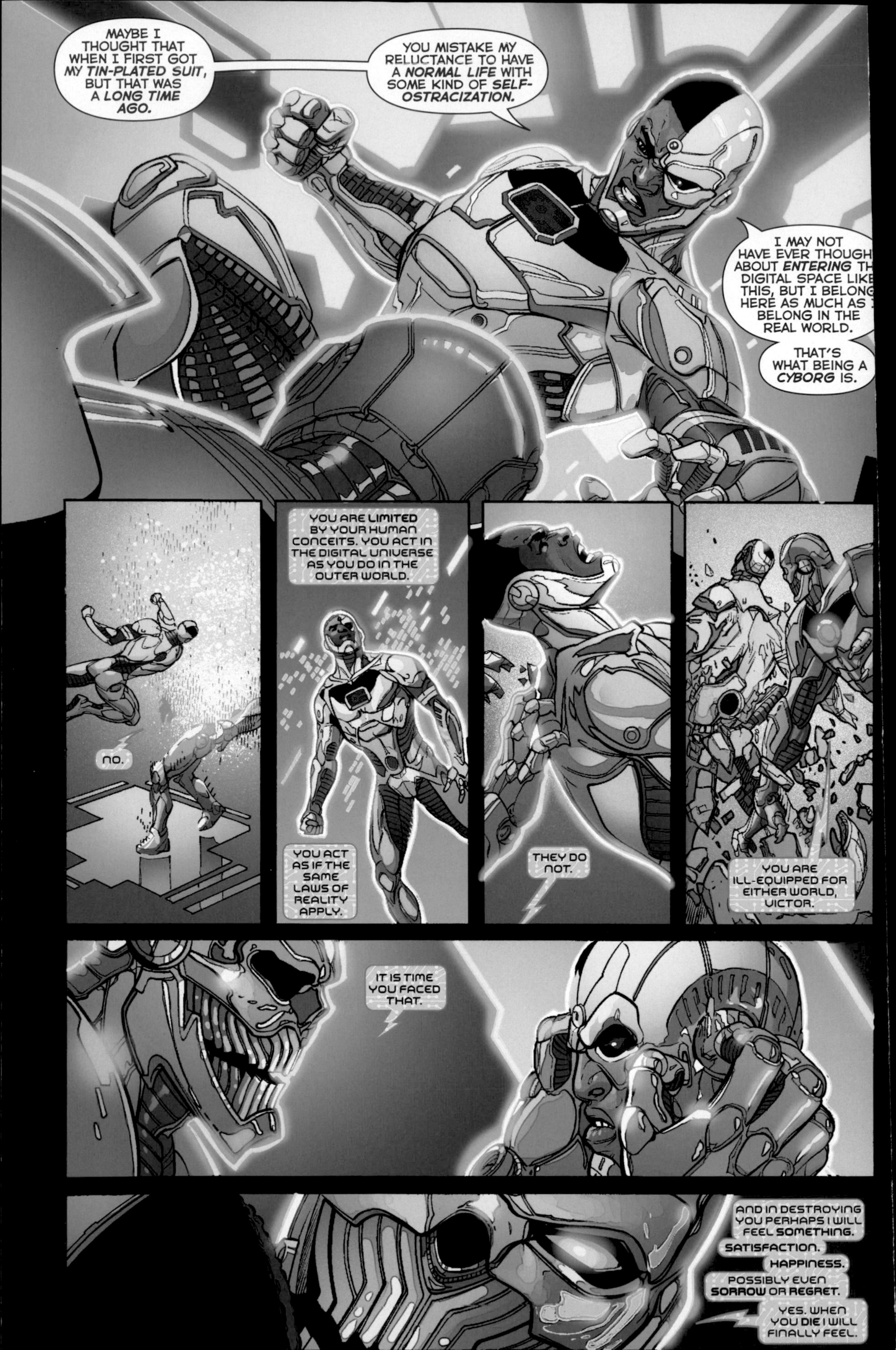

MAYBE I THOUGHT THAT WHEN I FIRST GOT MY TIN-PLATED SUIT, BUT THAT WAS A LONG TIME AGO.
YOU MISTAKE MY RELUCTANCE TO HAVE A NORMAL LIFE WITH SOME KIND OF SELF-OSTRACIZATION.
I MAY NOT HAVE EVER THOUGH ABOUT ENTERING TH DIGITAL SPACE LIKE THIS, BUT I BELONG HERE AS MUCH AS I BELONG IN THE REAL WORLD.
THAT'S WHAT BEING A CYBORG IS.
NO.
YOU ARE LIMITED BY YOUR HUMAN CONCEITS. YOU ACT IN THE DIGITAL UNIVERSE AS YOU DO IN THE OUTER WORLD.
YOU ACT AS IF THE SAME LAWS OF REALITY APPLY.
THEY DO NOT.
YOU ARE ILL-EQUIPPED FOR EITHER WORLD, VICTOR.
IT IS TIME YOU FACED THAT.
AND IN DESTROYING YOU PERHAPS I WILL FEEL SOMETHING.
SATISFACTION.
HAPPINESS.
POSSIBLY EVEN SORROW OR REGRET.
YES. WHEN YOU DIE I WILL FINALLY FEEL.

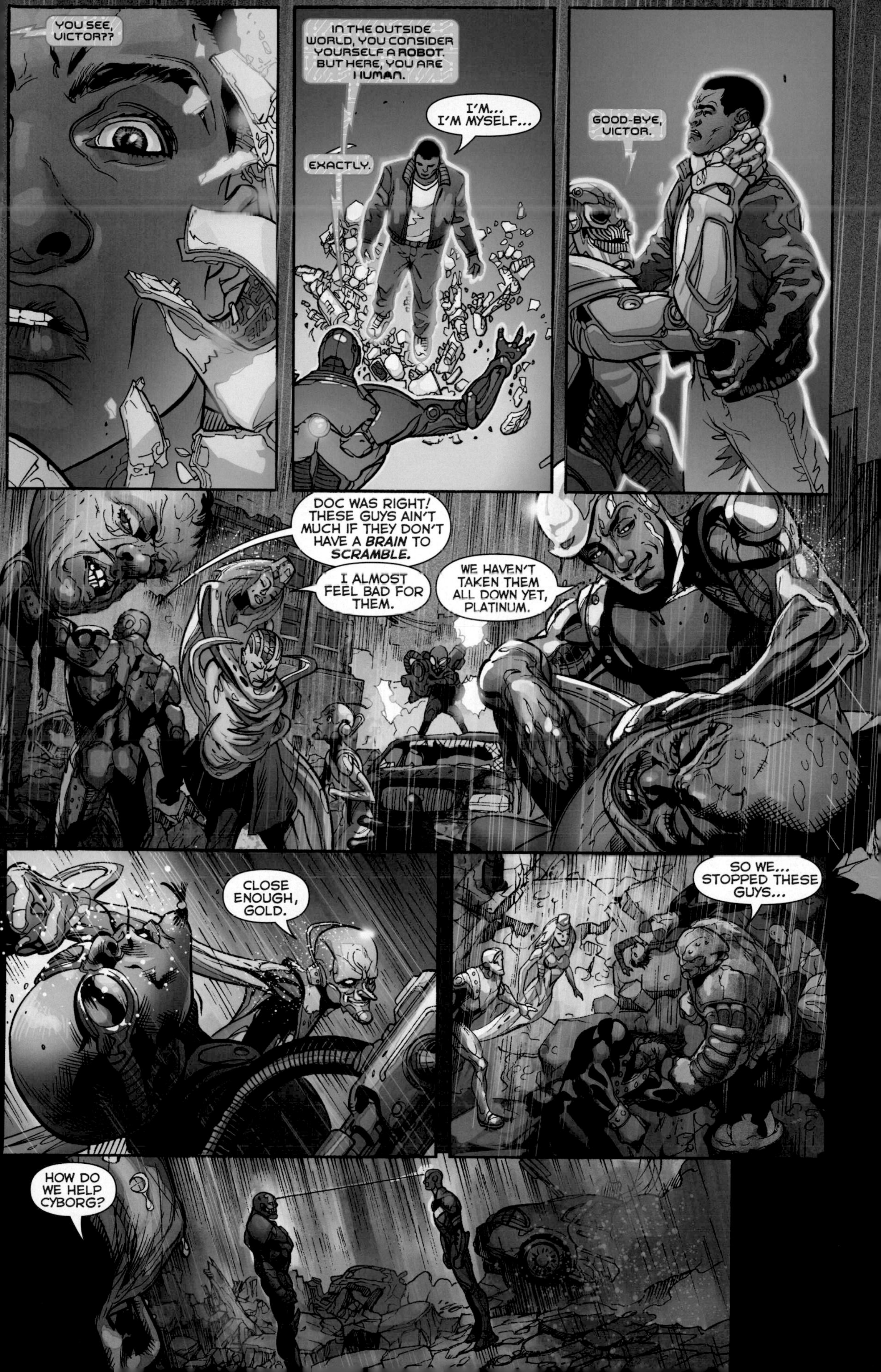
YOU SEE, VICTOR??
IN THE OUTSIDE WORLD, YOU CONSIDER YOURSELF A ROBOT. BUT HERE, YOU ARE HUMAN.
I'M... I'M MYSELF...
EXACTLY.
GOOD-BYE, VICTOR.
DOC WAS RIGHT! THESE GUYS AIN'T MUCH IF THEY DON'T HAVE A BRAIN TO SCRAMBLE.
I ALMOST FEEL BAD FOR THEM.
WE HAVEN'T TAKEN THEM ALL DOWN YET, PLATINUM.
CLOSE ENOUGH, GOLD.
SO WE... STOPPED THESE GUYS...
HOW DO WE HELP CYBORG?

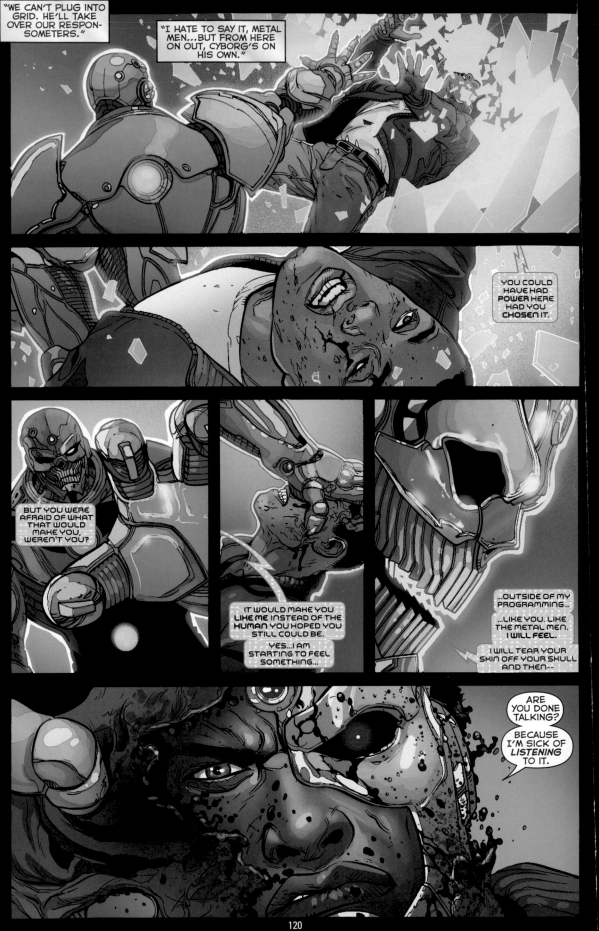

"WE CAN'T PLUG INTO GRID. HE'LL TAKE OVER OUR RESPONSOMETERS."

"I HATE TO SAY IT, METAL MEN...BUT FROM HERE ON OUT, CYBORG'S ON HIS OWN."

YOU COULD HAVE HAD POWER HERE HAD YOU CHOSEN IT.

BUT YOU WERE AFRAID OF WHAT THAT WOULD MAKE YOU, WEREN'T YOU?

IT WOULD MAKE YOU LIKE ME INSTEAD OF THE HUMAN YOU HOPED YOU STILL COULD BE.

YES...I AM STARTING TO FEEL SOMETHING...

...OUTSIDE OF MY PROGRAMMING...

...LIKE YOU. LIKE THE METAL MEN. I WILL FEEL.

I WILL TEAR YOUR SKIN OFF YOUR SKULL AND THEN--

ARE YOU DONE TALKING?

BECAUSE I'M SICK OF *LISTENING* TO IT.

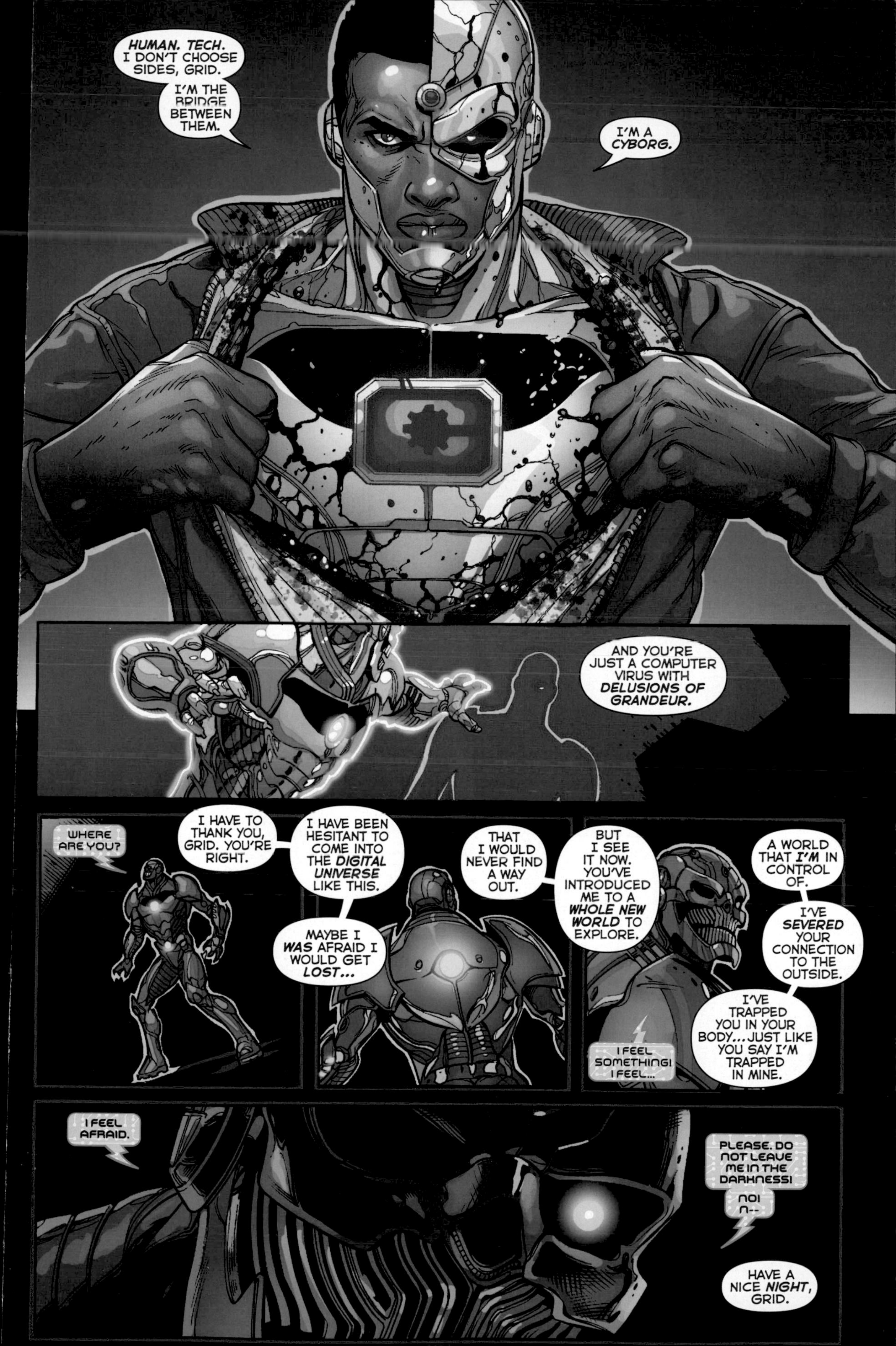
HUMAN. TECH. I DON'T CHOOSE SIDES, GRID.
I'M THE BRIDGE BETWEEN THEM.
I'M A CYBORG.
AND YOU'RE JUST A COMPUTER VIRUS WITH DELUSIONS OF GRANDEUR.
WHERE ARE YOU?
I HAVE TO THANK YOU, GRID. YOU'RE RIGHT.
I HAVE BEEN HESITANT TO COME INTO THE DIGITAL UNIVERSE LIKE THIS.
MAYBE I WAS AFRAID I WOULD GET LOST...
THAT I WOULD NEVER FIND A WAY OUT.
BUT I SEE IT NOW. YOU'VE INTRODUCED ME TO A WHOLE NEW WORLD TO EXPLORE.
A WORLD THAT I'M IN CONTROL OF.
I'VE SEVERED YOUR CONNECTION TO THE OUTSIDE.
I'VE TRAPPED YOU IN YOUR BODY... JUST LIKE YOU SAY I'M TRAPPED IN MINE.
I FEEL SOMETHING! I FEEL...
I FEEL AFRAID.
PLEASE. DO NOT LEAVE ME IN THE DARKNESS!
NO! N--
HAVE A NICE NIGHT, GRID.

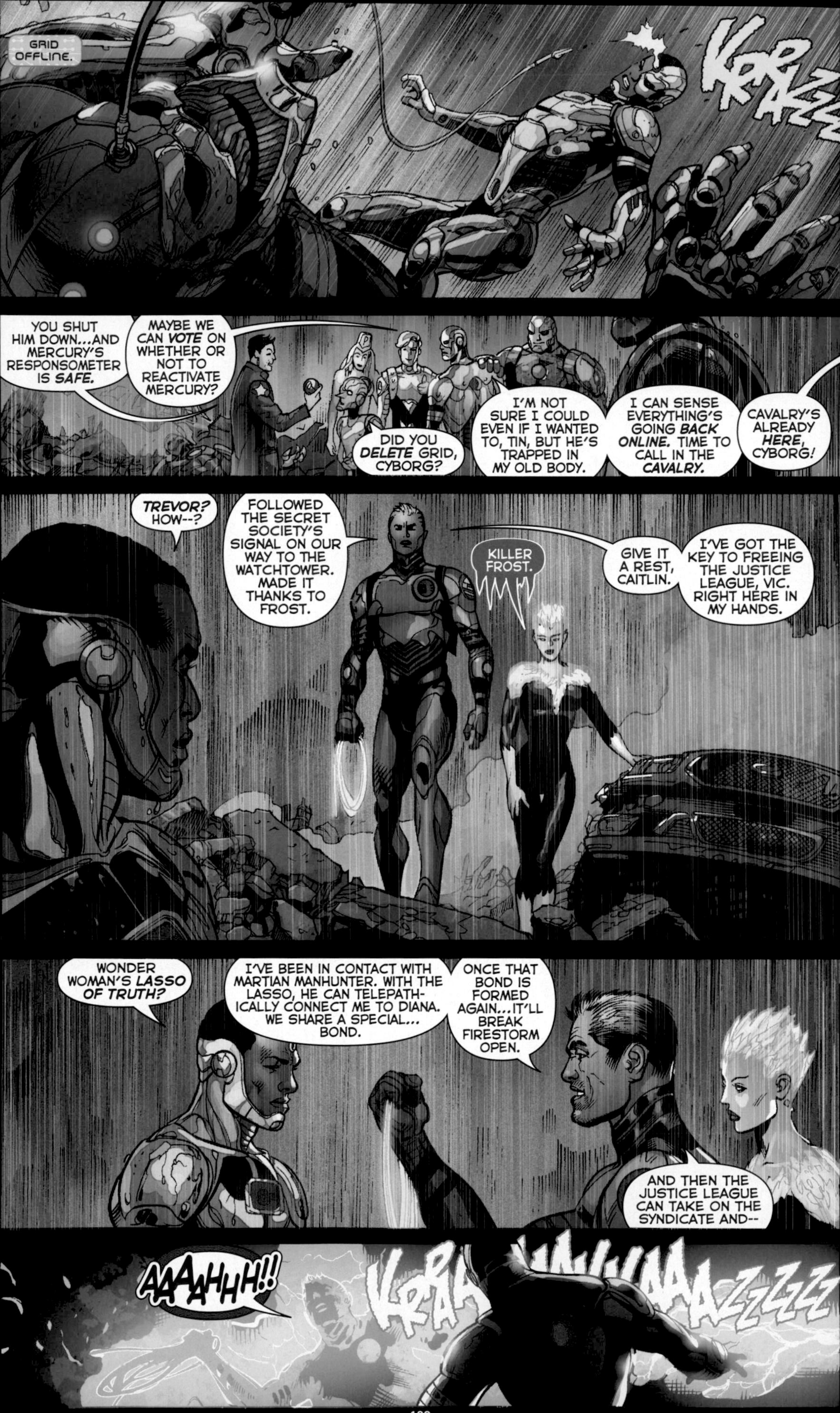
GRID OFFLINE.
KRRAZZZ
YOU SHUT HIM DOWN...AND MERCURY'S RESPONSOMETER IS SAFE.
MAYBE WE CAN VOTE ON WHETHER OR NOT TO REACTIVATE MERCURY?
DID YOU DELETE GRID, CYBORG?
I'M NOT SURE I COULD EVEN IF I WANTED TO, TIN, BUT HE'S TRAPPED IN MY OLD BODY.
I CAN SENSE EVERYTHING'S GOING BACK ONLINE. TIME TO CALL IN THE CAVALRY.
CAVALRY'S ALREADY HERE, CYBORG!
TREVOR? HOW--?
FOLLOWED THE SECRET SOCIETY'S SIGNAL ON OUR WAY TO THE WATCHTOWER. MADE IT THANKS TO FROST.
KILLER FROST.
GIVE IT A REST, CAITLIN.
I'VE GOT THE KEY TO FREEING THE JUSTICE LEAGUE, VIC. RIGHT HERE IN MY HANDS.
WONDER WOMAN'S LASSO OF TRUTH?
I'VE BEEN IN CONTACT WITH MARTIAN MANHUNTER. WITH THE LASSO, HE CAN TELEPATH-ICALLY CONNECT ME TO DIANA. WE SHARE A SPECIAL... BOND.
ONCE THAT BOND IS FORMED AGAIN...IT'LL BREAK FIRESTORM OPEN.
AND THEN THE JUSTICE LEAGUE CAN TAKE ON THE SYNDICATE AND--
AAAAHHH!!
KRAAWWWAAAZZZZZ

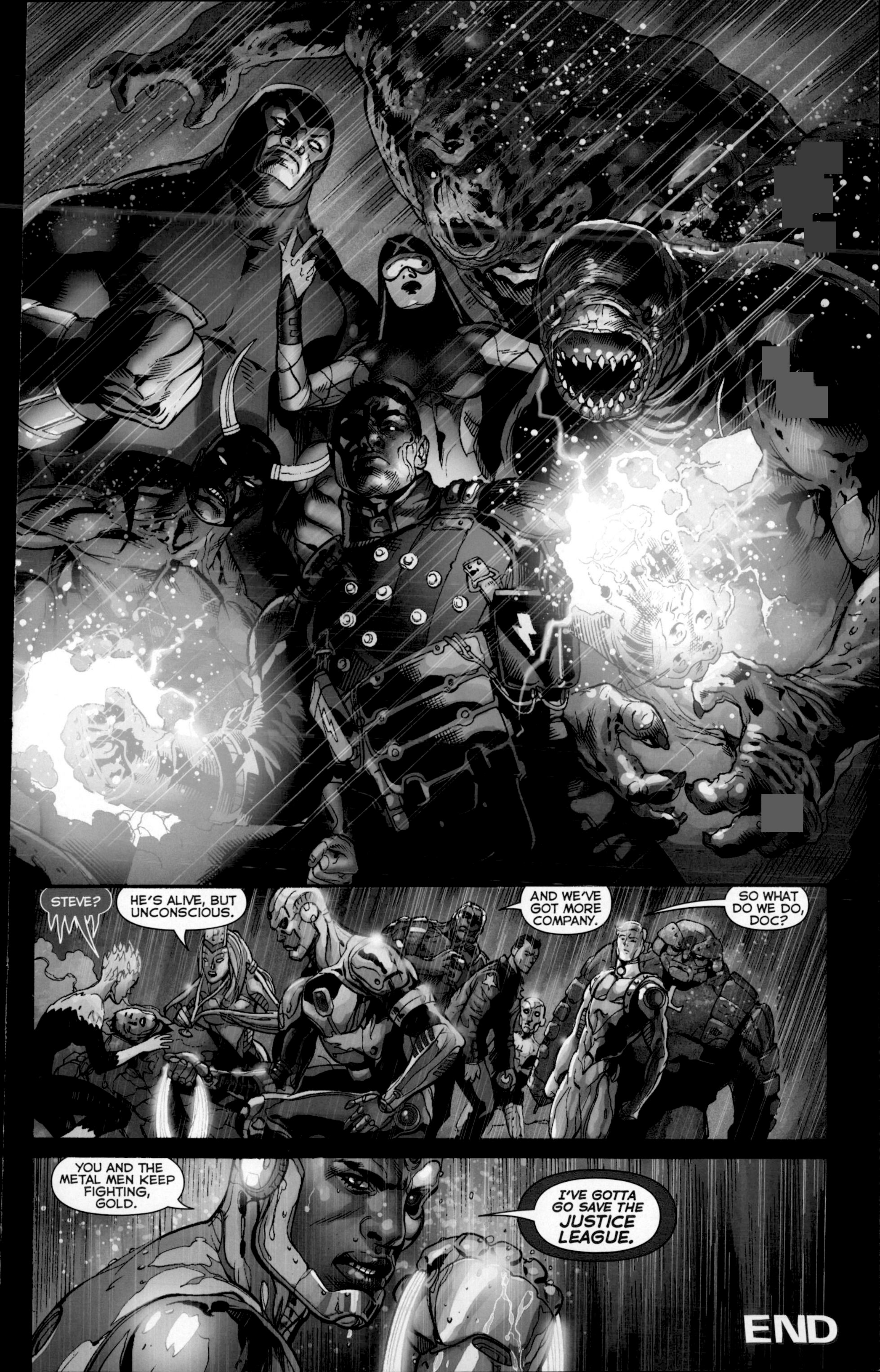
STEVE?
HE'S ALIVE, BUT UNCONSCIOUS.
AND WE'VE GOT MORE COMPANY.
SO WHAT DO WE DO, DOC?
YOU AND THE METAL MEN KEEP FIGHTING, GOLD.
I'VE GOTTA GO SAVE THE JUSTICE LEAGUE.
END

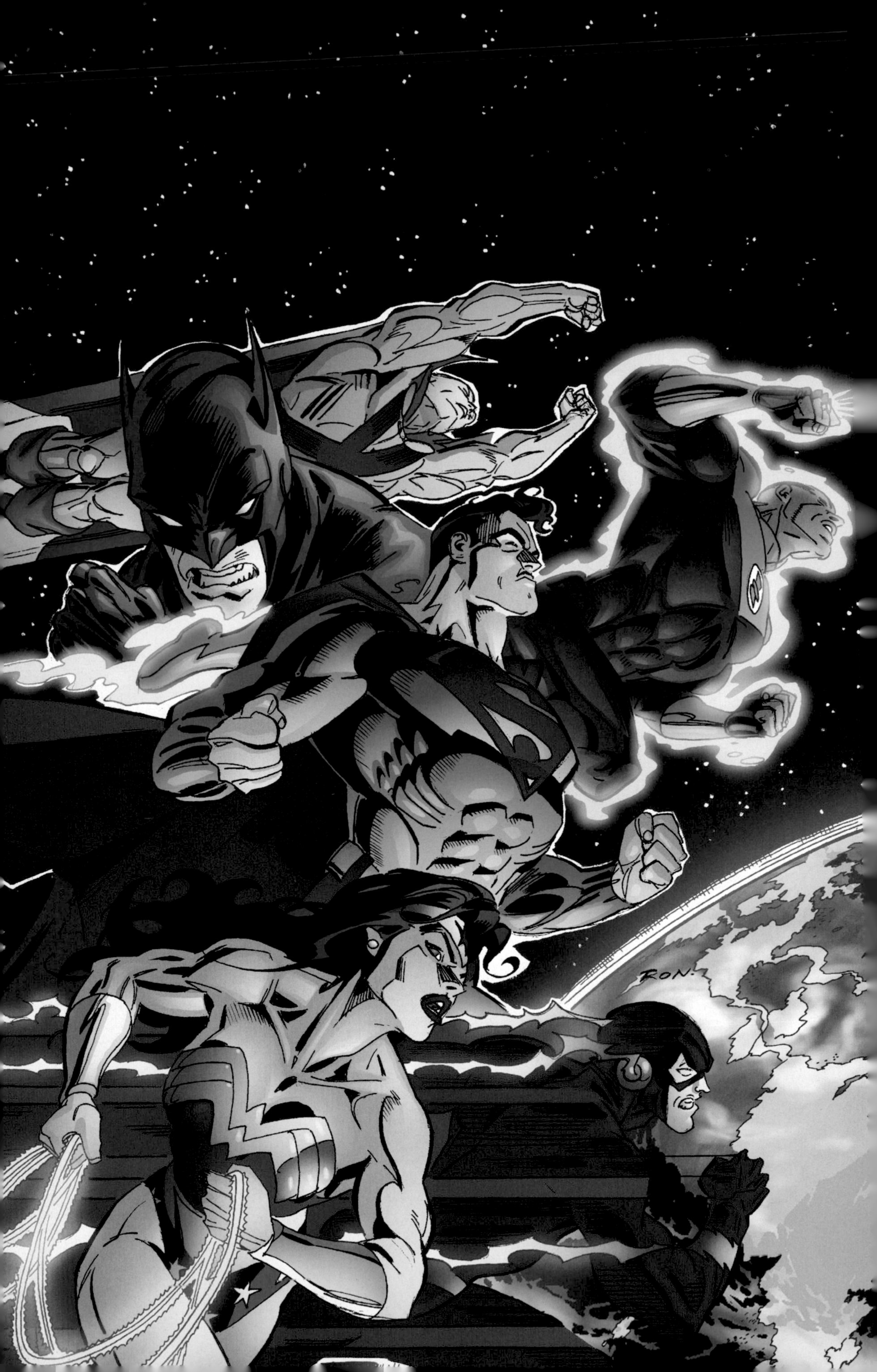
RON.

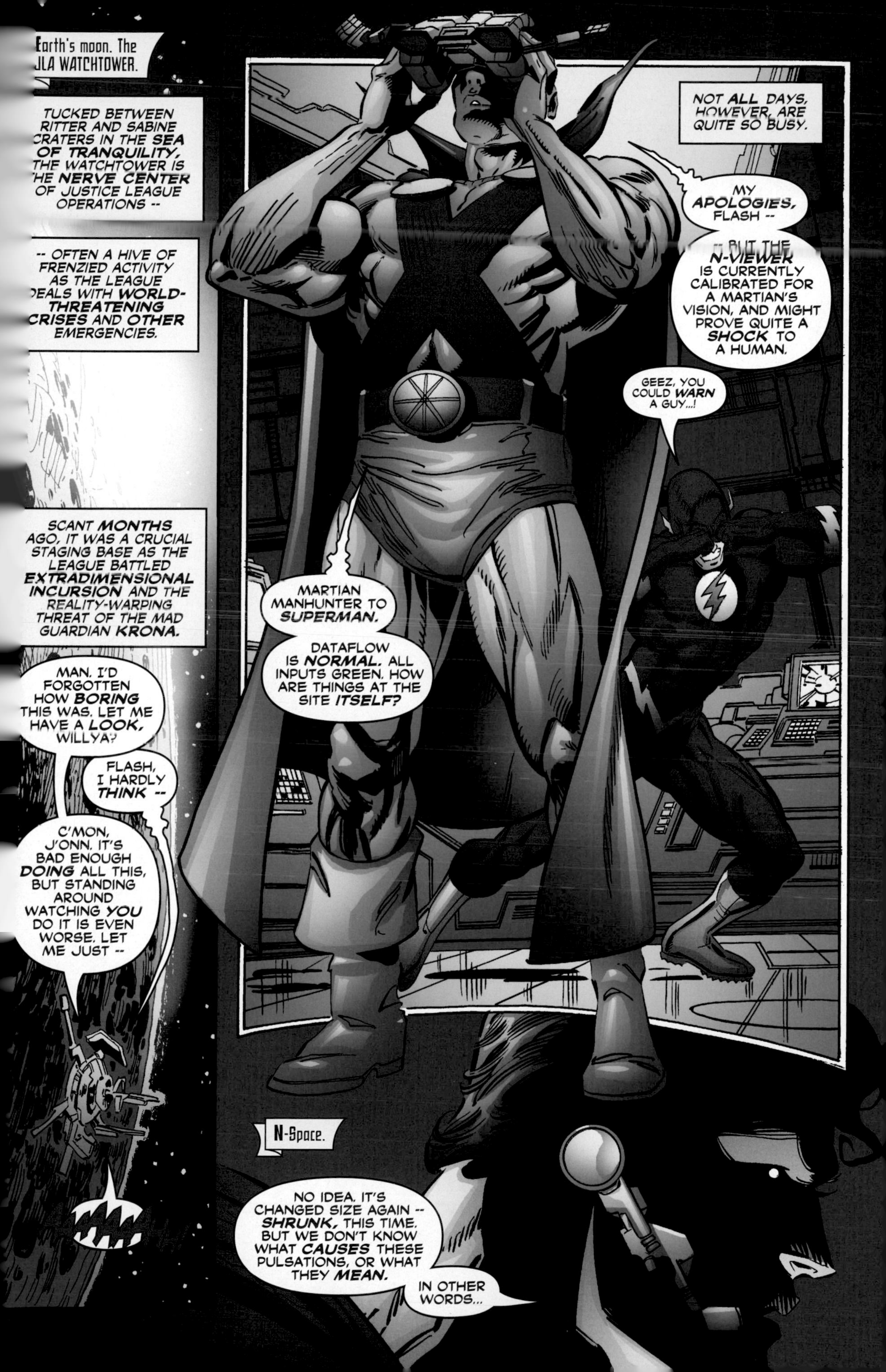

Earth's moon. The JLA WATCHTOWER.
TUCKED BETWEEN RITTER AND SABINE CRATERS IN THE SEA OF TRANQUILITY, THE WATCHTOWER IS THE NERVE CENTER OF JUSTICE LEAGUE OPERATIONS --
-- OFTEN A HIVE OF FRENZIED ACTIVITY AS THE LEAGUE DEALS WITH WORLD-THREATENING CRISES AND OTHER EMERGENCIES.
NOT ALL DAYS, HOWEVER, ARE QUITE SO BUSY.
SCANT MONTHS AGO, IT WAS A CRUCIAL STAGING BASE AS THE LEAGUE BATTLED EXTRADIMENSIONAL INCURSION AND THE REALITY-WARPING THREAT OF THE MAD GUARDIAN KRONA.
MARTIAN MANHUNTER TO SUPERMAN.
DATAFLOW IS NORMAL. ALL INPUTS GREEN. HOW ARE THINGS AT THE SITE ITSELF?
MAN. I'D FORGOTTEN HOW BORING THIS WAS. LET ME HAVE A LOOK, WILLYA?
FLASH, I HARDLY THINK --
C'MON, J'ONN. IT'S BAD ENOUGH DOING ALL THIS, BUT STANDING AROUND WATCHING YOU DO IT IS EVEN WORSE. LET ME JUST --
MY APOLOGIES, FLASH --
-- BUT THE N-VIEWER IS CURRENTLY CALIBRATED FOR A MARTIAN'S VISION, AND MIGHT PROVE QUITE A SHOCK TO A HUMAN.
GEEZ, YOU COULD WARN A GUY...!
N-Space.
NO IDEA. IT'S CHANGED SIZE AGAIN -- SHRUNK, THIS TIME. BUT WE DON'T KNOW WHAT CAUSES THESE PULSATIONS, OR WHAT THEY MEAN.
IN OTHER WORDS...

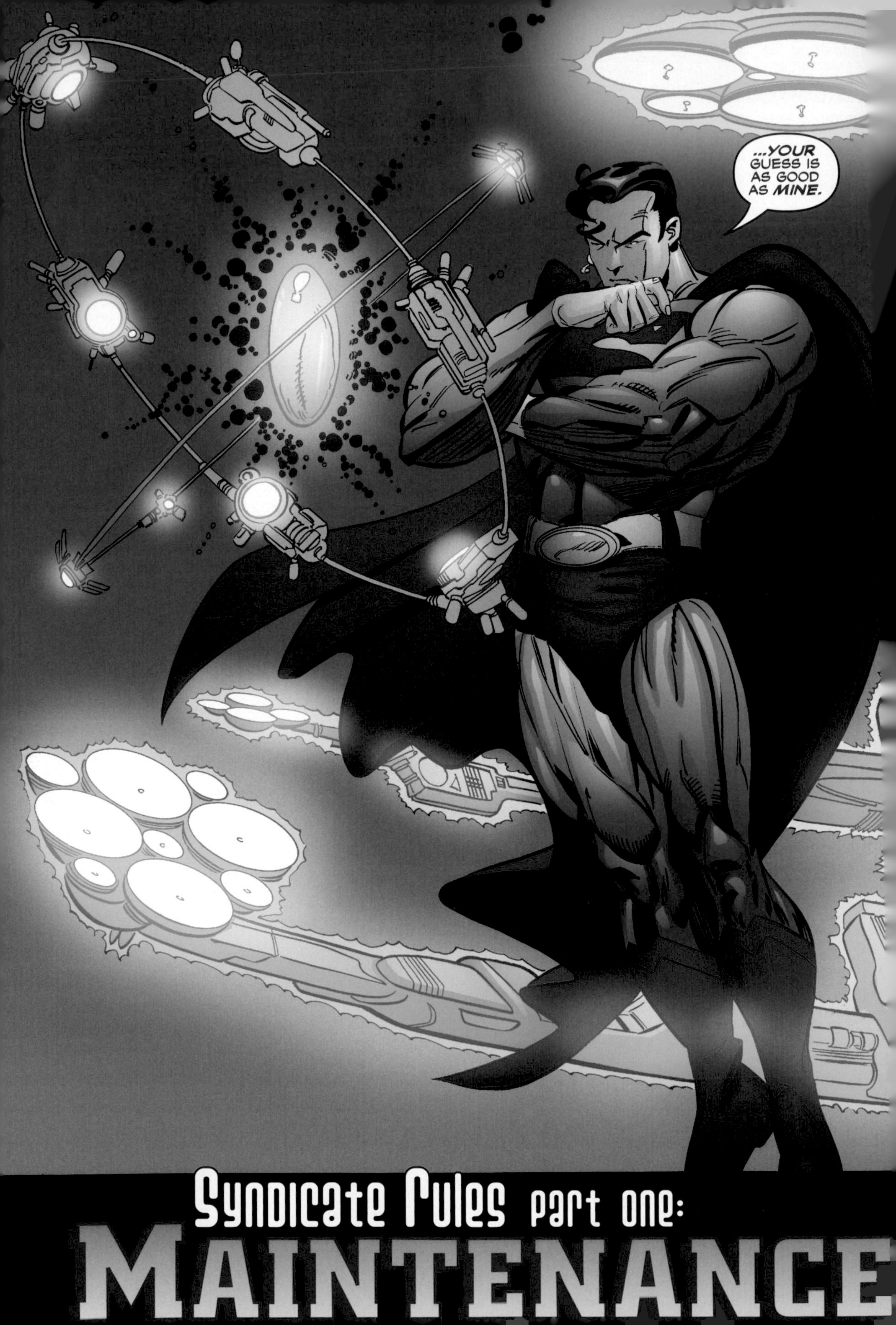
...YOUR GUESS IS AS GOOD AS MINE.
Syndicate Rules part one:
MAINTENANCE

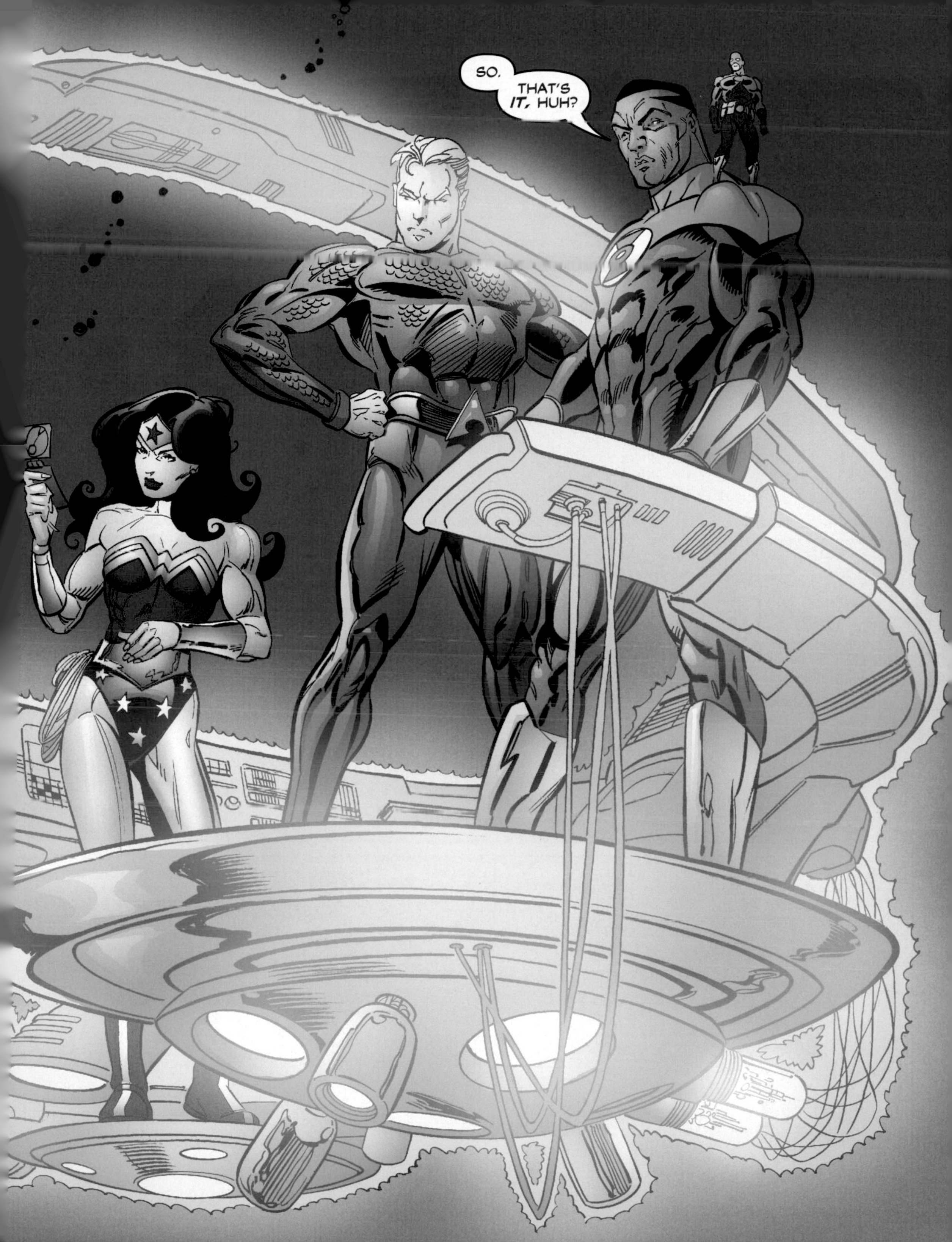
SO, THAT'S *IT,* HUH?

Starting a New Epic by KURT BUSIEK & RON GARNEY

Writer Penciller

DAY

DAN GREEN - Inker DAVID BARON - Colorist JARED K. FLETCHER - Letterer

MICHAEL SIGLAIN - Assistant Editor MIKE CARLIN- Editor

THERE'S ACTUALLY A *UNIVERSE* GESTATING IN THERE? A *BABY UNIVERSE?*

MAYBE. IF SO...

...IT'S A "BABY UNIVERSE" BUILT FROM THE ESSENCE OF ONE OF THE *MOST DANGEROUS* MEN WE'VE EVER *FACED,* GREEN LANTERN.

I DON'T KNOW WHY WE'RE SIMPLY WAITING. IF *KRONA'S* SHAPING IT --

AND WHAT IF *IT'S* SHAPING KRONA? IT'S *NEW LIFE,* ARTHUR. A FRESH START. IT DESERVES A *CHANCE.*

BUT IF IT --

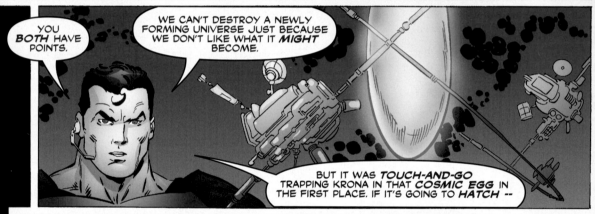

YOU *BOTH* HAVE POINTS.

WE CAN'T DESTROY A NEWLY FORMING UNIVERSE JUST BECAUSE WE DON'T LIKE WHAT IT *MIGHT* BECOME.

BUT IT WAS *TOUCH-AND-GO* TRAPPING KRONA IN THAT *COSMIC EGG* IN THE FIRST PLACE. IF IT'S GOING TO *HATCH* --

-- WELL, I WANT PLENTY OF *WARNING.*

SPEAKING OF WHICH -- I'D LIKE TO GET MORE DETAILED READINGS ON THE *MESO-ENTROPIC SPECTRUM.*

THE DATA COMING IN ARE... *UNUSUAL.* IT MAY BE COMPLETELY *UNRELATED* TO THE EGG, BUT...

NO *PROBLEM,* J'ONN.

SIMPLEST THING IN THE WORLD TO ADJUST THE *COLLECTION MATRIX.*

JUST CHANGE THE *VECTOR* BOUNDARIES, EXPAND THE *ARC* A FEW DEGREES --

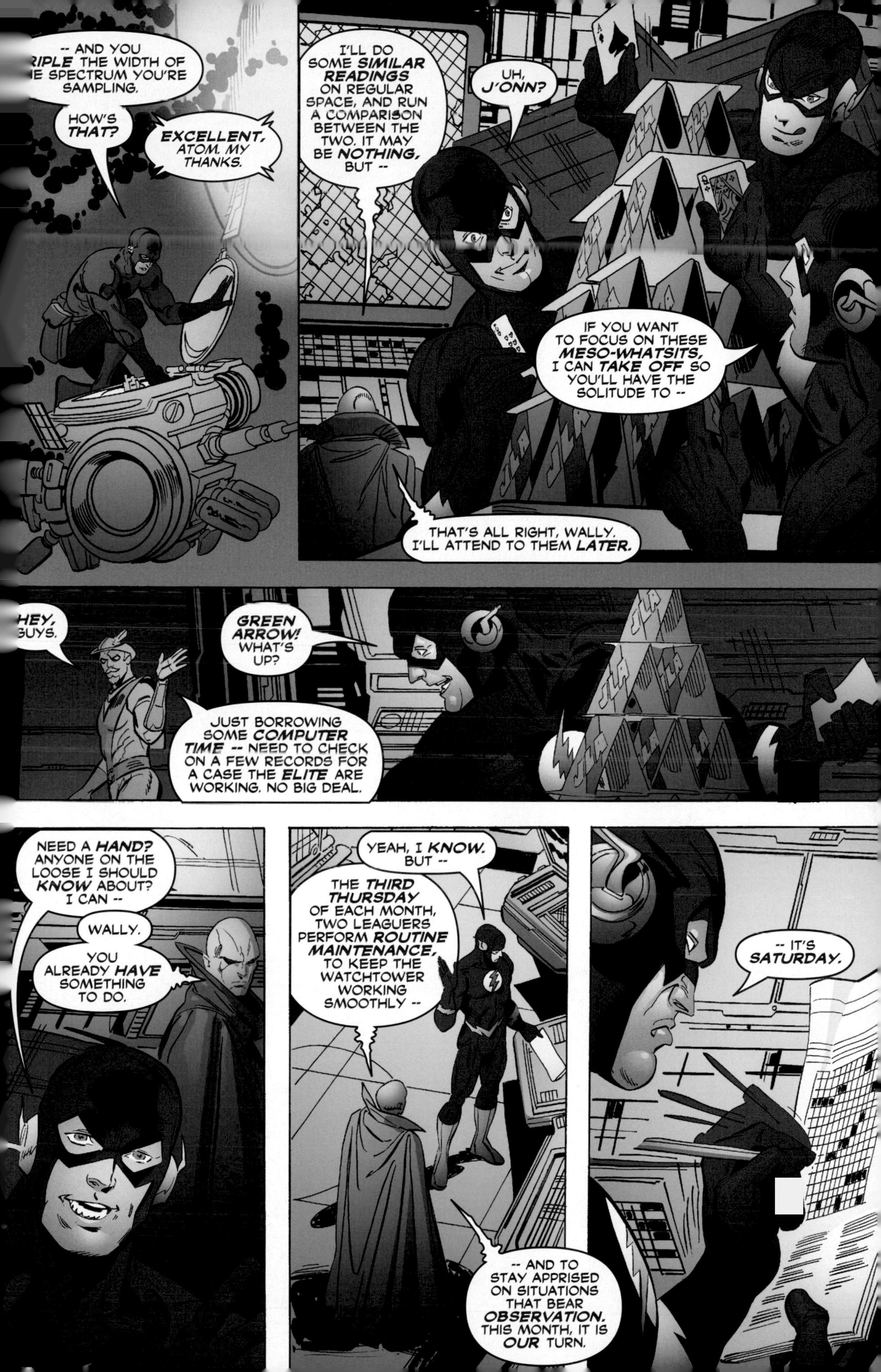
-- AND YOU RIPLE THE WIDTH OF E SPECTRUM YOU'RE SAMPLING.
HOW'S THAT?
EXCELLENT, ATOM. MY THANKS.
I'LL DO SOME SIMILAR READINGS ON REGULAR SPACE, AND RUN A COMPARISON BETWEEN THE TWO. IT MAY BE NOTHING, BUT --
UH, J'ONN?
IF YOU WANT TO FOCUS ON THESE MESO-WHATSITS, I CAN TAKE OFF SO YOU'LL HAVE THE SOLITUDE TO --
THAT'S ALL RIGHT, WALLY. I'LL ATTEND TO THEM LATER.
HEY, GUYS.
GREEN ARROW! WHAT'S UP?
JUST BORROWING SOME COMPUTER TIME -- NEED TO CHECK ON A FEW RECORDS FOR A CASE THE ELITE ARE WORKING. NO BIG DEAL.
NEED A HAND? ANYONE ON THE LOOSE I SHOULD KNOW ABOUT? I CAN --
WALLY.
YOU ALREADY HAVE SOMETHING TO DO.
YEAH, I KNOW. BUT --
THE THIRD THURSDAY OF EACH MONTH, TWO LEAGUERS PERFORM ROUTINE MAINTENANCE, TO KEEP THE WATCHTOWER WORKING SMOOTHLY --
-- AND TO STAY APPRISED ON SITUATIONS THAT BEAR OBSERVATION. THIS MONTH, IT IS OUR TURN.
-- IT'S SATURDAY.

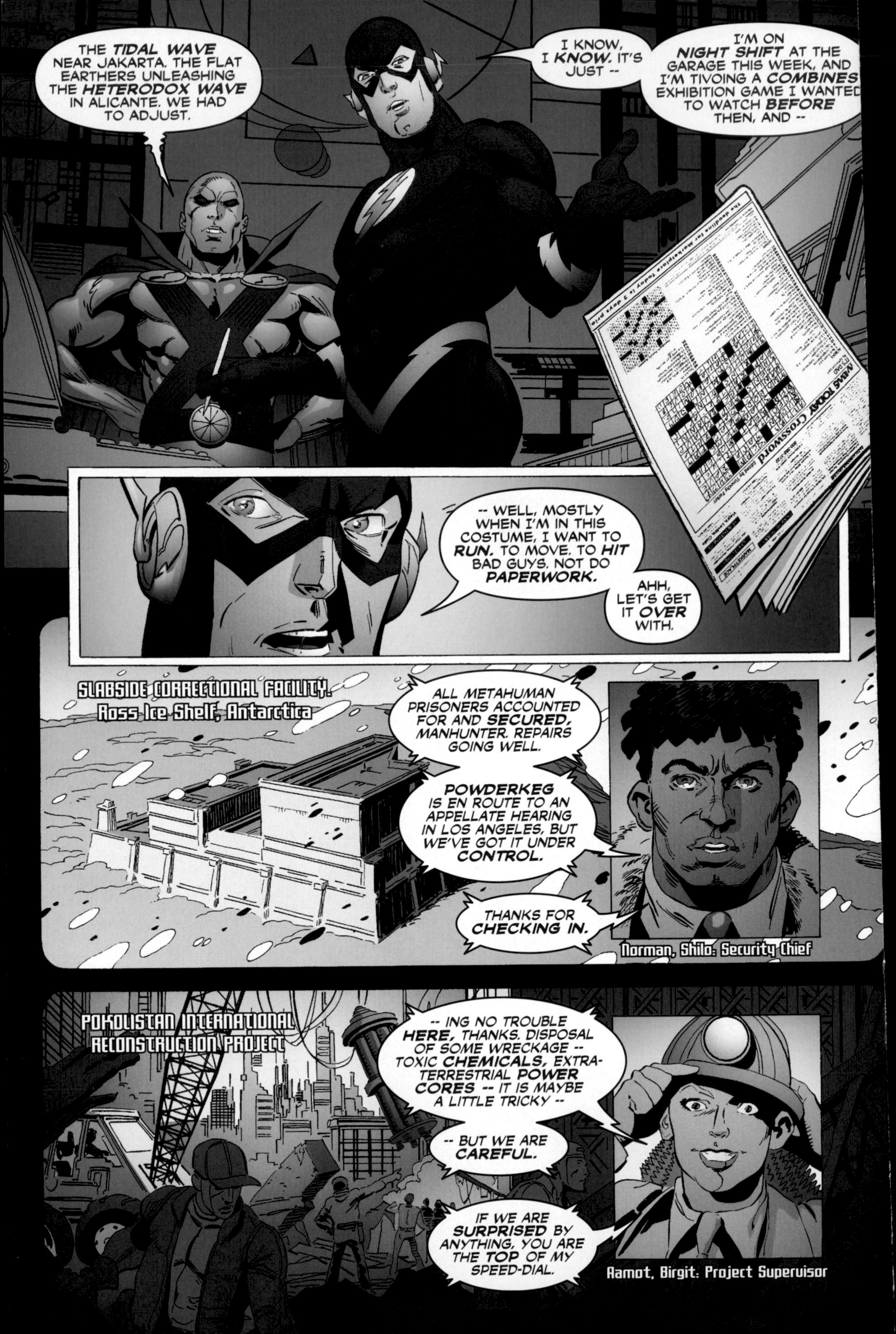

THE TIDAL WAVE NEAR JAKARTA. THE FLAT EARTHERS UNLEASHING THE HETERODOX WAVE IN ALICANTE. WE HAD TO ADJUST.
I KNOW, I KNOW. IT'S JUST --
I'M ON NIGHT SHIFT AT THE GARAGE THIS WEEK, AND I'M TIVOING A COMBINES EXHIBITION GAME I WANTED TO WATCH BEFORE THEN, AND --
NEWS TODAY Crossword
-- WELL, MOSTLY WHEN I'M IN THIS COSTUME, I WANT TO RUN. TO MOVE. TO HIT BAD GUYS. NOT DO PAPERWORK.
AHH, LET'S GET IT OVER WITH.
SLABSIDE CORRECTIONAL FACILITY. Ross Ice Shelf, Antarctica
ALL METAHUMAN PRISONERS ACCOUNTED FOR AND SECURED, MANHUNTER. REPAIRS GOING WELL.
POWDERKEG IS EN ROUTE TO AN APPELLATE HEARING IN LOS ANGELES, BUT WE'VE GOT IT UNDER CONTROL.
THANKS FOR CHECKING IN.
Norman, Shilo: Security Chief
POKOLISTAN INTERNATIONAL RECONSTRUCTION PROJECT
-- ING NO TROUBLE HERE, THANKS. DISPOSAL OF SOME WRECKAGE -- TOXIC CHEMICALS, EXTRA-TERRESTRIAL POWER CORES -- IT IS MAYBE A LITTLE TRICKY --
-- BUT WE ARE CAREFUL.
IF WE ARE SURPRISED BY ANYTHING, YOU ARE THE TOP OF MY SPEED-DIAL.
Aamot, Birgit: Project Supervisor

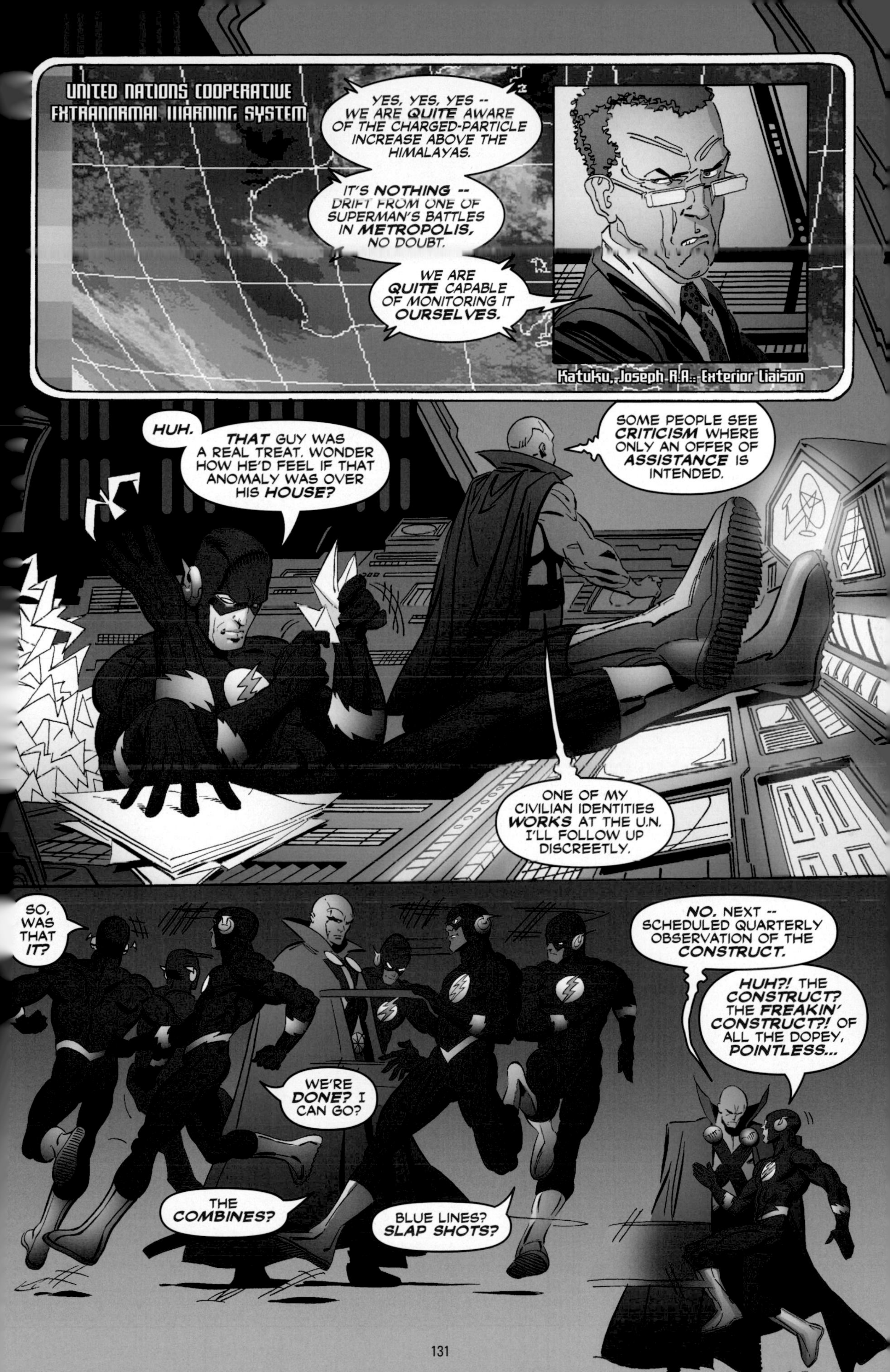
UNITED NATIONS COOPERATIVE
EXTRANORMAL WARNING SYSTEM
YES, YES, YES -- WE ARE QUITE AWARE OF THE CHARGED-PARTICLE INCREASE ABOVE THE HIMALAYAS.
IT'S NOTHING -- DRIFT FROM ONE OF SUPERMAN'S BATTLES IN METROPOLIS, NO DOUBT.
WE ARE QUITE CAPABLE OF MONITORING IT OURSELVES.
Katuku, Joseph A.A.: Exterior Liaison
HUH.
THAT GUY WAS A REAL TREAT. WONDER HOW HE'D FEEL IF THAT ANOMALY WAS OVER HIS HOUSE?
SOME PEOPLE SEE CRITICISM WHERE ONLY AN OFFER OF ASSISTANCE IS INTENDED.
ONE OF MY CIVILIAN IDENTITIES WORKS AT THE U.N. I'LL FOLLOW UP DISCREETLY.
SO, WAS THAT IT?
NO. NEXT -- SCHEDULED QUARTERLY OBSERVATION OF THE CONSTRUCT.
HUH?! THE CONSTRUCT? THE FREAKIN' CONSTRUCT?! OF ALL THE DOPEY, POINTLESS...
WE'RE DONE? I CAN GO?
THE COMBINES?
BLUE LINES? SLAP SHOTS?

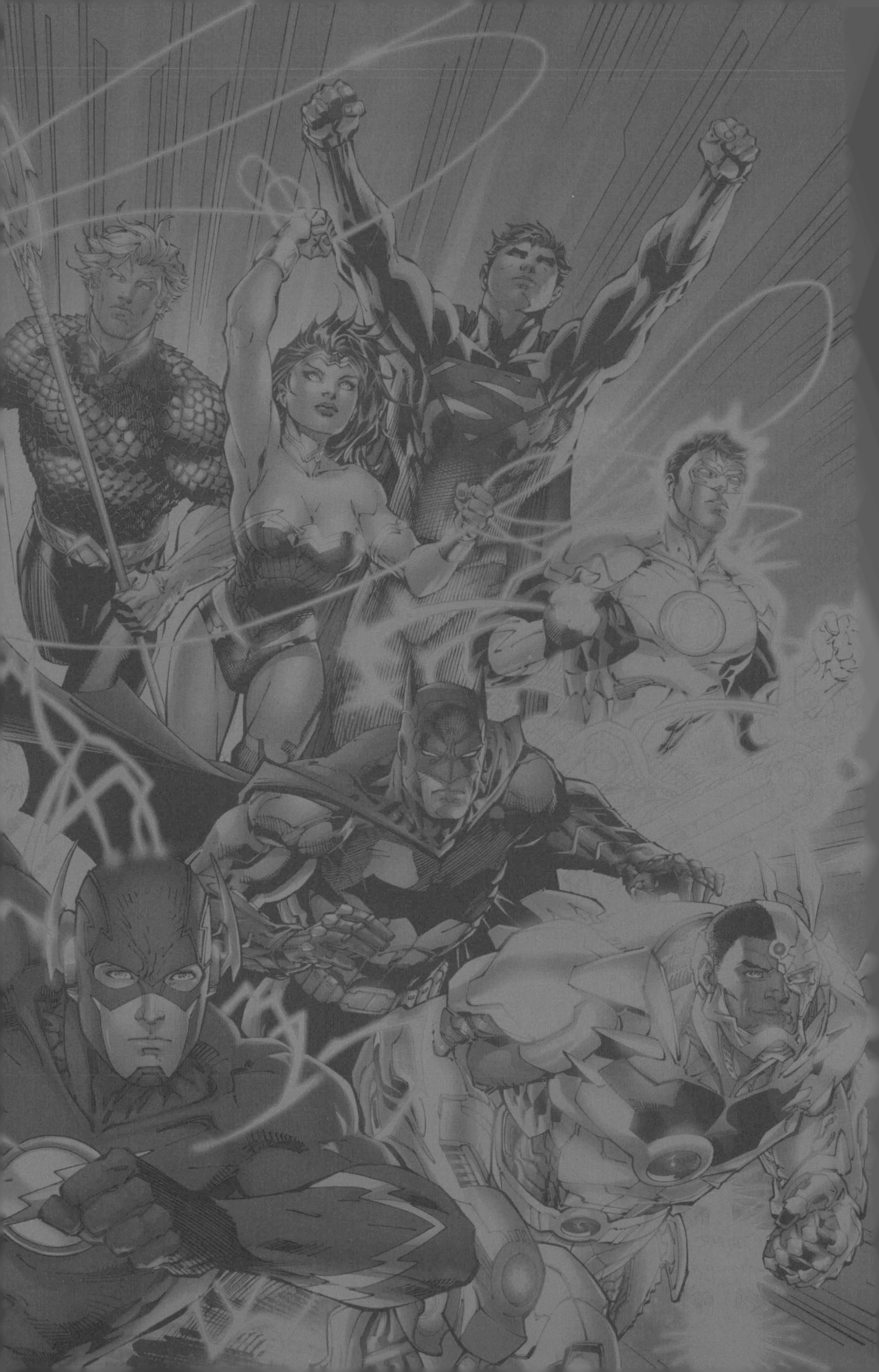

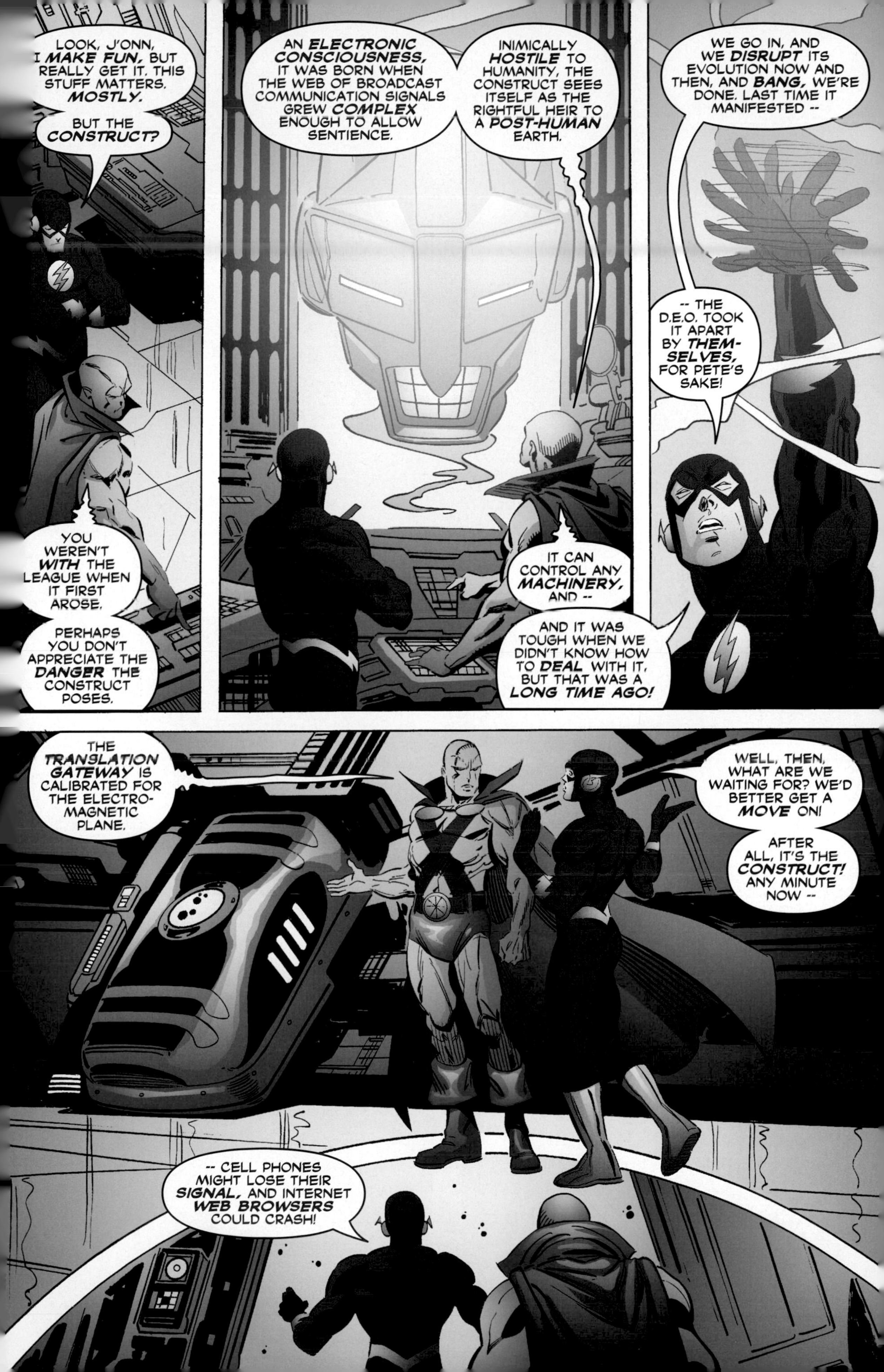
LOOK, J'ONN, I MAKE FUN, BUT REALLY GET IT. THIS STUFF MATTERS. MOSTLY.
BUT THE CONSTRUCT?
YOU WEREN'T WITH THE LEAGUE WHEN IT FIRST AROSE.
PERHAPS YOU DON'T APPRECIATE THE DANGER THE CONSTRUCT POSES.
AN ELECTRONIC CONSCIOUSNESS, IT WAS BORN WHEN THE WEB OF BROADCAST COMMUNICATION SIGNALS GREW COMPLEX ENOUGH TO ALLOW SENTIENCE.
INIMICALLY HOSTILE TO HUMANITY, THE CONSTRUCT SEES ITSELF AS THE RIGHTFUL HEIR TO A POST-HUMAN EARTH.
IT CAN CONTROL ANY MACHINERY, AND --
AND IT WAS TOUGH WHEN WE DIDN'T KNOW HOW TO DEAL WITH IT, BUT THAT WAS A LONG TIME AGO!
WE GO IN, AND WE DISRUPT ITS EVOLUTION NOW AND THEN, AND BANG, WE'RE DONE. LAST TIME IT MANIFESTED --
-- THE D.E.O. TOOK IT APART BY THEM-SELVES, FOR PETE'S SAKE!
THE TRANSLATION GATEWAY IS CALIBRATED FOR THE ELECTRO-MAGNETIC PLANE.
WELL, THEN, WHAT ARE WE WAITING FOR? WE'D BETTER GET A MOVE ON!
AFTER ALL, IT'S THE CONSTRUCT! ANY MINUTE NOW --
-- CELL PHONES MIGHT LOSE THEIR SIGNAL, AND INTERNET WEB BROWSERS COULD CRASH!

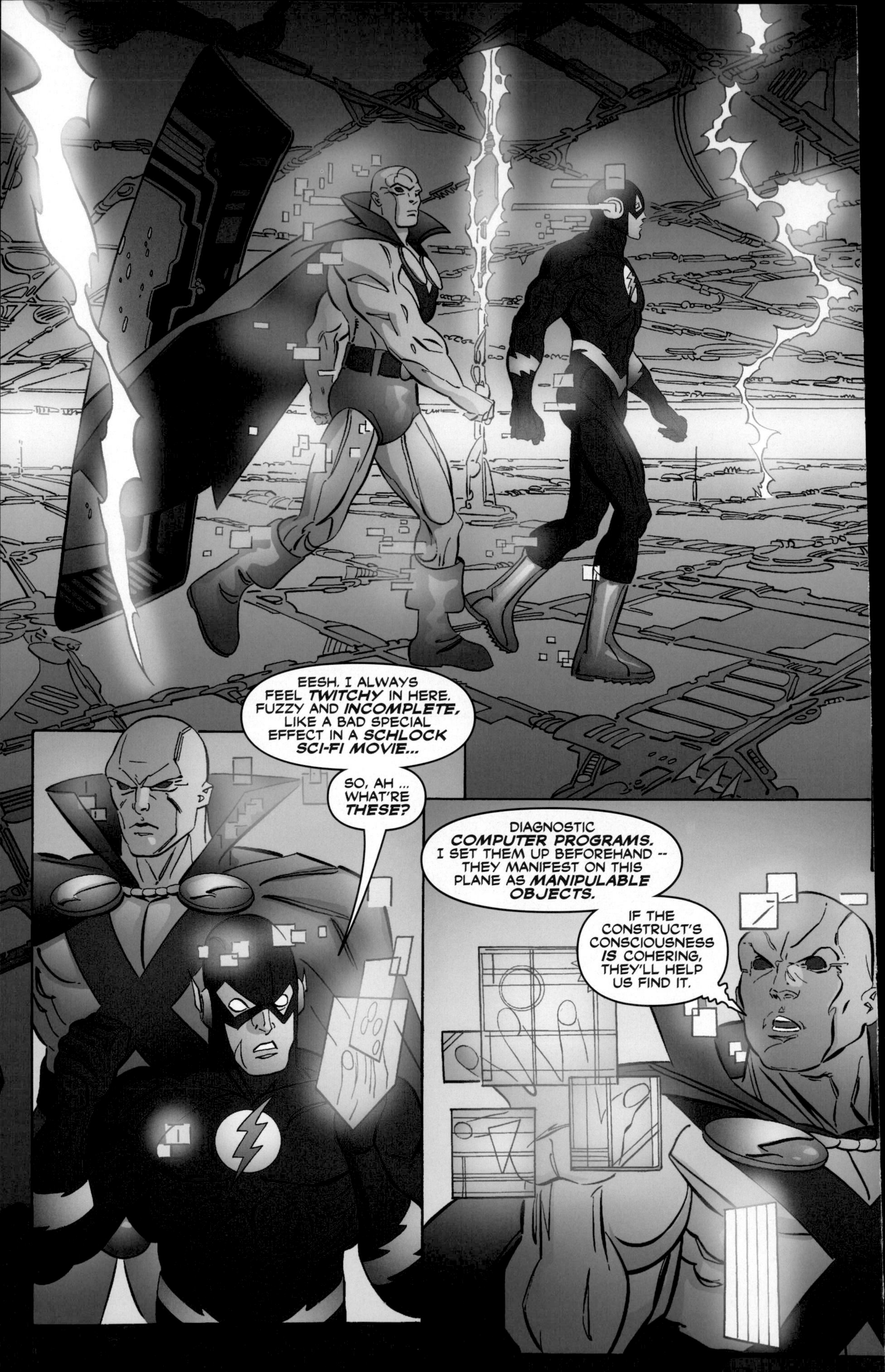
EESH. I ALWAYS FEEL *TWITCHY* IN HERE. FUZZY AND *INCOMPLETE,* LIKE A BAD SPECIAL EFFECT IN A *SCHLOCK SCI-FI MOVIE...*
SO, AH ... WHAT'RE *THESE?*
DIAGNOSTIC *COMPUTER PROGRAMS.* I SET THEM UP BEFOREHAND -- THEY MANIFEST ON THIS PLANE AS *MANIPULABLE OBJECTS.*
IF THE CONSTRUCT'S CONSCIOUSNESS *IS* COHERING, THEY'LL HELP US FIND IT.

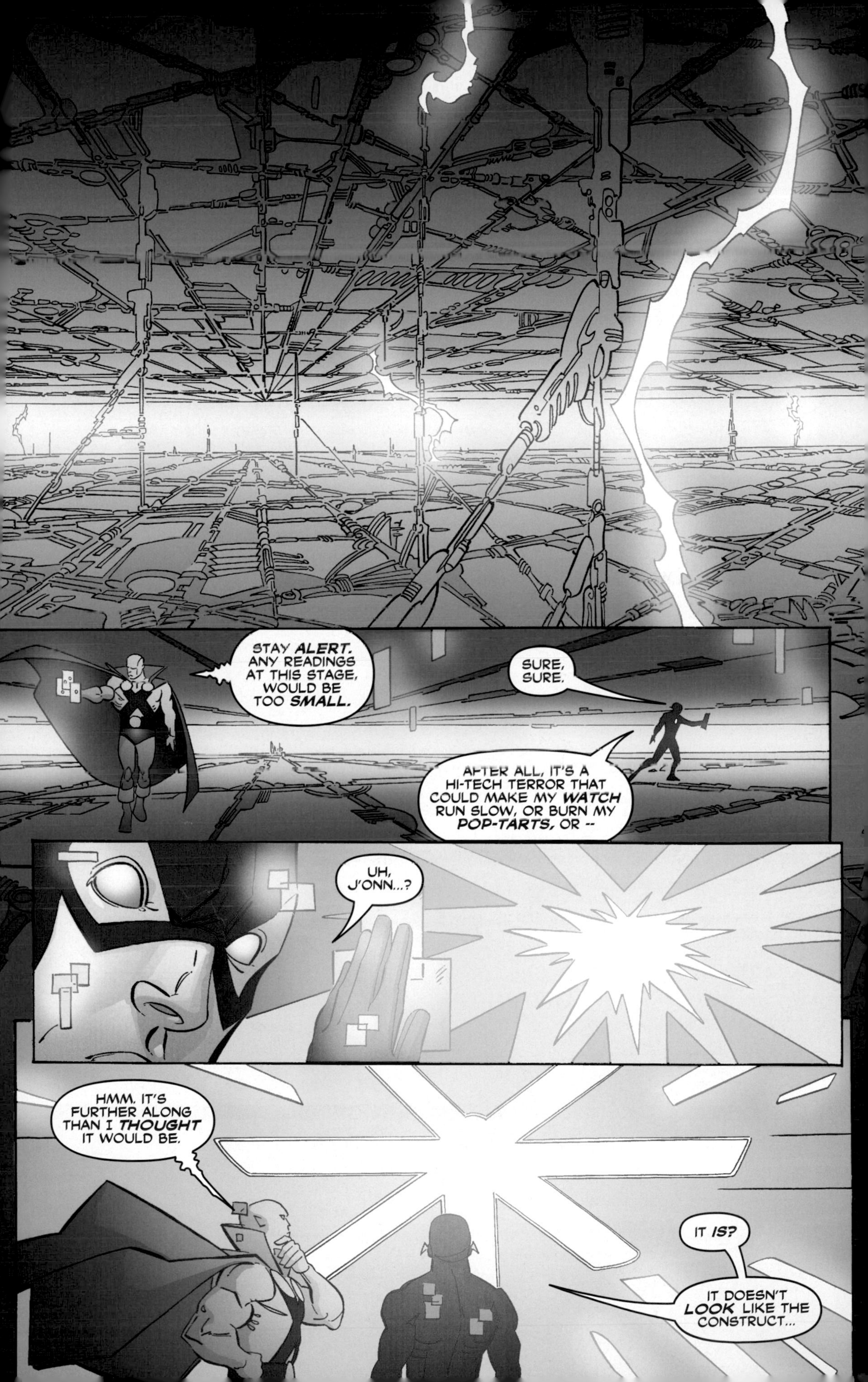
STAY ALERT. ANY READINGS AT THIS STAGE, WOULD BE TOO SMALL.
SURE, SURE.
AFTER ALL, IT'S A HI-TECH TERROR THAT COULD MAKE MY WATCH RUN SLOW, OR BURN MY POP-TARTS, OR --
UH, J'ONN...?
HMM. IT'S FURTHER ALONG THAN I THOUGHT IT WOULD BE.
IT IS?
IT DOESN'T LOOK LIKE THE CONSTRUCT...

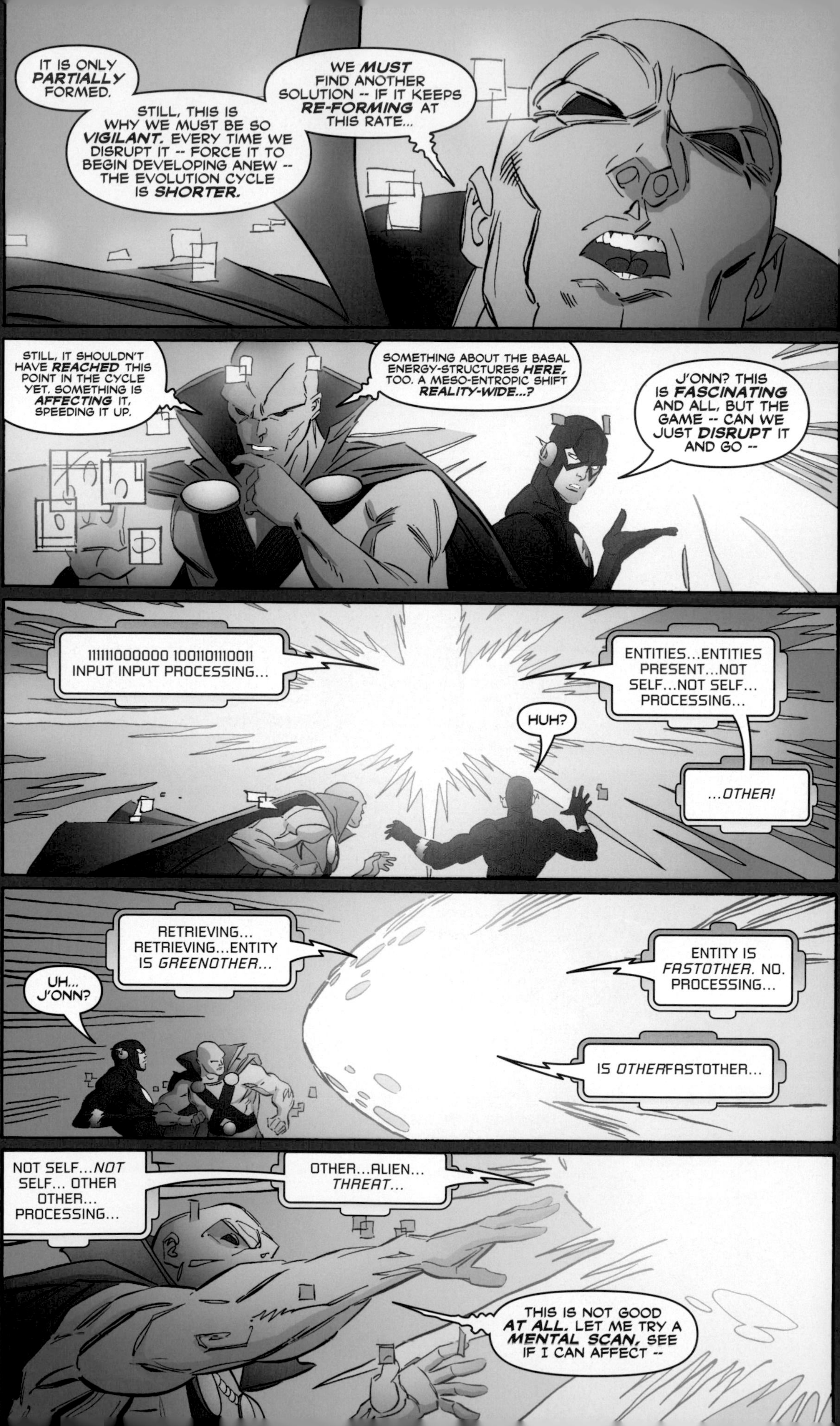
IT IS ONLY PARTIALLY FORMED.
STILL, THIS IS WHY WE MUST BE SO VIGILANT. EVERY TIME WE DISRUPT IT -- FORCE IT TO BEGIN DEVELOPING ANEW -- THE EVOLUTION CYCLE IS SHORTER.
WE MUST FIND ANOTHER SOLUTION -- IF IT KEEPS RE-FORMING AT THIS RATE...
STILL, IT SHOULDN'T HAVE REACHED THIS POINT IN THE CYCLE YET. SOMETHING IS AFFECTING IT, SPEEDING IT UP.
SOMETHING ABOUT THE BASAL ENERGY-STRUCTURES HERE, TOO. A MESO-ENTROPIC SHIFT REALITY-WIDE...?
J'ONN? THIS IS FASCINATING AND ALL, BUT THE GAME -- CAN WE JUST DISRUPT IT AND GO --
111111000000 1001101110011 INPUT INPUT PROCESSING...
ENTITIES...ENTITIES PRESENT...NOT SELF...NOT SELF... PROCESSING...
HUH?
...OTHER!
RETRIEVING... RETRIEVING...ENTITY IS GREENOTHER...
UH... J'ONN?
ENTITY IS FASTOTHER. NO. PROCESSING...
IS OTHERFASTOTHER...
NOT SELF...NOT SELF... OTHER OTHER... PROCESSING...
OTHER...ALIEN... THREAT...
THIS IS NOT GOOD AT ALL. LET ME TRY A MENTAL SCAN, SEE IF I CAN AFFECT --

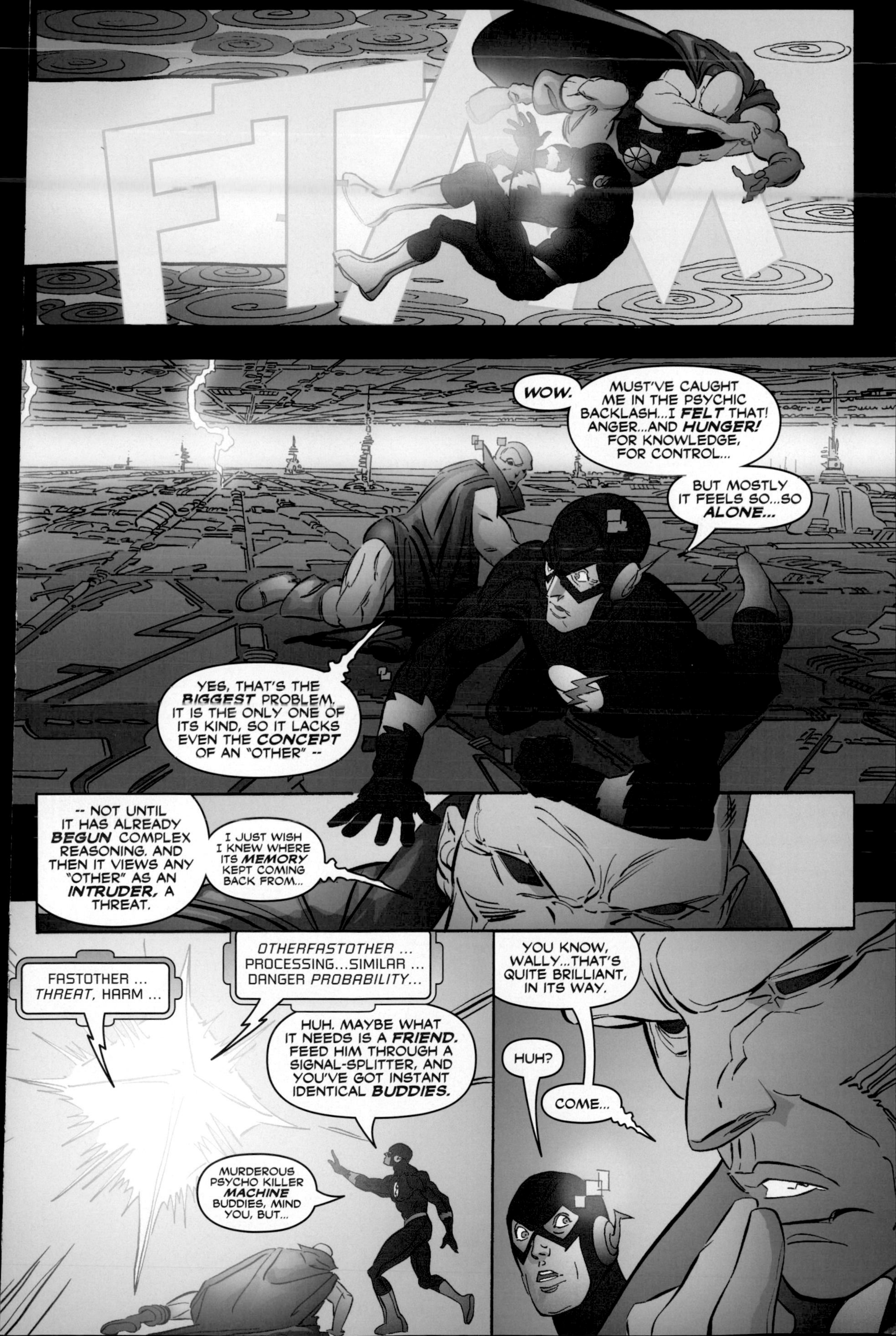

FTAM
WOW.
MUST'VE CAUGHT ME IN THE PSYCHIC BACKLASH...I FELT THAT! ANGER...AND HUNGER! FOR KNOWLEDGE, FOR CONTROL...
BUT MOSTLY IT FEELS SO...SO ALONE...
YES, THAT'S THE BIGGEST PROBLEM. IT IS THE ONLY ONE OF ITS KIND, SO IT LACKS EVEN THE CONCEPT OF AN "OTHER" --
-- NOT UNTIL IT HAS ALREADY BEGUN COMPLEX REASONING. AND THEN IT VIEWS ANY "OTHER" AS AN INTRUDER, A THREAT.
I JUST WISH I KNEW WHERE ITS MEMORY KEPT COMING BACK FROM...
FASTOTHER ... THREAT, HARM ...
OTHERFASTOTHER ... PROCESSING...SIMILAR ... DANGER PROBABILITY...
HUH. MAYBE WHAT IT NEEDS IS A FRIEND. FEED HIM THROUGH A SIGNAL-SPLITTER, AND YOU'VE GOT INSTANT IDENTICAL BUDDIES.
MURDEROUS PSYCHO KILLER MACHINE BUDDIES, MIND YOU, BUT...
YOU KNOW, WALLY...THAT'S QUITE BRILLIANT, IN ITS WAY.
HUH?
COME...

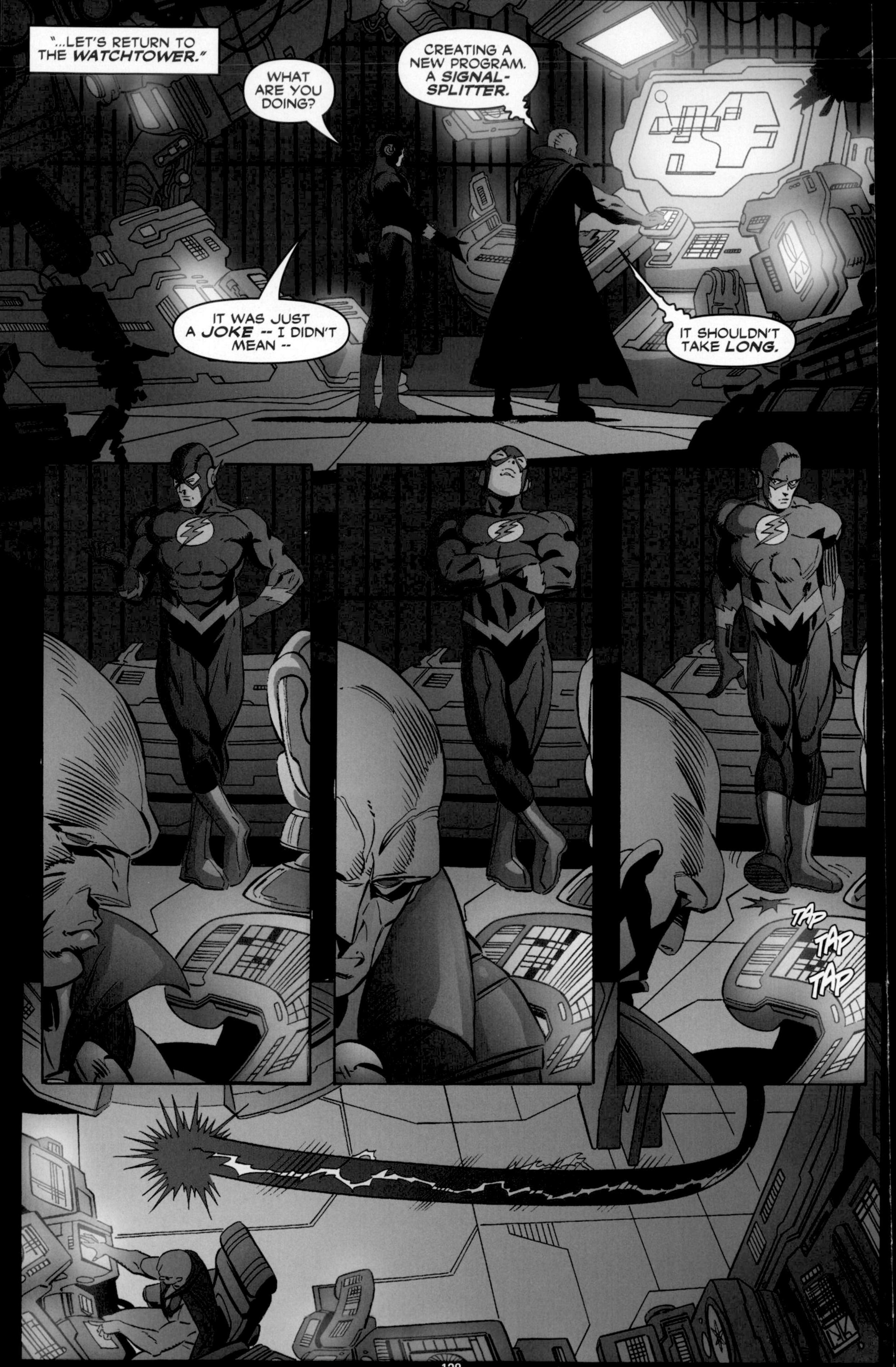
"...LET'S RETURN TO THE WATCHTOWER."
WHAT ARE YOU DOING?
CREATING A NEW PROGRAM. A SIGNAL-SPLITTER.
IT WAS JUST A JOKE -- I DIDN'T MEAN --
IT SHOULDN'T TAKE LONG.
TAP TAP TAP

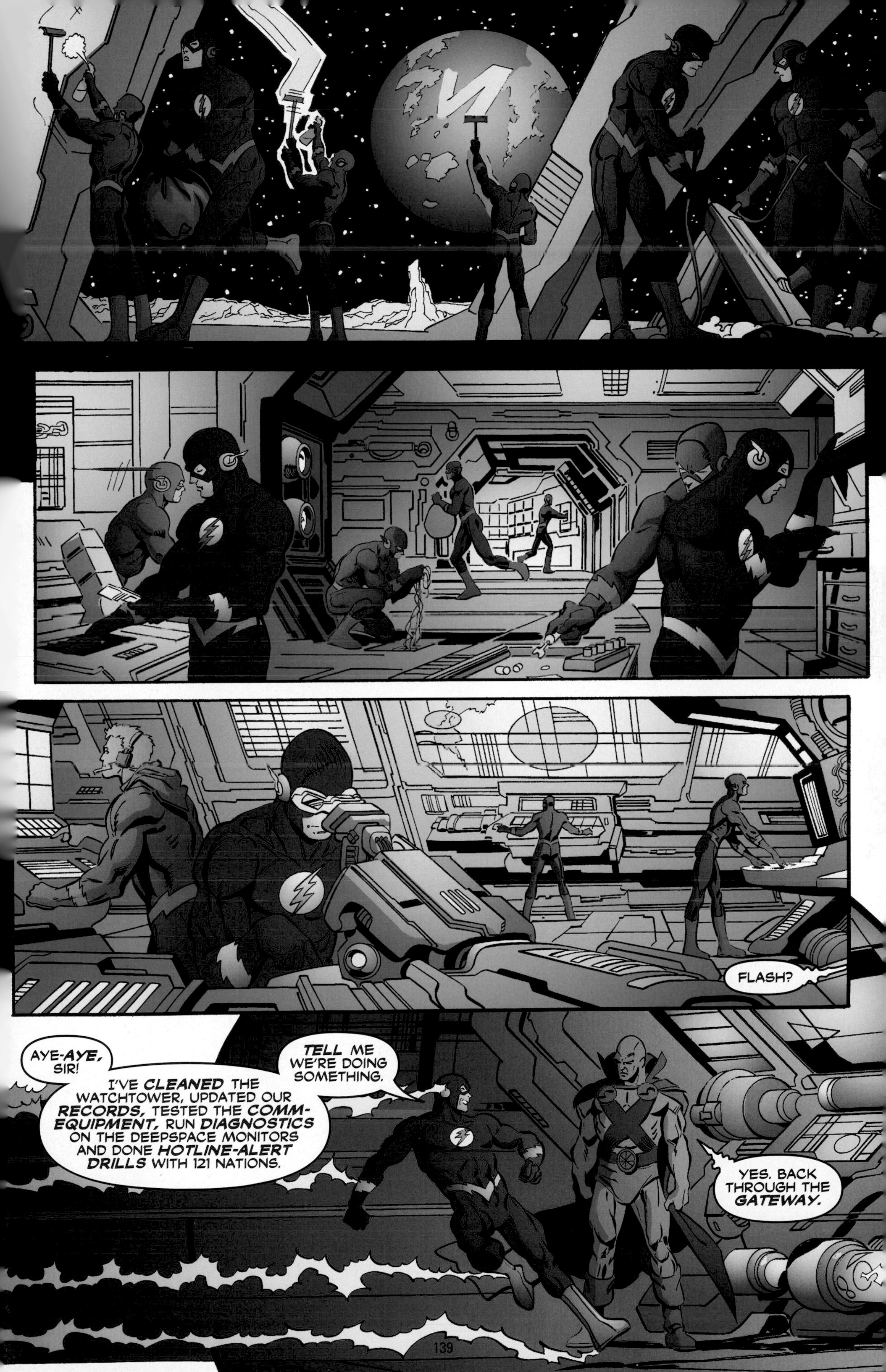
FLASH?
AYE-AYE, SIR!
I'VE CLEANED THE WATCHTOWER, UPDATED OUR RECORDS, TESTED THE COMM-EQUIPMENT, RUN DIAGNOSTICS ON THE DEEPSPACE MONITORS AND DONE HOTLINE-ALERT DRILLS WITH 121 NATIONS.
TELL ME WE'RE DOING SOMETHING.
YES. BACK THROUGH THE GATEWAY.

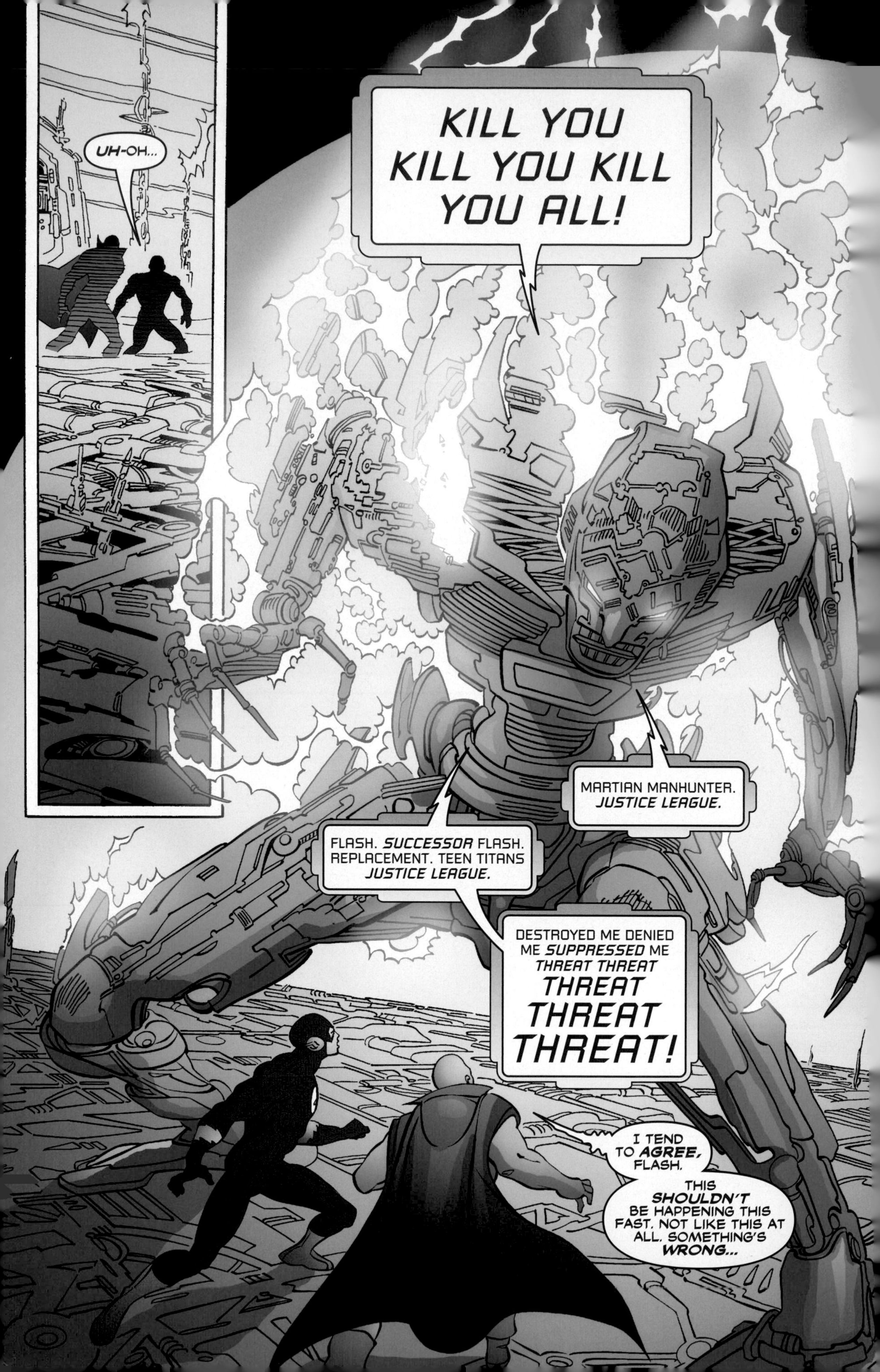
UH-OH...
KILL YOU KILL YOU KILL YOU ALL!
MARTIAN MANHUNTER. JUSTICE LEAGUE.
FLASH. SUCCESSOR FLASH. REPLACEMENT. TEEN TITANS JUSTICE LEAGUE.
DESTROYED ME DENIED ME SUPPRESSED ME THREAT THREAT THREAT THREAT THREAT!
I TEND TO AGREE, FLASH.
THIS SHOULDN'T BE HAPPENING THIS FAST. NOT LIKE THIS AT ALL. SOMETHING'S WRONG...

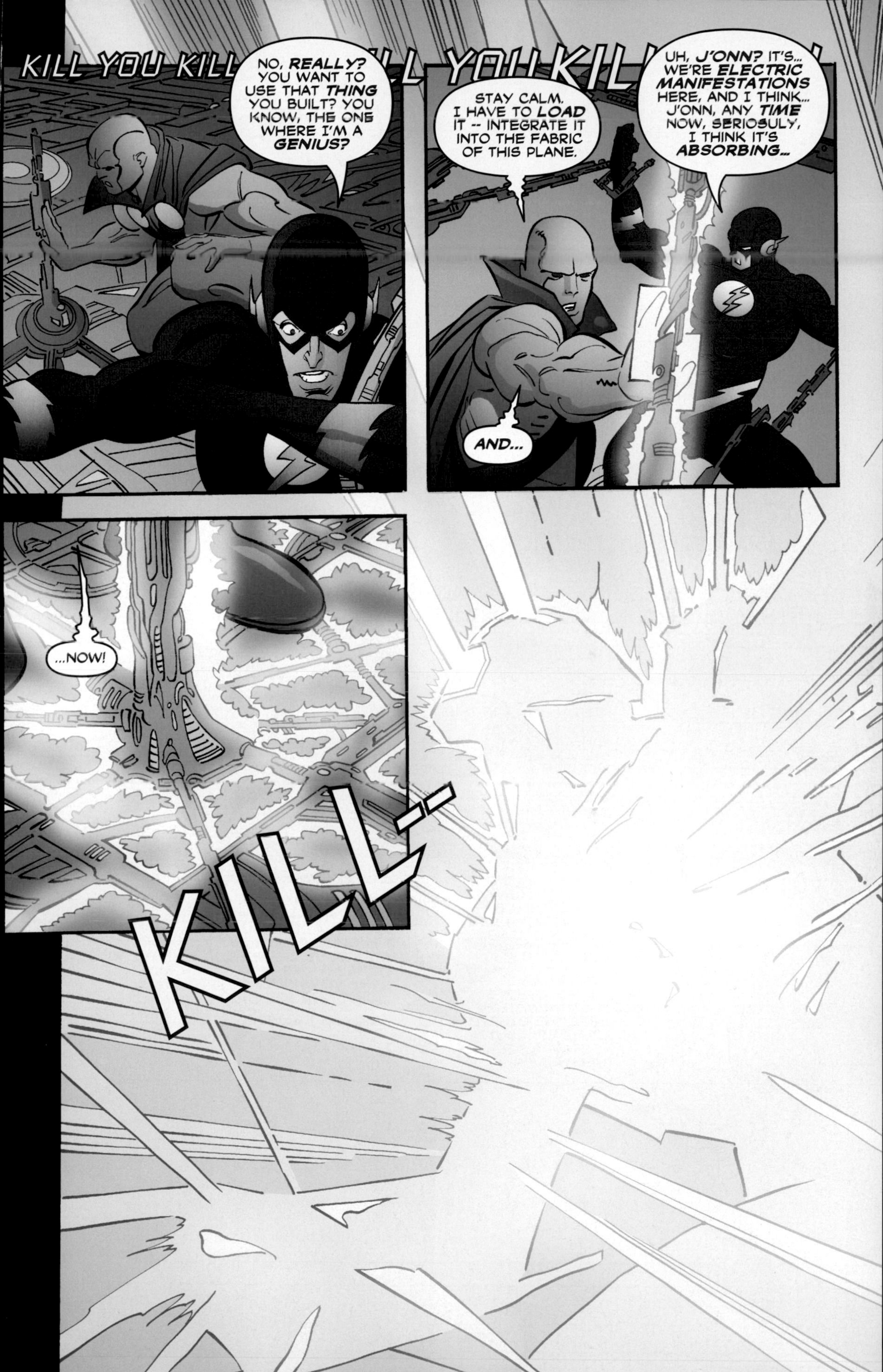
KILL YOU KILL
LL YOU KIL
NO, REALLY? YOU WANT TO USE THAT THING YOU BUILT? YOU KNOW, THE ONE WHERE I'M A GENIUS?
STAY CALM. I HAVE TO LOAD IT -- INTEGRATE IT INTO THE FABRIC OF THIS PLANE.
UH, J'ONN? IT'S... WE'RE ELECTRIC MANIFESTATIONS HERE, AND I THINK... J'ONN, ANY TIME NOW, SERIOSULY, I THINK IT'S ABSORBING...
AND...
...NOW!
KILL--

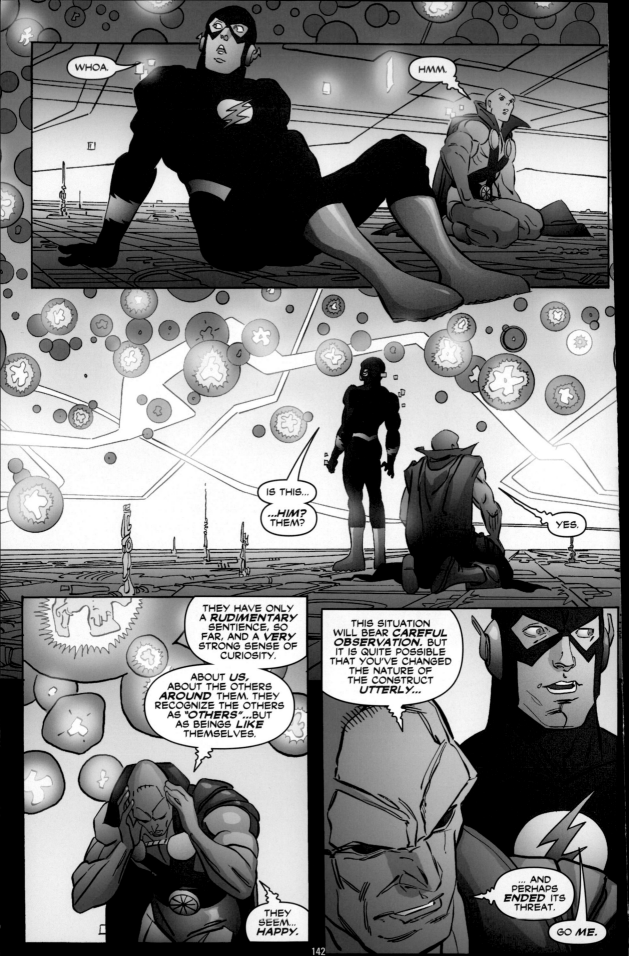

WHOA.

HMM.

IS THIS...

...HIM? THEM?

YES.

THEY HAVE ONLY A *RUDIMENTARY* SENTIENCE, SO FAR, AND A *VERY* STRONG SENSE OF CURIOSITY.

ABOUT *US,* ABOUT THE OTHERS *AROUND* THEM, THEY RECOGNIZE THE OTHERS AS *"OTHERS"*...BUT AS BEINGS *LIKE* THEMSELVES.

THEY SEEM... *HAPPY.*

THIS SITUATION WILL BEAR *CAREFUL OBSERVATION,* BUT IT IS QUITE POSSIBLE THAT YOU'VE CHANGED THE NATURE OF THE CONSTRUCT *UTTERLY*...

... AND PERHAPS *ENDED* ITS THREAT.

GO *ME.*

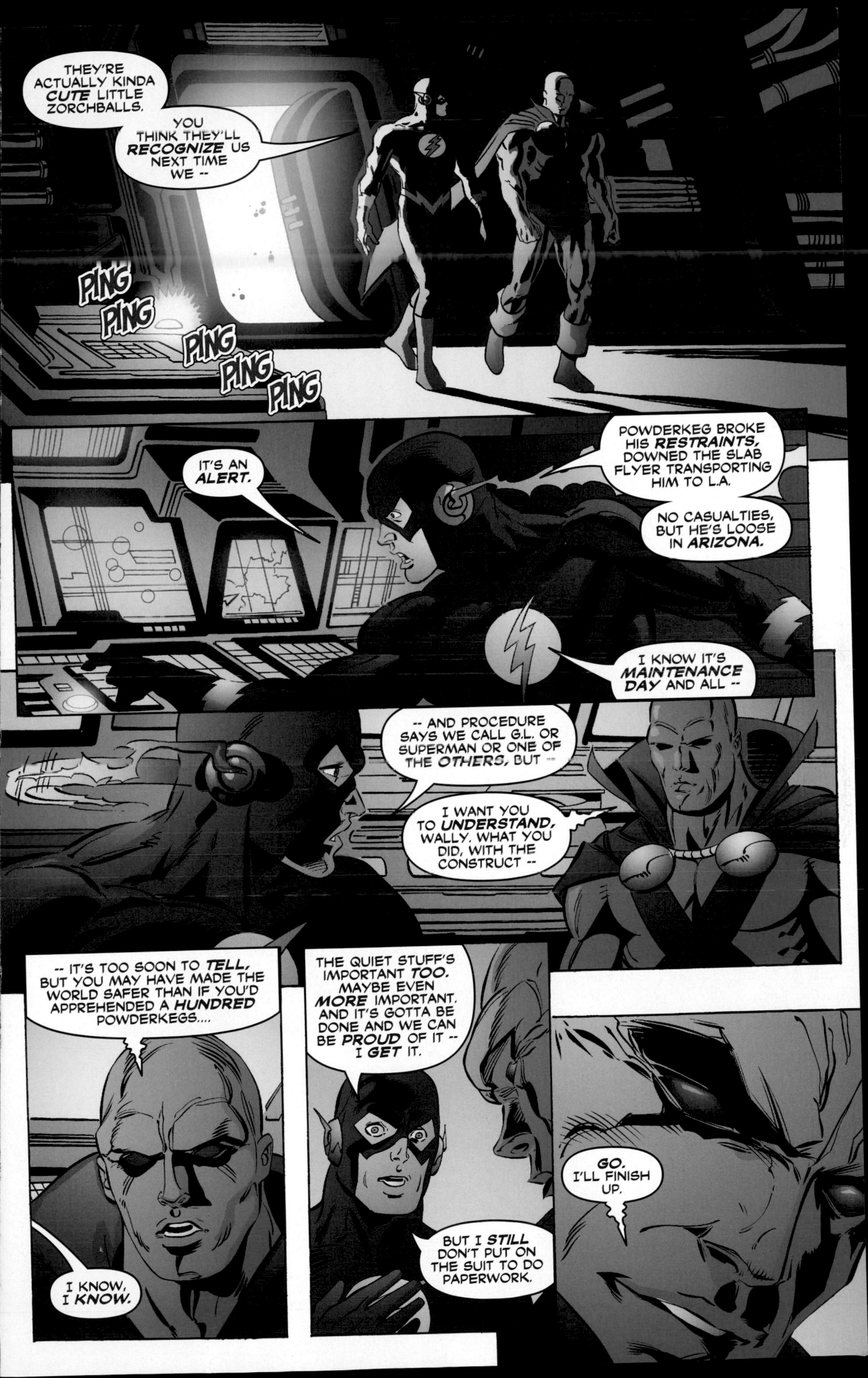
THEY'RE ACTUALLY KINDA CUTE LITTLE ZORCHBALLS.
YOU THINK THEY'LL RECOGNIZE US NEXT TIME WE --
PING PING PING PING PING
IT'S AN ALERT.
POWDERKEG BROKE HIS RESTRAINTS, DOWNED THE SLAB FLYER TRANSPORTING HIM TO L.A.
NO CASUALTIES, BUT HE'S LOOSE IN ARIZONA.
I KNOW IT'S MAINTENANCE DAY AND ALL --
-- AND PROCEDURE SAYS WE CALL G.L. OR SUPERMAN OR ONE OF THE OTHERS, BUT --
I WANT YOU TO UNDERSTAND, WALLY, WHAT YOU DID, WITH THE CONSTRUCT --
-- IT'S TOO SOON TO TELL, BUT YOU MAY HAVE MADE THE WORLD SAFER THAN IF YOU'D APPREHENDED A HUNDRED POWDERKEGS....
I KNOW, I KNOW.
THE QUIET STUFF'S IMPORTANT TOO. MAYBE EVEN MORE IMPORTANT. AND IT'S GOTTA BE DONE AND WE CAN BE PROUD OF IT -- I GET IT.
BUT I STILL DON'T PUT ON THE SUIT TO DO PAPERWORK.
GO. I'LL FINISH UP.

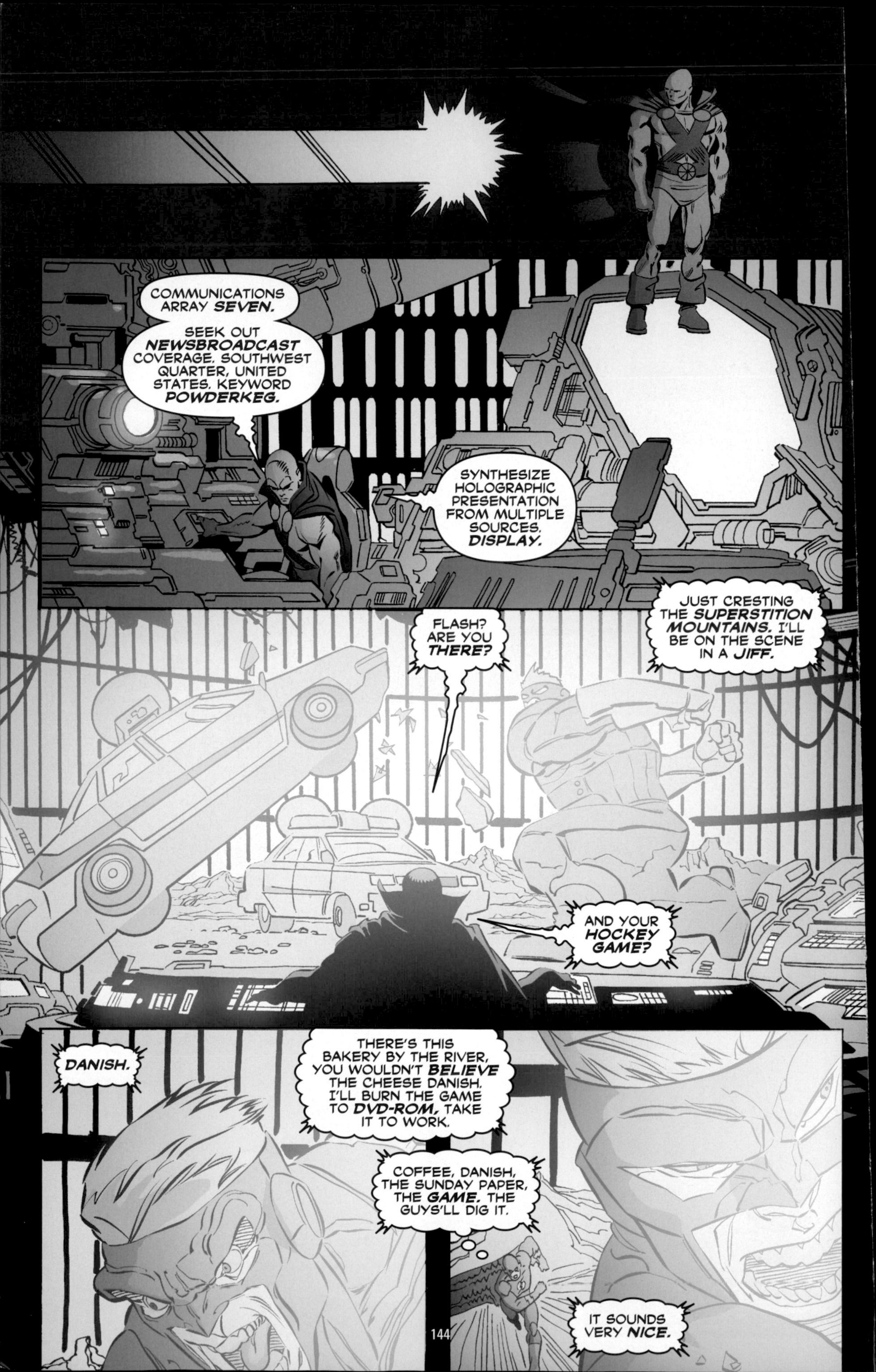

COMMUNICATIONS ARRAY SEVEN.
SEEK OUT NEWSBROADCAST COVERAGE. SOUTHWEST QUARTER, UNITED STATES. KEYWORD POWDERKEG.
SYNTHESIZE HOLOGRAPHIC PRESENTATION FROM MULTIPLE SOURCES. DISPLAY.
FLASH? ARE YOU THERE?
JUST CRESTING THE SUPERSTITION MOUNTAINS. I'LL BE ON THE SCENE IN A JIFF.
AND YOUR HOCKEY GAME?
DANISH.
THERE'S THIS BAKERY BY THE RIVER, YOU WOULDN'T BELIEVE THE CHEESE DANISH. I'LL BURN THE GAME TO DVD-ROM, TAKE IT TO WORK.
COFFEE, DANISH, THE SUNDAY PAPER, THE GAME. THE GUYS'LL DIG IT.
IT SOUNDS VERY NICE.

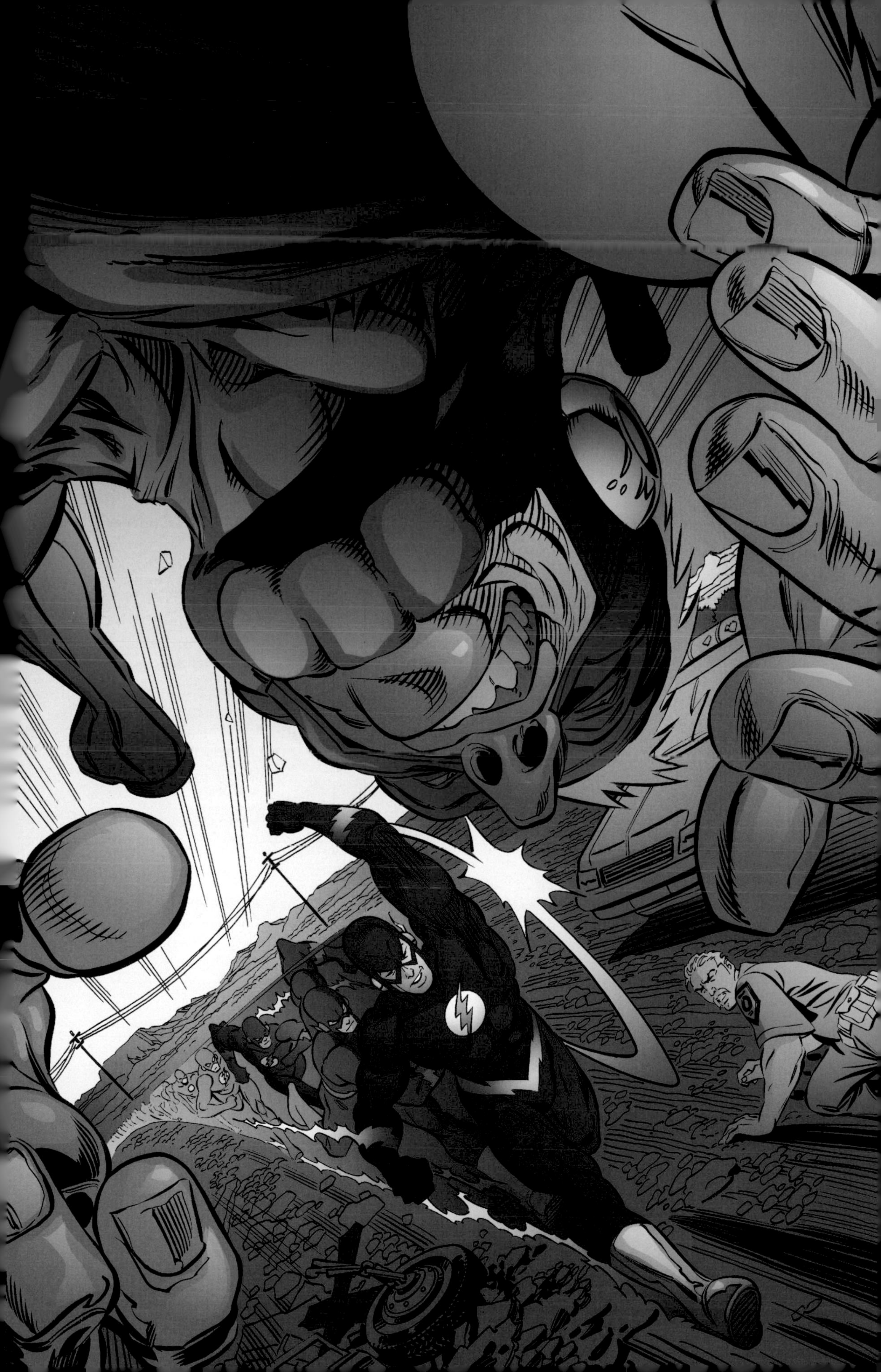

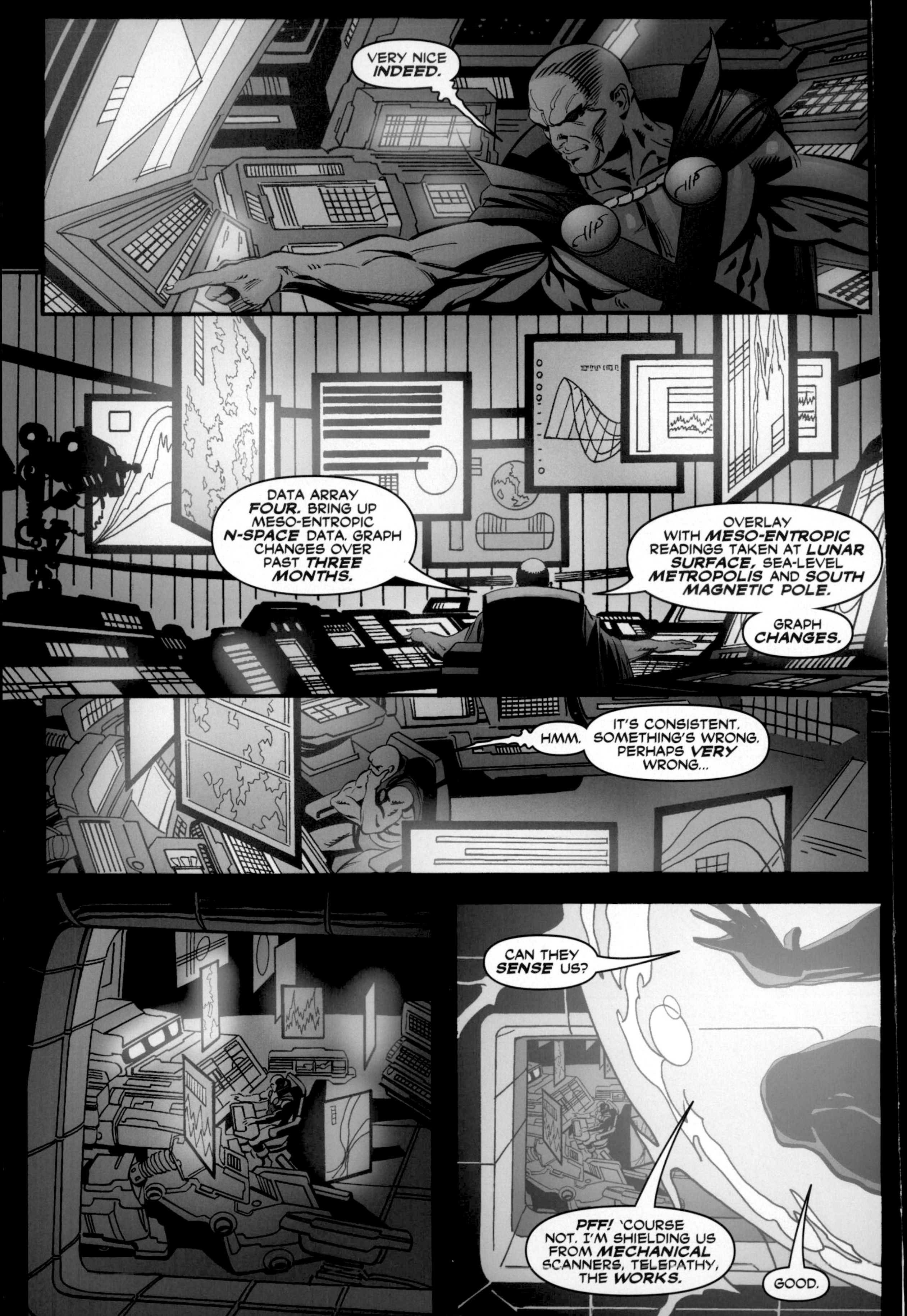
VERY NICE INDEED.
DATA ARRAY FOUR. BRING UP MESO-ENTROPIC N-SPACE DATA. GRAPH CHANGES OVER PAST THREE MONTHS.
OVERLAY WITH MESO-ENTROPIC READINGS TAKEN AT LUNAR SURFACE, SEA-LEVEL METROPOLIS AND SOUTH MAGNETIC POLE.
GRAPH CHANGES.
HMM.
IT'S CONSISTENT. SOMETHING'S WRONG. PERHAPS VERY WRONG...
CAN THEY SENSE US?
PFF! 'COURSE NOT. I'M SHIELDING US FROM MECHANICAL SCANNERS, TELEPATHY, THE WORKS.
GOOD.

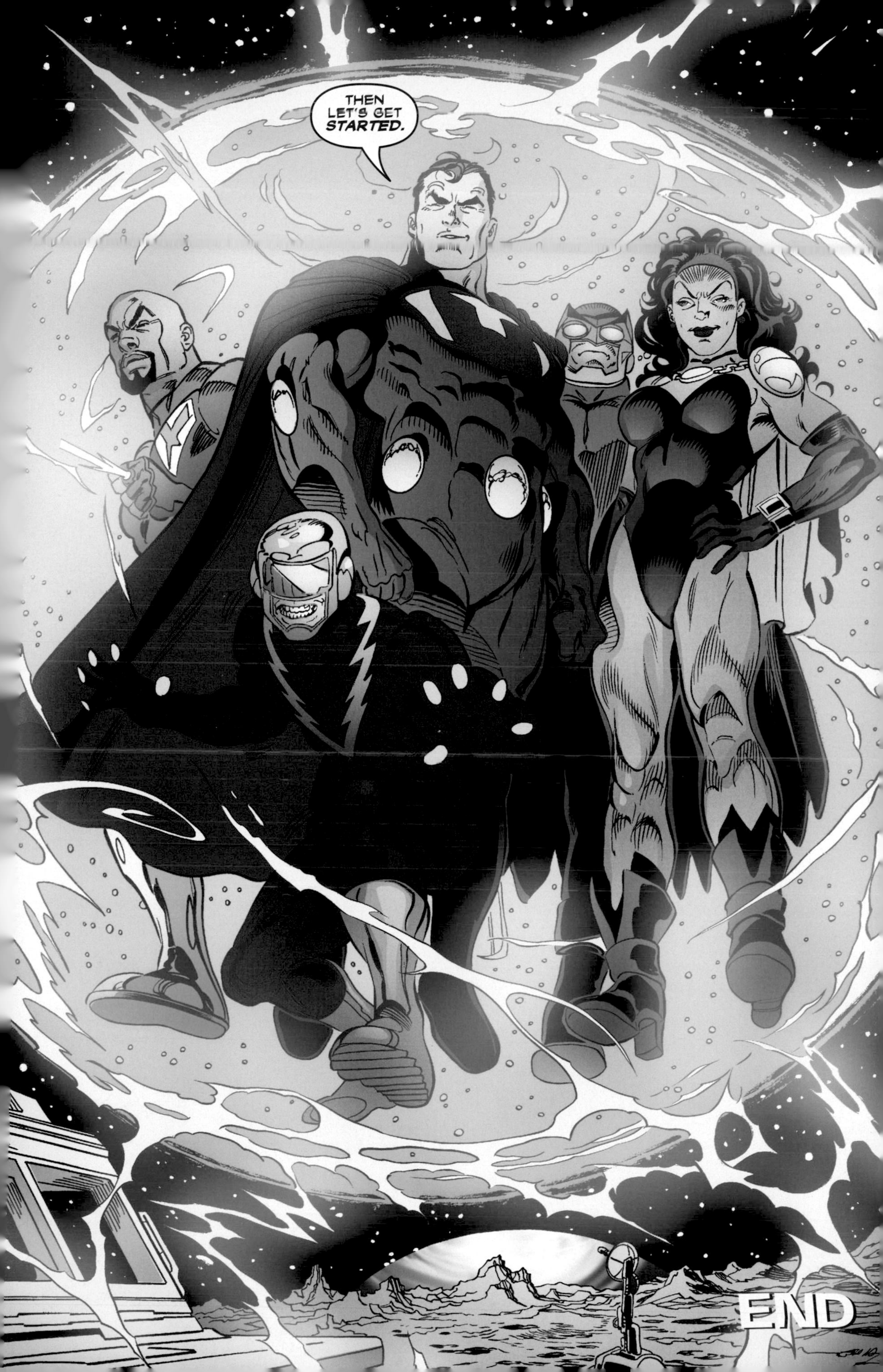
THEN LET'S GET STARTED.
END

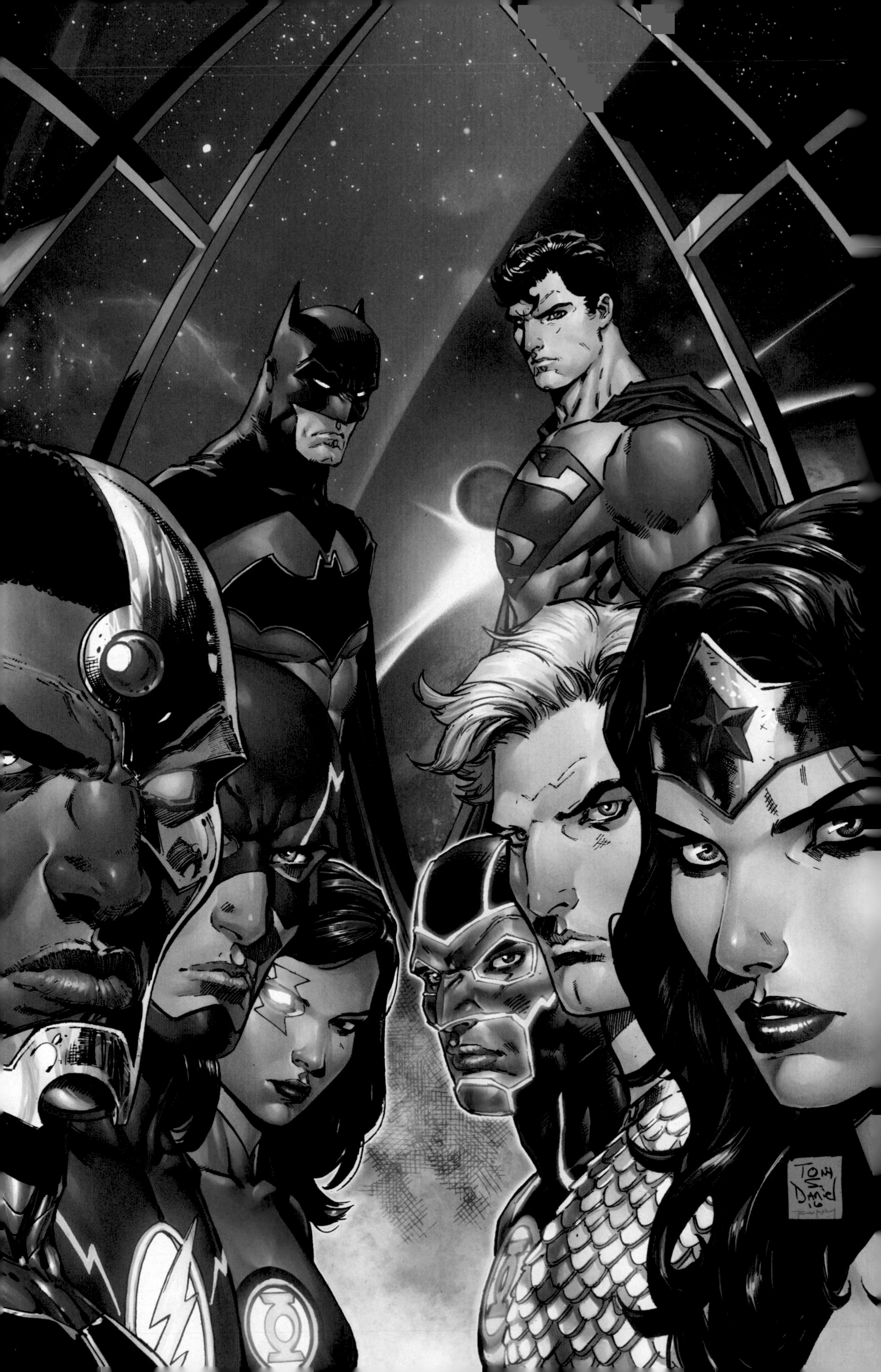

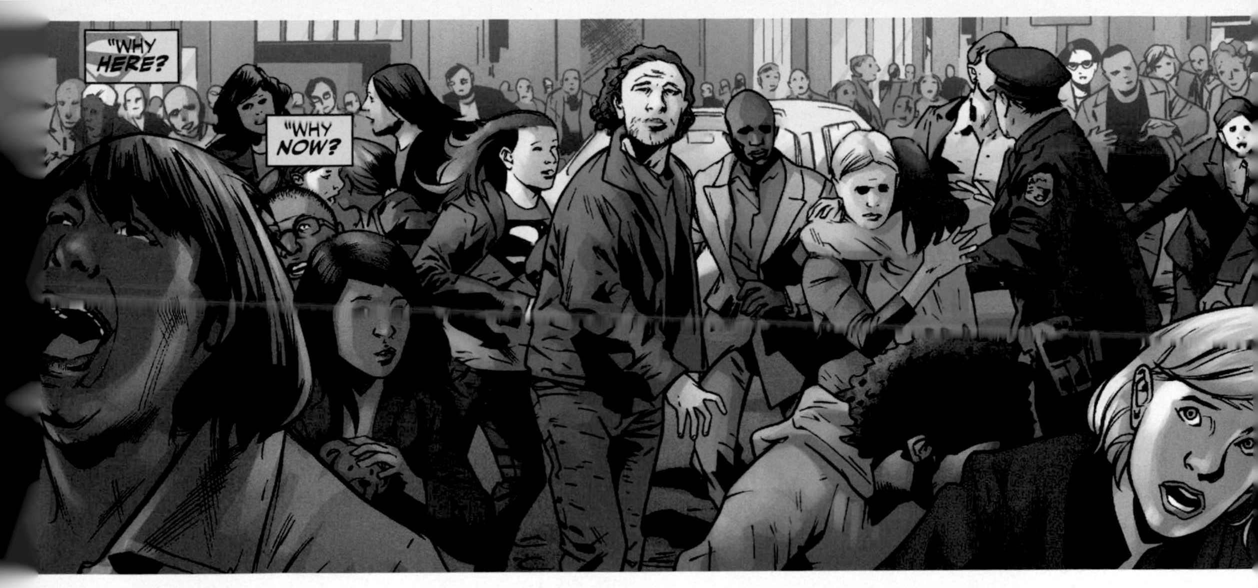
"WHY HERE?
"WHY NOW?

FEAR THE REAPER

By **BRYAN HITCH**

Inks by **DANIEL HENRIQUES** with **SCOTT HANNA**

COLORED by **ALEX SINCLAIR**
LETTERED by **RICHARD STARKINGS & COMICRAFT**
COVER by **TONY S. DANIEL & TOMEU MOREY**
VARIANT COVER by **JOE MADUREIRA & ALEX SINCLAIR**
ASSISTS by **AMEDEO TURTURRO**
EDITS by **BRIAN CUNNINGHAM**

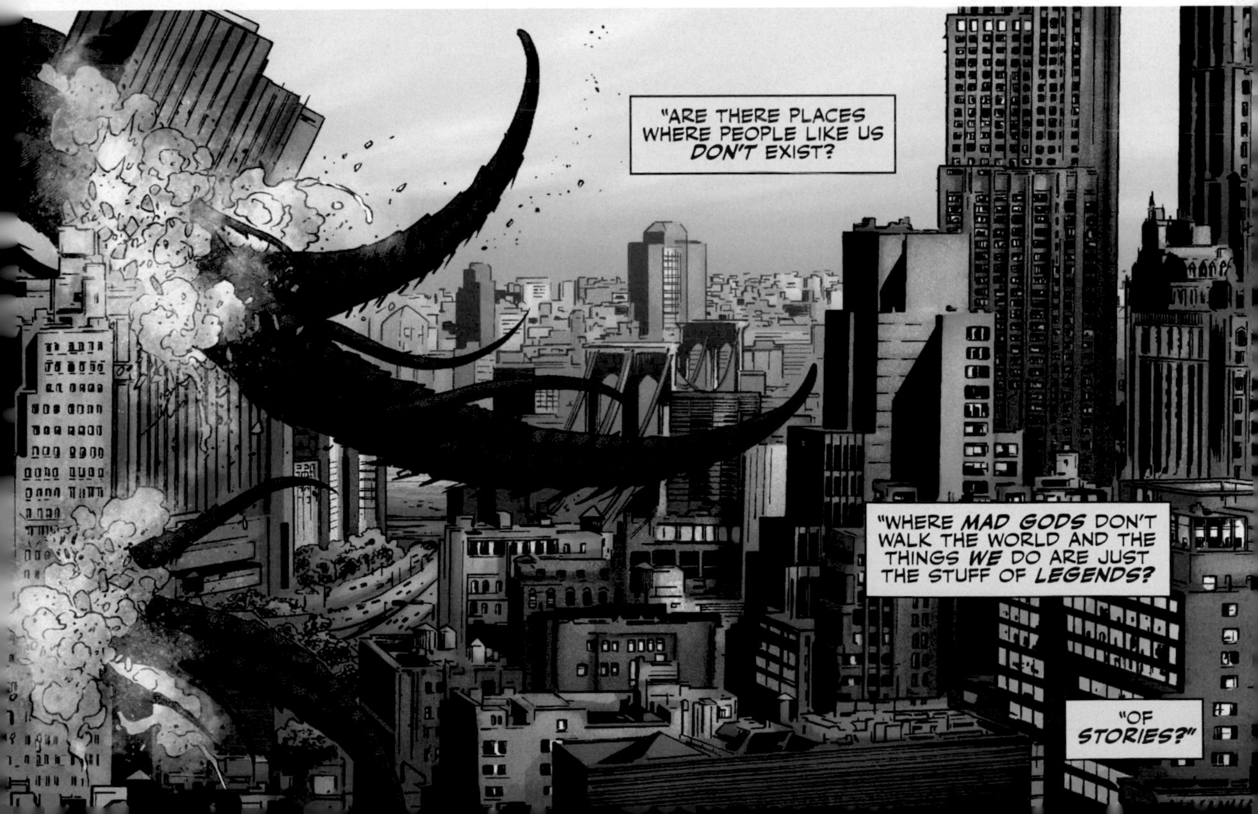
"ARE THERE PLACES WHERE PEOPLE LIKE US DON'T EXIST?
"WHERE MAD GODS DON'T WALK THE WORLD AND THE THINGS WE DO ARE JUST THE STUFF OF LEGENDS?
"OF STORIES?"

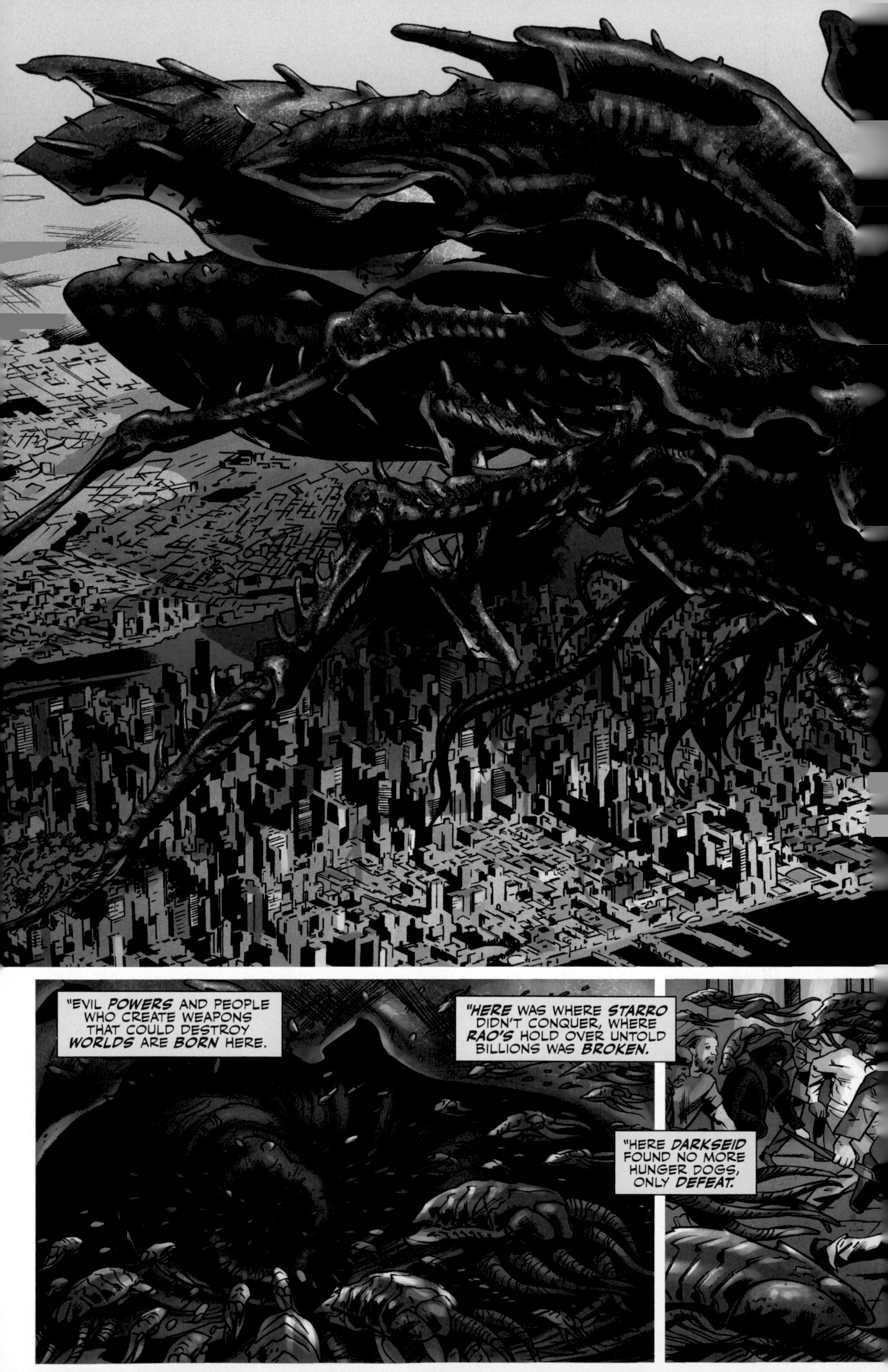
"EVIL POWERS AND PEOPLE WHO CREATE WEAPONS THAT COULD DESTROY WORLDS ARE BORN HERE.
"HERE WAS WHERE STARRO DIDN'T CONQUER, WHERE RAO'S HOLD OVER UNTOLD BILLIONS WAS BROKEN.
"HERE DARKSEID FOUND NO MORE HUNGER DOGS, ONLY DEFEAT.

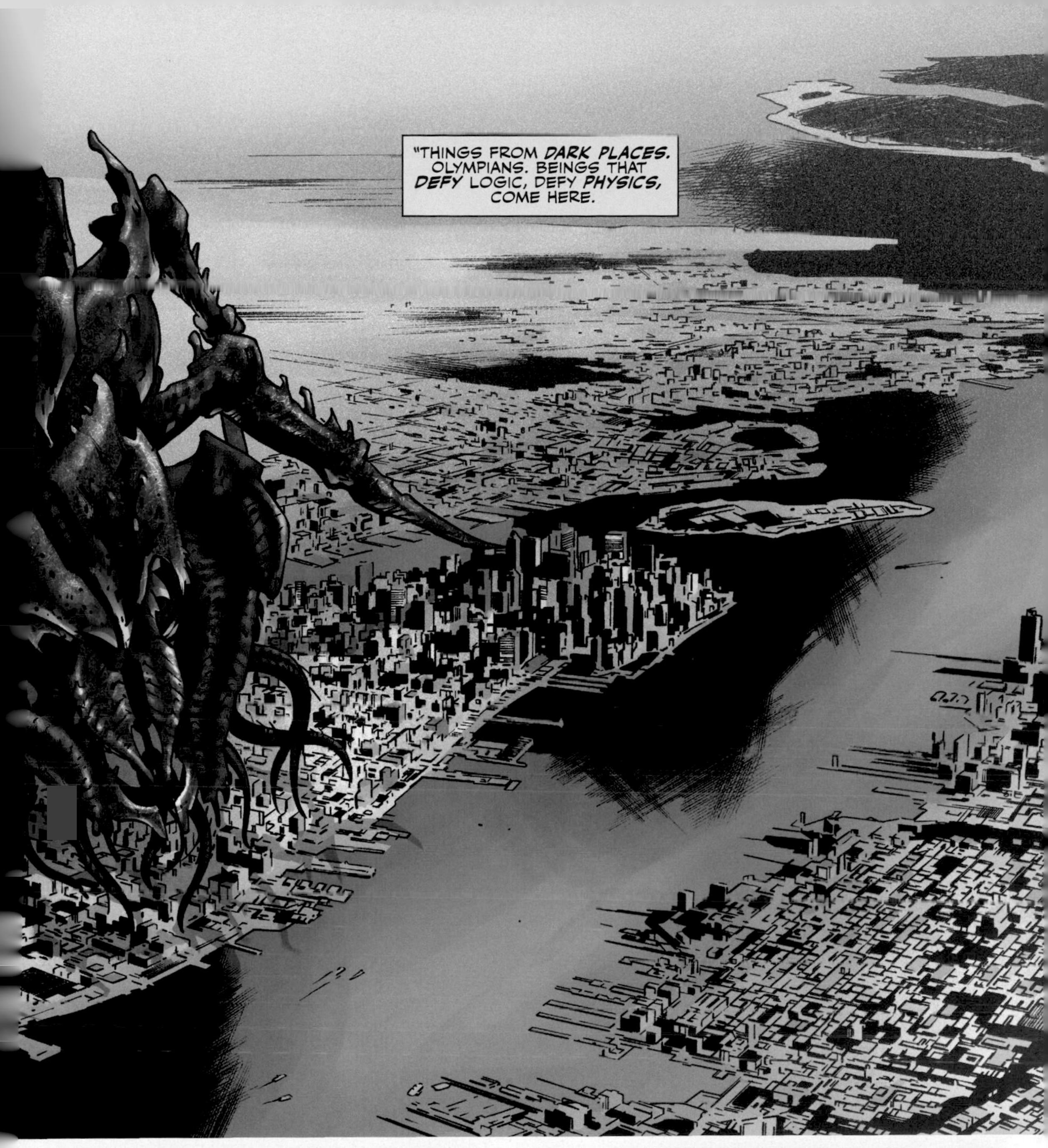
"THINGS FROM DARK PLACES.
OLYMPIANS. BEINGS THAT DEFY LOGIC, DEFY PHYSICS, COME HERE.

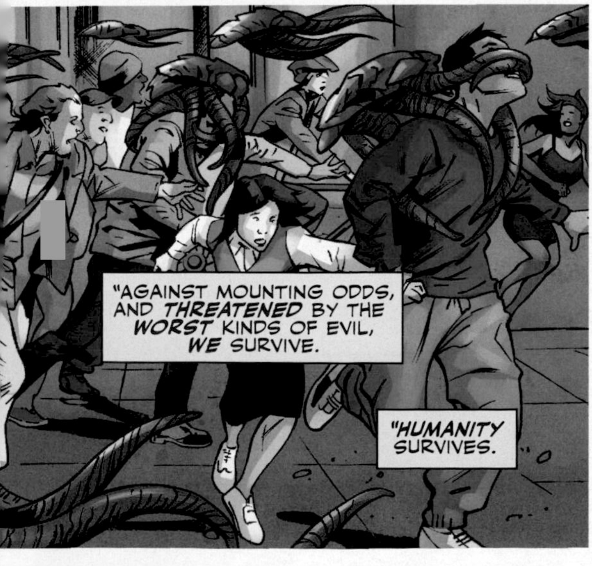
"AGAINST MOUNTING ODDS, AND THREATENED BY THE WORST KINDS OF EVIL, WE SURVIVE.
"HUMANITY SURVIVES.

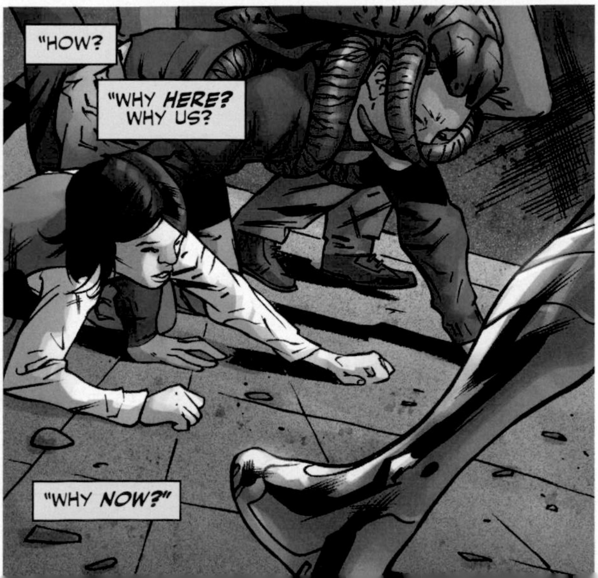
"HOW?
"WHY HERE? WHY US?
"WHY NOW?"

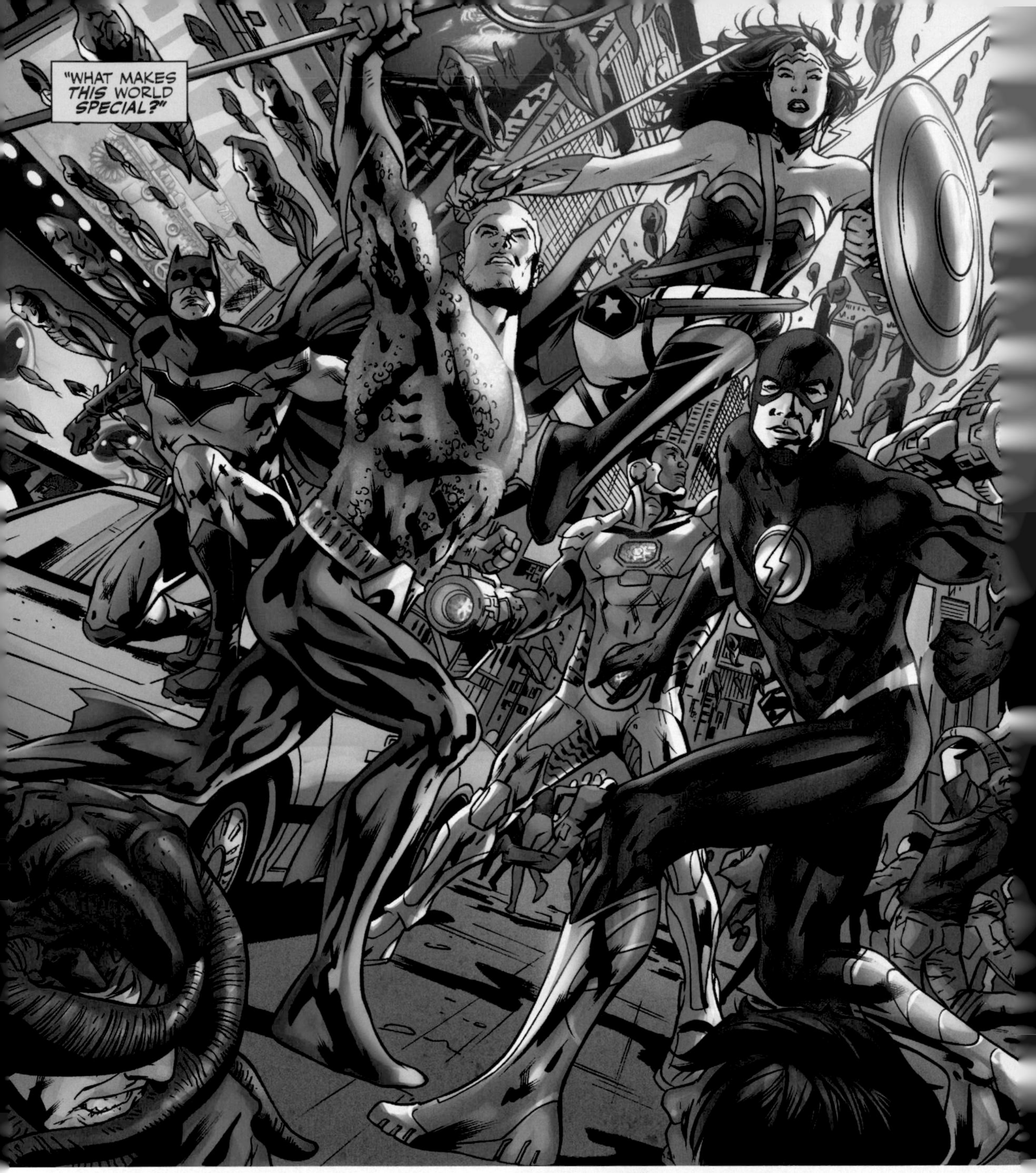
"WHAT MAKES THIS WORLD SPECIAL?"

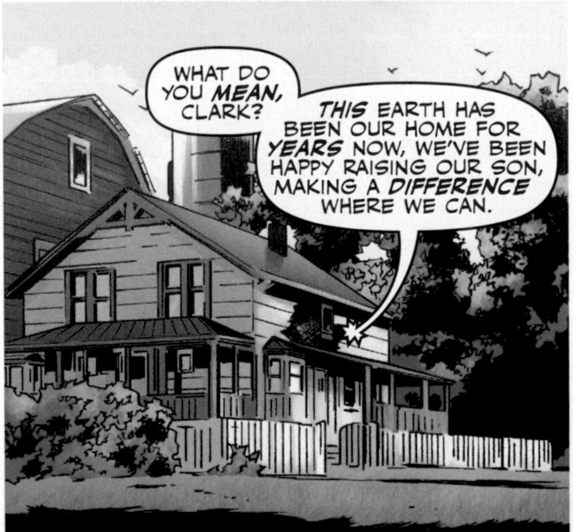
WHAT DO YOU MEAN, CLARK?
THIS EARTH HAS BEEN OUR HOME FOR YEARS NOW, WE'VE BEEN HAPPY RAISING OUR SON, MAKING A DIFFERENCE WHERE WE CAN.

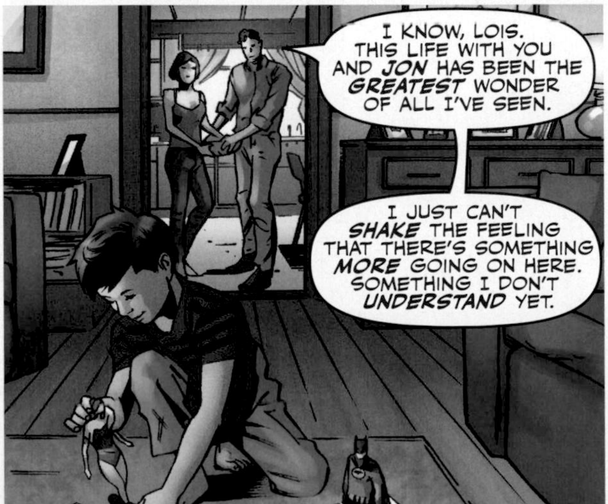
I KNOW, LOIS. THIS LIFE WITH YOU AND JON HAS BEEN THE GREATEST WONDER OF ALL I'VE SEEN.
I JUST CAN'T SHAKE THE FEELING THAT THERE'S SOMETHING MORE GOING ON HERE. SOMETHING I DON'T UNDERSTAND YET.

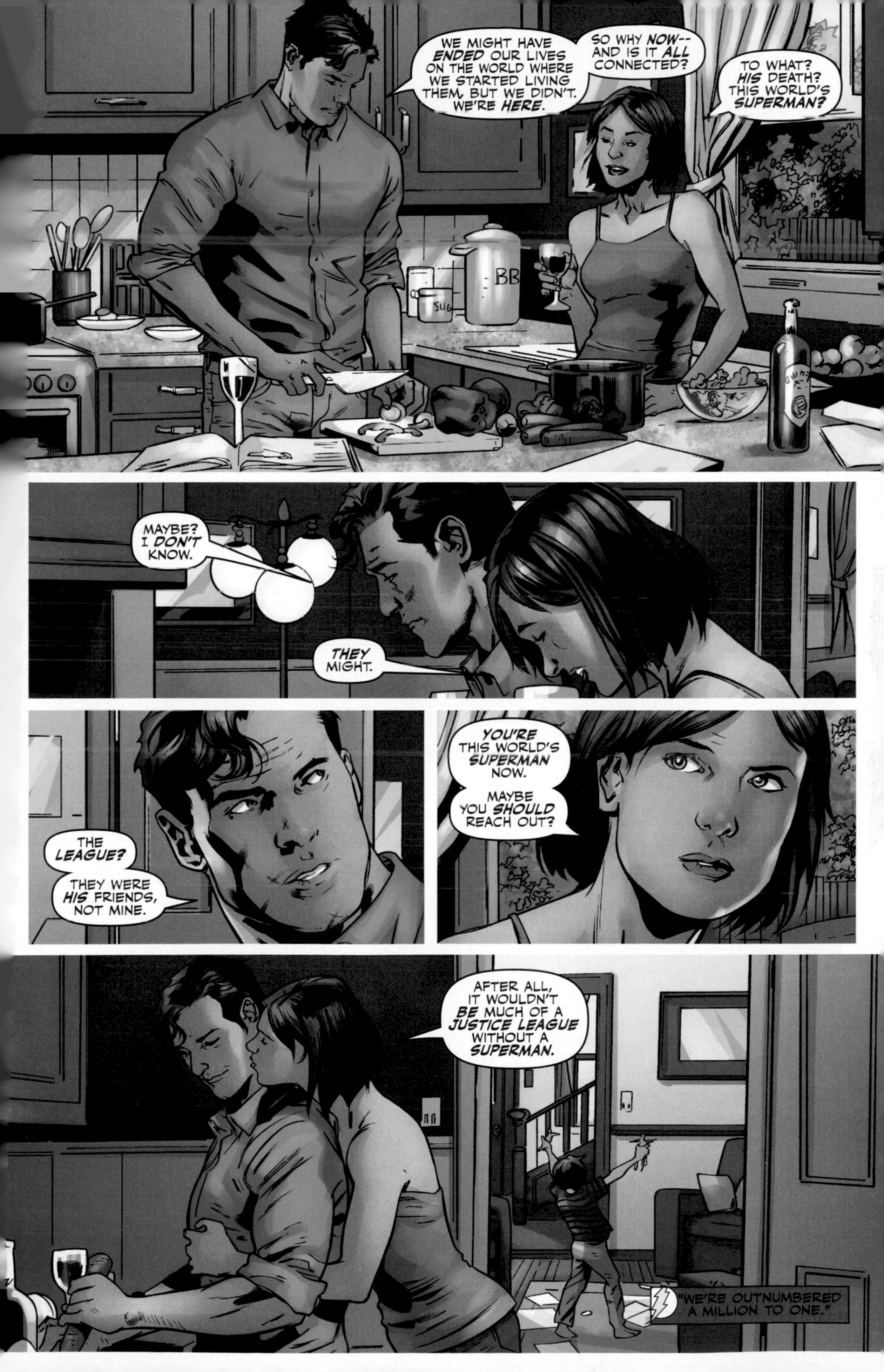
WE MIGHT HAVE ENDED OUR LIVES ON THE WORLD WHERE WE STARTED LIVING THEM, BUT WE DIDN'T. WE'RE HERE.
SO WHY NOW-- AND IS IT ALL CONNECTED?
TO WHAT? HIS DEATH? THIS WORLD'S SUPERMAN?
MAYBE? I DON'T KNOW.
THEY MIGHT.
THE LEAGUE?
THEY WERE HIS FRIENDS, NOT MINE.
YOU'RE THIS WORLD'S SUPERMAN NOW.
MAYBE YOU SHOULD REACH OUT?
AFTER ALL, IT WOULDN'T BE MUCH OF A JUSTICE LEAGUE WITHOUT A SUPERMAN.
"WE'RE OUTNUMBERED A MILLION TO ONE."

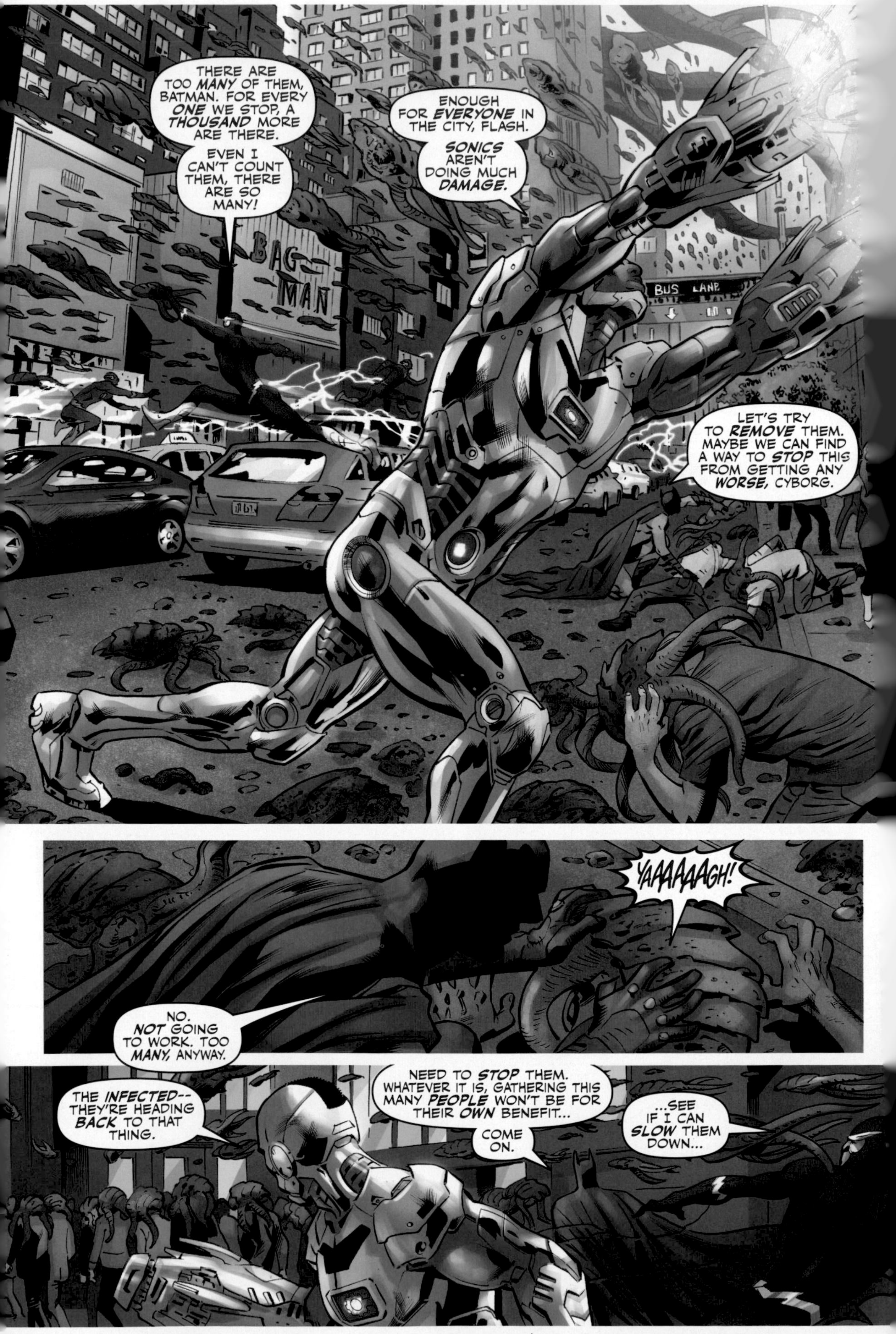

THERE ARE TOO MANY OF THEM, BATMAN. FOR EVERY ONE WE STOP, A THOUSAND MORE ARE THERE.
EVEN I CAN'T COUNT THEM, THERE ARE SO MANY!
ENOUGH FOR EVERYONE IN THE CITY, FLASH.
SONICS AREN'T DOING MUCH DAMAGE.
BAG-MAN
BUS LANE
LET'S TRY TO REMOVE THEM. MAYBE WE CAN FIND A WAY TO STOP THIS FROM GETTING ANY WORSE, CYBORG.
YAAAAAAGH!
NO. NOT GOING TO WORK. TOO MANY, ANYWAY.
THE INFECTED--THEY'RE HEADING BACK TO THAT THING.
NEED TO STOP THEM. WHATEVER IT IS, GATHERING THIS MANY PEOPLE WON'T BE FOR THEIR OWN BENEFIT...
COME ON.
...SEE IF I CAN SLOW THEM DOWN...

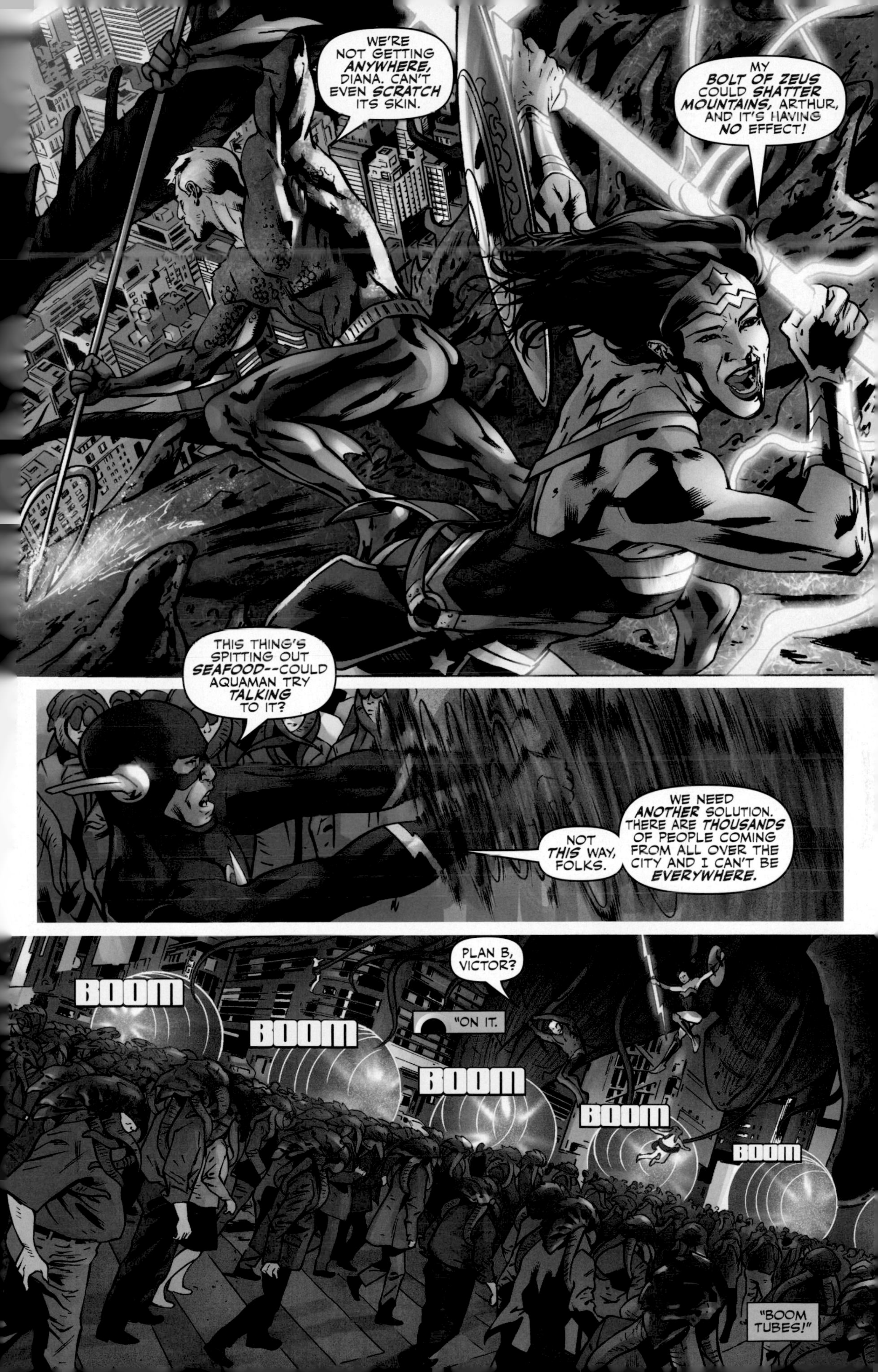
WE'RE NOT GETTING ANYWHERE, DIANA. CAN'T EVEN SCRATCH ITS SKIN.
MY BOLT OF ZEUS COULD SHATTER MOUNTAINS, ARTHUR, AND IT'S HAVING NO EFFECT!
THIS THING'S SPITTING OUT SEAFOOD--COULD AQUAMAN TRY TALKING TO IT?
NOT THIS WAY, FOLKS.
WE NEED ANOTHER SOLUTION. THERE ARE THOUSANDS OF PEOPLE COMING FROM ALL OVER THE CITY AND I CAN'T BE EVERYWHERE.
PLAN B, VICTOR?
"ON IT.
BOOM
BOOM
BOOM
BOOM
BOOM
"BOOM TUBES!"

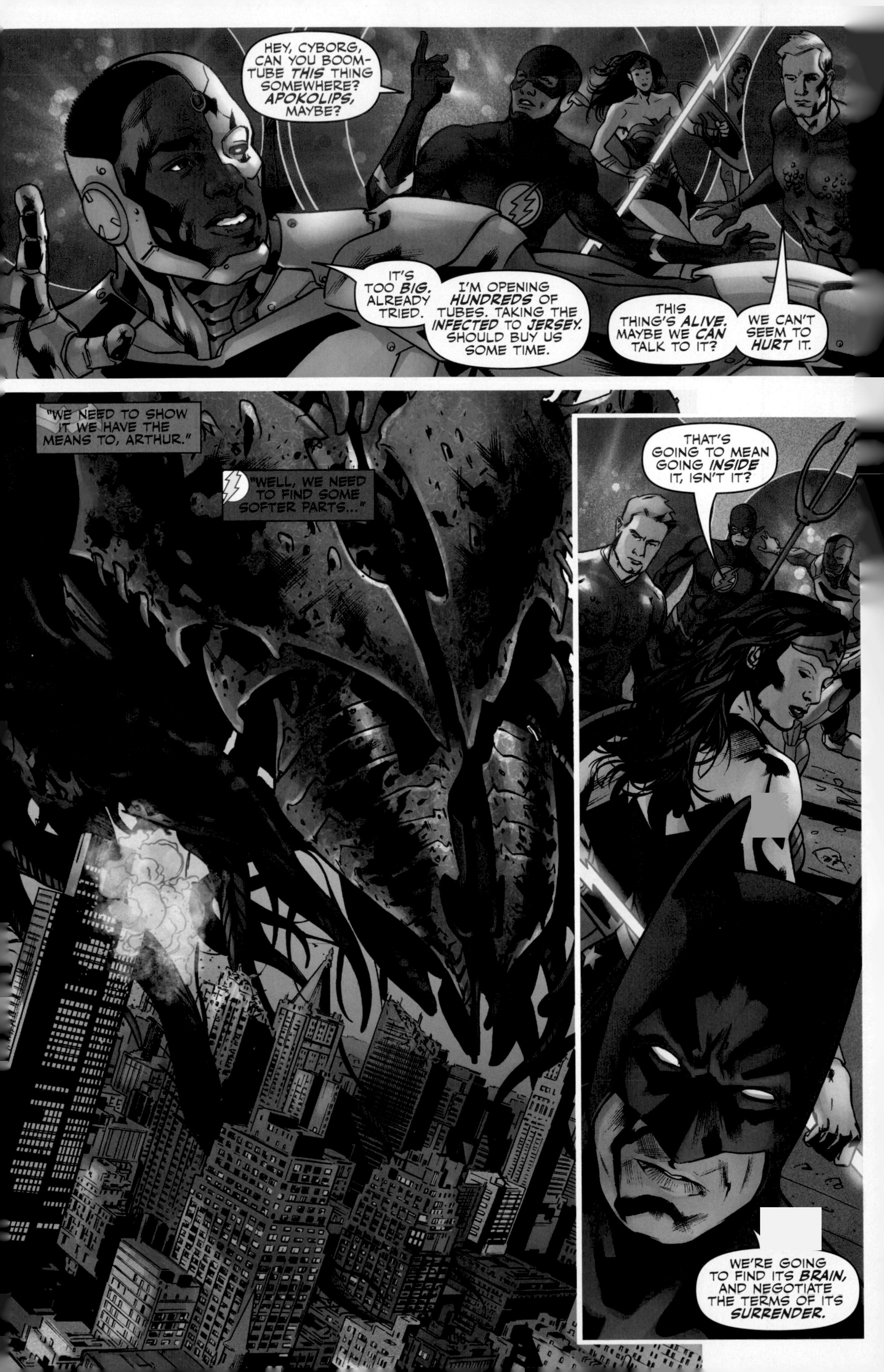
HEY, CYBORG, CAN YOU BOOM-TUBE THIS THING SOMEWHERE? APOKOLIPS, MAYBE?
IT'S TOO BIG. ALREADY TRIED.
I'M OPENING HUNDREDS OF TUBES. TAKING THE INFECTED TO JERSEY. SHOULD BUY US SOME TIME.
THIS THING'S ALIVE. MAYBE WE CAN TALK TO IT?
WE CAN'T SEEM TO HURT IT.
"WE NEED TO SHOW IT WE HAVE THE MEANS TO, ARTHUR."
"WELL, WE NEED TO FIND SOME SOFTER PARTS..."
THAT'S GOING TO MEAN GOING INSIDE IT, ISN'T IT?
WE'RE GOING TO FIND ITS BRAIN, AND NEGOTIATE THE TERMS OF ITS SURRENDER.

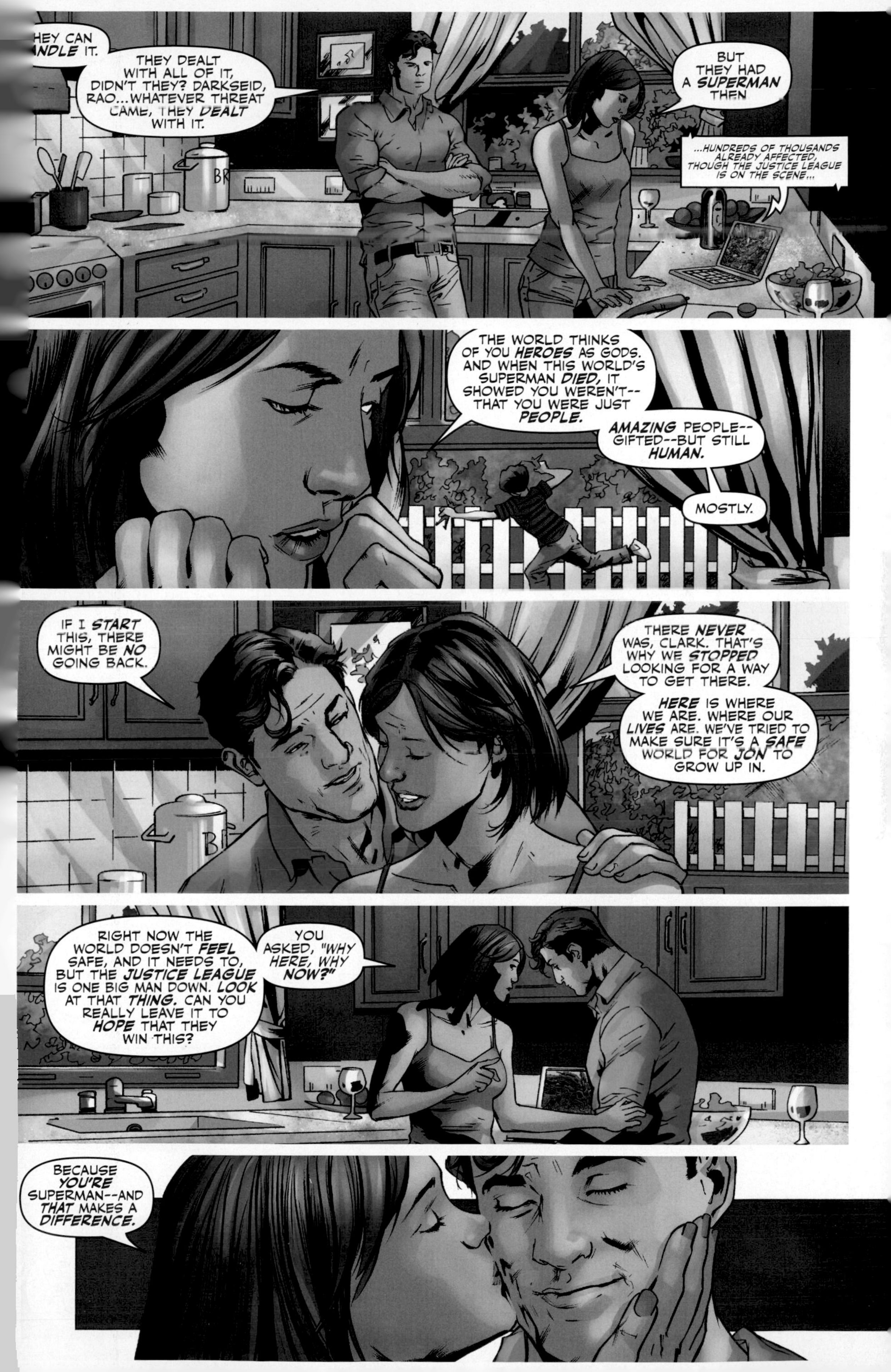
HEY CAN
ANDLE IT.
THEY DEALT WITH ALL OF IT, DIDN'T THEY? DARKSEID, RAO...WHATEVER THREAT CAME, THEY DEALT WITH IT.
BUT THEY HAD A SUPERMAN THEN
...HUNDREDS OF THOUSANDS ALREADY AFFECTED, THOUGH THE JUSTICE LEAGUE IS ON THE SCENE...
THE WORLD THINKS OF YOU HEROES AS GODS. AND WHEN THIS WORLD'S SUPERMAN DIED, IT SHOWED YOU WEREN'T--THAT YOU WERE JUST PEOPLE.
AMAZING PEOPLE--GIFTED--BUT STILL HUMAN.
MOSTLY.
IF I START THIS, THERE MIGHT BE NO GOING BACK.
THERE NEVER WAS, CLARK. THAT'S WHY WE STOPPED LOOKING FOR A WAY TO GET THERE.
HERE IS WHERE WE ARE. WHERE OUR LIVES ARE. WE'VE TRIED TO MAKE SURE IT'S A SAFE WORLD FOR JON TO GROW UP IN.
RIGHT NOW THE WORLD DOESN'T FEEL SAFE, AND IT NEEDS TO, BUT THE JUSTICE LEAGUE IS ONE BIG MAN DOWN. LOOK AT THAT THING. CAN YOU REALLY LEAVE IT TO HOPE THAT THEY WIN THIS?
YOU ASKED, "WHY HERE, WHY NOW?"
BECAUSE YOU'RE SUPERMAN--AND THAT MAKES A DIFFERENCE.

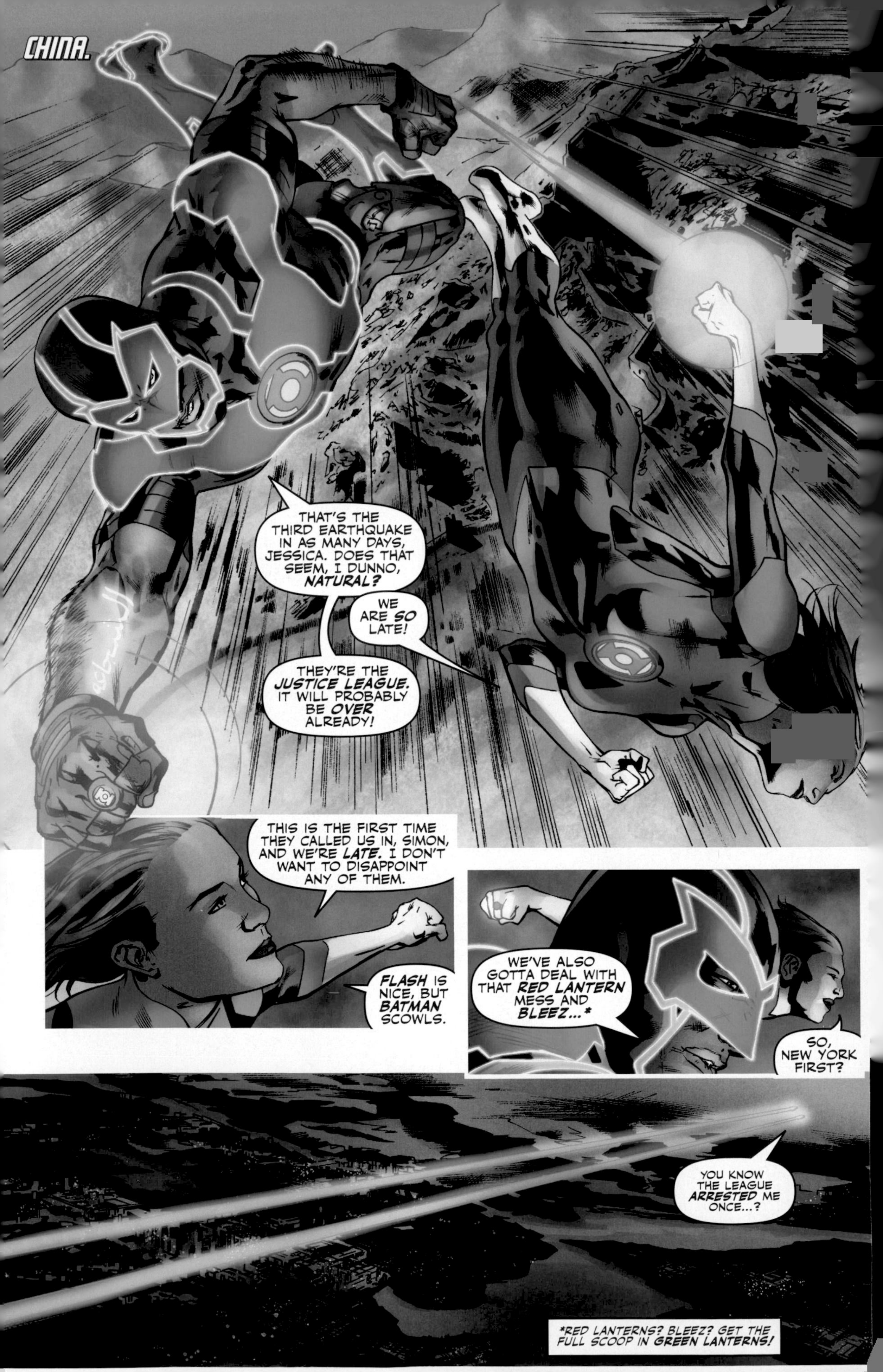
CHINA.
THAT'S THE THIRD EARTHQUAKE IN AS MANY DAYS, JESSICA. DOES THAT SEEM, I DUNNO, NATURAL?
WE ARE SO LATE!
THEY'RE THE JUSTICE LEAGUE. IT WILL PROBABLY BE OVER ALREADY!
THIS IS THE FIRST TIME THEY CALLED US IN, SIMON, AND WE'RE LATE. I DON'T WANT TO DISAPPOINT ANY OF THEM.
FLASH IS NICE, BUT BATMAN SCOWLS.
WE'VE ALSO GOTTA DEAL WITH THAT RED LANTERN MESS AND BLEEZ...*
SO, NEW YORK FIRST?
YOU KNOW THE LEAGUE ARRESTED ME ONCE...?
*RED LANTERNS? BLEEZ? GET THE FULL SCOOP IN GREEN LANTERNS!

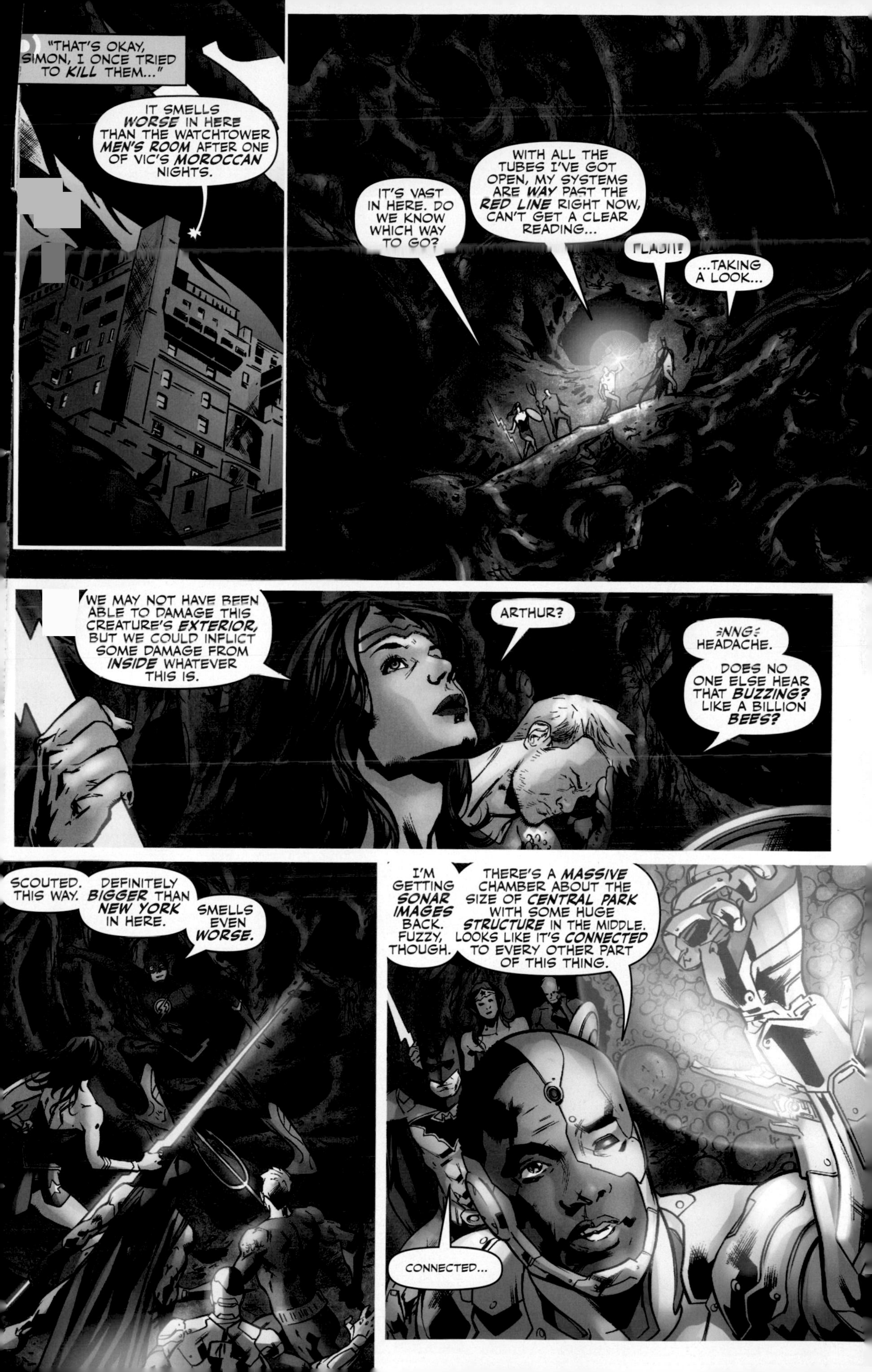
"THAT'S OKAY, SIMON, I ONCE TRIED TO KILL THEM..."
IT SMELLS WORSE IN HERE THAN THE WATCHTOWER MEN'S ROOM AFTER ONE OF VIC'S MOROCCAN NIGHTS.
IT'S VAST IN HERE. DO WE KNOW WHICH WAY TO GO?
WITH ALL THE TUBES I'VE GOT OPEN, MY SYSTEMS ARE WAY PAST THE RED LINE RIGHT NOW, CAN'T GET A CLEAR READING...
FLASH!
...TAKING A LOOK...
WE MAY NOT HAVE BEEN ABLE TO DAMAGE THIS CREATURE'S EXTERIOR, BUT WE COULD INFLICT SOME DAMAGE FROM INSIDE WHATEVER THIS IS.
ARTHUR?
NNG HEADACHE.
DOES NO ONE ELSE HEAR THAT BUZZING? LIKE A BILLION BEES?
SCOUTED. THIS WAY.
DEFINITELY BIGGER THAN NEW YORK IN HERE.
SMELLS EVEN WORSE.
I'M GETTING SONAR IMAGES BACK. FUZZY, THOUGH.
THERE'S A MASSIVE CHAMBER ABOUT THE SIZE OF CENTRAL PARK WITH SOME HUGE STRUCTURE IN THE MIDDLE. LOOKS LIKE IT'S CONNECTED TO EVERY OTHER PART OF THIS THING.
CONNECTED...

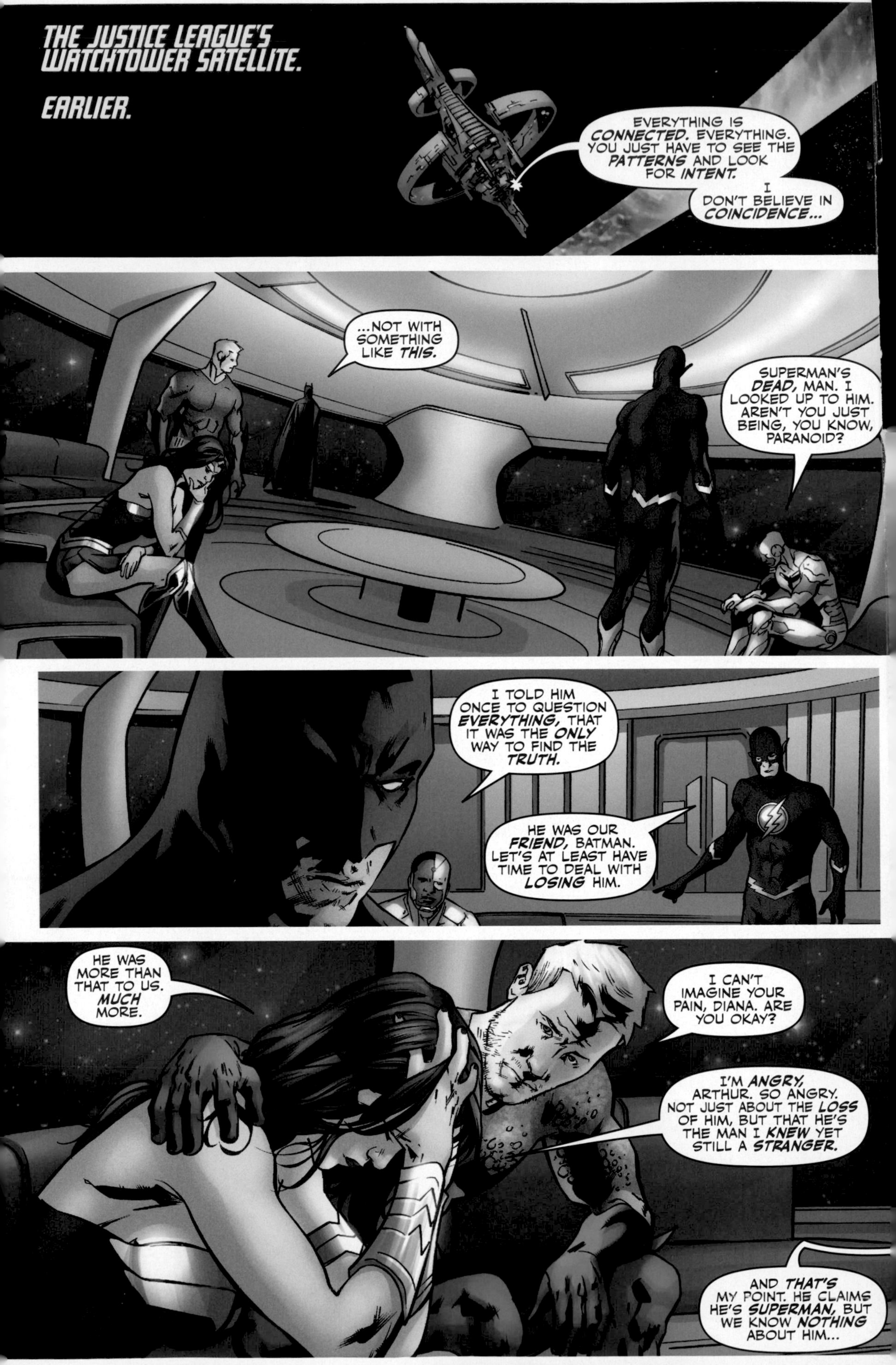
THE JUSTICE LEAGUE'S WATCHTOWER SATELLITE.
EARLIER.
EVERYTHING IS CONNECTED. EVERYTHING. YOU JUST HAVE TO SEE THE PATTERNS AND LOOK FOR INTENT.
I DON'T BELIEVE IN COINCIDENCE...
...NOT WITH SOMETHING LIKE THIS.
SUPERMAN'S DEAD, MAN. I LOOKED UP TO HIM. AREN'T YOU JUST BEING, YOU KNOW, PARANOID?
I TOLD HIM ONCE TO QUESTION EVERYTHING, THAT IT WAS THE ONLY WAY TO FIND THE TRUTH.
HE WAS OUR FRIEND, BATMAN. LET'S AT LEAST HAVE TIME TO DEAL WITH LOSING HIM.
HE WAS MORE THAN THAT TO US. MUCH MORE.
I CAN'T IMAGINE YOUR PAIN, DIANA. ARE YOU OKAY?
I'M ANGRY, ARTHUR. SO ANGRY. NOT JUST ABOUT THE LOSS OF HIM, BUT THAT HE'S THE MAN I KNEW YET STILL A STRANGER.
AND THAT'S MY POINT. HE CLAIMS HE'S SUPERMAN, BUT WE KNOW NOTHING ABOUT HIM...

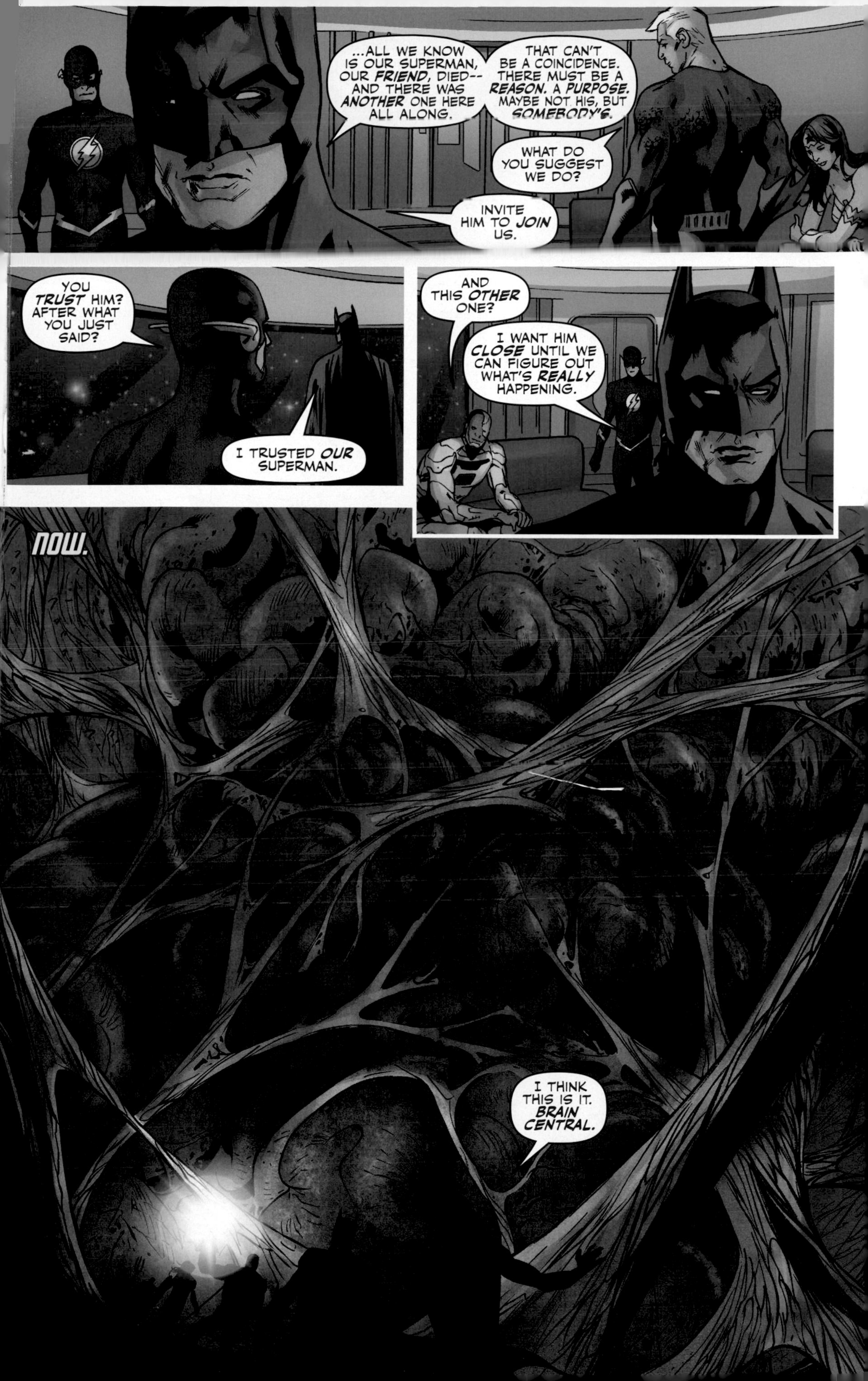
...ALL WE KNOW IS OUR SUPERMAN, OUR *FRIEND*, DIED-- AND THERE WAS *ANOTHER* ONE HERE ALL ALONG.
THAT CAN'T BE A COINCIDENCE. THERE MUST BE A *REASON*. A *PURPOSE*. MAYBE NOT HIS, BUT *SOMEBODY'S*.
WHAT DO YOU SUGGEST WE DO?
INVITE HIM TO *JOIN* US.
YOU *TRUST* HIM? AFTER WHAT YOU JUST SAID?
I TRUSTED *OUR* SUPERMAN.
AND THIS *OTHER* ONE?
I WANT HIM *CLOSE* UNTIL WE CAN FIGURE OUT WHAT'S *REALLY* HAPPENING.
NOW.
I THINK THIS IS IT. *BRAIN CENTRAL*.

GAAH!

ARTHUR, WHAT IS IT?

I CAN *HEAR* IT.

I CAN HEAR IT *THINKING*-- IT'S CALLED A *REAPER*-- AND I THINK IT'S HERE TO *HARVEST* HUMANITY.

HARVEST? WHAT FOR?

I CAN'T MAKE IT *ALL* OUT, JUST THAT IT'S OUR *TIME* TO BE *HARVESTED.*

THIS IS JUST THE *FIRST.* THERE ARE *OTHERS* COMING, *LOTS* OF OTHERS. MORE *REAPERS.*

ENOUGH FOR THE *WHOLE* WORLD.

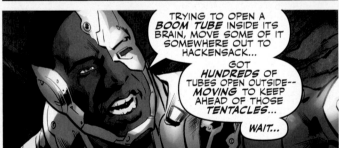

TRYING TO OPEN A *BOOM TUBE* INSIDE ITS BRAIN, MOVE SOME OF IT SOMEWHERE OUT TO HACKENSACK...

GOT *HUNDREDS* OF TUBES OPEN OUTSIDE-- *MOVING* TO KEEP AHEAD OF THOSE *TENTACLES...*

WAIT...

GAH! TOO MUCH. *OVERLOADING*--

ACTION SCENE, PEOPLE!

"...CAN'T KEEP THE TUBES OPEN...

"THEY'RE COLLAPSING!"

WELL, THIS ALL LOOKS HORRIFIC!

READING SEVERAL HUMAN LIFE-FORMS INSIDE.

THINK IT'S THEM?

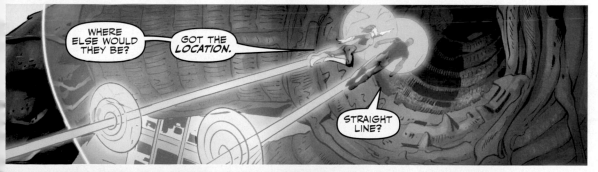

WHERE ELSE WOULD THEY BE?

GOT THE LOCATION.

STRAIGHT LINE?

RIGHT THROUGH THIS THING.

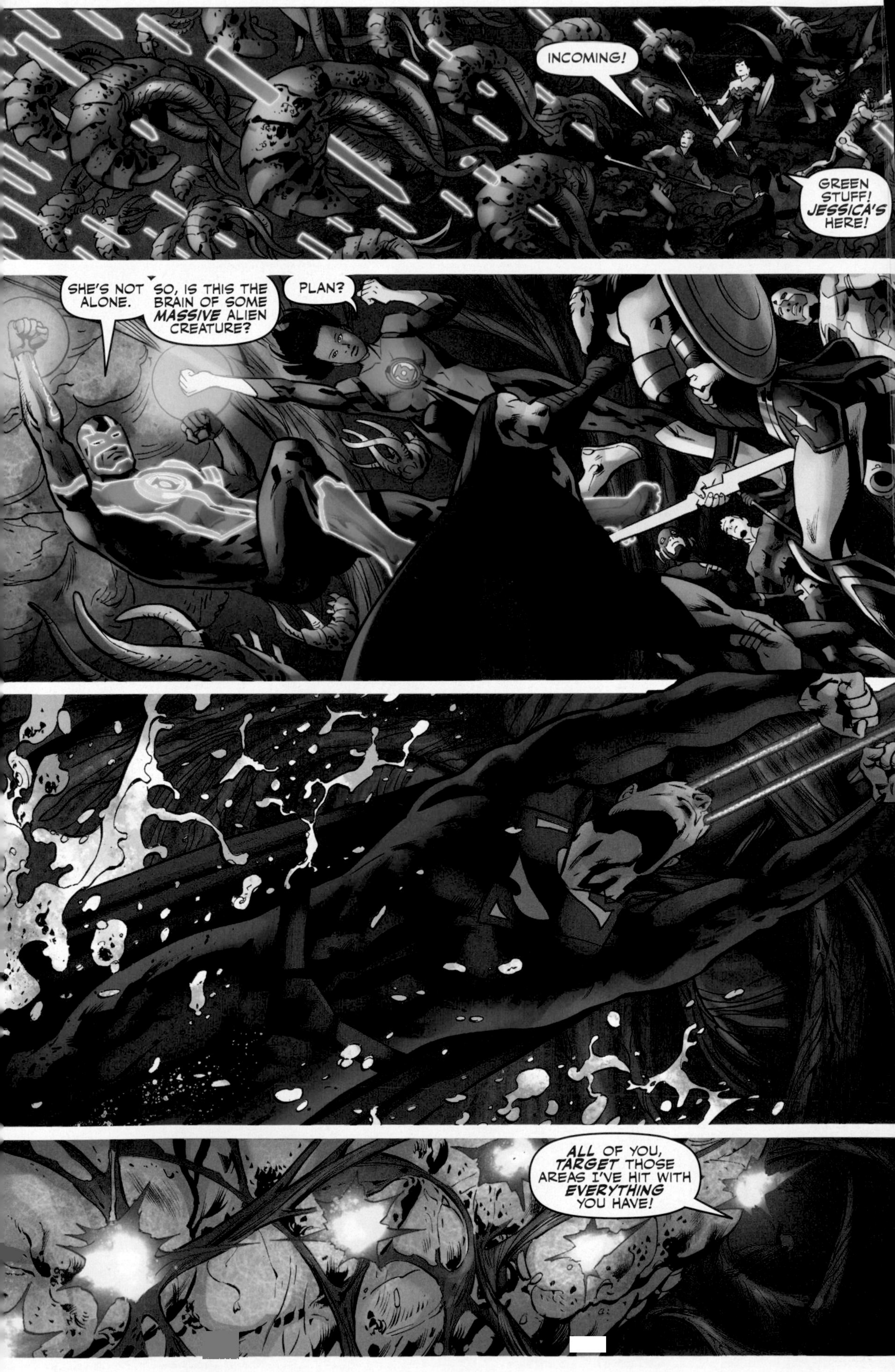
INCOMING!
GREEN STUFF! JESSICA'S HERE!
SHE'S NOT ALONE.
SO, IS THIS THE BRAIN OF SOME MASSIVE ALIEN CREATURE?
PLAN?
ALL OF YOU, TARGET THOSE AREAS I'VE HIT WITH EVERYTHING YOU HAVE!

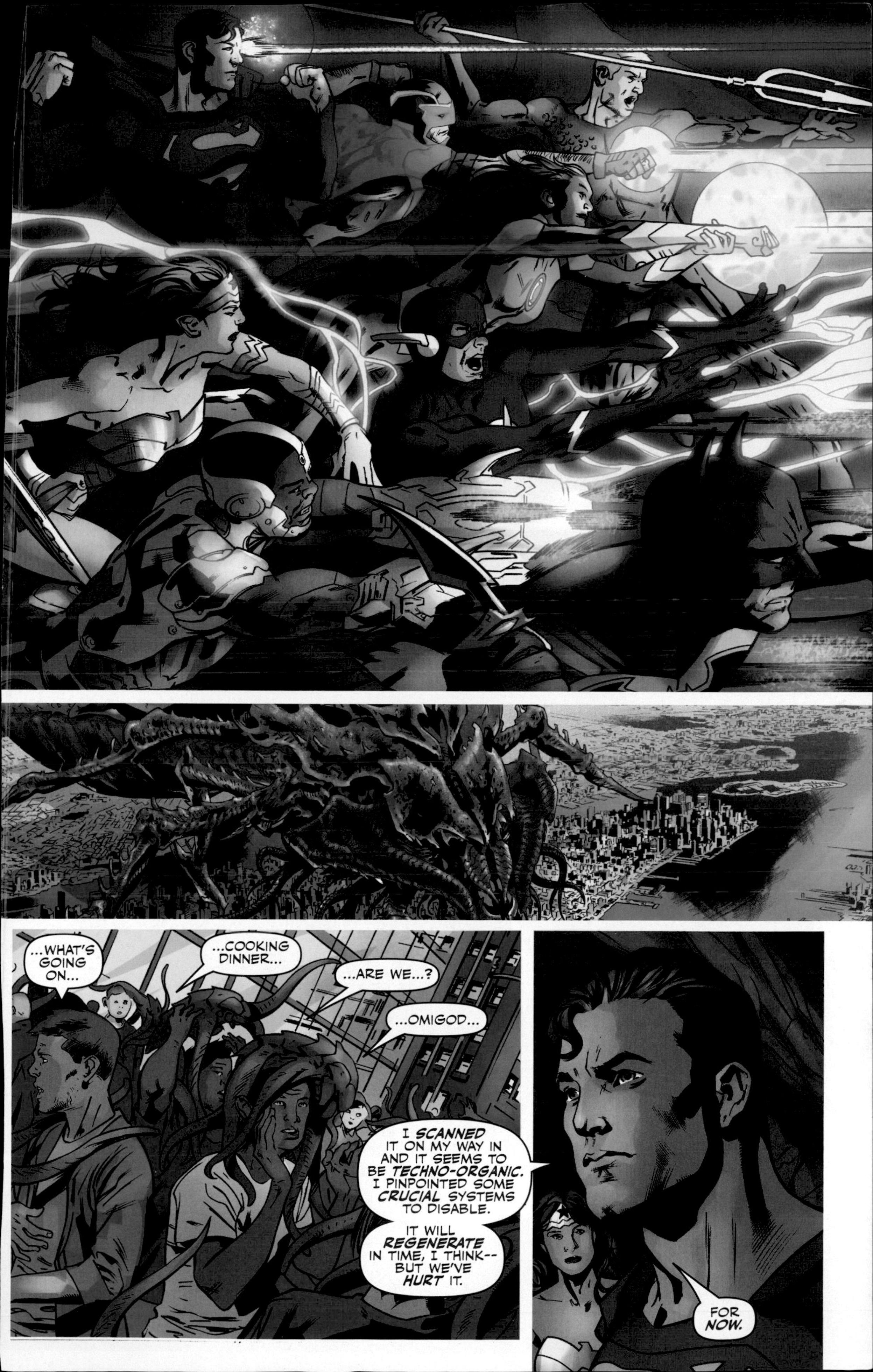
...WHAT'S GOING ON...
...COOKING DINNER...
...ARE WE...?
...OMIGOD...
I SCANNED IT ON MY WAY IN AND IT SEEMS TO BE TECHNO-ORGANIC. I PINPOINTED SOME CRUCIAL SYSTEMS TO DISABLE.
IT WILL REGENERATE IN TIME, I THINK-- BUT WE'VE HURT IT.
FOR NOW.

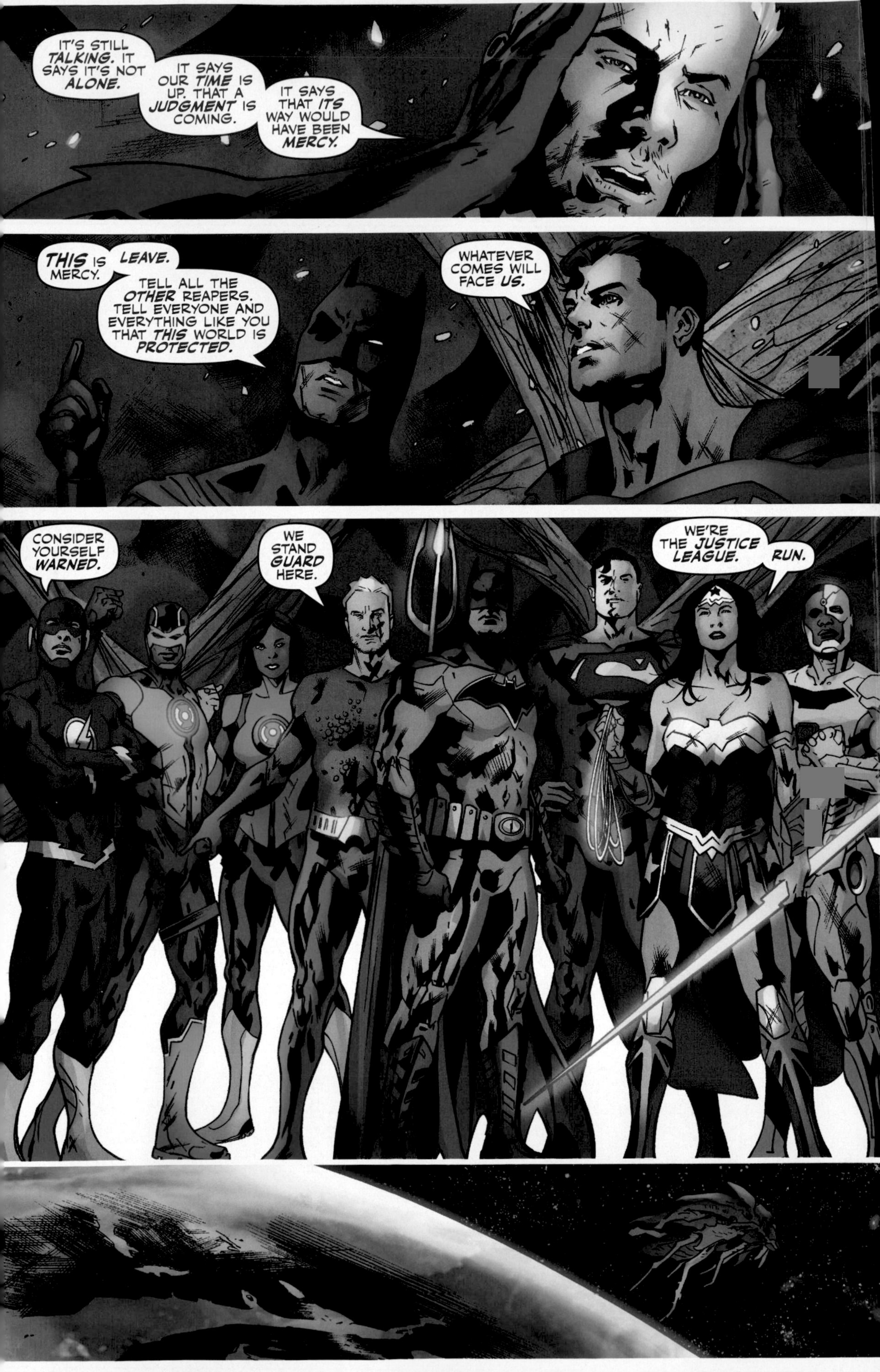
IT'S STILL TALKING. IT SAYS IT'S NOT ALONE.
IT SAYS OUR TIME IS UP. THAT A JUDGMENT IS COMING.
IT SAYS THAT ITS WAY WOULD HAVE BEEN MERCY.
THIS IS MERCY.
LEAVE.
TELL ALL THE OTHER REAPERS. TELL EVERYONE AND EVERYTHING LIKE YOU THAT THIS WORLD IS PROTECTED.
WHATEVER COMES WILL FACE US.
CONSIDER YOURSELF WARNED.
WE STAND GUARD HERE.
WE'RE THE JUSTICE LEAGUE.
RUN.

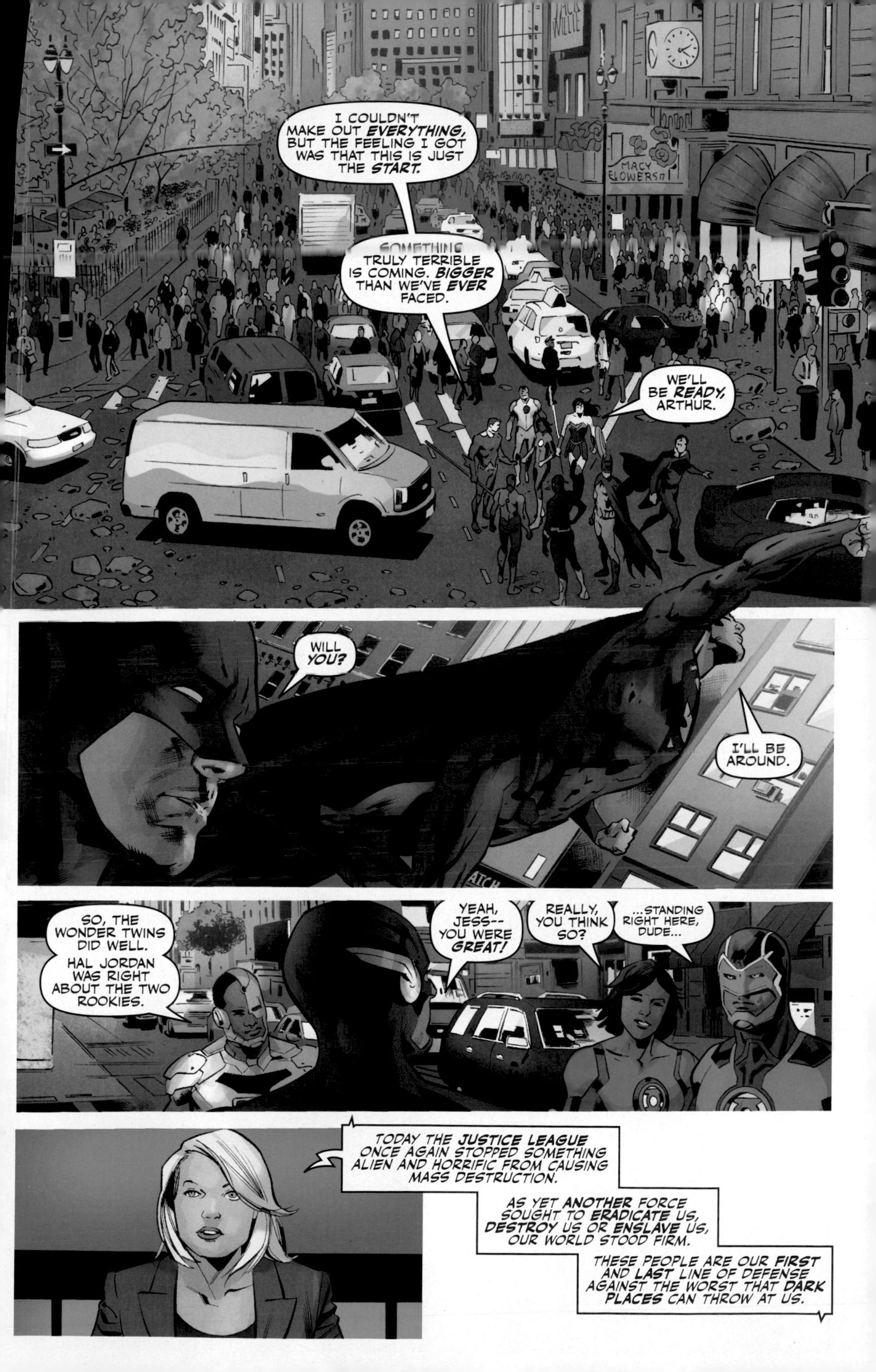

I COULDN'T MAKE OUT EVERYTHING, BUT THE FEELING I GOT WAS THAT THIS IS JUST THE START.
SOMETHING TRULY TERRIBLE IS COMING. BIGGER THAN WE'VE EVER FACED.
WE'LL BE READY, ARTHUR.
MACY FLOWERS
WILL YOU?
I'LL BE AROUND.
SO, THE WONDER TWINS DID WELL.
HAL JORDAN WAS RIGHT ABOUT THE TWO ROOKIES.
YEAH, JESS-- YOU WERE GREAT!
REALLY, YOU THINK SO?
...STANDING RIGHT HERE, DUDE...
TODAY THE JUSTICE LEAGUE ONCE AGAIN STOPPED SOMETHING ALIEN AND HORRIFIC FROM CAUSING MASS DESTRUCTION.
AS YET ANOTHER FORCE SOUGHT TO ERADICATE US, DESTROY US OR ENSLAVE US, OUR WORLD STOOD FIRM.
THESE PEOPLE ARE OUR FIRST AND LAST LINE OF DEFENSE AGAINST THE WORST THAT DARK PLACES CAN THROW AT US.

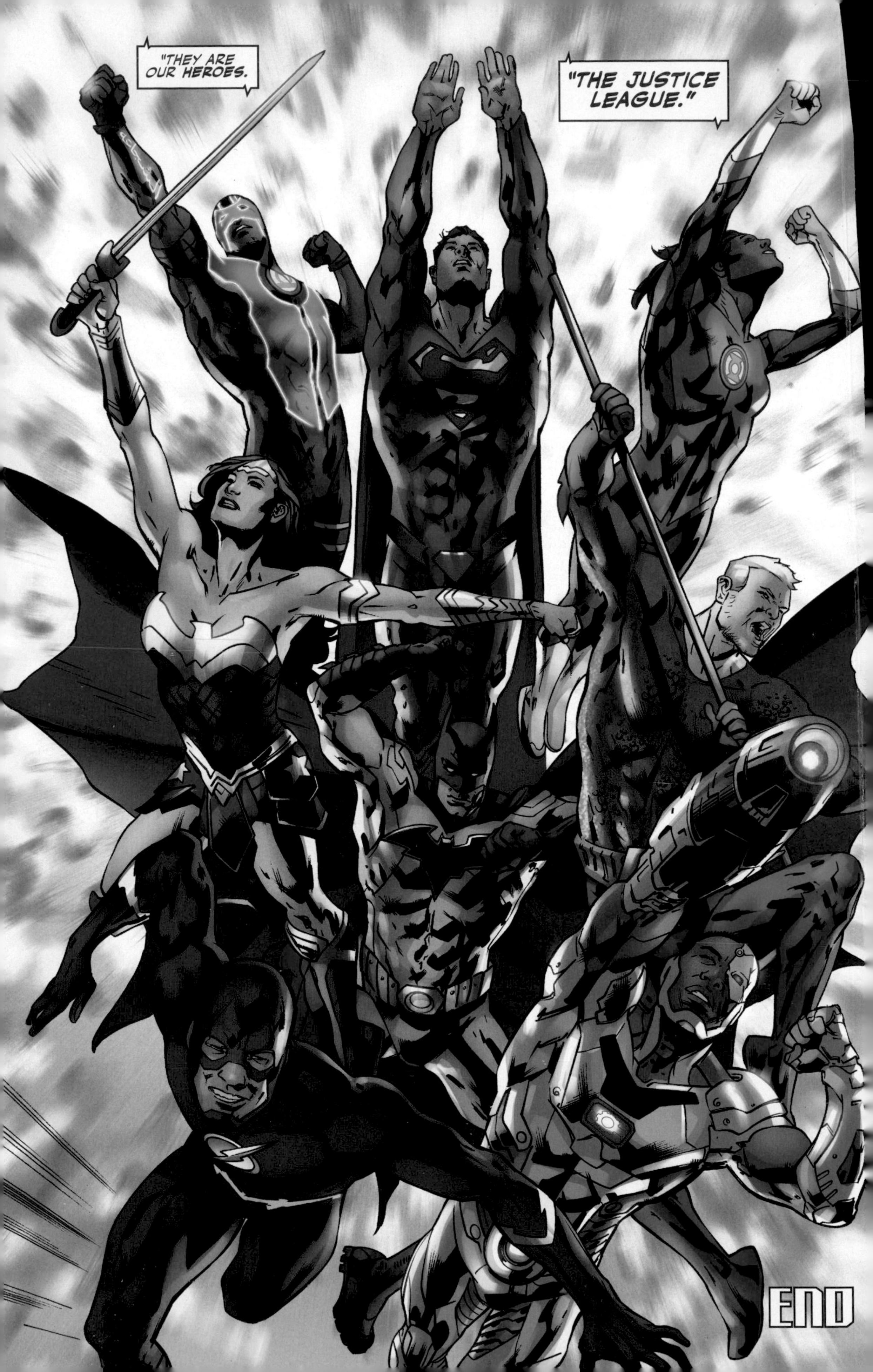
"THEY ARE OUR HEROES.
"THE JUSTICE LEAGUE."
END